The Complete INSTANT POT Cookbook

1000 Recipes For Easy & Delicious Pressure Cooker Homemade Meals

Patrick Jones

CONTENTS

POULTRY 31

BEEF & LAMB 69

FISH & SEAFOOD 87

PASTA & RICE 100

INTRODUCTION

Instant Pot is a magic pot which can transform a few, affordable ingredients into the most delicious dinner in the fastest and easiest way. If you are about to start using the Instant Pot that will be one of the best companion in your journey to a healthier and happier life. Even if you have a tight schedule, you can always find 5-10 minutes to prepare a bunch of ingredients and put them in the pot. You can steam the baby carrots, cook the lentils or produce the homemade yogurt from one single touch of the display. Instant Pot will make you love the world of food, so you will be more successful in sticking to your diet with way less efforts.

During the last century, the food industry provided us with too many options of tasty, but unhealthy processed foods full of artificial additives, colors, and preservatives. Long-term consumption of such products resulted in worsening health conditions of the population, so it's time to make a change. Home cooking can prevent the development of diabetes, stroke and heart failure, and it can also normalize blood pressure and cholesterol levels. Moreover, this magnificent cooking appliance can be used as a safe and effective tool for improving weight loss.

If you are reading this page, it means that you have already decided to start better eating habits and you chose the one of the healthies and fastest way to prepare the food - the Instant Pot pressure cooker. I congratulate you with the right choice to change your life for the better. This book contains 1000 recipes which will help you enjoy mouthwatering and healthy meals, everyday and for any occassion for the whole family and friends.

WHY THE INSTANT POT IS GREAT TO HAVE

Sometimes it's easier to buy ready-to-eat sausages in the supermarket or a quick cheesy burger at burger king. The combination of various unnatural additives, huge amounts of monosodium glutamate and sugar ruin the digestive system and affect some organs. Nothing bad will happen because of one or two "cheat meals", but repetetive consumption of processed foods over the course of months and years will affect you and your health.

The second thing you should do is to change your shopping behavior and buy fresh, organic and quality products so you can start cooking at home. I promise that you will find tons of mouthwatering recipes in this book which will excite you to cook and forget about the quick sugary snacks.

ONE-TOUCH COOKING MODES OF INSTANT POT

Instant Pot Pressure Cooker is your best friend in the kitchen that will help you immensely to achieve freedom in your kitchen - quickly and effortlessly. Thanks to one-touch cooking modes, the Instant Pot saves a lot of time and energy, and rewards you with tasty and nutritious meals.

- **Soup/Broth**. This pre-set method is for cooking soups or broths.

- **Meat/Stew**. This mode will be useful for stewing almost all kind of vegetables including peas, zucchini, spinach and other leafy veggies along with some juicy beef or park stew meat

- **Beans/Chili**. Lentils and beans are healthy plant-based sources of protein, so this setting will help you cook them in the fastest and hassle-free way.

- **Poultry**. Chicken and turkey should be prepared under this cooking mode. The meat will cook itself becoming tender and juicy.

- **Rice**. While rice is not considered as a part of the 20 healthiest foods, yet you can still utilize this setting for cooking quinoa or other nutritious grains.

- **Multigrain**. Wholegrains are full of the fiber, micro and macro elements, so you must add them to your everyday meals. The Instant Pot significantly reduces the cooking time of whole grains in comparison to a standard oven.

- **Porridge.** Tasty and nutritive oatmeal is a great way to start your day. This mode will help you cook the perfect breakfast.

- **Steam**. Steaming is the safest and the most effective cooking method, since it maximizes the amount of antioxidants and fiber in the food.

- **Sauté.** This mode allows stir-frying, browning or searing veggies, meat, poultry of fish.

- **Yogurt.** The best option for a homemade low-fat yogurt. When cooked at home, the yogurt is a very healthy food, without any added sugars and preservatives.

- **Pressure cook/Manual mode -** this is the most important Instant Pot setting. You can use this function for any kind of food preparation and adjust the pressure and cooking time as needed.

- **Slow cook**. The Instant Pot can also function as a Slow cooker. If you have plenty of time before a dinner, this method will help you to prepare the most delicious and tasty stews.

- **Pressure Level**. Depending on the amount of ingredients and their properties, you can adjust higher or lower pressure level to ensure the best cooking results.

- **Delay start.** You have a busy day and don't want to spend morning time in the kitchen? No problem, just prepare the ingredients, throw them in the Pot and set it to start cooking in 8h. And the dinner will be ready just in time. This function is also handy for soaking beans/grains.

- **Keep warm.** This function keeps the food warm. No need to microwave the meal anymore.

Note! Some Instant Pot models may have slightly different functions or buttons. Always check the manufacturer's manual before using any setting on your pressure cooker.

MORNING RECIPES

Chicken Sandwiches with Barbecue Sauce

Serving Size: 4 | Total Time: 50 minutes

4 chicken thighs, boneless and skinless

2 cups barbecue sauce	1 tbsp lemon juice
1 onion, minced	1 tbsp mayonnaise
2 garlic cloves, minced	2 cups lettuce, shredded
2 tbsp minced fresh parsley	4 burger buns

Into the pot, place the garlic, onion, and barbecue sauce. Add in the chicken and toss it to coat. Seal the lid and cook on High Pressure for 15 minutes. Do a natural release for 10 minutes. Use two forks to shred the chicken and mix it into the sauce. Press Keep Warm and let the mixture simmer for 15 minutes to thicken the sauce until the desired consistency.

In a bowl, mix lemon juice, mayonnaise, and parsley; toss lettuce into the mixture to coat. Separate the chicken into equal parts to match the burger buns; top with lettuce and complete the sandwiches.

Savory Roast Beef Sandwiches

Serving Size: 8 | Total Time: 1 hour 30 minutes

2 ½ lb beef roast	2 cups beef broth stock
2 tbsp olive oil	16 slices Fontina cheese
1 onion, chopped	8 split hoagie rolls
4 garlic cloves, minced	Salt and pepper to taste
½ cup dry red wine	

Season the beef with salt and pepper. Warm oil on Sauté and brown the beef for 2 to 3 minutes per side; reserve. Add onion and garlic to the pot and cook for 3 minutes until translucent. Set aside. Add red wine to deglaze. Mix in beef broth and take back the beef. Seal the lid and cook on High Pressure for 50 minutes. Release the pressure naturally for 10 minutes. Preheat a broiler.

Transfer the beef to a cutting board and slice. Roll the meat and top with onion. Each sandwich should be topped with 2 Fontina cheese slices. Place the sandwiches under the broiler for 2-3 minutes until the cheese melts.

Buckwheat Pancake with Yogurt & Berries

Serving Size: 4 | Total Time: 15 minutes

1 cup buckwheat flour	1 tsp vanilla sugar
2 tsp baking powder	1 tsp strawberry extract
1 ¼ cups milk	1 cup Greek yogurt
1 egg	1 cup fresh berries

In a bowl, whisk milk and egg until foamy. Gradually add flour and continue to beat until combined. Add baking powder, strawberry extract, and vanilla sugar. Spoon the batter in a greased cake pan. Pour 1 cup of water into the pot. Place a trivet. Lay the pan on the trivet. Seal the lid and cook for 5 minutes on High Pressure. Do a quick release. Top pancake with yogurt and berries.

Pumpkin Steel Cut Oats with Cinnamon

Serving Size: 4 | Total Time: 25 minutes

1 tbsp butter	1 cup pumpkin puree
2 cups steel-cut oats	3 tbsp maple syrup
¼ tsp cinnamon	2 tsp pumpkin seeds, toasted

Melt butter on Sauté. Add in cinnamon, oats, pumpkin puree, and 3 cups of water. Seal the lid, select Porridge and cook for 10 minutes on High Pressure to get a few bite oats or for 14 minutes to form soft oats. Do a quick release. Open the lid and stir in maple syrup. Top with pumpkin seeds and serve.

Vanilla Chai Latte Oatmeal

Serving Size: 4 | Total Time: 35 minutes

3 ½ cups milk	¼ tsp ground allspice
½ cup raw peanuts	¼ tsp ground cardamom
1 cup steel-cut oats	1 tsp vanilla extract
¼ cup agave syrup	2 tbsp chopped tea leaves
1 ½ tsp ground ginger	¼ tsp cloves
1 ¼ tsp ground cinnamon	

With a blender, puree peanuts and milk to obtain a smooth consistency. Transfer into the cooker. To the peanuts mixture, add agave syrup, oats, ginger, allspice, cinnamon, cardamom, tea leaves, and cloves and mix well. Seal the lid and cook on High Pressure for 12 minutes. Let pressure release naturally for 10 minutes. Stir in vanilla and serve.

Lazy Steel Cut Oats with Coconut

Serving Size: 2 | Total Time: 25 minutes

1 tsp coconut oil	¼ cup sugar
1 cup steel-cut oats	½ tsp vanilla extract
¾ cup coconut milk	1 tbsp shredded coconut

Warm coconut oil on Sauté in your Instant Pot. Add oats and cook as you stir until soft and toasted. Add in milk, sugar, vanilla, and 2 cups water and stir. Seal the lid and press Porridge. Cook for 12 minutes on High Pressure. Set steam vent to Venting to release the pressure quickly. Open the lid. Add oats as you stir to mix any extra liquid. Top with coconut and serve.

Banana & Vanilla Pancakes

Serving Size: 6 | Total Time: 15 minutes

2 bananas, mashed	1 ½ tsp baking powder
1 ¼ cups milk	1 tsp vanilla extract
2 eggs	2 tsp coconut oil
1 ½ cups rolled oats	1 tbsp honey

Combine the bananas, milk, eggs, oats, baking powder, vanilla, coconut oil, and honey in a blender and pulse until a completely smooth batter. Grease the inner pot with cooking spray. Spread 1 spoon batter at the bottom. Cook for 2 minutes on Sauté, flip the crepe, and cook for another minute. Repeat the process with the remaining batter. Serve immediately with your favorite topping.

Honey Butternut Squash Cake Oatmeal

Serving Size: 4 | Total Time: 35 minutes

3 ½ cups coconut milk	½ tsp salt
1 cup steel-cut oats	½ tsp orange zest
8 oz butternut squash, grated	¼ tsp ground nutmeg
½ cup sultanas	¼ cup walnuts, chopped
1/3 cup honey	½ tsp vanilla extract
¾ tsp ground ginger	½ tsp sugar

In the cooker, mix sultanas, orange zest, ginger, milk, honey, butternut squash, salt, oats, and nutmeg. Seal the lid and cook on High Pressure for 12 minutes. Do a natural release for 10 minutes. Into the oatmeal, stir in the vanilla extract and sugar. Top with walnuts and serve.

French Cheese & Spinach Quiche

Serving Size: 5 | Total Time: 20 minutes

1 lb spinach, chopped	½ cup goat cheese
½ cup mascarpone cheese	3 tbsp butter
½ cup feta cheese, shredded	½ cup milk
3 eggs, beaten	1 pack (6 sheets) pie dough

In a bowl, mix spinach, eggs, mascarpone, feta and goat cheeses. Dust a clean surface with flour and unfold the pie sheets onto it. Using a rolling pin, roll the dough to fit your Instant Pot. Repeat with the other sheets. Combine milk and butter in a skillet. Bring to a boil and melt the butter completely. Remove from the heat.

Grease a baking pan with oil. Place in 2 pie sheets and brush with milk mixture. Make the first layer of spinach mixture and cover with another two pie sheets. Again, brush with butter and milk mixture, and repeat until you have used all ingredients. Pour 1 cup water into your Instant Pot and insert a trivet. Lower the pan on the trivet. Seal the lid. Cook on High Pressure for 6 minutes. Do a quick release. Place parchment paper under the pie to use it as a lifting method to remove the pie. Serve cold.

Walnut & Pumpkin Strudel

Serving Size: 8 | Total Time: 55 minutes

2 cups pumpkin puree	2 tbsp brown sugar
1 tsp vanilla extract	2 tbsp butter, softened
2 cups Greek yogurt	2 puff pastry sheets
2 eggs	1 cup walnuts, chopped

In a bowl, mix butter, yogurt, and vanilla until smooth. Unfold the pastry and cut each sheet into 4-inch x 7-inch pieces; brush with some beaten eggs. Place approximately 2 tbsp of pumpkin puree, sugar, and 2 tbsp of the yogurt mixture at the middle of each pastry, sprinkle with walnuts. Fold the sheets and brush with the remaining eggs.

Cut the surface with a sharp knife and gently place each strudel into an oiled baking dish. Pour 1 cup of water into the pot and insert the trivet. Place the pan on top. Seal the lid and cook for 25 minutes on High Pressure. Release the pressure naturally for about 10 minutes. Let it chill for 10 minutes. Serve.

Italian Egg Cakes

Serving Size: 4 | Total Time: 25 minutes

¼ cup ricotta cheese, cubed	1 chopped tomato
½ cup mozzarella, shredded	Salt and pepper to taste
1 cup chopped baby spinach	2 tbsp basil, chopped
6 beaten eggs	

Pour 1 cup of water into the Instant Pot and fit in a trivet. Place spinach in small cups. Combine eggs, mozzarella cheese, ricotta cheese, tomato, salt, and pepper in a bowl. Fill 3/4 of each cup with the mixture and top with basil.

Place the cups on top of the trivet and seal the lid. Select Manual and cook for 15 minutes on High pressure. Once ready, perform a quick pressure release. Serve hot.

Smoked Salmon & Egg Muffins

Serving Size: 2 | Total Time: 15 minutes

4 beaten eggs	4 tbsp mozzarella, shredded
2 salmon slices, chopped	1 green onion, chopped

Beat eggs, salmon, mozzarella cheese, and onion in a bowl. Share into ramekins. Pour 1 cup of water into your Instant Pot and fit in a trivet.

Place the tins on top of the trivet and seal the lid. Select Manual and cook for 8 minutes on High pressure. Once done, let sit for 2 minutes, then perform a quick pressure release and unlock the lid. Serve immediately.

Breakfast Frittata

Serving Size: 4 | Total Time: 25 minutes

8 beaten eggs	1 cup mushrooms, chopped
1 cup cherry tomatoes, halved	Salt and pepper to taste
1 tbsp Dijon mustard	1 cup sharp cheddar, grated

Combine the eggs, mushrooms, mustard, salt, pepper, and ½ cup of cheddar cheese in a bowl. Pour in a greased baking pan and top with the remaining cheddar cheese and cherry tomatoes. Add 1 cup of water to your Instant Pot and fit in a trivet. Place the baking pan on the trivet.

Seal the lid. Select Manual and cook for 15 minutes on High. When ready, perform a quick pressure release and unlock the lid. Slice into wedges before serving.

Tofu Hash Brown Breakfast

Serving Size: 4 | Total Time: 21 minutes

1 cup tofu cubes	1 cup shredded cheddar
2 cups frozen hash browns	¼ cup milk
8 beaten eggs	Salt and pepper to taste

Set your Instant Pot to Sauté. Place in tofu and cook until browned on all sides, about 4 minutes. Add in hash brown and cook for 2 minutes. Beat eggs, cheddar cheese, milk, salt, and pepper in a bowl and pour over hash brown. Seal the lid, select Manual, and cook for 5 minutes on High. Once done, perform a quick pressure release. Cut into slices before serving.

Speedy Soft-Boiled Eggs

Serving Size: 4 | Total Time: 10 minutes

4 large eggs	Salt and pepper to taste

To the pressure cooker, add 1 cup of water and place a wire rack. Place eggs on it. Seal the lid, press Steam, and cook for 3 minutes on High Pressure. Do a quick release.

Allow to cool in an ice bath. Peel the eggs and season with salt and pepper before serving.

Spinach & Feta Pie with Cherry Tomatoes

Serving Size: 2 | Total Time: 35 minutes

4 eggs	1 cup baby spinach
Salt and pepper to taste	1 spring onion, chopped
½ cup heavy cream	¼ cup feta, crumbled
1 cup cherry tomatoes, halved	1 tbsp parsley, chopped

Grease a baking dish with cooking spray and add in the spinach and onion. In a bowl, whisk the eggs, heavy cream, salt, and pepper. Pour over the spinach and arrange the cherry tomato on top. Sprinkle with the feta.

Add a cup of water to the Instant Pot and insert a trivet. Place the dish on the trivet. Seal the lid, press Manual, and cook on High pressure for 15 minutes. Release pressure naturally for 10 minutes. Scatter parsley to serve.

Strawberry Jam

Serving Size: 6 | Total Time: 30 minutes

1 lb strawberries, chopped	½ lemon, juiced and zested
1 cup sugar	1 tbsp mint, chopped

Add the strawberries, sugar, lemon juice, and zest to the Instant Pot. Seal the lid, select manual, and cook for 2 minutes on High.

Release pressure naturally for 10 minutes. Open the lid and stir in chopped mint. Select Sauté and continue cooking until the jam thickens, about 10 minutes. Let to cool before serving.

Ricotta & Potato Breakfast

Serving Size: 4 | Total Time: 25 minutes

2 tbsp olive oil	½ tsp dried oregano
1 lb potatoes, chopped	1 tsp dried onion flakes
5 eggs, whisked	Salt and pepper to taste
1 cup ricotta, crumbled	

Warm the olive oil in your Instant Pot on Sauté.

Place the potatoes and cook for 3-4 minutes. Add in eggs, ricotta cheese, oregano, dried onion flakes, ¼ cup of water, salt, and pepper.

Seal the lid, select Manual, and cook for 10 minutes on High pressure.

Once ready, perform a quick pressure release and unlock the lid. Serve immediately.

Light & Fruity Yogurt

Serving Size: 12 | Total Time: 24hr

¼ cup Greek yogurt containing active cultures	
1 lb raspberries, mashed	1 tbsp fresh orange juice
1 cup sugar	8 cups milk
3 tbsp gelatin	

In a bowl, add sugar and raspberries and stir well to dissolve the sugar. Let sit for 30 minutes at room temperature. Add in orange juice and gelatin and mix well until dissolved. Remove the mixture and place in a sealable container, close, and allow to sit for 12 hrs to 24 hrs at room temperature before placing in the fridge. Refrigerate for a maximum of 2 weeks.

Into the cooker, add milk, and close the lid. The steam vent should be set to Venting then to Sealing. Select Yogurt until "Boil" is showed on display. When complete, there will be a display of "Yogurt" on the screen.

Open the lid and using a food thermometer, ensure the milk temperature is at least 185°F. Transfer the steel pot to a wire rack and allow to cool for 30 minutes until the milk has reached 110°F.

In a bowl, mix ½ cup warm milk and yogurt. Transfer the mixture into the remaining warm milk and stir without having to scrape the steel pot's bottom. Take the steel pot back to the base of the pot and seal the lid. Select Yogurt and cook for 8 hrs. Allow the yogurt to chill in a refrigerator for 1-2 hrs. Transfer the chilled yogurt to a bowl and stir in fresh raspberry jam.

Greek Yogurt with Honey & Walnuts

Serving Size: 10 | Total Time: 15hr

2 tbsp Greek yogurt	1 tsp vanilla extract
8 cups milk	1 cup walnuts, chopped
¼ cup sugar honey	

Add the milk to your Instant Pot. Seal the lid and press Yogurt until the display shows "Boil". When the cooking cycle is over, the display will show Yogurt. Open the lid and check that milk temperature is at least 175°F. Get rid of the skin lying on the milk's surface. Let cool in an ice bath until it becomes warm to the touch.

In a bowl, mix one cup of milk and yogurt to make a smooth consistency. Mix the milk with yogurt mixture. Transfer to the pot and place on your Pressure cooker.

Seal the lid, press Yogurt, and adjust the timer to 9 hrs. Once cooking is complete, strain the yogurt into a bowl using a strainer with cheesecloth. Chill for 4 hours. Add in vanilla and honey and gently stir well. Spoon the yogurt into glass jars. Serve sprinkled with walnuts and enjoy.

EGGS & VEGETABLES

Aioli Deviled Eggs

Serving Size: 4 | Total Time 20 minutes

1 tbsp aioli	1 tbsp Dijon mustard
8 eggs	Salt and pepper to taste
¼ cup heavy cream	2 tbsp dill, chopped

Pour 1 cup of water into your Instant Pot and fit in a trivet. Place eggs on the trivet and seal the lid. Select Manual and cook for 5 minutes on High pressure. Once ready, perform a quick pressure release. Remove the eggs and transfer to a bowl with cold water for 2-3 minutes.

Peel the eggs, slice them in half lengthwise, and remove the yolks to a bowl. Using a fork, mash the yolks into a fine crumble and combine with heavy cream, aioli, mustard, salt, and pepper. Pour into a pastry bag. Stuff each egg white with the mixture and top with dill.

Ham & Egg Cups

Serving Size: 4 | Total Time: 20 minutes

1 tbsp olive oil	Salt to taste
4 eggs	4 tbsp chives, chopped
4 ham slices, chopped	

Grease muffin cups with olive oil. Crack an egg in each and top with chopped ham. Sprinkle with salt and chives. Pour 1 cup of water into your Instant Pot and fit in a trivet. Place the cups on the trivet and seal the lid. Select Manual and cook for 8 minutes on High. Once done, perform a quick pressure release and unlock the lid.

Broccoli & Mushroom Egg Cups

Serving Size: 6 | Total Time: 15 minutes

1 tsp dried oregano	1 onion, chopped
10 eggs	1 cup sliced mushrooms
1 cup Pecorino cheese, grated	1 tbsp chopped parsley
1 cup heavy cream	Salt and pepper to taste
4 oz broccoli florets	

Pour 1 cup of water into your Instant Pot and fit in a trivet. In a bowl, whisk the eggs and heavy cream. Mix in Pecorino cheese, broccoli, onion, oregano, mushrooms, parsley, salt, and black pepper. Divide the egg mixture between small jars and seal the lids. Place them on the trivet and seal the lid. Select Manual and cook for 5 minutes on High pressure. When done, perform a quick pressure release and unlock the lid. Remove the jars carefully and serve.

Spanish Omelet with Cottage Cheese

Serving Size: 4 | Total Time: 25 minutes

1 lb tomatoes, peeled, diced	3 tbsp olive oil
1 tbsp tomato paste	1 tbsp Italian seasoning mix
1 cup cottage cheese	¼ cup parsley, chopped
4 eggs, beaten	¼ tbsp salt

Grease the inner pot with olive oil. Press Sauté and add tomatoes, Italian seasoning, parsley, tomato paste, and salt. Cook for 10 minutes, stirring occasionally. Mix eggs and cottage cheese and pour into the pot. Stir. Cook for 3 more minutes. Serve.

Kale & Parmesan Omelet

Serving Size: 6 | Total Time: 20 minutes

6 large eggs	Salt and pepper to taste
2 tbsp heavy cream	1 ½ cups kale, chopped
½ tsp freshly grated nutmeg	¼ cup grated Parmesan

In a bowl, beat eggs, heavy cream, nutmeg, salt, pepper, kale, and Parmesan. Place egg mixture into a greased baking pan. Pour in 1 cup of water and set a steamer rack over. Lay the pan onto the rack. Seal the lid and cook for 10 minutes on High. Release the pressure quickly. Serve.

Ham Omelet with Red Bell Pepper

Serving Size: 2 | Total Time: 20 minutes

1 red bell pepper, chopped	2 garlic cloves, crushed
4 eggs, beaten	½ cup ham, chopped
2 tbsp olive oil	1 tsp Italian seasoning

Grease the pot with olive oil. Stir-fry the pepper and garlic for 5 minutes. Mix the eggs with ham and season with Italian seasoning. Pour the mixture into the pot and cook for 2-3 minutes, or until set. Using a spatula, loosen the edges and gently slide onto a plate. Fold over to serve.

Power Swiss Chard & Spinach Omelet

Serving Size: 2 | Total Time: 20 minutes

1 cup spinach, chopped	2 tbsp olive oil
1 cup Swiss chard, chopped	½ tsp salt
4 eggs	¼ tsp red pepper flakes

Heat oil in the inner pot. Stir-fry the Swiss chard and spinach for 5 minutes on Sauté; reserve. Whisk the eggs, salt, and red pepper flakes. Pour the mixture into the pot. Cook for 3-4 minutes. Remove to a serving plate. Add the greens and fold over in half. Serve.

Mushroom & Goat Cheese Omelet

Serving Size: 2 | Total Time: 20 minutes

4 eggs	1 tsp dried oregano
½ cup fresh goat's cheese	¼ tsp salt
¼ cup milk	2 tsp olive oil
1 cup button mushrooms	1 tbsp parsley, chopped
1 onion, finely chopped	

Warm the olive oil. In your Instant Pot to Sauté. Stir-fry the onion for 3 minutes. Stir in the oregano, salt, and mushrooms. Cook for 5 minutes, stirring occasionally. Crack the eggs into a bowl and mix with goat cheese and milk. Remove the mushrooms to a plate. Pour the egg mixture into the pot and cook for 2 minutes on Sauté. Top with button mushrooms and parsley and serve.

Meat Lover's Omelet

Serving Size: 6 | Total Time: 45 minutes

10 beaten eggs	Salt and pepper to taste
3 sausage links, sliced	3 bacon slices, cooked
1 onion, diced	½ cup smoked sliced ham
1 tsp garlic powder	½ cup shredded cheddar

Beat eggs in a bowl. Stir in sausages, onion, salt, garlic powder, salt, and pepper. Pour in a greased baking pan and cover with aluminum foil. Pour 1 cup of water into your Instant Pot and fit in a trivet. Place the pan on top of the trivet. Seal the lid, select Manual, and cook for 15 minutes on High pressure.

Once done, allow a natural release for 10 minutes and unlock the lid. Remove the foil and scatter with cooked bacon, smoked ham, and cheddar cheese. Broil for 4-6 minutes until the cheese is melt. Serve hot!

Spicy Mozzarella Omelet Cups

Serving Size: 2 | Total Time 20 minutes

¼ cup shredded mozzarella	Salt and pepper to taste
1 tsp olive oil	1 onion, chopped
4 eggs, beaten	1 chili pepper, chopped

Grease two ramekins with olive oil. Beat eggs, salt, and black pepper in a bowl. Mix in onion and chili pepper. Divide the mixture into the ramekins and top with mozzarella cheese. Pour 1 cup of water into your Instant Pot and fit in a trivet. Place the ramekins on top of the trivet and seal the lid. Select Manual and cook for 15 minutes on High pressure. When ready, perform a quick pressure release and unlock the lid. Serve immediately.

Emmental Hot Dog Frittata

Serving Size: 4 | Total Time: 25 minutes

2 turkey hot dogs, sliced	¼ cup Emmental cheese, grated
1 tbsp butter	
8 beaten eggs	Salt and pepper to taste
2 tbsp sour cream	

Grease a baking dish with the butter. Pour 1 cup of water into your Instant Pot and fit in a trivet. Beat eggs and sour cream in a bowl. Mix in Emmental cheese, hot dogs, salt, and pepper. Pour in the dish and cover with aluminum foil. Place on top of the trivet and seal the lid.

Select Manual and cook for 15 minutes on High. Once ready, perform a quick pressure release. Serve warm.

Frittata with Vegetables & Cheese

Serving Size: 4 | Total Time: 30 minutes

4 eggs	1 cup chopped broccoli
8 oz spinach, finely chopped	4 tbsp olive oil
½ cup cheddar, shredded	Salt and pepper to taste
½ cup ricotta, crumbled	¼ tsp dried oregano
3 cherry tomatoes, halved	2 tsp celery leaves, chopped
¼ cup bell pepper, chopped	

Heat olive oil on Sauté. Add spinach and cook for 5 minutes, stirring occasionally. Add tomatoes, peppers, and broccoli and stir-fry for 3-4 more minutes. In a bowl, Whisk eggs, cheddar cheese, and ricotta cheese. Pour in the pot and cook for 5-7 minutes. Season with salt, black pepper, and oregano; press Cancel. Serve with celery.

Colby Cheese & Beef Egg Scramble

Serving Size: 4 | Total Time: 25 minutes

1 lb ground beef	¼ cup Colby cheese, grated
1 onion, chopped	¼ tsp garlic powder
6 eggs	1 tbsp tomato paste
¼ cup skim milk	2 tbsp olive oil

Warm the olive oil in your Instant Pot on Sauté and stir-fry the onion for 4 minutes until translucent. Add beef and tomato paste. Cook for 5 minutes, stirring occasionally. Whisk the eggs, milk, Colby cheese, and garlic. Pour the mixture into the pot and stir slowly with a wooden spatula. Cook until slightly underdone. Remove from the heat and serve.

Creamy Baked Eggs

Serving Size: 4 | Total Time: 40 minutes

1 tsp hot paprika	2 tbsp chopped cilantro
4 eggs	¼ tsp garlic powder
1 cup shredded cheddar	¼ tsp onion powder
1 cup heavy cream	¼ tsp cumin
¼ cup diced canned chilies	Salt and pepper to taste

Pour 1 cup of water into your Instant Pot and fit in a trivet. In a bowl, whisk the eggs. Mix in the cheddar cheese, heavy cream, chilies, garlic powder, onion powder, cumin, hot paprika, salt, and black pepper.

Grease with cooking spray a baking dish and pour in the egg mixture. Place the dish on the trivet and seal the lid. Select Manual and cook for 20 minutes on High. When done, allow a natural release for 10 minutes. Unlock the lid. Remove the dish and serve topped with cilantro.

Spicy Egg Casserole with Cheddar Cheese

Serving Size: 4 | Total Time: 35 minutes

½ lb cheddar, shredded	Salt and pepper to taste
5 eggs, whisked	¼ tbsp dried basil
1 onion, sliced	2 tbsp butter
1 green chili, chopped	¼ cup parsley, chopped
1 red bell pepper, chopped	

Melt butter in your Instant Pot on Sauté. Add in onion and cook for 2-3 minutes until tender. Put in bell pepper and cook for 2 minutes. Transfer to a baking dish. Add in whisked eggs, cheddar cheese, green chilies, basil, salt, and pepper. Pour 1 cup of water into the pot and insert a trivet. Place the dish on the trivet and seal the lid.

Select Manual and cook for 10 minutes on High pressure. When done, allow a natural release for 10 minutes and unlock the lid. Garnish with fresh parsley and serve.

Pancetta & Egg Casserole

Serving Size: 4 | Total Time: 27 minutes

2 tbsp olive oil	1 cup cheddar, shredded
6 slices pancetta, cubed	8 beaten eggs
1 tsp oregano	½ cup milk
2 cups frozen hash browns	Salt to taste

Warm the olive oil in your Instant Pot on Sauté. Place in pancetta and cook for 1-2 minutes. Add in a layer of potato hash brown and half of the cheddar cheese. Beat eggs, milk, oregano, and salt in a bowl and pour over cheese. Top with remaining cheddar and seal the lid.

Select Manual and cook for 15 minutes on High pressure. When ready, perform a quick pressure release and unlock the lid. Adjust seasoning. Serve right away.

Sausage & Egg Casserole

Serving Size: 4 | Total Time: 25 minutes

½ lb smoked sausages, sliced	1 cup cheddar, shredded
6 beaten eggs	¼ cup chives, chopped
½ cup plain yogurt	Salt and pepper to taste

Beat eggs and yogurt in a bowl. Add in cheddar cheese, smoked sausages, salt, and pepper and mix until combined. Pour 1 cup of water into your Instant Pot and fit in a trivet. Pour egg mixture into a baking dish and place it on top of the trivet. Seal the lid, select Manual, and cook for 15 minutes on High pressure. Once ready, perform a quick pressure release and unlock the lid. Top with chives and serve.

Tangy Egg Snacks

Serving Size: 6 | Total Time: 14 minutes

¼ tsp onion powder	¼ tsp garlic powder
6 eggs	Salt and black pepper to taste
½ tsp chili powder	
¼ tsp sea salt	

Grease a baking dish with cooking spray, crack the eggs, and whisk them. Sprinkle with salt, pepper, onion powder, chili powder, and garlic powder. Pour in 1 cup of water in your Instant Pot and fit in a trivet. Place the dish on the trivet and seal the lid. Select Manual and cook for 4 minutes on High pressure. When done, perform a quick pressure release and unlock the lid. Remove onto a cutting board and slice into cubes before serving.

Bacon & Spinach Eggs

Serving Size: 4 | Total Time: 25 minutes

8 eggs, beaten	2 tbsp chopped basil
½ cup chopped Spinach	3 tbsp heavy cream
4 bacon slices, diced	Salt and pepper to taste

Place the bacon in your Instant Pot and cook for 5 minutes on Sauté. Transfer to a bowl and mix in spinach, eggs, basil, heavy cream, salt, and pepper. Grease a baking dish with cooking spray and pour in the egg mixture.

Pour 1 cup of water into your Instant Pot and fit in a trivet. Place the dish on the trivet and seal the lid. Select Manual and cook for 8 minutes on High pressure. When done, perform a quick pressure release. Serve right away.

Mushroom & Egg Stuffed Bell Peppers

Serving Size: 4 | Total Time: 20 minutes

4 mushrooms, sliced	Salt and pepper to taste
4 bell peppers, top removed	2 tbsp mozzarella, grated
4 eggs	1 tbsp rosemary, chopped

Fill the peppers with the mushrooms. Crack an egg on each one and season with salt and pepper. Cover with aluminum foil. Pour 1 cup of water into your Instant Pot and fit in a trivet. Place bell peppers on the trivet and seal the lid. Select Manual and cook for 12 minutes on High.

Once done, perform a quick pressure release and unlock the lid. Remove to serving plates and scatter with mozzarella cheese and rosemary. Serve right away.

Egg & Ham Traybake

Serving Size: 4 | Total Time: 30 minutes

2 tbsp olive oil	1 cup canned black beans
2 shallots, chopped	1 cup feta cheese
½ lb ham, chopped	1 cup fontina cheese
8 large eggs, beaten	2 tbsp cilantro, chopped
½ cup flour	½ cup green onions

Warm the olive oil in your Instant Pot on Sauté. Add in shallots and cook for 2-3 minutes. Stir in ham and cook for 3-4 minutes more. In a bowl, whisk eggs with flour and pour over the ham. Top with beans, feta cheese, and fontina cheese. Seal the lid, select Manual, and cook for 15 minutes on High pressure. When over, allow a natural release for 10 minutes and unlock the lid. Scatter with cilantro and green onions. Serve chilled.

Spring Potato Salad with Eggs

Serving Size: 4 | Total Time: 20 minutes

4 eggs	2 spring onions, sliced
6 Yukon Gold potatoes	1 tbsp yellow mustard
1 cup mayonnaise	¼ cup pickle relish
2 tbsp dill, chopped	Salt and pepper to taste

Pour 1 cup of water into your Instant Pot and fit in a trivet. Place the eggs and potatoes on the trivet; seal the lid. Select Manual and cook for 5 minutes on High. When done, perform a quick pressure release and unlock the lid. Remove the eggs to a bowl filled with cold water and let them cool for 5 minutes. Peel and slice the potatoes.

Mix the pickle relish, mayonnaise, half of the dill, spring onions, and mustard in a bowl. Add in potatoes and toss to coat; season with salt and pepper. Peel and cut the eggs in half lengthwise. Transfer the salad to a serving plate and arrange the egg halves on top. Sprinkle with salt and dill and serve.

Green Bean & Feta Salad

Serving Size: 4 | Total Time: 25 minutes

1 cup feta cheese, crumbled	2 tbsp white wine vinegar
1 lb green beans, washed	3 garlic cloves, sliced
2 tbsp olive oil	Salt and pepper to taste

Place 1 cup of water in your Instant Pot and fit in a steamer basket. Put in green beans and seal the lid. Select Manual and cook for 2 minutes on High pressure. Whisk olive oil, vinegar, garlic, salt, and pepper in a bowl.

Once ready, perform a quick pressure release and unlock the lid. Remove the beans to a bowl and pour in the vinegar mixture. Mix it and let sit for 10 minutes. Discard garlic slices and scatter with feta cheese. Serve.

Potato & Salmon Salad

Serving Size: 6 | Total Time: 20 minutes

½ lb smoked salmon, chopped	
6 eggs	2 tbsp capers
3 lb red potatoes, cubed	1 tbsp chives, chopped
2 cups mayonnaise	Salt and pepper to taste

Pour 1 cup of water into your Instant Pot and fit in a steamer basket. Place in the eggs and potatoes and seal the lid. Select Manual and cook for 5 minutes on High.

Once ready, perform a quick pressure release and unlock the lid. Remove the egg to a bowl with iced water and let cool for a few minutes.

In another bowl, mix cooked potatoes, mayonnaise, smoked salmon, and capers. Peel and chop the eggs and mix them in the salad bowl. Sprinkle with salt and pepper. Serve topped with chives.

Potato, Green Bean & Egg Salad

Serving Size: 4 | Total Time: 30 minutes

1 lb potatoes, sliced to 1 inch thick	
2 tbsp toasted almonds, chopped	
2 large eggs	2 tbsp olive oil
1 lb green beans, trimmed	1 tbsp balsamic vinegar
Salt and pepper to taste	2 tbsp basil, chopped

Cover the potatoes with salted water in your Instant Pot. Seal the lid, select Manual, and cook for 12 minutes on High. Once ready, perform a quick pressure release and unlock the lid. Remove cooked potatoes to a bowl and set aside. Place eggs in the cooking water and fit in a steamer basket. Place in the green beans.

Seal the lid, select Manual, and cook for 6 minutes on High. When over, perform a quick pressure release. Remove the green beans and transfer them into the potato bowl. Combine with salt, pepper, olive oil, and vinegar.

Cool and peel the eggs, then cut them in half lengthways. Top the vegetables with egg halves, almonds, and basil. Serve right away.

Broccoli & Cherry Tomato Salad

Serving Size: 4 | Total Time: 20 minutes

2 tbsp olive oil	10 oz broccoli florets
1 cup mushrooms, sliced	1 cup cherry tomatoes, halved
1 tbsp soy sauce	1 cup vegetable broth

Warm the olive oil in your Instant Pot on Sauté. Place the mushrooms and cook for 5 minutes. Add in soy sauce and broccoli and Sauté for 1 more minute.

Stir in vegetable broth and seal the lid. Select Manual and cook for 2 minutes on High. Once ready, perform a quick pressure release and unlock the lid. Let cool for a few minutes, top with cherry tomatoes, and serve.

Carrot & Broccoli Salad with Hazelnuts

Serving Size: 4 | Total Time: 15 minutes

1 lb broccoli florets	1 tsp garlic powder
2 carrots, sliced	2 tbsp hazelnuts, chopped
2 green onions, sliced	2 tbsp olive oil
1 tbsp lemon juice	Salt to taste
1 tsp oregano	

Pour 1 cup of water into your Instant Pot and fit in a steamer basket. Place in the broccoli and carrots and seal the lid. Select Manual and cook for 2 minutes.

When done, perform a quick pressure release and unlock the lid. Remove the vegetables to iced water for a few minutes. Drain and place in a serving bowl. Add in green onions, lemon juice, oregano, garlic powder, salt, and olive oil and stir to combine. Serve topped with hazelnuts.

Broccoli & Egg Salad

Serving Size: 4 | Total Time: 20 minutes

1 lb small broccoli florets	¼ cup onion, chopped
4 large eggs	1 tbsp dill pickle juice
1 cup mayonnaise	1 tbsp yellow mustard
2 tbsp parsley, chopped	Salt and pepper to taste

Pour 1 cup water into your Instant Pot and fit in a trivet. Place broccoli and eggs on the trivet. Seal the lid, select Manual, and cook for 5 minutes on High. When over, perform a quick pressure release. Remove the eggs and transfer to a bowl with cold water for 2-3 minutes.

Meanwhile, mix mayonnaise, parsley, onion, dill pickle juice, and mustard in a bowl. Sprinkle with salt and pepper. Peel and slice the eggs. Place sliced egg and broccoli into mayonnaise mixture and toss to coat. Serve.

Cheesy Vegetable Medley

Serving Size: 4 | Total Time: 20 minutes

2 tbsp canola oil	2 tomatoes, chopped
1 red onion, sliced	Salt and pepper to taste
1 cup broccoli florets	2 garlic cloves, minced
2 red bell peppers, sliced	2 tbsp parsley, chopped
2 green bell pepper, sliced	3 tbsp mozzarella, shredded
1 yellow bell peppers, sliced	

Warm the canola oil in your Instant Pot on Sauté. Place the onion and garlic and cook for 3 minutes until softened. Add in bell peppers and Sauté for 5 minutes.

Stir in tomatoes, broccoli, salt, and pepper and seal the lid. Select Manual and cook for 2 minutes on High pressure. When done, perform a quick pressure release and unlock the lid. Remove the vegetables to a bowl and top with mozzarella cheese and parsley. Serve immediately.

Zucchini & Bacon Cheese Quiche

Serving Size: 4 | Total Time: 40 minutes

4 slices cooked and crumbled bacon
1 zucchini, chopped	1 cup diced ham
6 large eggs, beaten	1 cup Parmesan, shredded
½ cup milk	2 spring onions, chopped
Salt and pepper to taste	

Pour 1 cup of water into your Instant Pot and fit in a trivet. Mix eggs, milk, salt, and pepper in a bowl. Add in ham, bacon, zucchini, Parmesan cheese, and spring onions and stir. Cover with aluminum foil and place it on top of the trivet. Seal the lid, select Manual, and cook for 20 minutes on High pressure. When done, allow a natural release for 10 minutes and unlock the lid. Serve.

Asparagus & Tomato Tart

Serving Size: 4 | Total Time: 40 minutes

10 eggs	1 cup tomatoes, chopped
½ cup milk	4 green onions, chopped
Salt and pepper to taste	3 tomato slices
1 lb chopped asparagus	¼ cup Parmesan, shredded

Crack the eggs in a bowl and beat them with milk, salt, and pepper. In a separated bowl, mix asparagus, chopped tomatoes, and green onions and transfer to a baking dish. Pour the egg mixture over and toss to combine. Top with tomato slices and Parmesan cheese. Pour 1 cup of water into your Instant Pot and fit in a trivet.

Place the dish on top of the trivet and seal the lid. Select Manual and cook for 20 minutes on High pressure. Once ready, allow a natural release for 10 minutes, then perform a quick pressure release, and unlock the lid. Serve warm.

Baby Spinach & Gruyère Gratin

Serving Size: 4 | Total Time: 25 minutes

¼ cup Gruyère, grated	1 cup tomato, diced
8 beaten eggs	3 cups baby spinach
Salt and pepper to taste	3 green onions, sliced
½ cup milk	4 tomatoes, sliced

Pour 1 cup of water into your Instant Pot and fit in a trivet. Combine eggs, salt, pepper, and milk in a bowl. Place diced tomato, spinach, and green onions in a baking dish. Pour egg mixture over and top with tomato slices and Gruyère cheese. Place the dish on top of the trivet and seal the lid. Select Manual and cook for 15 minutes on High pressure. Perform a quick pressure release.

Spinach & Potato Gratin

Serving Size: 4 | Total Time: 30 minutes

2 tbsp olive oil	1 cup cheddar, shredded
2 cups spinach, torn	Salt and pepper to taste
½ yellow onion, chopped	1 cup breadcrumbs
1 lb potatoes	3 tbsp melted butter

Heat oil in your Instant Pot on Sauté. Place the onions and cook for 5 minutes; reserve. Pour 1 cup water in the pot and fit in a trivet. Place the potatoes on the trivet. Seal the lid. Select Manual and cook for 5 minutes on High.

Mix the breadcrumbs with butter. Once ready, perform a quick pressure release. Peel and slice the potatoes and transfer them to a baking sheet. Mix in the spinach. Sprinkle with cooked onion and cheddar cheese, season with salt and black pepper, and top with breadcrumb mixture. Place under a preheated broiler for about 8 minutes until crisp. Serve.

Mushroom-Potato Hash Casserole

Serving Size: 4 | Total Time: 20 minutes

1 onion, chopped	Salt and pepper to taste
2 garlic cloves, minced	½ tsp paprika
1 lb potatoes, peeled	½ tsp porcini powder
1 cup mushrooms, sliced	¼ tsp chili pepper powder

Place the potatoes in your Instant Pot and cover them with water. Seal the lid, select Manual, and cook for 5 minutes on High. Perform a quick pressure release. Unlock the lid. Remove the potatoes with a slotted spoon, then shred them with a cheese grater into a bowl.

Add in the mushrooms, garlic, onion, paprika, porcini powder, chili pepper powder, salt, and pepper and stir to combine. Transfer the mixture to a greased baking dish. Insert a trivet in the pot over the potato water and place the dish on the trivet. Seal the lid, select Manual, and cook for 7 minutes. Perform a quick pressure release.

Baby Spinach with Beets & Cheese

Serving Size: 4 | Total Time: 32 minutes

2 medium beets	1 tbsp apple cider vinegar
Salt and pepper to taste	¼ tsp brown sugar
¼ cup Goat cheese, crumbled	2 tbsp extra-virgin olive oil
2 cups baby spinach	2 tbsp walnuts, chopped

Pour 1 cup of water into your Instant Pot and fit in a steamer basket. Place in the beets and seal the lid. Select Manual and cook for 12 minutes on High pressure. When over, allow a natural release for 10 minutes, then perform a quick pressure release, and unlock the lid.

Remove the beets to a bowl and let cool. Peel and slice them into wedges. In a bowl, beat the apple cider vinegar, brown sugar, olive oil, salt, and pepper. Place the spinach, beets, and goat cheese in a serving bowl. Drizzle the dressing all over and toss lightly to coat. Sprinkle with walnuts and serve.

Potatoes with Creamy Arugula Sauce

Serving Size: 4 | Total Time: 30 minutes

2 lb potatoes, peeled, halved	1 tbsp basil, chopped
1 garlic clove, chopped	¼ cup extra-virgin olive oil
1 tbsp pine nuts, toasted	2 tbsp Parmesan, grated
1 cup arugula	2 tbsp heavy cream

Pour 1 cup water into your Instant Pot and fit in a trivet. Place the potatoes on the trivet and seal the lid. Select Manual and cook for 10 minutes on High. When over, allow a natural release for 10 minutes. Remove to a bowl.

Add garlic, pine nuts, arugula, and basil to a food processor and pulse until smooth. While the food processor is running, gradually pour the olive. Mix in the Parmesan cheese and heavy cream; adjust the seasonings. Pour the arugula sauce over the potatoes and serve.

Cheesy Potatoes with Herbs

Serving Size: 4 | Total Time: 30 minutes

½ cup Pecorino Romano cheese, shredded	
2 tbsp butter	½ tsp thyme
1 lb potatoes, cubed	½ tsp basil
1 cup chicken broth	½ tsp cayenne pepper
½ tsp rosemary	Salt to taste

Melt the butter in your Instant Pot on Sauté. Place the potatoes and cook for 5 minutes. Add in chicken broth, rosemary, thyme, and basil and seal the lid.

Select Manual and cook for 5 minutes on High. Once over, allow a natural release for 10 minutes and unlock the lid. Sprinkle with salt and cayenne pepper and transfer to a plate. Scatter Romano cheese over and serve.

Dill Potatoes with Butter & Olives

Serving Size: 4 | Total Time: 40 minutes

1 lb potatoes, chopped	1 tsp sea salt flakes
2 tbsp butter	3 tbsp sliced Kalamata olives
2 tbsp dill, chopped	

Cover the potatoes with enough in your Instant Pot and seal the lid. Select Manual and cook for 12 minutes on High pressure. Once over, allow a natural release for 10 minutes, then perform a quick pressure release, and unlock the lid. Drain potatoes leave them to dry.

Press Sauté and melt the butter. Put the dried potatoes back and cook for 3-4 minutes until lightly browned. Remove to a serving bowl and add in Kalamata olives and salt; toss to combine, and sprinkle with dill to serve.

Feta & Onion Layered Potatoes

Serving Size: 4 | Total Time: 30 minutes

1 tbsp butter, melted	Salt and pepper to taste
1 lb potatoes, sliced	2 tbsp scallions, chopped
½ tsp garlic powder	
½ lb onions, finely sliced	
1 cup feta cheese, grated	

Pour 1 cup of water into your Instant Pot and fit in a trivet. Add a layer of potatoes on a greased baking pan, sprinkle with salt and pepper, then add onions and half of the feta cheese. Top with another layer of potatoes and finish with the remaining feta cheese. Sprinkle with garlic powder and drizzle melted butter all over.

Cover with aluminum foil and lower the pan onto the trivet. Seal the lid, select Manual, and cook for 20 minutes on High. When done, perform a quick pressure release and unlock the lid. Garnish with scallions and serve.

Crushed Potatoes with Aioli

Serving Size: 4 | Total Time: 25 minutes

1 lb Russet potatoes, pierced	4 tbsp mayonnaise
Salt and pepper to taste	1 tsp garlic paste
2 tbsp olive oil	1 tbsp lemon juice

Mix the olive oil, salt, and pepper in a bowl. Add in the potatoes and toss to coat. Pour 1 cup of water into your Instant Pot and fit in a trivet. Place the potatoes on the trivet and seal the lid. Select Manual and cook for 12 minutes on High. Once ready, perform a quick release.

In a small bowl, combine the mayonnaise, garlic paste, and lemon juice and whisk well. Peel and crush the potatoes and transfer to a serving bowl. Serve with aioli.

Rosemary Sweet Potatoes with Butter

Serving Size: 4 | Total Time: 25 minutes

2 tbsp olive oil	Salt and pepper to taste
1 tbsp butter, melted	½ tsp rosemary
2 lb sweet potatoes, halved	

Warm the olive oil in your Instant Pot on Sauté. Place the sweet potatoes and cook for 10 minutes until golden brown. Sprinkle with salt and pepper. Pour in ¼ cup of water and seal the lid. Select Manual and cook for 6 minutes on High pressure. Once over, allow a natural release for 10 minutes, then perform a quick pressure release, and unlock the lid. Adjust the seasonings. Garnish with butter and rosemary and serve warm.

Parsley New Potatoes with Radishes

Serving Size: 4 | Total Time: 30 minutes

3 tbsp olive oil	2 tbsp parsley, chopped
2 lb baby potatoes, washed	Salt and pepper to taste
2 oz radishes, sliced	½ cup chicken broth

Warm the olive oil in your Instant Pot on Sauté. Place the potatoes and cook for 6-7 minutes. Make some holes with a fork. Season with salt and pepper. Pour in chicken broth and seal the lid.

Select Manual and cook for 10 minutes on High pressure. When done, perform a quick pressure release and unlock the lid. Remove the potatoes to a serving plate and scatter with radishes and parsley to serve.

Chive & Truffle Potato Mash

Serving Size: 4 | Total Time: 35 minutes

1 lb potatoes, quartered	Salt and pepper to taste
½ cup milk	2 tbsp chives, chopped
2 tbsp truffle oil	

Pour 1 cup of water into your Instant Pot and fit in a trivet. Place the potatoes on the trivet and seal the lid. Select Manual and cook for 15 minutes on High pressure.

Once over, allow a natural release for 10 minutes, then perform a quick pressure release, and unlock the lid. Remove potatoes to a bowl and mash them until smooth. Stir in milk and truffle oil; season with salt and pepper. Sprinkle with chives and serve.

Potato & Carrot Puree

Serving Size: 4 | Total Time: 20 minutes

1 lb potatoes, cubed	½ cup buttermilk
2 carrots, chopped	2 tbsp butter, melted
Salt and pepper to taste	

Pour 1 cups of water in your Instant Pot and fit in a trivet. Place the potatoes and carrots on the trivet. Seal the lid. Select Manual and cook for 12 minutes on High.

Once ready, perform a quick pressure release. Remove potatoes and carrots to a bowl and sprinkle with salt and pepper. Add in buttermilk and butter and mash them using a potato masher until smooth. Serve.

Chipotle & Garlic Mashed Potatoes

Serving Size: 4 | Total Time: 25 minutes

1 lb potatoes, cubed	¼ cup milk
2 garlic cloves	1 tbsp butter
1 tbsp chipotle paste	1 tbsp chili oil
1 cup chicken broth	Salt to taste

Place the potatoes, garlic, and chicken broth in your Instant Pot and seal the lid. Select Manual and cook for 15 minutes on High pressure. When done, perform a quick pressure release and unlock the lid.

Drain potatoes and transfer to a bowl. Add in milk, chipotle paste, chili oil, and butter and mash them using a potato masher until smooth. Sprinkle with salt. Serve.

Pumpkin & Potato Mash

Serving Size: 4 | Total Time: 20 minutes

½ lb pumpkin, cubed	¼ tsp dried sage
½ lb sweet potatoes, cubed	½ cup milk
2 garlic cloves	2 tbsp butter
¼ tsp dried tarragon	½ cup Parmesan, grated

Pour 1 cup of water into your Instant Pot and fit in a steamer basket. Place the pumpkin, sweet potatoes, and garlic in the steamer basket and seal the lid. Select Manual and cook for 12 minutes on High pressure.

Once ready, perform a quick pressure release and unlock the lid. Remove the veggies to a bowl. Stir in tarragon and sage. Pour in milk and butter and them using a potato masher until smooth; adjust the seasonings. Sprinkle with Parmesan cheese and serve.

Creamy Potatoes

Serving Size: 4 | Total Time: 25 minutes

6 potatoes, sliced	¼ cup buttermilk
1 tsp scallions	¼ cup milk
2 tbsp butter	2 tbsp potato starch
1 cup chicken broth	¼ tsp cayenne pepper

Place the potatoes and broth in your Instant Pot and seal the lid. Select Manual and cook for 5 minutes on High. Once ready, perform a quick pressure release and unlock the lid. Remove potatoes to a greased baking sheet.

Select Sauté on the pot and mix in the remaining cooking liquid with buttermilk, butter, milk, scallions, and potato starch and cook for 2-3 minutes until the sauce thickens. Pour it over the potatoes and place under the broiler for about 4 minutes. Sprinkle with cayenne pepper and serve.

Chili Coconut Potatoes

Serving Size: 4 | Total Time: 20 minutes

1 lb new potatoes	3 tbsp coconut oil, melted
½ tsp mustard seeds	1 red chili pepper flakes
2 garlic cloves, diced	Salt and pepper to taste

Pour 1 cup of water into your Instant Pot and fit in a trivet. Place the potatoes in a baking pan with garlic, mustard seeds, coconut oil, salt, and pepper; stir to combine. Lower the pan onto the trivet. Seal the lid, select Manual.

Cook for 4 minutes on High. When done, let sit for 5 minutes, then perform a quick pressure release and unlock the lid. Remove the potatoes to a bowl. Sprinkle with red chili pepper flakes and serve.

Mediterreanean Asparagus

Serving Size: 4 | Total Time: 15 minutes

1 lb asparagus, trimmed	3 tbsp feta cheese, crumbled
3 tbsp butter, melted	2 tsp parsley, chopped
2 garlic cloves, chopped	¼ tsp red pepper flakes
Salt and pepper to taste	

Pour 1 cup of water into your Instant Pot and fit in a trivet. Place the asparagus on a foil and brush with butter, garlic, salt, and pepper.

Fold up the sides of the foil to seal asparagus. Place the asparagus on the trivet and seal the lid. Select Manual and cook for 4 minutes on High.

Once ready, perform a quick pressure release and unlock the lid. Remove the asparagus from the foil and arrange them on a serving platter. Scatter with feta cheese, red pepper flakes, and parsley and serve.

Thyme & Garlic Potatoes

Serving Size: 4 | Total Time: 30 minutes

3 tbsp canola oil
2 garlic cloves
2 lb baby potatoes
1 thyme spring

½ cup stock
Salt and pepper to taste
2 tbsp toasted almonds, chopped

Warm the canola oil in your Instant Pot on Sauté. Place the garlic, potatoes, and thyme and Sauté for 10 minutes, stirring occasionally. Stir in stock, salt, and pepper and seal the lid. Select Manual and cook for 7 minutes on High pressure. Once ready, perform a quick pressure release and unlock the lid. Serve topped with almonds.

Rosemary Potato Fries

Serving Size: 4 | Total Time: 15 minutes

1 lb potatoes, cut into ½ inch sticks
Sea salt to taste
4 tbsp olive oil

2 tbsp rosemary, chopped

Place 1 cup of water in your Instant Pot and fit in a steamer basket. Place the potatoes in the basket and seal the lid. Select Manual and cook for 3 minutes on High.

Once ready, perform a quick pressure release. Unlock the lid. Remove potatoes to a bowl and pat them dry.

Discard the water and dry the pot. Warm the olive oil in the pot on Sauté. Place the potato sticks and cook until golden brown. Sprinkle with salt and rosemary to serve.

Sumac Red Potatoes

Serving Size: 4 | Total Time: 16 minutes

2 tbsp butter
1 lb red potatoes wedges

2 tbsp sumac
Salt and pepper to taste

Melt the butter in your Instant Pot on Sauté. Mix the potatoes, sumac, and ½ cup of water and seal the lid. Select Manual and cook for 6 minutes on High pressure. Once ready, perform a quick pressure release and unlock the lid. Sprinkle with salt and pepper. Serve immediately.

Steamed Sweet Potatoes with Cilantro

Serving Size: 4 | Total Time: 20 minutes

2 tbsp butter, melted
1 lb sweet potatoes, scrubbed

2 tbsp cilantro, chopped

Pour 1 cup water into your Instant Pot and fit in a trivet. Place the potatoes on the trivet. Seal the lid, select Manual, and cook for 12 minutes on High. When done, perform a quick pressure release and unlock the lid. Drizzle with melted butter and sprinkle with cilantro to serve.

Cheesy Jalapeño Sweet Potatoes

Serving Size: 4 | Total Time: 35 minutes

1 lb sweet potatoes, sliced
2 tbsp olive oil

Salt to taste
1 jalapeño pepper, sliced

Pour 1 cup of water into your Instant Pot and fit in a steamer basket. Place in the sweet potatoes and seal the lid. Select Manual and cook for 15 minutes on High.

Once ready, perform a quick pressure release and unlock the lid. Warm the olive oil in the pot on Sauté. Add in sweet potatoes and Sauté for 3-5 minutes. Sprinkle salt and pepper. Serve scattered with jalapeño slices.

Nutty Potatoes

Serving Size: 4 | Total Time: 20 minutes

1 tbsp lemon zest
Sea salt to taste
1 lb baby potatoes
¼ cup butter

¼ cup honey
1 tbsp cornstarch
1 cup mixed nuts, chopped

Mix the potatoes, lemon zest, salt, and 2 cups of of water in your Instant Pot and seal the lid. Select Manual and cook for 10 minutes on High pressure. When done, perform a quick pressure release and unlock the lid. Remove potatoes to a bowl. Melt the butter in the pot on Sauté. Stir in honey, cornstarch, and mixed nuts and cook for 2 minutes. Top the potatoes with sauce to serve.

Hazelnut Brussels Sprouts with Parmesan

Serving Size: 4 | Total Time: 15 minutes

1 lb Brussels sprouts, halved
2 tbsp butter
2 garlic cloves, minced
¼ cup hazelnuts, chopped

½ tsp thyme
¼ cup grated Parmesan cheese
Salt and pepper to taste

Pour 1 cup of water into your Instant Pot and fit in a steamer basket. Place in the sprouts halves and seal the lid. Select Manual and cook for 3 minutes on High.

Once ready, perform a quick pressure release. Unlock the lid. Clean the pot and melt the butter on Sauté. Add in Brussels sprouts and garlic and Sauté for 2-3 minutes, stirring occasionally. Season with salt, pepper, and thyme and mix in hazelnuts. Serve topped with Parmesan cheese.

Butternut Squash & Kale Pot

Serving Size: 4 | Total Time: 25 minutes

2 tbsp olive oil
1 onion, diced
2 garlic cloves, minced
1 tsp cumin seeds
1 tsp coriander seeds
½ tsp hot paprika

1 cup canned white beans
1 lb butternut squash, cubed
1 cup canned diced tomatoes
3 cups vegetable stock
3 cups kale, chopped

Warm olive oil in your Instant Pot on Sauté. Add in the onion, garlic, cumin and coriander seeds and Sauté for 3 minutes until tender. Stir in paprika, butternut squash, tomatoes, white beans, and vegetable stock and seal the lid. Select Manual and cook for 10 minutes on High.

When done, perform a quick pressure release and unlock the lid. Adjust the seasonings. Stir in kale and close the lid. Let it sit in the residual heat until the kale wilts. Serve.

Spicy Cauliflower Cakes

Serving Size: 4 | Total Time: 20 minutes

1 cauliflower head, chopped Salt and pepper to taste
1 cup panko breadcrumbs ½ tsp cayenne pepper
1 cup Parmesan, shredded 2 tbsp olive oil

Pour 1 cup of water into your Instant Pot and fit in a steamer basket. Place in the cauliflower and seal the lid. Select Manual and cook for 3 minutes on High pressure.

Once ready, perform a quick pressure release and unlock the lid. Mash the cauliflower with a fork in a bowl. Add in breadcrumbs, Parmesan cheese, cayenne pepper, salt, and black pepper and mix to combine. Form the meat mixture into patties. Clean the pot and warm the olive oil on Sauté. Fry the cakes for 4-5 minutes, flipping once until golden brown. Serve warm.

Steamed Vegetables with Chile Butter

Serving Size: 4 | Total Time: 10 minutes

10 oz broccoli florets Salt to taste
2 red bell peppers, sliced 2 tbsp butter
2 garlic cloves, minced 1 serrano chile, minced
1 tbsp Italian seasoning

Pour 1 cup of water into your Instant Pot and fit in a steamer basket. Place in the broccoli and bell peppers. Sprinkle with Italian seasoning. Seal the lid. Cook for 1 minute on Steam. When done, perform a quick release.

Clean the pot and melt in the butter on Sauté. Add in serrano chile, garlic, and salt and stir-fry for 1-2 minutes. Drizzle the chile butter over the veggies and serve.

Steamed Cauliflower with Cheese

Serving Size: 4 | Total Time: 10 minutes

1 lb cauliflower florets 1 cup shredded cheddar
Salt and pepper to taste

Pour 1 cup water into your Instant Pot and fit in a steamer basket. Place in the cauliflower and seal the lid. Select Manual and cook for 2 minutes on Steam. When done, perform a quick pressure release. Sprinkle the cauliflower with salt and pepper. Top with cheese to serve.

Italian-Style Brussels Sprouts

Serving Size: 4 | Total Time: 15 minutes

1 lb Brussels sprouts, halved Salt and pepper to taste
2 garlic cloves, minced 1 tsp olive oil
1 tbsp mustard seeds 2 tbsp rosemary, chopped
1 cup vegetable broth

Heat the olive oil in your Instant Pot and on Sauté. Cook Brussels sprouts, garlic, and mustard seeds for 2 minutes, stirring often. Pour in vegetable broth, salt, and pepper and seal the lid. Select Manual and cook for 4 minutes on High pressure. When done, perform a quick pressure release and unlock the lid. Serve topped with rosemary.

Brussels Sprouts with Cranberries

Serving Size: 4 | Total Time: 20 minutes

1 lb Brussels sprouts, halved 1 tbsp apple cider
Salt and pepper to taste ½ tsp brown sugar
¼ cup pine nuts, toasted 2 tbsp olive oil
2 tbsp dried cranberries

Pour 1 cup of water into your Instant Pot and fit in a steamer basket. Place in the Brussels sprouts and seal the lid. Select Manual and cook for 4 minutes on High.

Once ready, perform a quick pressure release and unlock the lid. Remove the sprouts to a bowl. Clean the pot and heat in the olive oil. Add in the dried cranberries, apple cider, and brown sugar and cook for 1 minute. Stir in Brussels sprouts and fry for another 2-3 minutes. Sprinkle with salt, pepper, and pine nuts and serve.

Chili Corn On the Cob

Serving Size: 4 | Total Time: 10 minutes

4 ears corn on the cob, husked
1 Poblano chili pepper, chopped
4 tbsp butter, softened 2 tbsp parsley, chopped

Pour 1 cup of water into your Instant Pot and fit in a trivet. Mix the chili pepper, parsley, and butter in a blender until smooth. Rub the mixture all over the corn and place on the trivet. Seal the lid, select Manual, and cook for 2 minutes on High pressure. Serve right away.

Provençal Ratatouille

Serving Size: 4 | Total Time: 20 minutes

2 tbsp olive oil ½ fennel bulb, sliced
1 red onion, sliced 2 red bell peppers, sliced
2 garlic cloves, minced 1 cup vegetable broth
2 eggplants, sliced 14 oz canned tomatoes, diced
3 zucchini, sliced ½ tbsp herbs de Provence

Warm the olive oil in your Instant Pot on Sauté. Place the onion, garlic, eggplants, zucchini, fennel, and bell peppers and cook for 3-4 minutes. Stir in tomatoes, vegetable broth, and herbs de Provence and seal the lid. Select Manual and cook for 5 minutes on High pressure. When done, perform a quick pressure release. Serve.

Cauliflower & Kale Curry

Serving Size: 4 | Total Time: 10 minutes

1 lb cauliflower florets 2 tsp garam masala
1 can coconut milk 1 cup tomato sauce
½ tsp fresh ginger, grated 1cup vegetable broth
1 lb kale, chopped Salt and pepper to taste

Mix the cauliflower, coconut milk, kale, garam masala, tomato sauce, ginger, broth, salt, and pepper in your Instant Pot. Seal the lid, select Manual, and cook for 4 minutes on High pressure. When done, perform a quick pressure release and unlock the lid. Serve immediately.

Parsnip & Cauliflower Mash

Serving Size: 4 | Total Time: 15 minutes

1 cauliflower, cut into florets   2 tbsp safflower oil
2 parsnips, chopped   1 green onion, chopped
Salt and pepper to taste

Pour 1 cup water into your Instant Pot and fit in a steamer basket. Place in the cauliflower and parsnips and seal the lid. Select Manual and cook for 3 minutes on High.

Once over, perform a quick pressure release and unlock the lid. Mash the cauliflower and parsnips with a potato masher and mix in salt, pepper, and safflower oil. Serve topped with green onion.

Fall Vegetable Mash

Serving Size: 4 | Total Time: 25 minutes

1 lb pumpkin, cubed   ½ tsp dried rosemary
¼ lb celeriac, cubed   2 tbsp butter
1 parsnip, cubed   1 tsp garlic powder
2 potatoes, cubed   ¼ cup milk
½ tsp dried thyme   Salt to taste

Pour 1 cup of water into your Instant Pot and fit in a steamer basket. Place in pumpkin, celeriac, parsnip, and potatoes and seal the lid. Select Manual and cook for 12 minutes on High. Once ready, perform a quick pressure release and unlock the lid. Transfer the vegetable to a bowl and mash them with a potato mash. Mix in milk, butter, garlic powder, rosemary, thyme, and salt. Serve.

Zucchini with Asparagus

Serving Size: 4 | Total Time: 15 minutes

1 lb asparagus, trimmed and chopped
2 tbsp olive oil   ½ cup vegetable broth
2 garlic cloves, minced   Salt and pepper to taste
2 zucchinis, sliced   2 tbsp fresh dill, chopped
½ cup whipping cream

Warm the olive oil in your Instant Pot on Sauté. Place the garlic and cook for 2 minutes. Stir in zucchinis, asparagus, vegetable broth, salt, and pepper. Seal the lid, select Manual, and cook for 4 minutes on High pressure. When done, perform a quick pressure release and unlock the lid. Stir in whipping cream. Serve topped with dill.

Mango & Pumpkin Porridge

Serving Size: 4 | Total Time: 20 minutes

1 lb pumpkin, chopped   2 tbsp maple syrup
1 mango, chopped   2 tbsp walnuts, chopped
1 cup milk   A pinch of salt
2 tbsp cinnamon powder

Mix the pumpkin, mango, cinnamon powder, maple syrup, milk, and salt in your Instant Pot. Seal the lid, select Manual, and cook for 12 minutes on High pressure. Once ready, perform a quick pressure release and unlock the lid. Serve topped with walnuts.

Steamed Asparagus with Salsa Verde

Serving Size: 4 | Total Time: 15 minutes

1 lb asparagus, trimmed   4 anchovy fillets, chopped
1 tbsp onion, chopped   2 tbsp extra-virgin olive oil
Salt and pepper to taste   1 tbsp sherry vinegar
2 tbsp parsley, chopped   2 tsp capers, chopped

Pour 1 cup of water into your Instant Pot and fit in a trivet. Place the asparagus on the trivet. Season with salt and pepper. Seal the lid and cook for 2 minutes on Steam. Once ready, perform a quick pressure release. Add parsley, onion, sherry vinegar, olive oil, anchovies, and capers in a blender and process until everything is well mixed. Drizzle the asparagus with the sauce.

Steamed Artichokes with Salsa Roquefort

Serving Size: 4 | Total Time: 25 minutes

1 lb artichokes, trimmed   ½ cup Roquefort cheese
1 lemon wedge   1 cup heavy cream

Pour 1 cup of water into your Instant Pot and fit in a steamer basket. Place in artichokes and seal the lid. Select Manual and cook for 10 minutes on High pressure.

When over, perform a quick pressure release. Remove artichokes to a plate to cool. Clean the pot and heat the heavy cream on Sauté. Add in the Roquefort cheese and stir constantly until the cheese melts, about 3-4 minutes. Pour the sauce over the artichokes and serve with lemon.

Coconut Pumpkin Chili

Serving Size: 4 | Total Time: 20 minutes

½ lb pumpkin, chopped   1 tsp cumin
2 cups tomatoes, diced   1 tbsp chili powder
1 cup coconut milk   Salt and pepper to taste
1 tsp red chili flakes   2 tbsp cilantro, chopped
1 tbsp red curry paste

Mix the pumpkin, tomatoes, cumin, coconut milk, chili powder, curry paste, salt, pepper, and 2 cups of water in your Instant Pot and seal the lid. Select Manual and cook for 10 minutes on High pressure. Once ready, perform a quick pressure release and unlock the lid. Top with red chili flakes and cilantro and serve.

Mascarpone Mashed Turnips

Serving Size: 4 | Total Time: 32 minutes

1 lb turnips, cubed   Salt and pepper to taste
1 onion, chopped   ¼ cup sour cream
½ tsp ground nutmeg   2 tbsp mascarpone
½ cup chicken stock

Place the turnips, onion, and chicken stock in your Instant Pot and seal the lid. Select Manual and cook for 12 minutes on High. Once over, allow a natural release for 10 minutes and unlock the lid. Add in sour cream, nutmeg, and mascarpone and mash it using a potato masher until smooth. Sprinkle with salt and pepper.

Tarragon Baby Carrots with Parsnips

Serving Size: 4 | Total Time: 25 minutes

1 tbsp olive oil	1 tsp ground cumin
1 small onion, chopped	1 tsp lemon juice
½ lb baby carrots, sliced	Salt and pepper to taste
2 parsnips, sliced	2 tbsp tarragon, chopped

Warm the olive oil in your Instant Pot on Sauté. Place the onion and cook for 3 minutes. Add in baby carrots, parsnips, cumin, and lemon juice and sauté for 1 more minute; season with salt and pepper.

Add in 1 cup of water and seal the lid. Select Manual and cook for 7 minutes on High pressure. When done, perform a quick pressure release and unlock the lid. Serve topped with tarragon.

Carrot & Beet Medley

Serving Size: 4 | Total Time: 20 minutes

2 tbsp olive oil	1 cup vegetable broth
2 shallots, chopped	1 tbsp caraway seeds
1 lb carrots, sliced	Salt and pepper to taste
2 beets, peeled and cubed	

Warm the olive oil in your Instant Pot on Sauté. Place the shallots and cook for 3 minutes. Stir in caraway seeds, carrots, beets, vegetable broth, salt, and pepper. Seal the lid, select Manual, and cook for 8 minutes on High pressure. Once ready, perform a quick pressure release and unlock the lid. Serve warm.

Orange Glazed Carrots

Serving Size: 4 | Total Time: 25 minutes

1 tbsp butter	1 tbsp orange marmalade
6 carrots, sliced diagonally	Salt and black pepper to taste
¼ tsp orange zest	
½ cup orange juice	

Pour 1 cup of water into your Instant Pot and fit in a steamer basket. Place in the carrots and seal the lid. Select Manual and cook for 8 minutes on High. When done, perform a quick release. Remove carrots to a bowl.

Clean the pot and melt in the butter on Sauté. Add in orange zest, orange juice, orange marmalade, salt, and pepper and stir to combine. Add in carrots and cook until they are caramelized and sticky, 5-8 minutes. Serve.

Garlic Eggplants with Parmesan

Serving Size: 4 | Total Time: 20 minutes

2 tbsp olive oil	Salt and pepper to taste
1 onion, chopped	1 cup tomato sauce
3 garlic cloves, minced	½ tsp dried oregano
1 lb eggplants, cubed	¼ cup Parmesan, grated

Warm the olive oil in your Instant Pot on Sauté. Place the onion and garlic and cook for 3 minutes. Add in the eggplants, salt, pepper, tomato sauce, oregano, and ½ of water. Season with salt and pepper.

Seal the lid, select Manual, and cook for 8 minutes on High. Once ready, perform a quick pressure release and unlock the lid. Serve topped with Parmesan cheese.

Yogurt Eggplant Dip

Serving Size: 4 | Total Time: 20 minutes

3 tbsp olive oil	1 cup Greek yogurt
3 eggplants, chopped	1 tsp ground cumin
4 garlic cloves, sliced	1 cup vegetable broth
Salt to taste	2 tbsp cilantro, chopped
1 lemon, juiced	

Warm the olive oil in your Instant Pot on Sauté. Place the eggplants and cook for 3 minutes, stirring occasionally. Add in garlic and Sauté for another 30 seconds. Season with salt and pour in vegetable broth

Seal the lid. Select Manual and cook for 6 minutes on High pressure. When over, perform a quick pressure release and unlock the lid. Transfer the mixture to a food processor and lemon juice, cumin, and yogurt and blend until smooth. Sprinkle with cilantro and serve.

Spicy Okra & Eggplant Dish

Serving Size: 4 | Total Time: 25 minutes

2 tbsp olive oil	1 tsp ground coriander
1 onion, chopped	½ tsp chili powder
2 garlic cloves, minced	½ cup diced tomatoes
2 eggplants, cubed	¾ cup vegetable stock
½ lb okra, tops removed	Fresh scallions, chopped

Warm the olive oil in your Instant Pot on Sauté. Place the onion, garlic, okra, and eggplants and cook for 3-4 minutes, stirring often. Add in the coriander, chili powder, tomatoes, and vegetable stock. Seal the lid, select Manual, and cook for 8 minutes on High pressure.

Once over, perform a quick pressure release and open the lid. Adjust the seasonings and serve topped with fresh scallions.

Winter Root Vegetables with Feta

Serving Size: 4 | Total Time: 40 minutes

½ lb beets	2 tbsp parsley, chopped
½ lb carrots	Salt and pepper to taste
1 tbsp olive oil	3 tbsp raspberry vinaigrette
1 clove garlic, minced	½ cup feta, crumbled

Pour 1 cup of water into your Instant Pot and fit in a steamer basket. Place in the beets and carrots and seal the lid. Select Manual and cook for 12 minutes on High pressure. Mix the garlic, parsley, salt, pepper, and raspberry vinaigrette in a bowl.

When over, allow a natural release for 10 minutes. Peel and slice the vegetables. Arrange on a greased baking sheet, drizzle with olive oil, and season with salt and pepper. Place under a preheated broiler for 4-5 minutes. Add in the dressing and feta and toss to coat. Serve.

Orange & Thyme Beet Wedges

Serving Size: 4 | Total Time: 25 minutes

1 lb beets	2 thyme sprigs
2 tbsp butter, melted	1 orange, juiced

Pour 1 cup of water into your Instant Pot and fit in a steamer basket. Place in the beets and seal the lid. Select Manual and cook for 12 minutes on High pressure. Once ready, perform a quick pressure release and unlock the lid. Remove the beets to a plate and let cool. Peel and cut into wedges. Clean the pot and melt the butter on Sauté. Add in the thyme sprigs and cook for 30-40 seconds. Pour in the orange juice and beets and stir for 2-3 minutes. Discard the thyme sprigs and serve.

Butter-Braised Cabbage

Serving Size: 4 | Total Time: 30 minutes

4 tbsp butter	½ tsp herbs de Provence
1 head cabbage, shredded	1 carrot, grated
1 ½ cups vegetable broth	2 tsp cornstarch
½ tsp red pepper flakes	

Melt the butter in your Instant Pot on Sauté. Add in the cabbage and 2-3 tbsp of the vegetable broth and cook for 6 minutes, stirring occasionally. Mix in carrots, herbs de Provence, and the remaining vegetable broth.

Seal the lid, select Manual, and cook for 6 minutes on High pressure. When done, perform a quick pressure release and unlock the lid. Remove the cabbage and carrot to a bowl with a slotted spoon.

Combine the cornstarch with some of the cooking liquid and pour it into the pot. Press Sauté and cook until the sauce thickens, about 3-4 minutes. Stir in red pepper flakes and pour over the cabbage. Serve warm.

Mushroom & Bell Pepper Casserole

Serving Size: 4 | Total Time: 30 minutes

1 ½ cups cremini mushrooms, sliced	
2 tbsp butter	½ cup heavy cream
1 onion, chopped	½ cup chicken broth
1 red bell pepper, sliced	½ cup crispy onions

Melt butter in your Instant Pot on Sauté. Place in onion, bell pepper, and mushrooms and cook for 3-4 minutes. Stir in heavy cream and chicken broth. Seal the lid, select Manual, and cook for 15 minutes on High pressure. Once over, perform a quick pressure release and unlock the lid. Serve topped with crispy onions.

Curried Tofu with Vegetables

Serving Size: 4 | Total Time: 20 minutes

2 tbsp sesame oil	1 red bell pepper, chopped
3 green onions, sliced	¼ tsp curry powder
3 garlic cloves, minced	28 oz firm tofu, cubed
1 celery stalk, chopped	1 cup bbq sauce
1 cup mushrooms, sliced	1 tbsp sesame seeds, toasted

Warm the sesame oil in your Instant Pot on Sauté. Place the green onions, garlic celery, mushrooms, and bell pepper and cook for 3 minutes. Stir in salt and curry powder and cook for 2 more minutes.

Add in tofu, and bbq sauce, and ½ cup of water. Seal the lid, select Manual, and cook for 5 minutes on High. Once ready, perform a quick pressure release and unlock the lid. Serve warm topped with sesame seeds.

Asparagus & Mushrooms with Bacon

Serving Size: 4 | Total Time: 30 minutes

1 lb asparagus, trimmed	8 oz mushrooms, sliced
6 oz bacon, chopped	Salt and pepper to taste
1 clove garlic, minced	1 tbsp balsamic vinegar
1 yellow onion, chopped	

Place asparagus in your Instant Pot and pour in water. Seal the lid, select Manual, and cook for 3 minutes on High pressure. When ready, allow a natural release for 10 minutes and unlock the lid. Strain asparagus; set aside.

Press Sauté on the pot and add bacon; cook for 1-2 minutes. Stir in garlic and onion and sauté for 2 minutes. Mix in mushrooms and cook until they are soft. Mix in cooked asparagus, salt, pepper, and balsamic vinegar and combine. Serve immediately.

Green Vegetables with Tomatoes

Serving Size: 6 | Total Time: 15 minutes

1 tsp olive oil	½ lb green beans, trimmed
1 clove garlic, minced	½ cup green peas
2 cups chopped tomatoes	½ lb asparagus, trimmed
½ cup vegetable stock	Salt and pepper to taste

Warm the olive oil in your Instant Pot on Sauté. Place in garlic and cook for 30 seconds until fragrant. Stir in tomatoes. Pour in vegetable stock, green beans, green peas, and asparagus; season with salt, and pepper. Seal the lid, select Manual, and cook for 5 minutes on High pressure. When done, perform a quick pressure release.

Yummy Vegetable Soup

Serving Size: 4 | Total Time: 25 minutes

2 tbsp olive oil	1 cup broccoli florets
1 cup leeks, chopped	1 cup cauliflower florets
2 garlic cloves, minced	½ red bell pepper, diced
4 cups vegetable stock	¼ head cabbage, chopped
1 carrot, diced	½ cup green beans
1 parsnip, diced	2 tbsp nutritional yeast
1 celery stalk, diced	Salt and pepper to taste
1 cup mushrooms	½ cup parsley, chopped

Heat oil on Sauté. Add in garlic and leeks and cook for 6 minutes until slightly browned. Add in stock, carrot, celery, broccoli, bell pepper, green beans, salt, nutritional yeast, cabbage, cauliflower, mushrooms, parsnip, and pepper. Seal the lid and cook on High Pressure for 6 minutes. Release pressure naturally. Stir in parsley to serve.

POULTRY

Chicken Salad The "Hawaiian Style"

Serving Size: 4 | Total Time: 1 hour 35 minutes

PINEAPPLE SALAD

¼ cup apple cider vinegar	½ head cabbage, shredded
¼ cup canola oil	2 cups arugula
1 pineapple, chopped	4 green onions, chopped

HAWAIIAN-STYLE CHICKEN

1 tsp brown sugar	2 tbsp grated fresh ginger
½ cup chicken broth	1 tsp black pepper
½ cup soy sauce	1 lb chicken breasts, halved
½ cup honey	1 tbsp cornstarch
2 tbsp orange juice	2 tbsp water
2 garlic cloves, minced	4 Hawaiian bread rolls

In a bowl, mix oil and vinegar; add pineapple, green onions, cabbage, and arugula and toss well to coat. Refrigerate for 1 hour while the bowl is covered. In the pot, mix sugar, soy sauce, garlic, pepper, ginger, honey, broth, and orange juice. Press Sauté on your Instant Pot. Allow to a simmer. Cook until the honey and sugar dissolve. Toss the chicken into the sauce.

Seal the lid and cook on High Pressure for 16 minutes. Release the pressure quickly. Shred the chicken with 2 forks. Preheat your oven's broiler. In a small bowl, mix water and cornstarch; stir into the sauce in the cooker. Set the cooker to Sauté and cook the sauce for 2 to 3 minutes until it thickens. Stir in the shredded chicken. Halve the loaf of Hawaiian rolls.

Set the halves, cut-side up, onto a baking sheet. Under the preheated broiler, toast the rolls for 3 minutes until golden brown. Transfer the shredded chicken to the bottom half of the rolls and apply a topping of salad. Replace the top half of the rolls and cut into them individual sliders before serving.

Lebanese-Style Chicken with Couscous

Serving Size: 4 | Total Time: 50 minutes

4 chicken thighs	1 onion, chopped
2 tbsp za'atar mix	1 garlic clove, minced
1 tbsp ground sumac	1 ½ cups couscous
Salt and pepper to taste	Juice from 1 lemon
2 tbsp butter	2 tbsp parsley, chopped
2 ½ cups chicken stock	

Season the chicken with salt, sumac, za'atar, and pepper. Melt butter on Sauté in your Instant Pot. Sear the chicken in batches for 5 minutes until lightly browned. Set aside.

Into the pot, add ¼ cup chicken stock to deglaze the pan, scrape the bottom to get rid of any browned bits of food. Add in garlic and onion and cook for 3 minutes until soft. Add the remaining chicken stock, chicken, lemon juice, and couscous into the pan and stir. Seal the lid and cook on High pressure for 10 minutes. Naturally release the pressure for 10 minutes. Garnish with parsley.

Crispy Bacon & Bean Chicken

Serving Size: 4 | Total Time: 65 minutes

4 boneless, skinless chicken thighs	
1 cup shredded Monterey Jack cheese	
2 tbsp olive oil	½ tsp cayenne pepper
4 slices bacon, crumbled	1 (14.5-oz) can tomatoes
1 onion, diced	1 cup chicken broth
4 garlic cloves, minced	1 tsp salt
1 tbsp tomato paste	1 cup cooked corn
1 tbsp oregano	1 red bell pepper, chopped
1 tbsp ground cumin	15 oz red kidney beans
1 tsp chili powder	2 tbsp chopped cilantro

Warm oil on Sauté in your Instant Pot. Sear the chicken for 3 minutes for each side until browned. Set aside. In the same oil, fry bacon until crispy, about 5 minutes; set aside. Add in onion and cook for 3 minutes until fragrant. Stir in garlic, oregano, cayenne, cumin, tomato paste, bell pepper, and chili and cook for 30 more seconds.

Pour in the broth, salt, and tomatoes. Bring to a boil. Take back the chicken and bacon to the pot and ensure it is submerged in the braising liquid. Seal the lid and cook on High Pressure for 15 minutes. Release the pressure quickly. Pour the corn and kidney beans into the cooker, Press Sauté and bring the liquid to a boil; cook for 10 minutes. Serve topped with shredded cheese and cilantro.

Ginger & Potato Chicken Thighs

Serving Size: 4 | Total Time: 35 minutes

4 chicken thighs, boneless	1 tbsp cayenne pepper
3 large potatoes, wedged	1 tsp fresh mint, chopped
1 tbsp lemon juice	¼ cup olive oil
2 garlic cloves, crushed	½ tsp salt
1 tsp ginger, ground	

In a bowl, combine olive oil, lemon juice, garlic, ginger, mint, cayenne, and salt. Brush each chicken piece with the mixture. Spread the remaining mixture on the inner pot of your Instant Pot. Place the potatoes and top with chicken. Add 1½ cups of water and seal the lid. Cook on Manual for 15 minutes on High. When ready, release the pressure naturally for 10 minutes. Serve.

Fabulous Orange Chicken Stew

Serving Size: 4 | Total Time: 55 minutes

1 cup fire-roasted tomatoes, diced	
1 lb chicken breasts	1 cup orange juice
1 tbsp chili powder	2 cups chicken broth
Salt and pepper to taste	

Season the chicken with chili powder, salt, and pepper, and place in your Instant Pot. Add fire-roasted tomatoes and cook on Sauté for 10 minutes, stirring occasionally. Pour in the broth and orange juice. Seal the lid and cook on Poultry for 25 minutes on High. Release the pressure naturally for 10 minutes. Serve immediately.

Buttered Chicken with Artichokes

Serving Size: 4 | Total Time: 35 minutes

1 lb chicken breasts, chopped	1 lemon, juiced
2 artichokes, trimmed, halved	Salt and pepper to taste
3 tbsp butter, melted	1 tbsp rosemary, chopped

Heat 1 tbsp butter on Sauté in your Instant Pot and cook the chicken for a minute per side until slightly golden. Pour in 1 cup of water, seal the lid, and cook on High Pressure for 13 minutes. Do a quick release. Set aside.

Insert a trivet in the pot. Rub the artichoke halves with half of the lemon juice and arrange on the trivet. Seal the lid and cook on Steam for 3 minutes. Do a quick release. Combine artichoke and chicken in a large bowl. Stir in salt, pepper, and lemon juice. Drizzle the remaining butter over and sprinkle with rosemary to serve.

Chicken Drumsticks with Potatoes

Serving Size: 4 | Total Time: 30 minutes

4 boneless skinless chicken drumsticks	
4 potatoes, peeled and quartered	
½ cup cherry tomatoes, quartered	
2 lemons, zested and juiced	1 cup watercress
1 tbsp olive oil	1 cucumber, sliced
1 tsp red pepper flakes	¼ cup Kalamata olives, pitted
Salt and pepper to taste	¼ cup hummus
2 serrano peppers, chopped	¼ cup feta, crumbled
3 tbsp chopped parsley	Lemon wedges, for serving

In your Instant Pot, place the potatoes and cover with water. Set trivet over them. In a baking bowl, mix lemon juice, olive oil, pepper, zest, salt, and red pepper flakes. Add in chicken drumsticks and stir to coat. Set the bowl with chicken on the trivet. Seal the lid, select Manual, and cook for 15 minutes on High. Do a quick release.

Take out the chicken and the trivet from the pot. Drain potatoes and add parsley and salt. Divide the potatoes between serving plates and top with watercress, cucumber slices, hummus, cherry tomatoes, chicken, olives, serrano peppers, and feta. Garnish with lemon wedges and serve.

Lemon Chicken Wings

Serving Size: 4 | Total Time: 20 minutes

2 tbsp olive oil	½ tsp cayenne pepper
8 chicken wings	Salt and pepper to taste
½ tsp chili powder	½ cup chicken broth
½ tsp garlic powder	2 lemons, juiced
½ tsp onion powder	

Coat the chicken wings with olive oil. Season with chili powder, onion powder, salt, garlic powder, cayenne, and pepper. In your Instant Pot, add the wings and chicken broth. Seal the lid and cook on High Pressure for 4 minutes. Do a quick pressure release.

Preheat the oven to 380 F. Onto a greased baking sheet, place the wings in a single layer and drizzle over the lemon juice. Bake for 5 minutes until the skin is crispy.

Sweet & Citrusy Chicken Breasts

Serving Size: 4 | Total Time: 20 minutes

2 chicken breasts, cubed	1 garlic clove, minced
½ cup honey	2 tsp cornstarch
½ cup orange juice	2 tsp water
1/3 cup soy sauce	1 cup diced orange
1/3 cup chicken stock	3 cups cooked quinoa
1/3 cup hoisin sauce	

Arrange the chicken at the bottom of your Instant Pot. In a bowl, stir honey, soy sauce, garlic, hoisin sauce, stock, and orange juice until the honey is dissolved. Pour the mixture over the chicken. Seal the lid and cook on High Pressure for 7 minutes. Release the pressure quickly.

Take the chicken from the pot and set it in a bowl. Press Sauté. In a small bowl, mix water with cornstarch. Pour into the liquid within the pot and cook for 3 minutes until thick. Stir diced orange and chicken into the sauce until well coated. Serve with quinoa.

White Wine Chicken with Fresh Herbs

Serving Size: 4 | Total Time: 30 minutes

4 chicken breasts	½ tsp rosemary, chopped
½ tsp salt	½ tsp marjoram, chopped
¼ cup dry white wine	½ tsp sage, chopped

Rub the chicken with salt, rosemary, marjoram, and sage and set in your Instant Pot. Mix in white wine, and 1 cup water. Seal the lid and cook for 6 minutes on High Pressure. Release the pressure naturally for 10 minutes. Serve warm.

Delicious Pulled Chicken with Peach Sauce

Serving Size: 4 | Total Time: 30 minutes

4 boneless, skinless chicken thighs	
15 oz canned peach chunks	½ tsp salt
14 oz canned diced tomatoes	Cheddar shredded cheese
2 cloves garlic, minced	2 tbsp chopped mint leaves
½ tsp cumin	

Strain canned peach chunks. Reserve the juice and set aside. In your Instant Pot, add chicken, tomatoes, cumin, garlic, peach juice (about 1 cup), and salt. Seal the lid, press Manual, and cook for 15 minutes on High. Do a quick pressure release. Shred chicken with two forks.

Transfer to a serving plate. Add peach chunks to the cooking juices and mix until well combined. Pour the peach salsa over the chicken, top with chopped mint leaves and shredded cheese, and serve.

Pancetta & Cabbage Chicken Thighs

Serving Size: 4 | Total Time: 30 minutes

4 chicken thighs, boneless skinless	
1 tbsp lard	1 tbsp Dijon mustard
4 slices pancetta, diced	1 lb green cabbage, shredded
Salt and pepper to taste	2 tbsp parsley, chopped
1 cup chicken broth	

Melt lard on Sauté in your Instant Pot. Fry pancetta for 5 minutes until crisp. Set aside. Season chicken with pepper and salt. Sear in the cooker for 2 minutes on each side until browned. In a bowl, mix mustard and broth.

In the cooker, add pancetta, and chicken broth mixture. Seal the lid and cook on High Pressure for 6 minutes. Release the pressure quickly. Open the lid, mix in green cabbage, seal again, and cook again on High Pressure for 2 minutes. Release the pressure quickly. Serve with sprinkled parsley.

Honey-Lemon Chicken with Vegetables

Serving Size: 4 | Total Time: 35 minutes

4 skin-on, bone-in chicken legs

2 tbsp olive oil	1 cup carrots, chopped
Salt and pepper to taste	1 cup parsnips, chopped
4 cloves garlic, minced	3 tomatoes, chopped
1 tsp fresh chopped thyme	1 tbsp honey
½ cup dry white wine	4 lemon slices
1 ¼ cups chicken stock	

Season the chicken with pepper and salt. Warm oil on Sauté in your Instant Pot. Cook the chicken legs for 6-8 minutes on all sides until browned; reserve. Sauté thyme and garlic in the chicken fat for 1 minute until soft and lightly golden. Add in wine to deglaze, scrape the pot's bottom to get rid of any brown bits of food. Simmer for 2-3 minutes until slightly reduced in volume.

Add stock, carrots, parsnip, tomatoes, pepper, and salt into the pot. Lay steam rack over veggies. Put the chicken legs on the rack. Drizzle with honey, then top with lemon slices. Seal the lid and cook on High Pressure for 12 minutes. Release pressure quickly. On a large platter, arrange the chicken legs and drained veggies. Sprinkle with thyme and serve.

Savory Orange Chicken

Serving Size: 6 | Total Time: 25 minutes

2 tbsp olive oil	1 tbsp garlic powder
6 chicken breasts, cubed	1 tsp chili sauce
1/3 cup chicken stock	1 cup orange juice
¼ cup soy sauce	Salt and pepper to taste
2 tbsp brown sugar	1 tbsp cornstarch
1 tbsp lemon juice	

Warm oil on Sauté in your Instant Pot. Sear the chicken for 5 minutes until browned, stirring occasionally. Set aside in a bowl. In the pot, mix orange juice, chicken stock, sugar, chili sauce, garlic powder, lemon juice, and soy sauce. Stir in chicken to coat. Seal the lid.

Cook on High Pressure for 7 minutes. Release the pressure quickly. Take ¼ cup liquid from the pot to a bowl and stir in cornstarch to dissolve. Pour the sauce in the pot and stir until the color is consistent. Press Sauté and cook the sauce for 2-3 minutes until thickened. Season with pepper and salt. Serve warm.

Green Salsa on Chicken Breasts

Serving Size: 4 | Total Time: 35 minutes

GREEN SALSA

1 jalapeño pepper, chopped	1 lime, juiced
½ cup capers	1 tsp salt
¼ cup parsley	¼ cup extra virgin olive oil

CHICKEN

4 chicken breasts	1 cup quinoa, rinsed

In a blender, mix olive oil, salt, lime juice, jalapeño pepper, capers, and parsley and blend until smooth. Arrange chicken breasts at the bottom of your Instant Pot. Over the chicken, pour salsa verde mixture. In a bowl that can fit in the cooker, mix quinoa and 2 cups water.

Set a steamer rack onto chicken and sauce. Set the bowl onto the rack. Seal the lid and cook on High Pressure for 20 minutes. Release the pressure quickly. Remove the quinoa. Using two forks, shred chicken into the pot. Stir to coat. Divide the quinoa between plates. Top with chicken and salsa verde before serving.

Chicken & Quinoa Soup

Serving Size: 6 | Total Time: 30 minutes

2 tbsp butter	6 oz quinoa, rinsed
1 cup red onion, chopped	2 tbsp parsley, chopped
1 cup carrots, chopped	Salt and pepper to taste
1 cup celery, chopped	4 oz mascarpone cheese
2 chicken breasts, cubed	1 cup milk
4 cups chicken broth	1 cup heavy cream

Melt butter on Sauté in your Instant Pot. Add carrots, onion, and celery and cook for 5 minutes. Add in broth, parsley, quinoa, and chicken. Season with pepper and salt. Seal the lid. Cook on High Pressure for 10 minutes. Release the pressure quickly. Add mascarpone to the soup and stir to melt it completely. Stir in heavy cream and milk until the soup is thickened and creamy.

Macaroni with Chicken & Pesto Sauce

Serving Size: 4 | Total Time: 20 minutes

3 ½ cups water	1 cup cherry tomatoes, halved
4 chicken breasts, cubed	½ cup basil pesto sauce
8 oz macaroni pasta	¼ cup cream cheese
1 tbsp butter	1 garlic clove, minced
Salt and pepper to taste	¼ cup asiago cheese, grated
1 lb collard greens, trimmed	2 tbsp chopped basil

Mix water, chicken, salt, butter, and macaroni in the Instant Pot. Seal the lid and cook for 2 minutes on High Pressure. Release the pressure quickly. Carefully open the lid, get rid of ¼ cup water from the pot. Set to Sauté.

Into the pot, mix in collard greens, pesto sauce, garlic, salt, cream cheese, cherry tomatoes, and black pepper. Cook for 1-2 minutes as you stir until sauce is creamy. Place the pasta into serving plates. Top with asiago cheese and basil before serving.

Okra & Rice Chicken with Spring Onions

Serving Size: 4 | Total Time: 30 minutes

6 garlic cloves, grated	1 cup rice, rinsed
¼ cup tomato puree	½ tsp salt
½ cup soy sauce	2 cups frozen okra
2 tbsp rice vinegar	1 tbsp cornstarch
2 tbsp olive oil	2 tsp toasted sesame seeds
4 chicken breasts, chopped	4 spring onions, chopped

In your Instant Pot, mix garlic, tomato puree, vinegar, soy sauce, ½ cup of water, and oil. Add in the chicken and toss it to coat. In an ovenproof bowl, mix 2 cups of water, salt, and rice. Set a steamer rack on top of the chicken. Lower the bowl onto the rack. Seal the lid.

Cook on High Pressure for 10 minutes. Release the pressure quickly. Stir in okra. Allow the okra steam in the residual heat for 3 minutes. Take the trivet and bowl from the pot. Set the chicken on a plate. Press Sauté.

In a bowl, mix 1 tbsp water and cornstarch until smooth. Stir into the sauce and cook for 3-4 minutes until thickened. Divide the rice, chicken, and okra between 4 bowls. Drizzle with sauce, garnish with spring onions and sesame seeds, and serve.

Tasty Indian Chicken Curry

Serving Size: 6 | Total Time: 30 minutes

1 (14.5 oz) can coconut milk, refrigerated overnight
2 lb boneless, skinless chicken legs

2 tbsp butter	3 tomatoes, pureed
1 large onion, minced	2 tbsp Indian curry paste
1 tbsp grated fresh ginger	2 tbsp dried fenugreek
1 tbsp minced fresh garlic	1 tsp garam masala
½ tsp ground turmeric	Salt to taste
1 tbsp Kashmiri chili powder	

Melt butter on Sauté in your Instant Pot. Add in onion and cook for 3 minutes until fragrant. Stir in ginger, turmeric, garlic, and red chili powder for 2 minutes. Place the water from the coconut milk can in a bowl and mix with pureed tomatoes and chicken. Pour in the onion mixture.

Seal the lid and cook on High Pressure for 8 minutes. Release the pressure quickly. Stir in coconut milk, fenugreek, salt, curry paste, and garam masala. Simmer for 10 minutes until the sauce thickens on Sauté. Serve.

Tasty Chicken Breasts with BBQ Sauce

Serving Size: 6 | Total Time: 20 minutes

2 lb chicken breasts	1 small onion, minced
1 tsp salt	1 cup carrots, chopped
1 ½ cups barbecue sauce	4 garlic cloves

Rub salt onto the chicken and place it in the Instant Pot. Add onion, carrots, garlic, and barbeque sauce; toss to coat. Seal the lid, press Manual, and cook on High for 15 minutes. Do a quick release. Shred the chicken and stir into the sauce. Serve.

Pumpkin & Wild Rice Cajun Chicken

Serving Size: 6 | Total Time: 30 minutes

6 chicken thighs, skinless	2 tbsp olive oil
Salt and pepper to taste	1 cup pumpkin, cubed
½ tsp ground red pepper	2 celery stalks, diced
½ tsp onion powder	2 onions, diced
1 tsp Cajun seasoning	3 cups chicken broth
1/8 tsp smoked paprika	1 ½ cups wild rice

Season the chicken with salt, onion powder, Cajun seasoning, white pepper, red pepper, and paprika. Warm oil on Sauté in your Instant Pot. Cook celery and pumpkin for 5 minutes; set aside. In the pot, sear chicken for 3 minutes per side until golden brown; reserve.

Into the cooker, add ¼ cup chicken stock to deglaze the pan, scrape away any browned bits from the bottom. Add in onion and cook for 2 minutes until fragrant. Take back the celery and pumpkin to the cooker and add the wild rice and remaining chicken stock. Place the chicken over the rice mixture. Seal the lid and cook for 10 minutes on High Pressure. Release the pressure quickly. Place rice and chicken pieces in serving plates and serve.

Avocado Fajitas

Serving Size: 4 | Total Time: 20 minutes

4 chicken breasts	4 garlic cloves, minced
1 taco seasoning	Juice of 1 lemon
1 tbsp olive oil	Salt and pepper to taste
24-oz can diced tomatoes	4 flour tortillas
3 bell peppers, julienned	2 tbsp cilantro, chopped
1 shallot, chopped	1 avocado, sliced

In a bowl, mix taco seasoning and chicken until evenly coated. Warm oil on Sauté. Sear chicken for 2 minutes per side until browned. To the chicken, add tomatoes, cilantro, shallot, lemon juice, garlic, and bell peppers. Season with pepper and salt. Seal the lid and press Manual.

Cook for 4 minutes on High Pressure. Release the pressure quickly. Move the bell peppers and chicken to tortillas. Add avocado slices and serve.

Sweet Chicken Carnitas in Lettuce Wraps

Serving Size: 6 | Total Time: 40 minutes

2 lb chicken thighs, boneless, skinless

2 tbsp canola oil	1 tsp chili-garlic sauce
1 cup pineapple juice	3 tbsp cornstarch
¼ cup soy sauce	Salt and pepper to taste
2 tbsp maple syrup	12 lettuce large leaves
1 tbsp rice vinegar	2 cups canned pinto beans

Warm oil on Sauté in your Instant Pot. In batches, stir chicken in the oil for 5 minutes until browned. Set aside in a bowl. Into your pot, mix chili-garlic sauce, pineapple juice, soy sauce, vinegar, maple syrup, and 1/3 cup water. Stir in chicken to coat. Seal the lid and cook on High Pressure for 7 minutes. Release pressure naturally for 10 minutes. Shred the chicken with two forks.

Take ¼ cup liquid from the pot to a bowl. Stir in cornstarch to dissolve. Mix the cornstarch mixture with the mixture in the pot and return the chicken. Select Sauté and cook for 5 minutes until the sauce thickens; add pepper and salt for seasoning. Transfer beans into lettuce leaves, top with chicken carnitas, and serve.

Hot Chicken with Coriander & Ginger

Serving Size: 6 | Total Time: 45 minutes

2 lb chicken thighs	6 cups chicken broth
1 tbsp ancho chili powder	1 tbsp ginger, freshly grated
1 tsp fresh basil	1 tbsp coriander seeds
Salt and pepper to taste	3 garlic cloves, crushed

Season the chicken with chili powder, salt, and pepper and place in the Instant Pot. Add the chicken broth broth, ginger, garlic, and coriander seeds; stir. Seal the lid and cook on Meat/Stew for 25 minutes on High. Do a natural release for 10 minutes. Serve topped with basil.

Savory Chicken Chili with Chickpeas

Serving Size: 4 | Total Time: 25 minutes

1 tbsp olive oil	1 tsp minced fresh garlic
3 serrano peppers, diced	1 tsp salt
1 onion, diced	2 (14.5 oz) cans chickpeas
1 jalapeño pepper, diced	2 tbsp chili powder
1 lb chicken breasts, cubed	½ cup chopped cilantro
1 tsp ground cumin	½ cup grated Monterey Jack

Warm oil on Sauté in your Instant Pot. Add in onion, serrano peppers, and jalapeño pepper and cook for 5 minutes until tender. Season with salt, cumin, and garlic. Stir in chicken for 3 to 6 minutes until no longer pink; add 2 cups water and chickpeas. Mix well. Seal the lid and cook for 5 minutes on High Pressure. Release pressure naturally. Stir chili powder with ½ cup water. Press Sauté. Boil the chili as you stir and cook until slightly thickened. Top with cheese and cilantro to serve.

Thyme Chicken with White Wine

Serving Size: 6 | Total Time: 45 minutes

1 cup chicken stock	Salt and pepper to taste
½ cup white wine	½ tsp dried thyme
½ onion, chopped	3 tbsp butter, melted
2 cloves garlic, minced	½ tsp paprika
3.5-pound whole chicken	

Into your Instant Pot, add onion, stock, wine, and garlic. Over the mixture, place a steamer rack. Rub pepper, salt, and thyme onto chicken. Put it on the rack breast-side up. Seal the lid, press Manual, and cook for 26 minutes. Release the pressure quickly. Preheat oven broiler. In a bowl, mix paprika and butter. Remove the chicken from your pot. Get rid of onion and stock. Brush butter mixture onto the chicken and cook under the broiler for 5 minutes until chicken skin is crispy and browned. Set chicken to a cutting board to cool for about 5 minutes, then carve, and transfer to a serving platter. Serve.

Easy Chicken with Capers & Tomatoes

Serving Size: 4 | Total Time: 35 minutes

4 chicken legs	1/3 cup red wine
Salt and pepper to taste	2 cups diced tomatoes
2 tbsp olive oil	1/3 cup capers
1 onion, diced	2 pickles, chopped
2 garlic cloves, minced	

Sprinkle pepper and salt over the chicken. Warm oil on Sauté in your Instant Pot. Add in onion and Sauté for 3 minutes until fragrant. Add in garlic and cook for 30 seconds. Mix the chicken with vegetables and cook for 6 to 7 minutes until lightly browned.

Add the red wine to the pan to deglaze, scraping the pan's bottom to eliminate any browned bits of food. Stir in tomatoes. Seal the lid and cook on High Pressure for 12 minutes. Release the pressure quickly. To the chicken mixture, add the capers and pickles. Serve the chicken topped with the tomato sauce and enjoy!

Best Italian Chicken Balls

Serving Size: 4 | Total Time: 35 minutes

1/3 cup blue cheese, crumbled	
¼ cup Pecorino Romano cheese, shredded	
1 lb ground chicken	1 tbsp fresh basil, chopped
3 tbsp red hot sauce	Salt and pepper to taste
1 egg	15 oz canned tomato sauce
¼ cup breadcrumbs	1 cup chicken broth
1 tbsp ranch dressing	2 tbsp olive oil

In a bowl, mix ground chicken, egg, Pecorino cheese, pepper, salt, ranch dressing, blue cheese, hot sauce, and breadcrumbs. Shape the mixture into balls. Warm oil on Sauté in your Instant Pot. Add in the meatballs and cook for 2-3 minutes until browned on all sides.

Add in tomato sauce and broth. Seal the lid and cook on High Pressure for 7 minutes. Release the pressure quickly. Remove meatballs carefully and place them on a serving plate. Top with basil and serve.

Chicken with Honey-Lime Sauce

Serving Size: 4 | Total Time: 30 minutes

4 chicken breasts, cut into chunks	
1 onion, diced	2 tsp sesame oil
4 garlic cloves, smashed	1 tsp rice vinegar
1 tbsp honey	1 tbsp cornstarch
3 tbsp soy sauce	Salt and pepper to taste
2 tbsp lime juice	

Mix garlic, onion, and chicken in your Instant Pot. In a bowl, combine honey, sesame oil, lime juice, soy sauce, and rice vinegar. Pour over the chicken mixture. Seal the lid and cook on High Pressure for 15 minutes. Release the pressure quickly. Mix 1 tbsp water and cornstarch until well dissolved; Stir into the sauce, add salt and pepper to taste. Press Sauté. Simmer the sauce and cook for 2 to 3 minutes as you stir until thickened.

Tasty Chicken Breasts

Serving Size: 4 | Total Time: 30 minutes

4 chicken breasts
Salt and pepper to taste
2 tbsp olive oil
2 tbsp soy sauce
2 tbsp tomato paste
2 tbsp honey
2 tbsp minced garlic
1 tbsp cornstarch
½ cup chives, chopped

Season the chicken with pepper and salt. Warm oil on Sauté in your Instant Pot. Add in chicken and cook for 5 minutes until lightly browned. In a small bowl, mix garlic, soy sauce, honey, and tomato paste. Pour the mixture over the chicken. Stir in ½ cup water.

Seal the lid and cook on High Pressure for 12 minutes. Release the pressure quickly. Remove the chicken. Mix 1 tbsp water and cornstarch to create a slurry. Stir it in the sauce for 2 minutes until thickened. Serve the chicken with sauce and chives.

Chicken Alla Italiana

Serving Size: 4 | Total Time: 45 minutes

1 lb chicken drumsticks, boneless, skinless
2 tsp olive oil
Salt and pepper to taste
1 carrot, chopped
1 red bell pepper, chopped
1 yellow bell pepper, chopped
1 onion, chopped
4 garlic cloves, chopped
2 tsp dried oregano
1 tsp dried basil
1 tsp dried parsley
1 tsp red pepper flakes
28-oz can diced tomatoes
½ cup dry red wine
¾ cup chicken stock
1 cup black olives, chopped
2 bay leaves

Warm oil on Sauté in your Instant Pot. Season the drumsticks with pepper and salt. In batches, sear the chicken for 5-6 minutes until golden brown. Set aside on a plate. Drain the pot and remain with 1 tablespoon of fat. In the hot oil, sauté onion, garlic, carrot, and bell peppers for 4 minutes until softened. Add red pepper flakes, basil, parsley, and oregano, and cook for 30 more seconds. Season with salt and pepper. Stir in tomatoes, black olives, chicken stock, red wine, and bay leaves. Return chicken to the pot. Seal the lid and cook on High Pressure for 15 minutes. Release the pressure quickly. Top with tomato mixture before serving.

Tarragon & Garlic Chicken

Serving Size: 4 | Total Time: 30 minutes

1 ¼ lb chicken breasts
Salt and pepper to taste
2 garlic cloves, crushed
3 tbsp tarragon, chopped
2 tbsp olive oil
1 onion, finely chopped

Warm oil on Sauté in your Instant Pot. Stir-fry the onion and garlic for 3 minutes until fragrant. Add in the chicken, salt, and pepper. Pour in 2 cups of water and adjust the seasoning. Seal the lid and cook on High Pressure for 15 minutes. When ready, do a quick pressure release. Slice the chicken and serve topped with fresh tarragon.

Chicken Drumsticks in Sriracha Sauce

Serving Size: 4 | Total Time: 20 minutes

4 boneless, skinless chicken drumsticks
½ cup soy sauce
½ cup chicken broth
3 tbsp honey
2 tbsp tomato paste
1 tbsp sriracha
1-inch piece ginger, grated
3 garlic cloves, grated
1 tbsp cornstarch
1 tbsp water
2 tbsp toasted sesame seeds
1 tbsp sesame oil
2 cups canned black beans
2 green onions, chopped

In your Instant Pot, mix soy sauce, honey, ginger, tomato paste, chicken broth, sriracha, and garlic. Stir until smooth; toss in chicken to coat. Seal the lid and cook for 3 minutes on High Pressure. Release the pressure quickly.

Open the lid and press Sauté. In a small bowl, mix water and cornstarch until no lumps remain, stir into the sauce and cook for 5 minutes until thickened. Stir sesame oil and 1½ tablespoons sesame seeds through the chicken mixture; garnish with extra sesame seeds and green onions. Serve with black beans.

Chicken & Zucchini Pilaf

Serving Size: 4 | Total Time: 25 minutes

1 lb boneless, skinless chicken legs
2 tsp olive oil
1 zucchini, chopped
1 cup leeks, chopped
2 garlic cloves, minced
1 tbsp chopped rosemary
2 tsp chopped fresh thyme
Salt and pepper to taste
2 cups chicken stock
1 cup rice, rinsed

Warm oil on Sauté in your Instant Pot. Add in zucchini and cook for 5 minutes. Stir in thyme, leeks, rosemary, pepper, salt, and garlic. Cook the mixture for 4 minutes. Add in ½ cup chicken stock to deglaze, scrape the bottom to get rid of any browned bits of food.

When liquid stops simmering, add in the remaining stock, rice, and chicken with more pepper and salt. Seal the lid and cook on High Pressure for 5 minutes. Do a quick release. Carefully open the lid. Serve warm.

Rice & Lentil Chicken with Parsley

Serving Size: 4 | Total Time: 30 minutes

4 boneless, skinless chicken thighs
1 tsp olive oil
1 garlic clove, minced
1 yellow onion, chopped
3 cups chicken broth
1 cup white rice
½ cup dried lentils
Salt and pepper to taste
2 tbsp chopped parsley

Warm oil on Sauté in your Instant Pot. Stir-fry onion and garlic for 3 minutes. Add in broth, rice, lentils, chicken, pepper, and salt. Seal the lid and cook on High Pressure for 15 minutes. Do a quick release.

Remove and shred the chicken in a large bowl. Set the lentils and rice into serving plates. Top with chicken and parsley to serve.

Rosemary Chicken with Asparagus Sauce

Serving Size: 4 | Total Time: 40 minutes

1 (3 ½ lb) whole chicken	8 oz asparagus, chopped
4 garlic cloves, minced	1 onion, chopped
2 tbsp olive oil	1 cup chicken stock
4 fresh thyme, minced	1 tbsp soy sauce
3 fresh rosemary, minced	1 fresh thyme sprig
2 lemons, zested, quartered	1 tbsp flour
Salt and pepper to taste	Chopped parsley to garnish
2 tbsp olive oil	

Rub all sides of the chicken with garlic, rosemary, black pepper, lemon zest, thyme, and salt. Into the chicken cavity, insert lemon wedges. Warm the olive oil on Sauté in your Instant Pot. Add in onion and asparagus, and sauté for 5 minutes until softened. Mix chicken stock, thyme sprig, black pepper, soy sauce, and salt. Into the inner pot, set trivet over asparagus mixture.

On top of the trivet, place the chicken with breast-side up. Seal the lid, select Manual, and cook for 20 minutes on High. Do a quick release. Remove the chicken to a serving platter. In the inner pot, sprinkle flour over asparagus mixture and blend the sauce with an immersion blender until desired consistency. Top the chicken with asparagus sauce and garnish with parsley.

Chicken Wings with Worcestershire Sauce

Serving Size: 4 | Total Time: 35 minutes

8 chicken wings	1/3 cup Worcestershire sauce
3 cups chicken broth	2 spring onions, chopped
1 tsp fresh ginger, grated	2 garlic cloves, crushed
1 tbsp honey	1 tsp salt
2 tbsp olive oil	

Add the chicken to your Instant Pot and pour in broth. Seal the lid and cook on Poultry for 15 minutes on High. Do a quick release. Remove chicken and broth and wipe the pot clean. Heat oil on Sauté and stir-fry onions and garlic for 3 minutes. Add Worcestershire sauce, honey, salt, and ginger. Cook for 1 minute and return the wings. Stir for 2 minutes until nice. Serve.

Grilled Chicken Drumsticks with Salad

Serving Size: 4 | Total Time: 60 minutes

4 chicken drumsticks	3 tbsp olive oil
3 cups chicken broth	1 tbsp Dijon mustard
1 tomato, roughly chopped	¼ cup white wine
2 oz lettuce, torn	1 tsp lemon juice
1 cup kalamata olives	1 tbsp Italian seasoning mix
1 cucumber, chopped	Salt and pepper to taste

In a bowl, mix mustard, 2 tbsp olive oil, Italian mix, salt, and pepper. Brush the chicken with the mixture. Cover and refrigerate for 30 minutes. Place the tomato, lettuce, cucumber, and kalamata olive in a serving bowl. Season with salt and pepper and add in the remaining olive oil and lemon juice. Stir and set aside.

Remove the drumsticks from the fridge and transfer them to your Instant Pot. Pour in the broth and wine. Seal the lid and cook on Manual for 15 minutes on High. Do a quick release and remove the drumsticks. Preheat a non-stick grill pan over high heat. Brown the drumsticks for 6-7 minutes, turning once. Serve with the salad.

Picante Chicken with Lemon

Serving Size: 2 | Total Time: 60 minutes

1 lb chicken breasts, sliced	3 garlic cloves, crushed
1 cup olive oil	1 tbsp cayenne pepper
1 cup chicken broth	1 tsp dried oregano
½ cup lemon juice	½ tsp salt
1 tbsp parsley, chopped	

In a bowl, mix olive oil, lemon juice, parsley, garlic, cayenne, oregano, and salt. Add in the chicken slices, toss to coat, and cover. Chill for 30 minutes. Remove from the fridge and place all inside your Instant Pot. Add in the broth. Seal the lid and cook on High Pressure for 7 minutes. Release the pressure naturally for about 10 minutes and serve immediately.

Hot Chicken with Garlic & Mushrooms

Serving Size: 4 | Total Time: 30 minutes

1 cup button mushrooms, chopped	
1 lb chicken breasts, cubed	Salt and pepper to taste
2 cups chicken broth	2 tbsp olive oil
2 tbsp flour	2 garlic cloves, chopped
1 tsp cayenne pepper	

Warm the olive oil in your Instant Pot on Sauté. Add mushrooms, garlic, and chicken, season with salt, and stir-fry for 5 minutes, stirring occasionally until the veggies are tender. Pour in the chicken broth. Seal the lid. Cook on High Pressure for 8 minutes. Release the steam naturally for 10 minutes and stir in flour, cayenne, and black pepper. Cook for 5 minutes on Sauté. Serve warm.

Corn & Sweet Potato Soup with Chicken

Serving Size: 4 | Total Time: 25 minutes

4 oz canned diced green chiles, drained	
2 chicken breasts, diced	1 tsp ground cumin
2 garlic cloves, minced	2 cups cheddar, shredded
1 cup chicken stock	2 cups creme fraiche
1 cup corn kernels	Salt and pepper to taste
1 sweet potato, peeled, cubed	Cilantro leaves, chopped
2 tsp chili powder	

Add chicken, corn, chili powder, cumin, chicken stock, sweet potato, green chiles, and garlic to your Instant Pot. Mix well. Seal the lid and cook on High Pressure for 10 minutes. Release the pressure quickly. Set the chicken to a cutting board and shred it. Return to the pot and stir well into the liquid. Stir in cheese and creme fraiche; Season with pepper and salt. Cook for 2-3 minutes until the cheese is melted. Place chowder into plates and top with cilantro. Serve warm.

Pea & Rice Chicken with Paprika & Herbs

Serving Size: 4 | Total Time: 30 minutes

4 chicken breasts, chopped	1 tbsp oil olive
1 garlic clove, minced	1 onion, chopped
½ tsp paprika	1 tbsp tomato puree
¼ tsp dried oregano	2 cups chicken broth
¼ tsp dried thyme	1 cup rice
1 tsp cayenne pepper	1 celery stalk, diced
Salt and pepper to taste	1 cup frozen green peas

Season chicken with garlic, oregano, white pepper, thyme, paprika, cayenne pepper, and salt. Warm the oil on Sauté in your Instant Pot. Add in onion and cook for 4 minutes until fragrant. Mix in tomato puree to coat. Add ¼ cup chicken broth into the cooker to deglaze the pan, scrape the pan's bottom to get rid of browned bits of food. Mix in celery, rice, and seasoned chicken. Add in the remaining broth to the chicken mixture. Seal the lid and cook on High Pressure for 8 minutes. Do a quick release. Mix in green peas, cover with the lid, and let sit for 5 minutes. Serve warm.

Chicken Sausage & Navy Bean Chili

Serving Size: 6 | Total Time: 50 minutes

1 (14-oz) can diced tomatoes with green chilies	
3 tbsp olive oil	2 tsp ground cumin
1 shallot, diced	Salt and pepper to taste
½ cup fennel, chopped	28-oz can crushed tomatoes
¼ cup minced garlic	2 lb chicken sausages, sliced
1 tbsp smoked paprika	¾ cup buffalo wing sauce
2 tsp chili powder	2 (14-oz) cans navy beans

Warm oil on Sauté in your Instant Pot. Add the sausages and brown for 5 minutes, turning frequently. Set aside on a plate. In the same fat, sauté shallot, roasted fennel, and garlic for 4 minutes until soft. Season with paprika, cumin, pepper, salt, and chili powder.

Stir in crushed tomatoes, diced tomatoes with green chilies, buffalo sauce, and navy beans. Return the sausages to the pot. Seal the lid and cook on High Pressure for 30 minutes. Do a quick pressure release. Serve.

Savory Tropical Chicken

Serving Size: 4 | Total Time: 20 minutes

4 boneless, skinless chicken thighs	
2 tbsp olive oil	1 garlic clove, minced
¼ cup pineapple juice	1 tsp cornstarch
2 tbsp ketchup	2 tsp water
2 tbsp Worcestershire sauce	2 tbsp cilantro, chopped

Warm oil on Sauté in your Instant Pot. In batches, sear the chicken in oil for 3 minutes until golden brown and set aside on a plate. Mix pineapple juice, Worcestershire sauce, garlic, and ketchup. Add to the pot to deglaze, scraping the bottom to get rid of any browned bits of food. Place the chicken into the sauce and stir well to coat. Seal the lid cook for 5 minutes on High Pressure.

Release the pressure quickly. In a bowl, mix water and cornstarch until well dissolved. Press Cancel and set to Sauté. Stir the cornstarch slurry into the sauce and cook for 2 minutes until the sauce is well thickened. Sprinkle with cilantro to serve.

Punjabi Chicken in Lemon-Honey Gravy

Serving Size: 4 | Total Time: 25 minutes + marinade time

PUNJABI CHICKEN

4 chicken thighs, skinless	1 tsp garam masala
½ cup Greek yogurt	½ tsp ground turmeric
1 tbsp olive oil	½ tbsp grated fresh ginger
1 tbsp lemon juice	½ tbsp minced garlic
1 tbsp red chili powder	

CILANTRO GRAVY

A handful of cilantro leaves	2 tsp lemon juice
1 tsp cumin seeds	¾ cup olive oil
½ jalapeño, chopped	1 tbsp of water
2-3 garlic cloves	Salt to taste
2 tsp honey	

In a bowl, mix yogurt, lemon juice, garam masala, garlic, turmeric, red chili powder, olive oil, and ginger. Use a paper towel to pat dry the thighs. Place into a resealable plastic bag. Add in yogurt mixture and seal. Massage bag to ensure the marinade coats the chicken completely and place in the refrigerator for 12 hours. Remove 30 minutes before cooking.

Add 1 cup water into your Instant Pot and insert a trivet. Arrange the drained chicken on the trivet. Seal the lid. Cook for 15 minutes on High Pressure. Quick-release the pressure. Unlock the lid. Blend the cilantro, cumin seeds, jalapeño, garlic, honey, lemon juice, olive oil, water, and salt in a food processor until smooth. Pour over the chicken and serve.

Awesome Chicken in Tikka Masala Sauce

Serving Size: 4 | Total Time: 30 minutes

2 lb boneless, skinless chicken thighs	
Salt and pepper to taste	½ tsp ground cumin
1 ½ tbsp olive oil	1 jalapeño pepper, minced
½ onion, chopped	29 oz canned tomato sauce
2 garlic cloves, minced	3 tomatoes, chopped
3 tbsp tomato puree	½ cup natural yogurt
1 tsp fresh ginger, minced	1 lemon, juiced
1 tbsp garam masala	¼ cup chopped cilantro
2 tsp curry powder	4 lemon wedges
1 tsp ground coriander	

Rub black pepper and salt onto the chicken. Warm oil on Sauté in your Instant Pot. Add garlic and onion and cook for 3 minutes until soft. Stir in tomato puree, garam masala, cumin, curry powder, ginger, coriander, and jalapeño pepper; cook for 30 seconds until fragrant.

Stir in tomato sauce and tomatoes. Simmer the mixture as you scrape the bottom to get rid of any browned bits. Stir in chicken to coat. Seal the lid and cook on High Pressure for 10 minutes. Release the pressure quickly.

Press Sauté and simmer the sauce and cook for 5 minutes until thickened. Stir lemon juice and yogurt through the sauce. Serve garnished with lemon wedges and cilantro.

Pesto Chicken with Green Beans

Serving Size: 4 | Total Time: 30 minutes

4 chicken breasts	¾ cup chicken stock
2 tbsp olive oil	Salt and pepper to taste
¼ cup dry white wine	1 cup green beans, chopped
FOR PESTO	
1 cup fresh basil	¼ cup Parmesan cheese
1 garlic clove, smashed	¼ cup extra virgin olive oil
2 tbsp pine nuts	Salt and pepper to taste

First, make the pesto - in a bowl, mix fresh basil, pine nuts, garlic, salt, pepper, and Parmesan cheese and place in a food processor. Add in oil and process until the desired consistency is attained. Apply a thin layer of pesto to one side of each chicken breast; tightly roll into a cylinder and fasten closed with small skewers.

Press Sauté. Heat oil in your Instant Pot. Cook chicken rolls for 1 to 2 minutes per side until browned. Add in wine and cook until the wine has evaporated, about 3-4 minutes. Add stock, salt and pepper, and top the chicken with green beans. Seal the lid, press Meat/Stew, and cook at High Pressure for 5 minutes. Release the pressure quickly. Serve chicken rolls with cooking liquid and green beans.

Chicken & Vegetable Stew

Serving Size: 4 | Total Time: 45 minutes

2 cups fire-roasted tomatoes, diced	
½ cup button mushrooms, sliced	
1 lb chicken breasts, chopped	2 tbsp tomato paste
1 tbsp fresh basil, chopped	2 celery stalks, chopped
2 cups coconut milk	2 carrots, chopped
1 cup chicken broth	2 tbsp coconut oil
Salt and pepper to taste	1 onion, finely chopped

Warm the coconut oil in your Instant Pot on Sauté. Add celery, onion, and carrots and cook for 7 minutes, stirring constantly. Add tomato paste, basil, and mushrooms. Continue to cook for 10 more minutes. Addin the tomatoes, chicken, coconut milk, chicken broth, salt, and pepper. Seal the lid and cook on Manual for 15 minutes on High. Do a quick release. Serve warm.

Colorful Vegetable & Chicken Rice

Serving Size: 4 | Total Time: 45 minutes

6 oz button mushrooms, chopped	
1 lb chicken breasts, cubed	2 carrots, chopped
1 cup rice	2 tbsp olive oil
1 red bell pepper, halved	1 tbsp butter
1 green bell pepper, halved	Salt and pepper to taste
1 yellow bell pepper, halved	1 tsp fresh basil, chopped
6 oz broccoli florets	Parmesan for topping
½ cup sweet corn	

Add the rice to your Instant Pot and pour in 2 cups of water. Stir in butter, pepper, and salt and seal the lid. Cook on Manual for 8 minutes on High. Do a quick release. Remove the rice. Heat oil on Sauté and add carrots and broccoli. Sauté for 10 minutes. Add sweet corn and bell peppers and cook for 5 minutes, stirring constantly. Stir in mushrooms and cook for 3-4 minutes.

Remove the vegetables, mix with the rice, and set aside. Add the chicken to the pot and pour in 2 cups of water. Season with salt and pepper. Seal the lid and cook on High pressure for 7 minutes. Do a quick release. Open the lid, stir in rice and vegetables and serve warm sprinkled with Parmesan cheese and fresh basil.

Chicken Thighs with Mushrooms & Garlic

Serving Size: 2 | Total Time: 30 minutes

2 chicken thighs, boneless and skinless	
6 oz button mushrooms	½ tsp salt
3 tbsp olive oil	1 tbsp butter
1 tsp rosemary, chopped	1 tbsp Italian seasoning
2 garlic cloves, crushed	

Heat a tablespoon of olive oil on Sauté in your Instant Pot. Add chicken thighs and sear for 5 minutes. Set aside. Pour in the remaining oil, and add mushrooms, rosemary, salt, and Italian seasoning mix. Stir-fry for 5 minutes. Add in butter, chicken, and 2 cups of water.

Seal the lid and cook on Pressure Cook for 13 minutes on High. Do a quick release. Remove the chicken and mushrooms from the cooker and serve with garlic.

Quinoa Pilaf with Chicken

Serving Size: 4 | Total Time: 35 minutes

1 lb chicken breasts, chopped	Salt and pepper to taste
1 cup quinoa	Greek yogurt for topping

Add chicken and 2 cups of water to your Instant Pot. Seal the lid. Cook on Manual for 15 minutes on High. Do a quick release; remove the chicken. Add the quinoa to the pot and seal the lid again. Cook on Manual for 8 minutes on High. Do a quick release. Stir in the chicken and adjust the seasoning with salt and pepper. Plate and top with yogurt. Serve immediately.

Brussels Sprouts & Zucchini Chicken

Serving Size: 4 | Total Time: 30 minutes

4 chicken thighs, boneless and skinless	
1 cup chicken stock	2 zucchinis, chopped
½ cauliflower head, chopped	1 onion, chopped
2 tomatoes, chopped	3 tbsp olive oil
½ lb Brussels sprouts	1 tsp salt

Heat the olive oil in your Instant Pot on Sauté. Stir-fry onion, cauliflower, tomatoes, sprouts, and zucchinis for 5 minutes until tender. Add in the chicken stock, chicken thighs, and salt and seal the lid. Cook on manual for 15 minutes on High. Do a quick release. Serve warm.

Tarragon Whole Chicken

Serving Size: 6 | Total Time: 45 minutes

1 (3 lb) whole chicken	Salt and pepper to taste
1 tsp tarragon, chopped	1 cup chicken broth
3 tbsp butter, softened	1 tbsp white wine
1 tbsp onion powder	2 tsp soy sauce
1 tbsp garlic powder	1 minced green onion
1 tbsp paprika	

Combine butter, tarragon, onion powder, garlic powder, paprika, salt, and pepper in a bowl. Pour the chicken broth, white wine, and soy sauce in your Instant Pot and fit in a trivet. Brush chicken with the butter mixture on all sides and place it on the trivet. Seal the lid, select Manual, and cook for 25 minutes on High pressure. When done, allow a natural release for 10 minutes and unlock the lid. Serve topped with minced green onion.

Tuscan Vegetable Chicken Stew

Serving Size: 4 | Total Time: 60 minutes

14 oz broccoli and cauliflower florets
A handful of yellow wax beans, whole

1 (3 lb) whole chicken	1 tomato, peeled, chopped
1 onion, peeled, chopped	¼ cup extra virgin olive oil
1 potato, peeled, chopped	Salt and pepper to taste
3 carrots, chopped	

Warm 3 tbsp olive oil in your Instant Pot on Sauté. Stir-fry the onion for 3-4 minutes on Sauté. Add the carrots and sauté for 5 more minutes. Add the remaining oil, broccoli, potato, wax beans, tomato, salt, and pepper and top with chicken. Add 1 cup of water and seal the lid. Cook on High Pressure for 30 minutes. Release the pressure naturally for about 10 minutes. Carefully unlock the lid. Serve warm.

Bell Pepper & Chicken Stew

Serving Size: 4 | Total Time: 30 minutes

1 lb chicken breasts, cubed	1 tomato, roughly chopped
2 potatoes, peeled, chopped	2 tbsp chopped parsley
5 bell peppers, chopped	3 tbsp extra virgin olive oil
2 carrots, chopped	1 tsp cayenne pepper
2 ½ cups chicken broth	

Warm the olive oil on Sauté in your Instant Pot. Stir-fry the bell peppers and carrots for 3 minutes. Add in the potatoes and tomato. Sprinkle with cayenne and stir well. Top with the chicken, pour in the broth, and seal the lid. Cook on High Pressure for 13 minutes. When ready, do a quick pressure release. Sprinkle with parsley and serve.

Spicy Chicken Thighs

Serving Size: 4 | Total Time: 45 minutes

1 lb chicken thighs	2 tsp lime zest
2 tbsp oil	1 tsp chili powder
4 cups chicken broth	½ cup tomato puree
1 tsp salt	1 tbsp sugar

Season the meat evenly with salt and chili powder on both sides. Warm oil on Sauté and add the thighs. Brown on both sides and then set aside. Add the tomato puree, sugar, and lime zest. Cook for 10 minutes to obtain a thick sauce. Add the chicken and pour in the broth. Seal the lid and cook on Poultry for 20 minutes on High pressure. Do a quick release. Unlock the lid. Serve.

Sage Chicken in Orange Gravy

Serving Size: 4 | Total Time: 50 minutes

1 (3.5 lb) whole chicken	3 cups chicken broth
¼ cup olive oil	1 cup red wine
2 tbsp fresh sage, minced	2 tbsp butter
2 tbsp lemon zest	1 cup orange juice
1 tsp garlic powder	½ cup flour
¼ tsp red pepper flakes	Salt and pepper to taste

Mix oil, sage, lemon zest, garlic, salt, pepper, and red pepper in a bowl. Rub the mixture onto chicken. Melt butter on Sauté in your Instant Pot and brown the chicken for 3-4 minutes. Pour in broth and wine. Seal the lid and cook on Manual for 30 minutes on High. Do a quick release and remove the chicken.

In a bowl, mix the orange juice, 1 cup of cooking liquid, and flour. Cook for 5 minutes on Sauté until the sauce has thickened. Scatter the sauce over the chicken to serve.

Easy Italian Chicken Stew with Potatoes

Serving Size: 4 | Total Time: 30 minutes

2 fire-roasted tomatoes, peeled, chopped
2 potatoes, peeled, cut into chunks

2 lb chicken wings	4 cups chicken broth
1 carrot, cut into chunks	2 tbsp parsley, chopped
2 garlic cloves, chopped	Salt and pepper to taste
2 tbsp olive oil	1 cup spinach, chopped
1 tsp smoked paprika	

Rub the chicken with salt, pepper, and paprika. Warm the olive oil on Sauté in your Instant Pot. Cook the wings for 5 minutes, stirring occasionally. Add in tomatoes, potatoes, carrot, garlic, and chicken broth and seal the lid. Cook on High Pressure for 12 minutes. When ready, do a quick release. Stir in spinach and cook for 5 minutes until wilted on Sauté. Sprinkle with parsley and serve hot.

Spiced Chicken Thighs with Garlic

Serving Size: 4 | Total Time: 30 minutes + marinating time

4 chicken thighs	1 tbsp fresh basil, chopped
1 cup olive oil	2 tbsp fresh thyme, chopped
¼ cup apple cider vinegar	1 tbsp rosemary, chopped
3 garlic cloves, crushed	1 tsp cayenne pepper
½ cup lemon juice	1 tsp salt

In a bowl, add oil, vinegar, garlic, juice, basil, thyme, rosemary, salt, and cayenne. Submerge thighs into this mixture and refrigerate for 1 hour. Remove from the fridge and pat dry with kitchen paper.

Pour 1 cup of water into your Instant Pot and set a trivet. Place the chicken on it. Seal the lid and cook on Manual for 15 minutes on High. Do a quick release. Remove the chicken and broth. Warm oil on Sauté and brown the chicken for 5 minutes, turning once until nice and golden.

Chimichurri Chicken

Serving Size: 6 | Total Time: 25 minutes

2 lb chicken breasts	1 tsp cumin
1 cup chicken broth	Salt and pepper to taste
1 tsp smoked paprika	2 cups chimichurri salsa

Sprinkle chicken breasts with paprika, cumin, salt, and pepper. Place the chicken broth with chicken breasts in your Instant Pot. Seal the lid, select Manual, and cook for 15 minutes on High pressure. Once done, perform a quick pressure release and unlock the lid. Cut the chicken into slices and top with chimichurri sauce. Serve.

Quick Swiss Chard & Chicken Stew

Serving Size: 4 | Total Time: 30 minutes

1 lb chicken breasts, cubed	2 tbsp butter, unsalted
1 lb Swiss chard, chopped	2 tbsp olive oil
2 cups chicken broth	Salt and pepper to taste

Add the chicken, oil, and broth to your Instant Pot. Season with salt and black pepper. Seal the lid and cook on Manual for 13 minutes on High. Do a quick release. Unlock the lid. Add Swiss chard and butter. Cook on Sauté for 5 minutes until the chard is wilted. Serve warm.

Easy Primavera Chicken Stew

Serving Size: 4 | Total Time: 55 minutes

4 green onions, chopped	Salt and pepper to taste
3 garlic cloves, minced	1 chicken breasts, chopped
3 new potatoes, chopped	2 cups chicken broth
1 cup baby carrots, chopped	2 tbsp olive oil
4 oz can tomato sauce	2 tbsp parsley, chopped

Heat the olive oil on Sauté in the Instant Pot. Stir-fry the onions, garlic, and carrots for 3 minutes until tender. Add in the chicken and brown for 5-6 minutes, stirring occasionally. Pour in the tomato sauce, potatoes, and chicken broth. Season with salt and pepper. Seal the lid and cook on Manual for 15 minutes on High. Do a natural release for 10 minutes. Top with parsley to serve.

Dijon Mustard Chicken Breast

Serving Size: 2 | Total Time: 40 minutes

1 lb chicken	Salt and pepper to taste
¼ cup apple cider vinegar	2 tbsp olive oil
2 tbsp Dijon mustard	2 cups chicken stock

Season the chicken with salt and black pepper. Place in your Instant Pot and pour in the stock. Seal the lid and cook on Manual for 20 minutes. Do a quick release and remove the meat along with the stock.

In a bowl, mix olive oil, mustard, and vinegar. Pour into the pot and press Sauté. Place the chicken in this mixture and cook for 10 minutes, turning once. When done, remove from the pot and drizzle with the sauce.

Festive Chicken with Bacon

Serving Size: 4 | Total Time: 55 minutes

1 whole chicken (3.5 lb)	2 cups chicken stock
3 tbsp butter	6 oz bacon
¼ cup Worcestershire sauce	1 tbsp flour

Place the chicken in your Instant Pot along with stock and Worcestershire sauce. Seal the lid and cook on High Pressure for 40 minutes. Do a quick release and remove to a bowl. Melt butter on Sauté. Stir-fry the bacon for 2 minutes until crispy.

Stir in flour and 1 cup of cooking juices and cook for 4 minutes until the sauce thickens. Transfer the chicken to a platter. Allow cooling for a few minutes, then carve, and serve drizzled with gravy.

Country Chicken with Vegetables

Serving Size: 4 | Total Time: 30 minutes

4 boneless, skinless chicken thighs	
1 cup quartered cremini mushrooms	
Salt and pepper to taste	1 tbsp tomato paste
2 tbsp olive oil	10 cherry tomatoes, halved
2 chopped carrots	½ cup pitted green olives
½ lb green peas	½ cup fresh basil, minced
1 chopped onion	¼ cup parsley, chopped
3 garlic cloves, smashed	

Sprinkle chicken thighs with salt and pepper. Warm the olive oil in your Instant Pot on Sauté and cook carrots, mushrooms, and onion for 5 minutes. Add in garlic and tomato paste and cook for another 30 seconds. Stir in cherry tomatoes, chicken thighs, and olives.

Pour in 1 cup of water. Seal the lid, select Manual, and cook for 10 minutes on High pressure. Once ready, perform a quick pressure release and unlock the lid. Select Sauté and mix in green peas; cook for 5 minutes. Serve topped with fresh basil and parsley.

Saucy Chicken Marsala

Serving Size: 4 | Total Time: 30 minutes

4 chicken breasts	½ cup soy sauce
¼ cup ketchup	2 green onions, chopped
¾ cup Marsala wine	

Place chicken breasts, 1 cup of water, ketchup, Marsala wine, and soy sauce in your Instant Pot and stir. Seal the lid and cook for 15 minutes on Manual.

When ready, perform a quick pressure release and unlock the lid. Simmer for 5 minutes on Sauté until the sauce thickens. Top with green onions and serve.

Garlic Chicken

Serving Size: 4 | Total Time: 35 minutes

1 lb chicken breasts	1 cup chicken broth
Salt and pepper to taste	2 garlic cloves, minced
2 tbsp butter	2 tbsp tarragon, chopped

Place chicken breasts in your Instant Pot. Sprinkle with garlic, salt, and pepper. Pour in the chicken broth and butter. Seal the lid, select Manual, and cook for 15 minutes on High pressure.

When over, allow a natural release for 10 minutes and unlock the lid. Remove the chicken and shred it. Top with tarragon and serve.

Herby Chicken with Peach Gravy

Serving Size: 4 | Total Time: 55 minutes

4 chicken breasts	½ tsp dried thyme
¼ cup olive oil	½ tsp dried sage
1 cup onions, chopped	2 cups chicken stock
2 celery stalks, chopped	Salt and pepper to taste
2 peaches, cut into chunks	

Heat oil on Sauté in your Instant Pot and stir-fry the onions for 2-3 minutes until soft. Add celery stalks and peaches and cook for 5 minutes, stirring occasionally.

Rub the meat with salt, pepper, thyme, and sage. Add it to the pot along with the stock. Seal the lid and cook on High Pressure for 35 minutes. Do a quick release. Serve.

Chicken Wings in Yogurt-Garlic Sauce

Serving Size: 6 | Total Time: 35 minutes

12 chicken wings	½ cup sour cream
3 tbsp olive oil	1 cup yogurt
Salt to taste	2 garlic cloves, minced
3 cups chicken broth	

Heat oil on Sauté in your Instant Pot. Brown the wings for 6 minutes, turning once. Pour in broth, salt, and seal the lid. Cook on Poultry for 15 minutes on High. Do a natural release. Unlock the lid. In a bowl, mix sour cream, yogurt, salt, and garlic. Drizzle with yogurt sauce. Serve.

Spinach Chicken Thighs

Serving Size: 4 | Total Time: 40 minutes

1 lb chicken thighs	½ cup white wine vinegar
1 lb spinach, chopped	2 bay leaves
2 garlic cloves, minced	Salt and pepper to taste
½ cup soy sauce	

Combine garlic, soy sauce, vinegar, bay leaves, salt, and pepper in a bowl. Add in chicken thighs and toss to coat. Transfer to your Instant Pot. Seal the lid and cook for 15 minutes on Poultry. Once ready, allow a natural release for 10 minutes and unlock the lid. Discard bay leaves and mix in spinach. Cook on Sauté for 4-5 minutes until the spinach wilts. Serve right away.

Thai Chicken

Serving Size: 4 | Total Time: 25 minutes

1 lb chicken thighs	1 red chili pepper, sliced
1 cup lime juice	2 tbsp olive oil
4 tbsp red curry paste	1 tsp ginger, grated
½ cup fish sauce	2 tbsp cilantro, chopped
2 tbsp brown sugar	

Combine lime juice, red curry paste, fish sauce, olive oil, brown sugar, ginger, and cilantro in a bowl. Add in chicken thighs and toss to coat. Transfer to your Instant Pot and pour in 1 cup water.

Seal the lid, select Manual, and cook for 15 minutes on High. When done, perform a quick pressure release. Top with red chili slices and serve.

Chicken Fricassee

Serving Size: 4 | Total Time: 40 minutes

4 chicken breasts	½ cup chicken broth
2 tbsp olive oil	¼ cup heavy cream
1 onion, chopped	2 tbsp capers
2 garlic cloves, minced	1 bay leaf
Salt and pepper to taste	2 tbsp tarragon, chopped
½ cup dry white wine	

Warm the olive oil in your Instant Pot on Sauté. Sprinkle chicken with salt and pepper and place in the pot. Cook for 6 minutes on all sides. Add in onion and garlic and cook for 3 minutes. Pour in chicken broth, white wine, and bay leaf. Seal the lid, select Manual, and cook for 15 minutes on High pressure.

When ready, perform a quick pressure release. Remove bay leaf and put in heavy cream and capers. Stir for 2-3 minutes and cook in the residual heat until thoroughly warmed. Ladle into bowls, top with tarragon, and serve.

Spring Onion Buffalo Wings

Serving Size: 6 | Total Time: 30 minutes

2 lb chicken wings, sectioned	
2 spring onions, sliced diagonally	
½ cup hot pepper sauce	Sea salt to taste
1 tbsp Worcestershire sauce	2 tbsp sugar, light brown
3 tbsp butter	

Combine hot sauce, Worcestershire sauce, butter, salt, and brown sugar in a bowl and microwave for 20 seconds until the butter melts. Pour 1 cup of water into your Instant Pot and fit in a trivet. Place the chicken wings on the trivet and seal the lid. Select Manual and cook for 10 minutes on High pressure.

Once done, perform a quick pressure release and unlock the lid. Remove chicken wings to a baking dish and brush the top with marinade. Broil for 4-5 minutes, turn the wings and brush more marinade. Broil for 4-5 minutes more. Top with spring onions and serve.

Curried Chicken with Mushrooms

Serving Size: 4 | Total Time: 25 minutes

1 cup shiitake mushrooms, sliced
1 cup white mushrooms, sliced
1 lb chicken breasts, cubed | 1 tbsp curry paste
2 tbsp olive oil | 1 cup chicken stock
1 yellow onion, thinly sliced | ½ bunch cilantro, chopped

Warm the olive oil in your Instant Pot on Sauté. Add in the chicken breasts and cook for 2 minutes until browned. Stir in onion and mushrooms and cook for another 3 minutes. Mix curry paste and chicken stock in a bowl and pour into the pot. Seal the lid, select Manual, and cook for 15 minutes on High pressure. Once ready, perform a quick pressure release and unlock the lid. Serve topped with cilantro.

Chili & Lemon Chicken Wings

Serving Size: 4 | Total Time: 20 minutes

1 lb chicken wings | ½ tsp cayenne pepper
2 tbsp olive oil | ½ chili pepper, chopped
1 tbsp honey | Salt and pepper to taste
1 lemon, zested and juiced | 1 ½ cups chicken broth
½ tsp garlic powder

Combine olive oil, lemon zest, lemon juice, red chili pepper, honey, garlic powder, cayenne pepper, black pepper, and salt in a bowl. Brush chicken wings with the mixture on all sides. Place the chicken broth and chicken wings in your Instant Pot. Seal the lid, select Manual, and cook for 10 minutes on High pressure. When over, perform a quick pressure release. Serve warm.

Sticky Chicken Wings

Serving Size: 6 | Total Time: 35 minutes + marinating time

2 lb chicken wings | 1 small lime, juiced
3 tbsp light brown sugar | ½ tsp sea salt
2 tbsp soy sauce | 1 tsp five-spice powder

Combine soy sauce, lime juice, five-spice powder, brown sugar, and salt in a bowl. Place chicken wing and marinade in a resealable bag and shake it. Transfer to the fridge and let marinate for 30 minutes.

Pour 1/2 cup of water and marinate chicken wings with the juices in your Instant Pot. Seal the lid, select Manual, and cook for 15 minutes on High pressure. When done, allow a natural release for 10 minutes and unlock the lid. Cook on Sauté until the sauce thickens. Serve.

Korean-Style Chicken

Serving Size: 6 | Total Time: 35 minutes

3 green onions, sliced diagonally
3 chicken breasts, halved | 1 tbsp rice vinegar
5 tbsp sweet chili sauce | 2 tbsp sesame seeds
5 tbsp sriracha sauce | 1 tbsp soy sauce
1 tbsp grated ginger | ½ cup chicken stock
4 garlic cloves

Combine chili sauce, sriracha sauce, ginger, garlic, vinegar, sesame seeds, soy sauce, and chicken stock in a bowl. Add in the chicken fillets and toss to coat. Transfer to your Instant Pot. Seal the lid, select Manual, and cook for 15 minutes on High pressure. Once ready, allow a natural release for 10 minutes and unlock the lid. Top with green onions and serve.

Chicken & Pepper Cacciatore

Serving Size: 4 | Total Time: 50 minutes

4 chicken thighs, with the bone, skin removed
3 mixed bell peppers, cut into strips
2 tbsp olive oil | 1 cup canned diced tomatoes
Salt and pepper to taste | 2 tbsp chopped rosemary
2 garlic cloves, minced | ½ tsp oregano
1 diced onion | 10 black olives, pitted

Warm olive oil in your Instant Pot on Sauté. Sprinkle chicken with salt and pepper and cook in the pot for 2-3 minutes per side; reserve. Add bell pepper, garlic, and onion to the pot and cook for 5 minutes. Stir in tomatoes, oregano, and 1 cup water and return the chicken. Seal the lid, select Manual, and cook for 20 minutes on High pressure. When done, allow a natural release for 10 minutes and unlock the lid. Serve topped with black olives and rosemary.

Spicy Honey Chicken

Serving Size: 4 | Total Time: 20 minutes

4 chicken drumsticks | 1 garlic clove, minced
5 tbsp soy sauce | 2 tbsp hot chili sauce
2 tbsp honey | 2 tbsp cornstarch
1 cup chicken broth | 1 lime, cut into wedges

Place soy sauce, honey, garlic, and chili sauce in your Instant Pot and stir. Add in chicken drumsticks and toss to coat. Pour in chicken broth and seal the lid. Select Manual and cook for 12 minutes on High pressure. Mix 2 tbsp of water and cornstarch in a bowl.

When over, perform a quick pressure release and unlock the lid. Add in the slurry and simmer on Sauté until the sauce thickens. Serve right away with lime wedges.

Chicken & Tomato Curry

Serving Size: 4 | Total Time: 35 minutes

2 lb chicken breasts | 1-inch piece ginger, grated
16 oz canned coconut milk | 1 onion, chopped
1 lb tomatoes, chopped | 2 tbsp red curry paste
1 tbsp tomato paste | 1 tsp salt
2 garlic cloves, minced | 2 tbsp cilantro, chopped

Place coconut milk, tomatoes, tomato paste, garlic cloves, ginger, onion, curry paste, salt, and cilantro in your Instant Pot and stir. Add in chicken and 1 cup of water and seal the lid and stir. Select Manual and cook for 15 minutes on High pressure. When over, allow a natural release for 10 minutes and unlock the lid. Top with cilantro and serve.

Creamy Mascarpone Chicken

Serving Size: 4 | Total Time: 30 minutes

8 bacon slices, cooked and crumbled
1 lb chicken breasts
8 oz mascarpone cheese
1 tbsp Dijon mustard

1 tsp ranch seasoning
3 tbsp cornstarch
½ cup cheddar, shredded

Place the chicken breasts, mustard, and mascarpone cheese in your Instant Pot. Add in ranch seasoning and 1 cup of water. Seal the lid, select Manual, and cook for 15 minutes on High pressure. Once ready, perform a quick pressure release and unlock the lid. Remove the chicken and shred it. Add in cornstarch, shredded chicken, cheese, and bacon and cook for 3 minutes on Sauté. Lock the lid and let chill for a few minutes. Serve.

Greek Chicken with Potatoes & Okra

Serving Size: 4 | Total Time: 45 minutes

2 lb chicken thighs, skinless and boneless
1 lb potatoes, peeled and cut into quarters
2 tbsp olive oil
¾ cup chicken stock

¼ lb okra, tops removed
¼ cup lemon juice
2 tbsp Greek seasoning
Salt and pepper to taste

Warm the olive oil in your Instant Pot on Sauté. Sprinkle chicken thighs with salt and pepper. Place in the pot and cook for 6 minutes on all sides. Combine chicken stock, lemon juice, and Greek seasoning in a bowl and pour over the chicken. Stir in potatoes, okra, salt, and pepper and seal the lid. Select Manual and cook for 15 minutes on High pressure. Once ready, allow a natural release for 10 minutes and unlock the lid. Serve warm.

Harissa Chicken Thighs

Serving Size: 4 | Total Time: 25 minutes

2 lb boneless chicken thighs
2 tbsp harissa
¼ cup soy sauce
1 tbsp ketchup
2 tbsp olive oil

¼ cup honey
2 tsp garlic powder
2 cups cooked rice
Salt and pepper to taste

Place soy sauce, ketchup, olive oil, honey, garlic powder, harissa, pepper, and salt in your Instant Pot and stir. Add in chicken thighs and pour in 1 cup of water. Seal the lid, select Manual, and cook for 20 minutes on High pressure.Once done, perform a quick pressure release and unlock the lid. Serve with a bed of rice.

Filipino-Style Chicken Congee

Serving Size: 6 | Total Time: 55 minutes

6 chicken drumsticks
1 cup Jasmine rice
1 tbsp fresh ginger, grated

1 tbsp fish sauce
4 green onions, chopped
3 hard-boiled eggs, halved

Place chicken, rice, 6 cups of water, fish sauce, and ginger in your Instant Pot and stir. Seal the lid, select Manual, and cook for 25 minutes on High pressure.

When done, allow a natural release for 10 minutes. Remove the chicken and shred it. Put shredded chicken back in the pot and cook for 10 minutes on Sauté. Top with eggs and green onions and serve.

Famous Chicken Adobo

Serving Size: 4 | Total Time: 50 minutes

4 chicken thighs
Salt and pepper to taste
2 tbsp olive oil
¼ cup white vinegar
¼ cup soy sauce

1 tbsp honey
1 onion, chopped
2 garlic cloves, crushed
2 bay leaves
2 tbsp cilantro, chopped

Warm the olive oil in your Instant Pot on Sauté. Sprinkle chicken with salt and pepper. Place it in the pot and brown for 8 minutes on all sides. Stir in vinegar, soy sauce, honey, onion, garlic, bay leaves, 1 cup of water, and pepper. Seal the lid, select Manual, and cook for 20 minutes on High pressure.

Once done, perform a quick pressure release and unlock the lid. Simmer for 10 minutes on Sauté until the sauce thickens. Discard bay leaves and top with cilantro. Serve.

Jamaican Chicken with Pineapple Sauce

Serving Size: 4 | Total Time: 40 minutes

1 lb chicken thighs
½ cup coconut cream
2 tbsp soy sauce
1 cup pineapple chunks
1 tsp Jamaican seasoning

1 tsp coriander seeds
¼ tsp salt
½ cup cilantro, chopped
1 tsp arrowroot starch

Place chicken thighs, coconut cream, soy sauce, Jamaican jerk seasoning, coriander seeds, and salt in your Instant Pot and stir. Pour in 1 cup of water and seal the lid; cook for 15 minutes on manual. Once over, allow a natural release for 10 minutes and unlock the lid.

Remove chicken to a bowl. Combine arrowroot starch and 1 tbsp of water in a cup and pour it into the pot. Add in pineapple chunks and cook for 4-5 minutes on Sauté. Top the chicken with cilantro and sauce. Serve.

Buffalo Chicken with Blue Cheese Sauce

Serving Size: 4 | Total Time: 30 minutes

1 lb chicken breasts, cut into thin strips
2 tbsp olive oil
1 tsp paprika
1 yellow onion, chopped
½ cup celery, chopped

½ cup buffalo sauce
½ cup chicken stock
¼ cup blue cheese, crumbled
4 tbsp sour cream

Place the chicken breasts, olive oil, paprika, onion, celery, buffalo sauce, and chicken stock in your Instant Pot. Seal the lid, select Manual, and cook for 12 minutes on High.

When ready, allow a natural release for 10 minutes and unlock the lid. In a bowl, combine the crumbled blue cheese and sour cream and add 1 cup of the cooking juice and stir. Pour into the pot. Serve right away.

Homemade Chicken Puttanesca

Serving Size: 6 | Total Time: 45 minutes

6 chicken thighs, skin on	½ tsp red chili flakes
2 tbsp olive oil	6 oz pitted black olives
2 anchovy fillets, chopped	1 tbsp capers
14 oz canned diced tomatoes	1 tbsp fresh basil, chopped
2 garlic cloves, crushed	Salt and pepper to taste

Warm the olive oil in your Instant Pot on Sauté. Place in the chicken thighs skin side-down and brown for 4-6 minutes. Remove to a bowl. Place tomatoes, garlic, chili flakes, anchovy fillets, black olives, capers, fresh basil, salt, and pepper into the pot. Pour in 1 cup of water.

Bring to a simmer. Add in back the chicken and seal the lid. Select Manual and cook for 20 minutes on High pressure. When ready, allow a natural release for 10 minutes and unlock the lid. Serve immediately.

Sweet & Spicy BBQ Chicken

Serving Size: 4 | Total Time: 35 minutes

6 chicken drumsticks	1 jalapeño pepper, minced
1 tbsp olive oil	½ cup sweet BBQ sauce
1 onion, chopped	1 tbsp arrowroot
1 tsp garlic, minced	

Warm the olive oil in your Instant Pot on Sauté. Add in the onion and cook for 3 minutes. Add in garlic and jalapeño pepper and cook for another minute. Stir in barbecue sauce and 1/2 cup of water. Put in chicken drumsticks and seal the lid. Select Manual and cook for 18 minutes on High pressure. When over, perform a quick pressure release and unlock the lid. Mix 2 tbsp of water and arrowroot and pour it into the pot. Cook for 5 minutes on Sauté until the liquid thickens. Top with sauce and serve.

Fennel Chicken with Tomato Sauce

Serving Size: 4 | Total Time: 35 minutes

1 lb chicken breasts	1 tbsp fennel seeds
½ cup chicken broth	2 tbsp olive oil
Salt and pepper to taste	2 cups tomato-basil sauce

Place the chicken breasts, olive oil, chicken broth, fennel seeds, salt, and pepper in your Instant Pot. Seal the lid, select Manual, and cook for 20 minutes on High pressure. When done, perform a quick pressure release and unlock the lid. Shred the chicken and add in tomato sauce. Simmer for 5 minutes on Saute. Serve immediately.

Chicken Gumbo

Serving Size: 4 | Total Time: 40 minutes

4 chicken thighs	Salt and pepper to taste
1 onion, diced	2 tbsp olive oil
2 garlic cloves, minced	1 ½ cups tomato sauce
2 sticks celery, finely diced	1 jalapeno, halved
2 green peppers, diced	2 tbsp sage, chopped
1 tsp Cajun seasoning	

Warm the olive oil in your Instant Pot on Sauté. Place in chicken and cook for 4-6 minutes on all sides; reserve. Add in onion, garlic, celery, and green peppers and cook for 5 minutes. Stir in Cajun seasoning, tomato sauce, salt, pepper, and 1 cup of water. Seal the lid, select Manual, and cook for 20 minutes on High pressure. When ready, perform a quick pressure release and unlock the lid. Top with sage and jalapeño pepper and serve.

Sticky Teriyaki Chicken

Serving Size: 4 | Total Time: 30 minutes

1 lb chicken breasts	½ cup chicken stock
2/3 cup teriyaki sauce	Salt and pepper to taste
1 tsp sesame seeds	3 green onions, chopped

Set your Instant Pot to Sauté. Place in teriyaki sauce and simmer for 1 minute. Stir in chicken stock, salt, and pepper and seal the lid. Select Manual and cook for 12 minutes on High pressure. Once over, allow a natural release for 10 minutes and unlock the lid. Transfer the chicken to a plate and shred it. Remove 1/2 cup of cooking liquid. Put chicken back in the pot and stir in green onions. Top with sesame seeds and serve.

Za'atar Chicken with Baby Potatoes

Serving Size: 4 | Total Time: 30 minutes

1 lb chicken thighs	1 garlic clove, minced
½ lb baby potatoes, halved	1 large onion, sliced
2 tbsp olive oil	Salt and pepper to taste
1 tbsp za'atar seasoning	

Warm the olive oil in your Instant Pot on Sauté. Place in onion and garlic and cook for 2 minutes. Add in chicken thighs and cook for 4-6 minutes on both sides. Scatter with za´atar seasoning, salt, pepper, potatoes, and pour in 1 cup of water. Seal the lid, select Manual, and cook for 15 minutes on High pressure.

Once ready, perform a quick pressure release and unlock the lid. Remove the chicken and shred it. Put chicken back to the pot and toss to coat. Serve right away.

Indian-Style Chicken

Serving Size: 6 | Total Time: 37 minutes + marinating time

6 chicken thighs, bone-in	Salt and pepper to taste
½ cup Greek yogurt	1 tbsp fresh ginger, grated
1 tbsp curry paste	2 tbsp cilantro, chopped
1 tbsp lemon juice	

Combine yogurt, lemon juice, curry paste, salt, and pepper in a bowl. Add in chicken thighs and toss to coat. Let marinate in the fridge for 2 hours. Place the chicken, marinade, ginger, and 1 cup of water in your Instant Pot. Seal the lid, select Manual, and cook for 12 minutes on High pressure. When over, allow a natural release for 10 minutes and unlock the lid. Transfer to a baking tray and put under the broiler 3-5 minutes. Top with cilantro.

Chicken with Chili & Lime

Serving Size: 4 | Total Time: 25 minutes

1 lb chicken breasts	1 tsp onion powder
¾ cup chicken broth	2 garlic cloves, minced
Juice and zest of 1 lime	1 tsp mustard powder
1 red chili, chopped	1 bay leaf
1 tsp cumin	Salt and pepper to taste

Place the chicken breasts, chicken broth, lime juice, lime zest, red chili, cumin, onion powder, garlic cloves, mustard powder, bay leaf, salt, and pepper in your Instant Pot. Seal the lid, select Manual, and cook for 10 minutes on High. When ready, allow a natural release. Remove chicken and shred it. Discard the bay leaf. Top the chicken with cooking juices and serve.

Cuban Mojo Chicken Tortillas

Serving Size: 4 | Total Time: 80 minutes + marinating time

4 chicken breasts	Salt and pepper to taste
2 tbsp olive oil	2 tbsp chopped cilantro
1 lime, juiced	4 tortillas
1 grapefruit, juiced	1 avocado, sliced
4 garlic cloves, minced	2 tbsp hot sauce
1 tsp ground cumin	

Combine olive oil, lime juice, grapefruit juice, garlic, cumin, cilantro, salt, and pepper in a bowl. Add in chicken breasts and let marinate covered for 30 minutes. Transfer chicken and marinade to your Instant Pot and pour in 1 cup of water. Seal the lid and cook for 20 minutes on Manual. Once done, allow a natural release for 10 minutes and unlock the lid. Remove the chicken and shred it, then add it back to the pot; stir. Divide the chicken between the tortillas and top with avocado slices and hot sauce. Serve right away.

Creole Chicken with Rice

Serving Size: 4 | Total Time: 45 minutes

2 tbsp olive oil	1 (14.5-oz) can tomato sauce
1 onion, diced	1 cup white rice, rinsed
3 garlic cloves, minced	1 bell pepper, chopped
1 lb chicken breasts, sliced	2 tsp creole seasoning
1 cup chicken broth	1 tbsp hot sauce

Warm the olive oil in your Instant Pot on Sauté. Place in onion and garlic and cook until fragrant, about 3 minutes. Stir in chicken breasts, bell pepper, hot sauce, and creole seasoning. Cook for 3 more minutes. Mix in chicken broth, tomato sauce, and rice and seal the lid. Select Manual and cook for 20 minutes on High pressure. When ready, allow a natural release for 10 minutes and unlock the lid. Serve warm.

Moroccan-Style Chicken

Serving Size: 4 | Total Time: 30 minutes

1 lb chicken thighs, skinless	Salt and pepper to taste
2 tbsp vegetable oil	3 garlic cloves, minced
1 large onion, chopped	1 tbsp fresh ginger, grated
¼ tsp cumin	½ tsp cinnamon, ground
½ cup chicken broth	2 tbsp cilantro, chopped
12 dried apricots, sliced	2 tbsp flaked almonds
1 lb canned tomatoes, diced	

Warm the vegetable oil in your Instant Pot on Sauté. Sprinkle chicken thighs with salt and pepper and place in the pot along with garlic and onion. Cook for 5 minutes. Stir in chicken broth, apricots, tomatoes, fresh ginger, cumin, and cinnamon. Seal the lid, select Manual, and cook for 12 minutes on High pressure. Once ready, perform a quick pressure release and unlock the lid. Serve topped with cilantro and almonds.

Chicken in Creamy Mushroom Sauce

Serving Size: 4 | Total Time: 50 minutes

1 lb chicken breasts	1 cup chicken stock
1 tbsp olive oil	Salt and pepper to taste
1 cup mushrooms, sliced	1 cup heavy cream
1 large onion, chopped	2 green onions, chopped
2 garlic cloves, minced	

Warm the olive oil in your Instant Pot on Sauté. Place in mushrooms, onion, and garlic and cook for 4-5 minutes. Sprinkle chicken breasts with salt and pepper and place in the pot. Cook for 6-8 minutes on all sides. Add in chicken stock and stir. Seal the lid, select Manual, and cook for 12 minutes on High pressure.

Once done, allow a natural release for 10 minutes. Remove the chicken. Add the heavy cream to the cooker and stir for 3 minutes on Sauté. Pour the sauce over the chicken, top with green onions, and serve warm.

Peppered Chicken with Chunky Salsa

Serving Size: 4 | Total Time: 30 minutes

3 mixed-color peppers, cut into strips	
1 lb chicken breasts	Salt and pepper to taste
2 tbsp olive oil	½ tsp oregano
2 jalapeño peppers, sliced	½ tsp cumin
1 onion, sliced	2 cups chunky salsa

Warm the olive oil in your Instant Pot on Sauté. Place in onion, peppers, and jalapeño peppers and sauté for 5 minutes. Sprinkle chicken breasts with salt and pepper and place them in the pot along with oregano, cumin, chunky salsa, and ½ cup of water. Seal the lid and cook for 15 minutes on Manual on High. When ready, perform a quick pressure release. Shred chicken before serving.

Chicken & Bacon Cacciatore

Serving Size: 4 | Total Time: 45 minutes

2 cups canned tomatoes and juice, crushed	
1 lb chicken drumsticks	1 tsp oregano, dried
4 oz bacon, chopped	1 bay leaf
1 red onion, chopped	Salt to taste
1 cup chicken stock	1 roasted pepper, chopped
1 garlic clove, minced	12 Kalamata olives, sliced

Set your Instant Pot to Sauté. Add in the bacon and cook for 5 minutes. Stir in onion and garlic and cook for 3 minutes. Pour in chicken stock, tomatoes, oregano, bay leaf, salt, and chicken. Seal the lid, select Manual, and cook for 15 minutes on High pressure. Once over, allow a natural release for 10 minutes and unlock the lid. Discard the bay leaf and mix in roasted pepper. Serve topped with olives.

Lemon & Thyme Chicken

Serving Size: 6 | Total Time: 40 minutes

3 lb red potatoes, peeled and quartered
2 lb chicken thighs   2 tbsp thyme, chopped
2 tbsp olive oil   ¾ cup chicken broth
1 onion, chopped   1 lemon, juiced and zested
2 garlic cloves, minced   Salt and pepper to taste

Warm the olive oil in your Instant Pot on Sauté. Place in the chicken thighs and brown for 2-3 minutes, stirring occasionally. Add in onion and garlic and cook for 3 minutes. Stir in chicken broth, lemon zest, lemon juice, potatoes, half of the thyme, salt, and pepper. Seal the lid and cook for 15 minutes on Poultry. Once ready, allow a natural release for 10 minutes and unlock the lid. Top with thyme and serve.

Cumin Chicken with Capers

Serving Size: 4 | Total Time: 30 minutes

4 chicken breasts   Juice of 1 lemon
½ cup butter   1 cup chicken broth
½ tsp cumin   ½ cup capers
Salt and pepper to taste

Melt butter in your Instant Pot on Sauté. Sprinkle chicken breasts with cumin, salt, and pepper and place in the pot. Cook for 7-8 minutes on all sides. Stir in lemon juice, chicken broth, and capers and seal the lid. Select Manual and cook for 10 minutes on High pressure. Once ready, allow a natural release for 5 minutes and unlock the lid.

Feta Cheese Turkey Balls

Serving Size: 6 | Total Time: 35 minutes

1 onion, minced   1 egg, lightly beaten
½ cup plain bread crumbs   1 tbsp olive oil
1/3 cup feta, crumbled   1 carrot, minced
Salt and pepper to taste   ½ celery stalk, minced
½ tsp dried oregano   3 cups tomato puree
1 lb ground turkey   2 cups water

In a mixing bowl, combine half the onion, oregano, turkey, salt, crumbs, pepper, and egg, and stir until everything is well incorporated. Heat oil on Sauté in your Instant Pot. Cook celery, remaining onion, and carrot for 5 minutes until soft. Pour in water and tomato puree. Adjust the seasonings. Roll the mixture into meatballs, and drop into the sauce. Seal the lid. Press Meat/Stew and cook on High Pressure for 5 minutes. Release the pressure naturally for 20 minutes. Serve topped with feta.

Chicken with Port Wine Sauce

Serving Size: 6 | Total Time: 41 minutes

1 (3 lb) chicken, cut into pieces
2 tbsp olive oil   ¼ cup Port wine
1 large onion, finely diced   Salt and pepper to taste
1 cup mushrooms   2 tbsp parsley, chopped

Warm olive oil in your IP on Sauté. Add in the chicken pieces and cook until the chicken is light brown, about 6-7 minutes; set aside. Add onion and mushrooms to the pot and sauté for 3-4 minutes. Deglaze with Port wine and pour in 1 cup of water. Season with salt and pepper and return the chicken. Seal the lid, select Manual, and cook for 20 minutes on High. Once ready, release pressure naturally. Sprinkle with parsley and serve.

Turkey Cakes with Ginger Gravy

Serving Size: 4 | Total Time: 25 minutes

1 lb ground turkey   Salt and pepper to taste
¼ cup breadcrumbs   2 tbsp olive oil
¼ cup grated Parmesan   2 cups tomatoes, diced
½ tsp garlic powder   ¼ cup chicken broth
2 green onions, chopped
GINGER SAUCE

4 tbsp soy sauce   1 tsp ginger, grated
2 tbsp canola oil   ½ tbsp honey
2 tbsp rice vinegar   ¼ tsp black pepper
1 garlic clove, minced   ½ tbsp cornstarch

Combine turkey, breadcrumbs, green onions, garlic powder, salt, pepper, and Parmesan cheese in a bowl. Mix with your hands and shape meatballs out of the mixture. In another bowl, mix soy sauce, canola oil, rice vinegar, garlic clove, ginger, honey, pepper, and cornstarch. Warm the olive oil in your Instant Pot on Sauté.

Place in meatballs and cook for 4 minutes on all sides. Pour in ginger gravy, tomatoes, and chicken stock and seal the lid. Select Manual and cook for 10 minutes on High pressure. Once over, perform a quick pressure release and unlock the lid. Serve in individual bowls.

Delicious Turkey Burgers

Serving Size: 4 | Total Time: 35 minutes

1 lb ground turkey   1 onion, finely chopped
2 egg   Salt and pepper to taste
1 tbsp flour   1 tbsp sour cream

In a bowl, add ground turkey, egg, flour, onion, salt, pepper, and sour cream and mix well. Form the mixture into patties. Line parchment paper over a baking dish and arrange the patties. Pour 1 cup of water into your Instant Pot. Lay the trivet and place the baking dish on top.

Seal the lid. Cook on Manual for 15 minutes on High. Release the pressure naturally for 10 minutes. Unlock the lid. Serve with lettuce and tomatoes.

Rigatoni with Turkey & Tomato Sauce

Serving Size: 4 | Total Time: 30 minutes

2 tbsp canola oil	1 tsp cumin
1 lb ground turkey	1 tsp red pepper flakes
1 egg	Salt and pepper to taste
¼ cup bread crumbs	3 cups tomato sauce
2 cloves garlic, minced	8 oz rigatoni
1 tsp dried oregano	2 tbsp grated Grana Padano

In a bowl, combine turkey, crumbs, cumin, garlic, and egg. Season with oregano, salt, red pepper flakes, and pepper. Form the mixture into meatballs. Warm the oil on Sauté in your Instant Pot. Cook the meatballs for 3-4 minutes until browned on all sides; set aside.

Add rigatoni to the cooker and pour the tomato sauce over. Cover with water. Stir well. Throw in the meatballs. Seal the lid and cook for 4 minutes on High Pressure. Release the pressure quickly. Serve topped with cheese.

Sunday Turkey Lettuce Wraps

Serving Size: 4 | Total Time: 35 minutes

¾ cup olive oil	1 tbsp Thai-style chili paste
4 cloves garlic, minced	1 lb turkey breast, boneless,
3 tbsp maple syrup	cut into strips
2 tbsp pineapple juice	1 lettuce, leaves separated
1 cup coconut milk	1/3 cup chopped peanuts
3 tbsp rice wine vinegar	¼ cup chopped cilantro
3 tbsp soy sauce	

In your Instant Pot, mix oil, garlic, rice wine vinegar, soy sauce, pineapple juice, maple syrup, coconut milk, and chili paste until smooth; add turkey strips and ensure they are submerged in the sauce. Seal the lid and cook on High Pressure for 12 minutes. Release the pressure quickly. Place the turkey at the center of each lettuce leaf. Top with cilantro and chopped peanuts.

Homemade Turkey Pepperoni Pizza

Serving Size: 4 | Total Time: 25 minutes

1 cup fire-roasted tomatoes, diced	
1 cup turkey pepperoni, chopped	
1 pizza crust	7 oz gouda cheese, grated
1 tsp oregano	2 tbsp olive oil

Grease a baking pan with oil. Line some parchment paper and place the pizza crust in it. Spread the fire-roasted tomatoes over the pizza crust and sprinkle with oregano. Make a layer with cheese and top with pepperoni. Add a trivet to your Instant Pot and pour in 1 cup water. Seal the lid and cook for 15 minutes on High Pressure. Do a quick release. Remove the pizza and serve.

Turkish-Style Roasted Turkey

Serving Size: 6 | Total Time: 70 minutes

2 lb boneless turkey breast, halved	
2 garlic cloves, crushed	Salt and pepper to taste
1 tsp dried basil	3 whole cloves

½ cup soy sauce	¼ cup oil
½ cup lemon juice	3 cups chicken broth

Place the turkey in a Ziploc bag and add basil, cloves, soy sauce, oil, salt, pepper, and lemon juice. Pour in 1 cup of broth and seal. Shake and refrigerate for 30 minutes. Heat oil on Sauté in your Instant Pot. Cook the garlic for 2 minutes. Add in turkey and 2 tbsp of the marinade and the remaining broth. Seal the lid. Cook on Manual for 25 minutes on High. Release the pressure naturally. Serve.

Spicy Turkey Casserole with Tomatoes

Serving Size: 4 | Total Time: 30 minutes

2 (14-oz) cans fire-roasted tomatoes	
2 bell peppers, cut into thick strips	
2 tbsp olive oil	1 cup salsa
½ sweet onion, diced	2 tsp chili powder
3 cloves garlic, minced	1 tsp ground cumin
1 jalapeño pepper, minced	Salt to taste
1 lb turkey breast, cubed	1 tbsp oregano, chopped

Warm oil on Sauté. Add in garlic, onion, and jalapeño and cook for 5 minutes until fragrant. Stir in turkey and cook for 5-6 minutes until browned. Add in salsa, tomatoes, bell peppers, and 1 ½ cups water. Season with salt, cumin, and chili powder. Seal the lid, press Manual, and cook for 10 minutes on High. Release the pressure quickly. Top with oregano and serve.

Cranberry Turkey with Hazelnuts

Serving Size: 4 | Total Time: 40 minutes

1 lb turkey breasts, sliced	1 tbsp rosemary, chopped
3 tbsp butter, softened	2 tbsp olive oil
2 cups fresh cranberries	2 tbsp orange zest
1 cup hazelnuts, chopped	Salt and pepper to taste
1 cup red wine	

Rub the turkey with oil and sprinkle with orange zest, salt, pepper, and rosemary. Melt butter in your Instant Pot on Sauté and brown turkey breast for 5-6 minutes. Pour in the wine, cranberries, and 1 cup of water. Seal the lid. Cook on High Pressure for 25 minutes. Do a quick release. Serve with chopped hazelnuts.

Parsley & Lemon Turkey Risotto

Serving Size: 4 | Total Time: 40 minutes

2 boneless turkey breasts, cut into strips	
2 lemons, zested and juiced	2 cups chicken broth
1 tbsp dried oregano	1 cup arborio rice, rinsed
2 garlic cloves, minced	Salt and pepper to taste
1 ½ tbsp olive oil	¼ cup chopped parsley
1 onion, diced	8 lemon slices

In a Ziploc bag, mix turkey, oregano, salt, garlic, juice and zest of two lemons. Marinate for 10 minutes. Warm oil on Sauté in your Instant Pot. Add onion and cook for 3 minutes. Stir in the rice and chicken broth and season with pepper and salt.

Empty the Ziploc having the chicken and marinade into the pot. Seal the lid and cook on High Pressure for 12 minutes. Release the pressure quickly. Garnish with lemon slices and parsley to serve.

Sage Turkey & Red Wine Casserole

Serving Size: 4 | Total Time: 50 minutes

1 lb boneless turkey breast, cubed
1 onion, sliced
1 celery stalk, sliced
2 tbsp olive oil
1 carrot, diced
½ cup red wine

Salt and pepper to taste
1 cup chicken broth
1 tbsp tomato puree
2 tbsp sage, chopped

Warm olive oil in your IP on Sauté. Add in the turkey cubes and brown for 4-5 minutes, stirring occasionally; set aside. Add onion, celery, and carrot to the pot and sauté for 3-4 minutes. Stir in tomato puree, red wine, salt, and pepper and pour in chicken broth. Stir and return the turkey. Seal the lid, select Manual, and cook for 20 minutes on High. Once ready, release pressure naturally for 10 minutes. Unlock the lid, top with sage and serve.

Spicy Ground Turkey Chili with Vegetables

Serving Size: 6 | Total Time: 60 minutes

1 tbsp olive oil
1 small onion, diced
2 garlic cloves, minced
1 lb ground turkey
2 bell peppers, chopped
6 potatoes, chopped
1 cup carrots, chopped

1 cup corn kernels, roasted
1 cup tomato puree
1 cup diced tomatoes
1 cup chicken broth
1 tbsp ground cumin
1 tbsp chili powder
Salt and pepper to taste

Warm oil on Sauté in your Instant Pot and stir-fry onion and garlic until soft for about 3 minutes. Stir in turkey and cook until thoroughly browned, about 5-6 minutes. Add the bell peppers, potatoes, carrots, corn, tomato puree, tomatoes, broth, cumin, chili powder, salt, and pepper, and stir to combine. Seal the lid and cook for 25 minutes on High Pressure. Do a quick release. Set to Sauté and cook uncovered for 15 more minutes. Serve.

Turkey & Black Bean Chili

Serving Size: 6 | Total Time: 30 minutes

2 lb chopped turkey breast
1 ½ cups vegetable stock
2 (14-oz) cans black beans
2 garlic cloves, peeled
1 onion, diced
1 yellow bell pepper, diced

1 (7 oz) green chiles, diced
1 (14 oz) can diced tomatoes
1 tbsp hot sauce
½ tsp cumin
½ tbsp chili powder
1 cup cheddar, shredded

Place turkey, vegetable stock, black beans, garlic, onion, bell pepper, tomatoes, chiles, cumin, hot sauce, and chili powder in your Instant Pot and stir. Seal the lid, select Manual, and cook for 20 minutes on High pressure. Once done, allow a natural release for 10 minutes, then a quick pressure release, and unlock the lid. Top with cheddar and serve.

Turkey Stew with Salsa Verde

Serving Size: 4 | Total Time: 52 minutes

1 lb turkey thighs, boneless and diced
2 tbsp olive oil
1 cup pearl onions
1 carrot, julienned
1 cup green peas

1 cup salsa verde
Salt and pepper to taste
¼ tsp turmeric
¼ tsp cumin

Warm olive oil in your IP on Sauté. Add in the turkey pieces and brown for 4-5 minutes, stirring occasionally; set aside. Add pearl onions and carrot to the pot and sauté for 3-4 minutes. Stir in the turmeric, cumin, salt, and pepper and pour in 1 cup of water. Return the turkey.

Seal the lid, select Manual, and cook for 20 minutes on High. Once ready, allow a natural pressure release for 10 minutes. Unlock the lid, add in the green peas and salsa verde, and stir. Press Sauté and cook for 3 minutes.

Potato Skins with Shredded Turkey

Serving Size: 4 | Total Time: 30 minutes

2 cups vegetable broth
1 tsp chili powder
1 tsp ground cumin
½ tsp onion powder
½ tsp garlic powder

1 lb turkey breast
4 potatoes
1 Fresno chili, minced
Salt and pepper to taste

In the pot, combine broth, cumin, garlic powder, onion powder, and chili powder. Toss in turkey to coat. Place a steamer rack over the turkey. On top of the rack, set the steamer basket. Use a fork to pierce the potatoes and transfer to the steamer basket. Seal the lid and cook for 20 minutes on High. Release the pressure quickly.

Remove rack and steamer basket from the cooker. Shred the turkey in a bowl. Place the potatoes on a plate. Cut in half each potato lengthwise and scoop out the insides. Season with salt and pepper. Stuff with shredded turkey. Top with chili pepper.

Turkey Soup with Noodle

Serving Size: 6 | Total Time: 40 minutes

1 tbsp olive oil
1 onion, minced
3 cloves garlic, minced
1 turnip, chopped
1 cup celery rib, chopped
1 tbsp dry basil

1 bay leaf
6 cups vegetable broth
1 lb turkey breasts, cubed
8 oz dry egg noodles
Salt and pepper to taste

Warm olive oil on Sauté. Stir-fry in garlic and onion for 3 minutes. Mix in celery, bay leaf, basil, and turnip. Pour in 3 cups of broth. Scrape any brown bits from the pan's bottom and add turkey. Seal the lid and cook on High Pressure for 10 minutes. Naturally release the pressure. Transfer turkey breasts to another bowl.

Do away with the skin and bones. Using two forks, shred the meat. Set the cooker on Sauté. Transfer the turkey to the pot; add noodles and the remaining broth. Simmer for 10 minutes until noodles are done. Season and serve.

Caribbean Turkey Wings

Serving Size: 4 | Total Time: 55 minutes

2 lb turkey wings	½ cup brown sugar
2 tbsp vegetable oil	1 tbsp bonnet pepper sauce
2 tbsp butter	¼ cup chives, chopped
Salt and pepper to taste	1 cup pineapple juice
1 yellow onion, sliced	1 tbsp cornstarch

Warm the vegetable oil and butter in your Instant Pot on Sauté. Sprinkle turkey wings with salt and pepper and place them in the pot. Sear for 5-6 minutes on all sides; set aside. Place onion in the pot and cook for 2 minutes. Stir in pineapple juice, bonnet pepper sauce, brown sugar, and 1/2 cup of water. Put in turkey wings and seal the lid. Select Manual and cook for 20 minutes on High.

When done, allow a natural release for 10 minutes and unlock the lid. Remove wings to a plate. Mix cornstarch and some cooking liquid in a bowl and pour into the pot. Simmer for 5 minutes on Sauté until the sauce thickens. Top with chives and serve with sauce.

Turkey Meatball Soup with Rice

Serving Size: 4 | Total Time: 30 minutes

1 green bell pepper, chopped	
1 habanero pepper, seeded and minced	
2 tbsp olive oil	½ tsp cumin
1 onion, chopped	½ tsp oregano
2 garlic cloves, minced	½ cup white rice, rinsed
½ lb ground turkey	Salt and pepper to taste
1 carrot, chopped	1 egg, beaten
1 (14-oz) can diced tomatoes	1 cup yogurt

Mix ground turkey with cumin, oregano, salt, and pepper in a bowl. Shape the mixture into 1-inch balls. Warm olive oil in your Instant Pot on Sauté. Add in onion, bell pepper, habanero pepper, carrot, and garlic. Cook for 3-4 minutes. Add in meatballs, tomatoes, 3 cups water, and rice. Seal the lid, select Manual and cook for 15 minutes.

Once ready, perform a quick pressure release and unlock the lid. Mix the egg and yogurt in a bowl, and temper with one cup of the soup liquid, adding it slowly and whisking constantly to prevent the egg from cooking. Stir this mixture into the pot. Ladle the soup into bowls and serve immediately.

Hungarian-Style Turkey Stew

Serving Size: 4 | Total Time: 40 minutes

1 lb chopped turkey pieces	1 red bell pepper, chopped
2 tbsp butter	1 green bell pepper, chopped
1 tsp paprika	1 cup chicken stock
1 can (15 oz) diced tomatoes	Salt and pepper to taste
1 red onion, sliced	6 tbsp sour cream
2 garlic cloves, chopped	2 tbsp parsley, chopped

Melt butter in your Instant Pot on Sauté and cook the turkey for 5 minutes, stirring occasionally. Add in onion, garlic, and bell peppers and sauté for another 3 minutes.

Stir in paprika, tomatoes, and stock and seal the lid. Select Manual and cook for 20 minutes on High pressure. Once over, perform a quick pressure release and unlock the lid. Adjust the seasoning. Top with sour cream and parsley.

Buffalo Turkey Chili

Serving Size: 4 | Total Time: 40 minutes

1 lb ground turkey	½ cup hot Buffalo sauce
2 tbsp olive oil	2 ½ cups chicken stock
1 onion, diced	1 tsp oregano
½ habanero pepper, diced	1 tbsp chili powder
½ cup red bell pepper, diced	Salt and pepper to taste
1 (14 oz) can pinto beans	2 tbsp cilantro, chopped

Warm the olive oil in your Instant Pot on Sauté and cook the onion, habanero pepper, and bell pepper until tender, about 3-4 minutes. Stir in ground turkey, beans, chicken stock, buffalo sauce, oregano, chili powder, salt, and pepper. Seal the lid and cook for 15 minutes on Bean/Chili on High pressure. When over, allow a natural release for 10 minutes, then perform a quick pressure release and unlock the lid. Serve topped with cilantro.

Turkey Sausage with Brussels Sprouts

Serving Size: 4 | Total Time: 40 minutes

1 lb turkey sausage, sliced	¼ cup chicken broth
2 tbsp olive oil	1 tsp yellow mustard
1 yellow onion, chopped	1 tsp balsamic vinegar
2 garlic cloves, minced	Salt and pepper to taste
½ lb Brussels sprouts, sliced	

Warm the olive oil in your Instant Pot on Sauté. Place in onion and garlic and cook for 2 minutes. Add in turkey sausage and cook for 5 more minutes. Stir in Brussels sprouts, mustard, vinegar, salt, and pepper for 3 minutes. Pour in chicken broth. Seal the lid, select Manual, and cook for 15 minutes on High pressure. When ready, allow a natural release for 5 minutes, then a quick pressure release, and unlock the lid. Serve right away.

Potato & Cauliflower Turkey Soup

Serving Size: 4 | Total Time: 35 minutes

1 tbsp olive oil	1 cup tomato sauce
1 lb ground turkey	½ tsp dried sage
2 garlic cloves, minced	½ tsp dried thyme
1 leek, chopped	4 cups chicken broth
1 cup cauliflower florets	3 potatoes, chopped
1 carrot, chopped	Salt and pepper to taste
1 celery stalk, chopped	

Warm the olive oil in your Instant Pot on Sauté. Place the ground turkey and garlic and cook for 5-6 minutes. Remove to a bowl. Add the leek, carrot, celery, cauliflower, tomato sauce, chicken broth, potatoes, sage, and thyme to the pot and return the turkey. Seal the lid, select Manual, and cook for 8 minutes on High. When over, allow a natural release for 10 minutes and unlock the lid. Sprinkle with salt and pepper. Serve right away.

North African Turkey Stew

Serving Size: 4 | Total Time: 60 minutes

1 lb turkey breast, cubed	2 celery stalks, chopped
2 tbsp butter	15.5 oz chickpeas, drained
1 onion, diced	2 oz green olives, pitted
½ tsp garlic powder	3 ½ cups chicken broth
2 tsp ras el hanout	Salt and pepper to taste
1 carrot, sliced	2 tbsp cilantro, chopped

Melt butter in your Instant Pot on Sauté and cook the onion, carrot, and celery for 3-4 minutes. Stir in turkey breast and cook until browned, about 4-5 minutes. Mix in garlic powder, ras el hanout, salt, pepper, chickpeas, and chicken broth. Seal the lid, select Manual, and cook for 25 minutes on High pressure. When done, allow a natural release for 10 minutes and unlock the lid. Serve topped with green olives and cilantro.

Weekend Turkey with Vegetables

Serving Size: 4 | Total Time: 35 minutes

1 lb turkey breast, chopped	3 garlic cloves, chopped
1 tsp red pepper flakes	1 onion, finely chopped
2 cups canned tomatoes	2 tbsp tomato paste
3 cups chicken broth	1 cup baby carrots, chopped
1 tsp honey	Salt and pepper to taste
2 cups zucchini, cubed	2 tbsp olive oil

Mix turkey, red pepper flakes, tomatoes, broth, honey, zucchini, garlic, onion, tomato paste, carrots, salt, pepper, and olive oil in your Instant Pot. Seal the lid and cook on Meat/Stew for 25 minutes on High Pressure. When ready, do a quick release and open the lid. Serve.

Turkey with Rice & Peas

Serving Size: 6 | Total Time: 45 minutes

1 ½ lb turkey breasts, sliced	1 cup green peas
1 tbsp olive oil	2 cups chicken broth
1 small onion, sliced	Salt and pepper to taste
1 cup brown rice	

Warm the olive oil in your Instant Pot on Sauté. Add in the onion and turkey and cook for 3 minutes, stirring occasionally. Stir in rice for 1 minute and pour in the broth; season with salt and pepper. Seal the lid, select Manual, and cook for 20 minutes on High.

Once ready, allow a natural release for 10 minutes, then perform a quick pressure release and unlock the lid. Mix in green peas and cook for 3-4 minutes on Sauté. Serve.

Mediterranean Duck with Olives

Serving Size: 4 | Total Time: 20 minutes

½ cup sun-dried tomatoes, chopped	
1 lb duck breasts, halved	½ cup chicken stock
2 tbsp olive oil	¾ cup heavy cream
½ tbsp Italian seasoning	1 cup kale, chopped
Salt and pepper to taste	½ cup Parmesan, grated
2 garlic cloves, minced	10 Kalamata olives, pitted

Combine olive oil, Italian seasoning, pepper, salt, and garlic in a bowl. Add in the duck breasts and toss to coat. Set your Instant Pot to Sauté. Place in duck breasts and cook for 5-6 minutes on both sides. Pour in chicken stock and seal the lid. Select Manual and cook for 4 minutes.

When done, perform a quick pressure release and unlock the lid. Mix in heavy cream, tomatoes, Kalamata olives, and kale and cook for 5 minutes on Sauté. Serve topped with Parmesan cheese.

Honey-Glazed Turkey

Serving Size: 4 | Total Time: 60 minutes

1 large turkey breast	2 cups chicken stock
½ cup honey	1 onion, diced
½ tsp cumin	2 garlic cloves, minced
½ tsp turmeric	1 tbsp dry sherry
Salt and pepper to taste	

Combine honey, cumin, turmeric, salt, and pepper in a bowl. Rub the mixture onto the turkey and let sit for 10 minutes. Place onion, garlic, and turkey in your Instant Pot. Add in chicken stock and sherry. Seal the lid and cook for 30 minutes on Manual. When ready, allow a natural release for 10 minutes. Slice turkey before serving.

Roast Goose with White Wine

Serving Size: 4 | Total Time: 40 minutes

1 lb goose fillets, sliced	1 cup white wine
1 onion, chopped	2 tbsp fresh celery, chopped
4 tbsp butter, softened	1 tsp dried thyme
2 garlic cloves, crushed	Salt and pepper to taste

Season the goose with salt and white pepper. Melt butter on Sauté in your Instant Pot and stir-fry onions, celery, and garlic for 3-4 minutes. Add the goose filletsand brown on both sides for 6-8 minutes. Add in the white wine and thyme. Pour in 1 cup of water, seal the lid, and set to Meat/Stew. Cook for 25 minutes on High Pressure. When ready, do a quick release and set aside. Serve.

Duck Breasts with Honey-Mustard Glaze

Serving Size: 4 | Total Time: 50 minutes

1 lb duck breast	¼ cup dry sherry
1 tbsp oil	1 tbsp Dijon mustard
1 tsp onion powder	3 cups chicken broth
1 cup honey	Salt and pepper to taste
¼ cup soy sauce	

Rub the duck with onion powder, salt, and pepper. Place it in the Instant Pot. Pour the broth, seal the lid and cook on Meat/Stew for 35 minutes on High Pressure.

Do a quick release. Remove the duck. Heat oil on Sauté, add soy sauce, honey, sherry, and mustard. Stir well and cook for 3-4 minutes. Add the meat and coat well. Serve the meat topped with the sauce.

PORK

Pork Chops with Creamy Gravy & Broccoli

Serving Size: 6 | Total Time: 35 minutes

PORK CHOPS

Salt and pepper to taste	10 broccoli florets
1 tsp garlic powder	1 cup vegetable stock
1 tsp onion powder	¼ cup butter, melted
1 tsp red pepper flakes	¼ cup milk
6 boneless pork chops	

GRAVY

3 tbsp flour	Salt and pepper to taste
½ cup heavy cream	

Combine salt, garlic powder, pepper flakes, onion, and pepper. Rub the mixture onto pork chops. Place stock, milk, and broccoli in the Instant Pot. Lay the pork chops on top. Seal the lid and cook for 15 minutes on High Pressure. Release the pressure quickly.

Transfer the pork chops and broccoli to a plate. Press Sauté and simmer the liquid remaining in the pot. Mix cream and flour. Pour into the simmering liquid and cook for 4 to 6 minutes until thickened and bubbly. Season with pepper and salt. Top the chops with gravy, drizzle butter over broccoli, and serve.

Pork Sausages with Potato & Celeriac Mash

Serving Size: 4 | Total Time: 40 minutes

1 tbsp olive oil	2 tbsp butter
4 pork sausages	¼ cup milk
1 onion	Salt and pepper to taste
2 cups vegetable broth	1 tbsp heavy cream
½ cup water	1 tsp Dijon mustard
4 potatoes, peeled, diced	½ tsp dry mustard powder
1 cup celeriac, chopped	2 tbsp parsley, chopped

Warm oil on Sauté in your Instant Pot. Add in sausages and cook for 1 to 2 minutes for each side until browned. Set the sausages to a plate. To the same pot, add onion and Sauté for 3 minutes until fragrant.

Add sausages on top of onion and pour water and broth over them. Place a trivet over onion and sausages. Put potatoes and celeriac in the steamer basket and transfer it to the trivet.

Seal the lid and cook for 11 minutes on High Pressure. Release the pressure quickly. Transfer potatoes and celeriac to a bowl. Set sausages on a plate and cover them with foil. With a potato masher, mash potatoes and celeriac. Stir in black pepper, milk, salt, and butter until mash becomes creamy and fluffy. Adjust the seasonings.

Set to Sauté. Add the onion mixture and bring to a boil. Cook for 5 to 10 minutes until the mixture is reduced and thickened. Into the gravy, stir in dry mustard, salt, pepper, mustard, and heavy cream. Top with sausage and gravy. Garnish with parsley. Serve immediately.

Cumin Pork Chops with Peach Sauce

Serving Size: 4 | Total Time: 20 minutes

4 pork chops	2 cups peaches, sliced
1 tsp cumin seeds	1 tbsp vegetable oil
Salt and pepper to taste	¾ cup vegetable stock

Sprinkle salt, cumin, and pepper on the pork chops. Set to Sauté and warm oil. Add the chops and cook for 3-5 minutes until browned and set aside on a bowl. Arrange peach slices at the bottom of the cooker.

Place the pork on top of the peaches. Add any juice from the plate over the pork and apply stock around the edges. Seal lid and cook on High Pressure for 8 minutes. Do a quick pressure release. Transfer the pork to a serving plate and spoon over the peach sauce before serving.

Apricot Jam-Glazed Ham

Serving Size: 4 | Total Time: 40 minutes

5 lb smoked ham	2 tsp mustard
¾ cup apricot jam	½ tsp ground cardamom
½ cup brown sugar	¼ tsp ground nutmeg
Juice from 1 lime	Black pepper to taste

To your Instant Pot, add ¼ cup water and ham. In a bowl, mix jam, lime juice, cardamom, pepper, nutmeg, mustard, and sugar. Pour the mixture over the ham. Seal the lid and cook on High Pressure for 10 minutes. Release the pressure quickly. Transfer the ham to a cutting board.

Allow to sit for 10 minutes. Press Sauté. Simmer the liquid and cook for 4 to 6 minutes until thickened into a sauce. Slice ham and place it onto a serving bowl. Drizzle with sauce before serving.

Paprika Pork Fajitas with Cotija Cheese

Serving Size: 4 | Total Time: 1 hour 30 minutes

½ cup queso Cotija, crumbled	
1 tbsp ground cumin	¾ cup vegetable broth
2 tsp dried oregano	¼ cup pineapple juice
1 tsp paprika	1 lime, juiced
1 tsp onion powder	4 cloves garlic, crushed
Salt and pepper to taste	2 bay leaves
½ tsp ground cinnamon	4 corn tortillas, warmed
2 lb boneless pork shoulder	

In a bowl, combine cumin, paprika, pepper, onion powder, oregano, salt, and cinnamon; toss in pork to coat. Place the pork, broth, garlic, lime juice, bay leaves, and pineapple juice in the Instant Pot. Seal the lid. Cook on High Pressure for 50 minutes. Release pressure quickly. Transfer the pork to a baking sheet and shred it with 2 forks. Reserve juices in the pot.

Preheat oven to 450 F. Bake in the oven for 10 minutes until crispy. Skim and get rid of fat from the liquid remaining in the pot. Dispose of the bay leaves. Over the pork, pour the liquid and serve alongside warm corn tortillas and queso Cotija.

Delicious Pork in Button Mushroom Gravy

Serving Size: 6 | Total Time: 60 minutes

1 cup button mushrooms, chopped
2 lb pork shoulder

2 tbsp butter, unsalted	¼ cup soy sauce
1 tbsp balsamic vinegar	2 bay leaves
Salt and garlic powder to taste	1 cup beef broth
	2 tbsp cornstarch

Rub the pork with salt and garlic powder. Melt butter on Sauté. Brown the meat for 5 minutes on each side. Stir in soy sauce and bay leaves. Cook for 2 minutes. Add in beef broth and balsamic vinegar. Seal the lid and set to Meat/Stew. Cook for 30 minutes on High Pressure.

When done, do a quick release. Remove and discard the bay leaves. Stir in mushrooms. Cook for about 8 minutes on Sauté. Stir in cornstarch and cook for 2 minutes.

Chickpea & Pork Stew with Bell Peppers

Serving Size: 6 | Total Time: 30 minutes

2 lb boneless pork shoulder, cubed

2 tbsp olive oil	1 tbsp chili powder
1 white onion, chopped	1 bay leaf
15 oz canned chickpeas	2 red bell peppers, diced
½ cup sweet paprika	6 cloves garlic, minced
2 tsp salt	1 tbsp cornstarch

Set to Sauté, add pork and oil, and allow cooking for 5 minutes until browned. Add in the onion, paprika, bay leaf, salt, 1 ½ cups of water, chickpeas, and chili powder. Seal the lid and cook on High Pressure for 8 minutes.

Do a quick release and discard bay leaf. Remove 1 cup of cooking liquid from the pot; add to a blender alongside garlic, water, cornstarch, and red bell peppers, and blend well until smooth. Add the blended mixture into the stew and mix well. Plate and serve immediately.

Authentic Cuban Pork Shoulder

Serving Size: 4 | Total Time: 70 minutes + marinating time

¼ cup lime juice	1 tbsp ground cumin
2 tbsp canola oil	1 tbsp fresh oregano
¼ cup chopped cilantro	Salt and pepper to taste
1 tsp red pepper flakes	2 lb pork shoulder
2 cloves garlic, minced	

In a large plastic bag, mix pork, canola oil, cumin, salt, pepper, oregano, pepper flakes, lime juice, and garlic. Seal and massage the bag to ensure the marinade covers the pork thoroughly. Place in the refrigerator for two hours.

In the Instant Pot, pour the pork. Seal the lid and cook on High Pressure for 50 minutes. Release pressure naturally for 10 minutes. Transfer the pork to a cutting board and use a fork to break into smaller pieces. Skim and get rid of the fat from the liquid in the cooker. Serve the liquid with pork and sprinkle with cilantro.

Classic Pork Goulash

Serving Size: 4 | Total Time: 40 minutes

12 oz pork neck, cut into bite-sized pieces

2 tbsp flour	10 oz button mushrooms
2 tbsp vegetable oil	4 cups beef broth
2 onions, peeled, chopped	1 chili pepper, chopped
1 carrot, chopped	1 tbsp cayenne pepper
1 chopped celery stalk	Salt and pepper to taste

Heat oil on Sauté. Add onions and cook for 2 minutes until translucent. Add flour, chili pepper, carrot, celery, cayenne pepper, and continue to cook for 2 minutes, stirring constantly. Add meat, mushrooms, and beef broth. Season with salt and pepper. Seal the lid and cook on Manual for 30 minutes on High Pressure. Do a quick release and serve immediately.

Pork Hot Dogs with Peppers & Beer

Serving Size: 6 | Total Time: 15 minutes

3 mixed-color peppers, cut into strips

1 tbsp olive oil	1 ½ cups beer
6 pork sausage links	6 hot dog rolls
2 spring onions, chopped	Salt and pepper to taste

Warm oil on Sauté in your Instant Pot. Add in sausage links and sear for 5 minutes until browned; set aside. Into the Instant Pot, add chopped peppers. Lay the sausages on top. Add beer into the pot and season with salt and pepper. Seal the lid and cook for on High Pressure 5 minutes. Release the pressure quickly. Serve sausages in hot dog rolls topped with onions and bell peppers.

Beer Pork Roast with Mushrooms

Serving Size: 4 | Total Time: 50 minutes

10 oz cream mushroom soup

3 lb pork roast	12 oz root beer
8 oz mushrooms, sliced	1 package dry onion soup

In the pressure cooker, whisk mushroom soup, dry onion soup mix, and root beer. Add the mushrooms and pork. Seal the lid, and set to Meat/Stew for 40 minutes on High. When ready, let sit for 5 minutes before doing a quick pressure release.

Pork Chops in Honey-Mustard Sauce

Serving Size: 4 | Total Time: 45 minutes

2 lb pork chops	1 tbsp Dijon mustard
1 cup beef broth	½ tsp cinnamon
2 tbsp oil	1 tsp ginger, grated
¼ cup honey	Salt and pepper to taste

Season the chops with salt and pepper. Heat oil on Sauté and brown the chops for 2-3 minutes on each side. In a bowl, mix honey, mustard, cinnamon, and ginger. Whisk together and drizzle over chops. Pour in broth and seal the lid. Cook on High Pressure for 30 minutes. Do a quick release and serve hot.

Beer Pulled Pork Tacos

Serving Size: 4 | Total Time: 1 hour + marinating time

3 tbsp sugar	2 tbsp lemon juice
3 tsp taco seasoning	¼ cup mayonnaise
Salt and pepper to taste	2 tbsp honey
2 lb pork shoulder, cubed	2 tsp mustard
1 cup beer	3 cups shredded cabbage
1 cup vegetable broth	4 taco tortillas

In a bowl, combine sugar, taco seasoning, salt, and black pepper. Rub onto pork pieces to coat well. Allow settling for 30 minutes. Into the pot, add broth, pork, and beer. Seal the lid and cook on High Pressure for 50 minutes. Release the pressure naturally for 10 minutes. Transfer the pork to a cutting board, allow cooling for a few minutes, and then shred with two forks.

In a bowl, mix mayonnaise, mustard, lemon juice, cabbage, and honey until well coated. Skim and get rid of fat from liquid in the pressure cooker. Return pork to the pot and mix with the juice. Toast the tortillas in a skillet over medium heat for about 30 seconds per side. Fill each tortilla with pork and slaw to serve.

Mushroom & Carrot Pork Stew

Serving Size: 2 | Total Time: 50 minutes

2 pork chops, bones removed and cubed
1 cup crimini mushrooms, sliced

2 carrots, chopped	1 cup beef broth
½ tsp garlic powder	1 tbsp apple cider vinegar
Salt and pepper to taste	2 tbsp cornstarch
2 tbsp butter	

Season the meat with salt and pepper. Add butter and pork chops to the pot and brown for 10 minutes, stirring occasionally on Sauté. Add mushrooms and cook for 5 minutes. Add carrots, garlic powder, broth, vinegar, and cornstarch and seal the lid. Cook on High Pressure for 25 minutes. Do a quick release. Carefully unlock the lid.

Honey & White Wine Pork

Serving Size: 4 | Total Time: 40 minutes

1 lb pork loin, cut into chunks
15 oz canned peaches, chopped

2 tbsp white wine	2 tbsp honey
¼ cup beef stock	2 tbsp soy sauce
2 tbsp sweet chili sauce	2 tbsp cornstarch

Into the pot, mix soy sauce, beef stock, wine, honey, the juice from the canned peaches, and sweet chili sauce. Stir in pork to coat. Seal the lid and cook on High Pressure for 5 minutes. Release pressure naturally for 10 minutes. Unlock the lid. Remove the pork to a serving plate.

In a bowl, mix ¼ cup water with cornstarch until well dissolved and stir it in the pot. Press Sauté. Cook for 5 minutes until you obtain the desired thick consistency. Add in the peaches and stir well for 2 minutes. Serve the pork topped with the peach sauce. Enjoy!

Christmas Ham with Honey-Mustard Glaze

Serving Size: 10 | Total Time: 35 minutes

½ cup apple cider	2 tbsp pineapple juice
¼ cup honey	½ tsp ground cinnamon
1 tbsp Dijon mustard	¼ tsp grated nutmeg
¼ cup brown sugar	1 (5-pound) ham, bone-in
2 tbsp orange juice	

Set to Sauté. Mix in apple cider, mustard, pineapple juice, cinnamon, sugar, honey, orange juice, and nutmeg. Cook until the sauce becomes warm, and the sugar and spices are completely dissolved. Lay ham into the sauce. Seal the lid and cook on High Pressure for 10 minutes. Release the pressure quickly. Transfer the ham to a baking sheet.

On Sauté, cook the remaining liquid for 4 to 6 minutes until you have a thick and syrupy glaze. Preheat the oven's broiler. Brush the glaze onto ham. Set the glazed ham in the preheated broiler and bake for 3 to 5 minutes until the glaze is caramelized. Place the ham on a cutting board and slice. Transfer to a serving bowl and drizzle glaze over the ham.

Saucy Baby Back Ribs

Serving Size: 4 | Total Time: 60 minutes

2 lb baby back pork ribs	Juice from 1 lemon
4 cups orange juice	

FOR BBQ SAUCE

2 tbsp honey	1tsp mustard
½ cup ketchup	2 tsp paprika
Juice from ½ lemon	½ tsp cayenne pepper
1 tbsp Worcestershire sauce	Salt to taste

Mix honey, ketchup, lemon juice, Worcestershire sauce, mustard paprika, cayenne pepper, and salt in a bowl until well incorporated. Place the ribs into your Instant Pot and add in the lemon and orange juices. Seal the lid, press Meat/Stew, and cook on High Pressure for 30 minutes. Release pressure naturally for 10 minutes. Carefully unlock the lid.

Meanwhile, preheat oven to 400°F. Line the sheet pan with aluminum foil. Transfer the ribs to the prepared sheet. Do away with the cooking liquid. Onto both sides of ribs, brush barbecue sauce. Bake ribs in the oven for 10 minutes until sauce is browned and caramelized; set the ribs aside and cut into individual bones to serve.

Steamed Red Cabbage with Crispy Bacon

Serving Size: 8 | Total Time: 35 minutes

1 lb red cabbage, chopped	2 tbsp butter
8 bacon slices, chopped	Salt and pepper to taste
1 ½ cups beef broth	

Add the bacon slices to your Instant Pot and cook for 5 minutes until crispy on Sauté. Stir in the cabbage, broth, salt, pepper, and butter. Seal the lid and cook on Steam for 10 minutes. Release the pressure naturally for 10 minutes. Serve.

Rice Chowder with Bacon & Green Peas

Serving Size: 4 | Total Time: 30 minutes

1 cup basmati rice
1 cup bacon, chopped
1 medium onion, chopped
½ cup green peas
3 tbsp olive oil
2 garlic cloves, chopped
1 tsp dried thyme
1 tsp salt
2 cups beef broth

Heat oil on Sauté in your Instant Pot. Stir-fry the onion and garlic for 3 minutes until translucent. Add in rice, bacon, green peas, thyme, salt, and broth and stir. Seal the lid. Cook on High Pressure for 5 minutes. Release the pressure naturally for 10 minutes. Plate and serve.

Caribean-Style Pork with Mango Sauce

Serving Size: 6 | Total Time: 70 minutes

1 ½ tsp onion powder
1 tsp dried thyme
Salt and pepper to taste
1 tsp cayenne pepper
1 tsp ground allspice
½ tsp ground nutmeg
½ tsp ground cinnamon
3 lb pork shoulder
1 mango, cut into chunks
1 tbsp olive oil
½ cup water
2 tbsp cilantro, minced

In a bowl, combine onion, thyme, allspice, cinnamon, pepper, sea salt, cayenne, and nutmeg. Coat the pork with olive oil. Season with seasoning mixture. Warm oil on Sauté in your Instant Pot. Add in the pork and cook for 5 minutes until browned completely. To the pot, add water and mango chunks. Seal the lid, press Meat/Stew, and cook on High Pressure for 45 minutes.

Release the pressure naturally for 10 minutes. Transfer the pork to a cutting board to cool. To make the sauce, pour the cooking liquid into a food processor and pulse until smooth. Shred the pork and arrange it on a serving platter. Serve topped with mango salsa and cilantro.

Pork Chops with Brussels Sprouts

Serving Size: 4 | Total Time: 35 minutes

1 lb pork chops
1 cup onions, sliced
1 cup carrots, sliced
1 tbsp butter
2 cups Brussels sprouts
1 tbsp arrowroot
1 garlic clove, minced
1 cup vegetable stock
Salt and pepper to taste

Melt butter on Sauté. Add the pork chops, and cook on all sides until golden in color. Transfer to a plate. Add the onions, and cook for 3 minutes, then add the garlic. Saute for one more minute. Return the pork chops to the pot and pour the stock over. Season with salt and pepper. Seal the lid and cook on High Pressure for 15 minutes.

When the timer goes off, do a quick pressure release. Stir in carrots and Brussel sprouts. Seal the lid again and cook for 3 minutes on High Pressure. Do a quick pressure release. Transfer the chops and veggies to a serving platter. Whisk the arrowroot into the pot and cook on Sauté until it thickens. Pour the sauce over the chops and veggies. Serve immediately.

Pork Tenderloin with Balsamic & Butter

Serving Size: 4 | Total Time: 50 minutes

2 lb pork tenderloin
2 tbsp butter, unsalted
2 tbsp brown sugar
2 tbsp balsamic vinegar
2 garlic cloves, crushed
1 cup beef broth
Salt and pepper to taste
1 tbsp cornstarch

Melt butter on Sauté in your Instant Pot. Stir-fry garlic for 1 minute. Add in sugar and vinegar and cook for 1 more minute. Rub the meat with salt and pepper. Place it in the pot and pour in the broth. Seal the lid. Cook on High Pressure for 35 minutes. Do a quick release and unlock the lid. Set the meat aside. Stir in cornstarch in the remaining liquid and cook for 1 minute on Sauté to thicken the sauce. Drizzle over meat and serve.

Spiced Pork with Orange & Cinnamon

Serving Size: 4 | Total Time: 70 minutes

2 tbsp olive oil
2 lb pork shoulder
1 cinnamon stick
1 cup orange juice
1 tbsp cumin
½ tsp garlic powder
¼ tsp onion powder
1 onion, chopped
1 jalapeño pepper, diced
2 tsp thyme
½ tsp oregano
Salt and pepper to taste

Place half of the oil in a small bowl. Add cumin, garlic powder, onion powder, thyme, oregano, salt, and pepper and stir well to combine the mixture. Rub it all over the meat, making sure that the pork is well-coated. Heat the remaining oil on Sauté. Add the pork and sear it on all sides until browned. Transfer to a plate. Pour the orange juice into the pan and deglaze the bottom with a spatula.

Add cinnamon stick, onion, and jalapeño and stir to combine well. Return the pork to the pot. Seal the lid, select Pressure Cook, and cook for 40 minutes. When ready, allow for a natural pressure release for about 10 minutes. Grab two forks and shred the pork inside the pot. Stir to combine with the juices and serve.

Pork Loin with Apples & Rutabaga

Serving Size: 4 | Total Time: 30 minutes

1 tbsp olive oil
1 lb pork loin, cubed
2 apples, peeled, chopped
1 large rutabaga, chopped
1 onion, diced
1 celery stalk, diced
1 tbsp parsley, chopped
½ cup leeks, sliced
1 ½ cups beef broth
½ tsp cumin
½ tsp thyme
Salt and pepper to taste

Heat half of the olive oil on Sauté in your Instant Pot. Add the pork and cook until it browned on all sides. Remove to a plate. Add leeks, onion, celery, and drizzle with the remaining oil. Stir to combine and cook for 3 minutes. Add the pork back to the cooker, pour the broth over, and stir in parsley, cumin, thyme, salt, and pepper. Seal the lid, and cook on High Pressure for 10 minutes. After the beep, do a quick pressure release. Stir in the rutabaga and apples. Seal the lid again and cook for 5 minutes on High. Do a quick pressure release. Serve.

Pork Loin with Pineapple Sauce

Serving Size: 6 | Total Time: 35 minutes

2 lb pork loin, cut into 6 equal pieces
16 oz canned pineapples | ½ tsp ginger, grated
1 cup vegetable broth | Salt and pepper to taste
1 tbsp brown sugar | ¼ cup tamari
3 tbsp olive oil | ¼ cup rice wine vinegar
½ cup tomato paste | ½ tbsp cornstarch
1 cup sliced onions

Heat the 2 tbsp oil on Sauté. Cook the onions for 3 minutes until translucent. Add the pork and stir in pineapples, sugar, broth, tomato paste, ginger, salt, pepper, tamari, and rice vinegar. Seal the lid and cook for 20 minutes on Soup/Broth on High. Release the pressure quickly. Mix cornstarch and 1 tbsp water and stir it in the pot. Cook for 2 minutes or until thickened on Sauté. Serve hot.

Pork Carnitas Wraps with Lime & Cilantro

Serving Size: 4 | Total Time: 65 minutes

1 (2-pound) boneless pork shoulder
2 tsp grapeseed oil | 1 tsp dried oregano
1 onion, chopped | 1 jalapeño pepper, chopped
2 garlic cloves, minced | 1 avocado, sliced
1 grapefruit, juiced | 2 tbsp cilantro, chopped
1 lime, juiced | 4 corn tortillas, warmed
1 tsp sweet smoked paprika

Warm oil on Sauté in your Instant Pot. Add in pork and cook for 5 minutes until golden brown. Transfer the pork to a plate. Add garlic and onion to the pot and cook for 3 minutes until soft. Add lime and grapefruit juices into the pan and scrape the bottom to eliminate any browned bits of food. Stir in paprika, oregano, and 1 cup water. Return the pork to pot and stir to coat.

Seal the lid and cook for 35 minutes on High Pressure. Release the pressure quickly. Press Sauté. When the liquid starts to simmer, use two forks to shred the pork. Cook for 10 more minutes until liquid is reduced by half. Serve in warmed tortillas topped with jalapeños, avocado slices, and cilantro. Enjoy!

Pork Shoulder with Honey & Ginger

Serving Size: 6 | Total Time: 1 hour

2 lb pork shoulder, boneless | 1 tbsp apple cider vinegar
Salt and pepper to taste | 1 tbsp honey
½ tsp red pepper flakes | 3 tbsp soy sauce
1 tbsp butter, unsalted | 1 tsp garlic powder
2 tsp fresh ginger, grated

In a bowl, combine apple cider, honey, soy sauce, garlic powder, and ginger. Brush the meat with the mixture. Brown it for 5 minutes on all sides on Sauté. Stir in 2 cups water, salt, pepper, and red pepper flakes. Seal the lid and cook on High Pressure for 35 minutes on High. Do a quick release. Press Sauté and add the butter. Cook until the liquid evaporates, 10 minutes. Serve warm.

Pork Chops on Puréed Butternut Squash

Serving Size: 4 | Total Time: 35 minutes

3 tbsp olive oil | 4 cloves garlic, minced
2 sprigs thyme, chopped | 1 cup vegetable broth
2 sprigs rosemary, chopped | 1 tbsp soy sauce
4 pork chops | 1 lb butternut squash, cubed
1 cup mushrooms, chopped | 1 tsp cornstarch

Set to Sauté and heat 2 tbsp of oil in your Instant Pot. Add the pork chops, rosemary, and thyme and sear for 1 minute for each side until lightly browned. Sauté garlic and mushrooms in the Instant Pot for 5-6 minutes until mushrooms are tender. Add soy sauce and broth. Over the chops, place a cake pan. Add in the butternut squash in the pan and drizzle with olive oil. Seal the lid.

Cook on High Pressure for 10 minutes. Release the pressure quickly. Remove the pan and trivet from the pot. Stir cornstarch into the mushroom mixture for 3 minutes until the sauce thickens. Transfer the mushroom sauce to a food processor. Blend until you attain the desired consistency. Scoop the sauce into a cup with a pour spout. Smash the squash into a purée and spoon into a serving platter. Top with the pork chops and drizzle with the gravy. Serve and enjoy!

Pulled Pork with Homemade BBQ Sauce

Serving Size: 4 | Total Time: 70 minutes

4 lb pork shoulder | 2 cups vegetable stock
1 tbsp onion powder | 6 dates, soaked
1 tbsp garlic powder | ¼ cup tomato paste
Salt and pepper to taste | ½ cup coconut aminos
1 tbsp chili powder

In a small bowl, combine onion powder, garlic powder, salt, black pepper, and chili powder. Rub the mixture onto the pork. Place the pork inside your pressure cooker. Pour the stock around the meat, not over it, and then seal the lid. Select Pressure Cook and set the timer to 60 minutes. Place the dates, tomato paste, and coconut aminos in a food processor; pulse until smooth. Release the pressure quickly. Grab two forks and shred the meat inside the pot. Pour the sauce over and stir to combine.

Spicy Garlic Pork

Serving Size: 4 | Total Time: 45 minutes

1 lb pork shoulder | 1 large onion, chopped
2 tbsp olive oil | 2 garlic cloves, crushed
3 Jalapeño peppers, minced | 3 cups beef broth
1 tsp ground cumin | Salt and pepper to taste

Heat oil on Sauté in your Instant Pot and cook the jalapeño peppers for 3 minutes. Add in cumin, salt, pepper, garlic, and onion and stir-fry for another 2 minutes until soft. Add in the pork shoulder, and beef broth. Seal the lid, and cook on Meat/Stew for 30 minutes on High. Release the pressure quickly and serve hot.

Spring Onion & Pork Egg Casserole

Serving Size: 4 | Total Time: 35 minutes

1 tbsp butter, melted	6 eggs
4 spring onions, chopped	Salt and pepper to taste
1 lb ground pork, chopped	1 cup water

In a bowl, break the eggs and whisk until frothy. Mix in the onions and ground meat and season with salt and pepper. Grease a casserole dish with melted butter. Pour the egg mixture into the dish. Place a trivet in the pressure cooker and add water. Select Manual and cook for 25 minutes on High. Do a quick pressure release.

Maple Pulled Pork with Tomatoes

Serving Size: 6 | Total Time: 50 minutes

½ cup sun-dried tomatoes, diced	
2 lb pork shoulder	½ cup brown sugar
½ cup maple syrup	2 tbsp salt
3 cups beef stock	1 cup cilantro, chopped
2 tbsp mustard powder	

Rub the meat with salt and sugar, and place it in the pot. Add mustard powder, stock, maple syrup, and tomatoes. Seal the lid and cook on High Pressure for 30 minutes. Allow the pressure to release naturally for 10 minutes. Shred the pork with two forks, transfer to a plate, and top with cilantro to serve.

Tasty Buckwheat & Pork Stew

Serving Size: 4 | Total Time: 57 minutes

1 cup buckwheat	3 tbsp vegetable oil
1 lb pork tenderloin	1 tsp dry marjoram
1 carrot, chopped	Salt and pepper to taste
1 onion, finely chopped	½ cup white wine
2 garlic cloves, minced	2 cups vegetable broth

Heat oil on Sauté. Add onion and garlic and stir-fry for 2 minutes until fragrant and translucent. Add carrot and pork. Cook for 5 minutes until lightly browned. Add buckwheat, marjoram, salt, pepper, wine, and broth. Seal the lid and cook on High Pressure for 35 minutes. Do a quick release. Stir and spoon onto bowls. Serve hot.

Sweet & Spicy Pulled Pork

Serving Size: 4 | Total Time: 60 minutes

1 lb pork shoulder	1 cup beef broth
1 onion, finely chopped	1 tsp maple syrup
2 tbsp butter, unsalted	2 tbsp soy sauce
1 tbsp cayenne pepper	¼ cup Worcestershire sauce
1 tsp salt	

Warm butter on Sauté and stir-fry onions, cayenne pepper, and salt for 4 minutes. Add in maple syrup, soy sauce, and Worcestershire sauce and stir. Cook for 5 minutes. Add pork and pour in the broth. Seal the lid and cook on High Pressure for 40 minutes. When done, do a quick release. Divide between plates and serve hot.

Garlic Pork Meatloaf with Ketchup Glaze

Serving Size: 6 | Total Time: 70 minutes

1 lb pork sausages	2 garlic cloves, minced
1 lb ground pork	1 onion, diced
1 cup cooked rice	Salt and pepper to taste
1 cup milk	2 tbsp brown sugar
½ tsp marjoram	1 cup ketchup
2 eggs, beaten	

In a bowl, crack the eggs and whisk them with milk. Stir in the meat, marjoram, rice, onion, salt, black pepper, and garlic. With hands, mix in the ingredients to combine and form a meatloaf. Add it to a greased baking dish. Whisk together the ketchup and sugar and pour over the meatloaf. Place a trivet inside your Instant Pot and pour 1 cup of water. Lay the dish on top, seal the lid and cook on Manual for 50 minutes on High. Do a quick release. Unlock the lid. Serve the meatloaf sliced.

Wine Pork Butt with Fennel & Mushrooms

Serving Size: 4 | Total Time: 30 minutes

3 tbsp olive oil	½ cup white wine
1 lb pork butt, sliced	1 tsp garlic, minced
2 cups mushrooms, sliced	½ cup vegetable broth
1 fennel bulb, chopped	

Heat the olive oil on Sauté. Brown the pork slices and for a few minutes. Stir in mushrooms, fennel, wine, garlic, and broth. Seal the lid and cook for 20 minutes on Manual on High. When done, do a quick release. Serve.

Short Ribs with Wine Mushroom Sauce

Serving Size: 4 | Total Time: 75 minutes

2 lb boneless pork short ribs, cut into 3-inch pieces	
Salt and pepper to taste	2 carrots, sliced
½ onion, chopped	2 cups mushrooms, sliced
½ cup red wine	1 tbsp cornstarch
3 tbsp olive oil	Minced parsley to garnish
½ tbsp tomato paste	

Rub the ribs on all sides with salt and pepper. Heat the oil on Sauté in your Instant Pot and brown short ribs on all sides, about 6-7 minutes. Remove to a plate. Add onion to the pot and cook for 3-5 minutes. Pour in wine and tomato paste to deglaze by scraping any browned bits from the bottom of the cooker. Cook for 2 minutes until the wine has reduced slightly. Return ribs to the pot and cover with carrots. Pour 1 cup of water over.

Seal the lid, and select Manual on High Pressure for 35 minutes. When ready, let the pressure release naturally for 10 minutes. Carefully unlock the lid. Transfer ribs and carrots to a plate. To the pot, add mushrooms. Press Sauté and cook them for 2-4 minutes. In a bowl, add 2 tbsp of water and cornstarch and mix until smooth. Pour this slurry into the pot, stirring constantly until it thickens slightly, 2 minutes. Season the gravy with salt and pepper. Pour over the ribs and garnish with parsley.

Pork Chops in Cinnamon Apple Sauce

Serving Size: 4 | Total Time: 55 minutes

4 pork loin chops	1 cup beef broth
2 tbsp oil	2 tbsp honey
1 tbsp butter	¼ tsp cinnamon
3 apples, peeled, chopped	Salt and pepper to taste
¼ cup soy sauce	

Heat oil on Sauté and briefly brown the chops for 3 minutes on each side. Remove and melt the butter. Add apples, soy sauce, broth, honey, and cinnamon. Cook until apples are slightly tender. Add the chops back, seal the lid and cook on Meat/Stew for 40 minutes on High. Do a quick release. Adjust the seasoning and serve.

White Peas with Jalapeño & Bacon

Serving Size: 4 | Total Time: 40 minutes

1 lb white peas	2 tbsp butter
4 slices bacon	1 tbsp cayenne pepper
1 onion, chopped	3 bay leaves, dried
1 jalapeño pepper, chopped	Salt and pepper to taste
2 tbsp flour	

Melt butter on Sauté, and stir-fry the onion for 2-3 minutes until translucent. Add bacon, peas, jalapeño pepper, bay leaves, salt, cayenne, and pepper. Stir in 2 tbsp of flour and add 3 cups of water. Seal the lid and cook on High Pressure for 15 minutes. Release the steam naturally for 10 minutes.

Homemade Braised Pork Belly

Serving Size: 4 | Total Time: 30 minutes

1 lb pork belly, sliced	¼ cup honey
2 tbsp oil	¼ cup red wine
½ tsp cinnamon, ground	2 cups orange juice
¼ tsp nutmeg, ground	1 cup water

Heat oil on Sauté, and brown the pork for 3 minutes. Add cinnamon, nutmeg, honey, wine, orange juice and water, seal the lid, and cook on High Pressure for 20 minutes. Do a quick release. Press Sauté and bring it to a boil. Let simmer until the excess liquid evaporates. Serve.

Pancetta Kale with Chickpeas

Serving Size: 4 | Total Time: 35 minutes

2 oz onion soup mix	½ lb pancetta slices, chopped
¼ cup olive oil	1 onion, chopped
1 tbsp garlic, minced	1 cup kale, chopped
1 cup canned chickpeas	Salt and pepper to taste
2 tsp mustard	

Heat the oil and cook the onion, garlic, and pancetta for 5 minutes on Sauté. Add 1 cup of water, soup mix, salt, and pepper, and cook for 5 more minutes. Then, add the chickpeas and 2 cups of water. Add in the kale and mustard. Seal the lid and cook for 15 minutes on Pressure Cook on High Pressure. Once done, perform a quick pressure release. Serve immediately.

Easy Pork Balls with Apple Sauce

Serving Size: 4 | Total Time: 40 minutes

1 lb ground pork	2 tsp honey
¼ cup tamari sauce	¼ cup apple juice
3 garlic cloves, minced	1 cup breadcrumbs
½ tbsp dried thyme	Salt and pepper to taste
½ cup diced onions	

Whisk together honey, tamari, apple juice, 1 ½ cups water, and thyme in the pressure cooker. Season with salt and pepper. Set to Sauté and cook for 15 minutes. Combine pork, garlic, onions, and breadcrumbs in a bowl. Shape meatballs out of the mixture and pour them into the sauce. Seal the lid and cook on Pressure Cook for 15 minutes. Release the pressure quickly. Serve.

Pork Meatloaf with Chili Tomato Sauce

Serving Size: 4 | Total Time: 45 minutes

2 lb ground pork	½ tsp dried oregano
2 garlic cloves, minced	2 tsp brown sugar
1 cup bread crumbs	2 tbsp olive oil
1 large-sized egg	1 shallot, finely chopped
½ cup milk	28 oz canned tomatoes
2 onions, finely chopped	½ red chili, finely chopped
Salt and pepper to taste	2 tbsp Worcestershire sauce
½ tsp turmeric powder	1 tbsp lemon juice

Place a trivet in your pressure cooker and pour in 1 cup of water. Combine ground pork, bread crumbs, milk, onions, egg, garlic, salt, pepper, oregano, and turmeric powder in a bowl. Shape into a loaf and place onto a greased sheet pan. Lower the sheet pan onto the trivet. Seal the lid, select Pressure Cook and cook for 20 minutes. Do a quick pressure release. Remove the meatloaf and set aside covered. Clean the pot and place the olive oil.

Select Sauté and add in the shallot and chili pepper. Stir-fry for 3 minutes until tender. Pour in tomatoes, brown sugar, Worcestershire sauce, and lemon juice and cook for 10 minutes. Blitz the mixture with an immersion blender. Adjust the seasoning with salt and pepper. Slice the meatloaf and spoon the sauce over to serve.

Pork with Onions & Cream Sauce

Serving Size: 6 | Total Time: 52 minutes

1 ½ lb pork shoulder, cut into pieces	
2 onions, chopped	¼ tsp cumin
1 ½ cups sour cream	¼ tsp cayenne pepper
1 cup tomato puree	1 garlic clove, minced
½ tbsp cilantro	Salt and pepper to taste

Coat with cooking spray the inner pot and add the pork. Cook for 3-4 minutes on Sauté until lightly browned. Add onions and garlic and cook for 3 minutes until fragrant. Press Cancel. Stir in sour cream, tomato puree, cilantro, cumin, cayenne pepper, salt, and pepper and seal the lid. Select Soup/Broth and cook for 30 minutes on High. Let sit for 5 minutes before quickly releasing the pressure.

Thyme Pork Loin with Apples & Daikon

Serving Size: 4 | Total Time: 40 minutes

1 lb pork loin, cubed	1 tbsp vegetable oil
1 onion, diced	1 celery stalk, diced
1 daikon, chopped	2 tbsp dried parsley
1 cup vegetable broth	¼ tsp thyme
½ cup white wine	½ tsp cumin
2 apples, peeled and diced	¼ tsp lemon zest
½ cup sliced leeks	Salt and pepper to taste

Heat oil on Sauté. Add pork and cook for 6 minutes until browned. Add the onion and cook for 2 more minutes. Stir in daikon, broth, wine, leeks, celery, parsley, thyme, cumin, lemon zest, salt, and pepper. Seal the lid and cook for 15 minutes on Pressure Cook. Release the pressure quickly. Stir in apples, seal the lid again, and cook on High for another 5 minutes. Do a quick release. Carefully unlock the lid. Serve warm.

Apple Pork Chops

Serving Size: 4 | Total Time: 42 minutes

2 leeks, white part only, cut into rings

1 lb pork fillets	1 tsp chili pepper
½ lb apples, cut into wedges	Salt and pepper to taste
2 tbsp olive oil	1 tsp dry rosemary
¼ cup apple cider vinegar	1 tsp dry thyme

Heat 1 tbsp of olive oil on Sauté. Season the pork with salt, black and chili pepper. Brown the fillets for about 4 minutes per side. Set aside. Heat the remaining oil in the pressure cooker. Add in leeks and Sauté until soft, about 4 minutes. Add in apples, rosemary, and thyme and pour in the vinegar and 1 cup of water. Place the pork loin along with the apples and leeks. Seal the lid.

Cook for 20 minutes on Meat/Stew on High. Once cooking is complete, perform a quick pressure release and remove the lid. To serve, arrange the pork on a plate and pour the apple leeks mixture over the pork.

Fennel Pork Butt with Mushrooms

Serving Size: 8 | Total Time: 30 minutes

1 lb pork butt, sliced	½ cup white wine
2 cups mushrooms, sliced	½ cup vegetable broth
1 fennel bulb, chopped	Salt and pepper to taste

Grease with cooking spray and heat on Sauté. Brown the pork slices and for a few minutes. Stir in mushrooms, fennel, wine, broth, salt, and pepper. Seal the lid and cook for 20 minutes on Meat/Stew on High. When done, do a quick release.

Vegetable Casserole with Smoked Bacon

Serving Size: 4 | Total Time: 30 minutes

½ lb smoked bacon, chopped	4 golden potatoes, peeled and chopped
½ cup carrots, sliced	
1 cup vegetable stock	4 endives, chopped
¾ cup half and half	Salt and pepper to taste

Set to Sauté and add the bacon. Cook for 2 minutes until slightly crispy. Add the potatoes, carrots, 2 cups water, and vegetable stock. Seal the lid and cook for 10 minutes on High Pressure. Release the pressure quickly. Add the endives and cook for 5 more minutes on Sauté. Stir in the half and half and season with salt and pepper. Cook for 3 more minutes. Serve.

Easy Pork Fillets with Peachy Sauce

Serving Size: 6 | Total Time: 30 minutes

1 lb pork loin fillets	½ tsp garlic, minced
16 oz canned peach	Salt and pepper to taste
½ tsp ground coriander	1 cup onions, sliced
½ tsp ginger, chopped	2 tbsp olive oil
½ cup Worcestershire sauce	1 cup tomato sauce
¼ cup apple cider vinegar	1 tbsp arrowroot slurry

On Sauté, heat oil. Cook onions until tender, about 4 minutes. Stir in pork, peaches, coriander, ginger, Worcestershire sauce, apple vinegar, garlic, salt, pepper, and tomato sauce. Seal the lid, Select Meat/Stew, and cook for 20 minutes. Do a quick pressure release. Stir in the slurry and cook on Sauté until the sauce thickens.

Garlic Mashed Potatoes with Sausages

Serving Size: 6 | Total Time: 30 minutes

4 potatoes, peeled and cut into chunks

6 Italian sausages	¼ cup milk
1 tbsp olive oil	Salt and pepper to taste
2 garlic cloves, smashed	1 tbsp chopped chives
⅓ cup butter, melted	

Select Sauté and heat olive oil. Cook sausages for 8-10 minutes, turning often until browned. Set aside. Wipe the pot with paper towels. Add in 1 cup of water and set steamer rack over water and steamer basket onto the rack. Add in the potatoes. Seal the lid and cook on High Pressure for 12 minutes. Release the pressure quickly. Remove basket and rack from the pot.

Drain water from the pot. Return potatoes to the pot. Add in salt, butter, pepper, garlic, and milk and use a hand masher to mash until no large lumps remain. Using an immersion blender, blend potatoes on Low for 1 minute until fluffy and light. Transfer the mash to a serving plate. Top with sausages and chives to serve.

Party Apple-Glazed Pork Ribs

Serving Size: 4 | Total Time: 45 minutes

½ cup apple cider vinegar	3 ½ cups apple juice
2 lb pork ribs	Salt and pepper to taste

Pour apple juice and apple cider vinegar into the pressure cooker and lower the trivet. Season the pork ribs with salt and pepper, and place on top of the trivet and seal the lid. Cook on High Pressure for 30 minutes. Once it goes off, let the valve drop on its own for a natural release for about 10 minutes. Serve.

Oregano Pork with Pears & Dijon Mustard

Serving Size: 6 | Total Time: 60 minutes

3 lb pork roast	½ cup white wine
2 pears, peeled and sliced	1 tbsp garlic, minced
3 tbsp Dijon mustard	1 tbsp olive oil
1 tbsp dried oregano	Salt and pepper to taste

Brush the pork with mustard. Heat oil on Sauté and sear the pork on all sides for 6minutes. Stir in pears, oregano, wine, 1 cup of water, garlic, salt, and pepper. Seal the lid and cook for 40 minutes on Meat/Stew on High Pressure. Release the pressure naturally for 10 minutes.

Pork Tenderloin with Cherries & Apples

Serving Size: 4 | Total Time: 55 minutes

1 ¼ lb pork tenderloin	½ cup water
1 chopped celery stalk	¼ cup onions, chopped
2 apples, peeled, chopped	Salt and pepper to taste
1 cup cherries, pitted	2 tbsp olive oil
½ cup apple juice	

Heat oil on Sauté and cook the onions and celery for 5 minutes until softened. Season the pork with salt and pepper, and add to the cooker. Brown for 2-3 minutes per side. Top with apples and cherries, and pour the water and apple juice. Seal the lid.

Cook on Meat/Stew for 40 minutes on High pressure. Once ready, do a quick pressure release. Slice the pork tenderloin and arrange it on a serving platter. Spoon the apple-cheery sauce over the pork slices to serve.

Tasty Cajun Pork Chops

Serving Size: 4 | Total Time: 80 minutes

2 lb pork chops	2 tbsp potato starch
1 cup beef broth	1 carrot, chopped
1 onion, diced	

MARINADE

2 tbsp fish sauce	½ cup soy sauce
½ tsp Cajun seasoning	1 tbsp sesame oil
2 tsp garlic, minced	

Combine fish sauce, Cajun seasoning, garlic, soy sauce, and sesame oil in a bowl. Add in the pork chops and let marinate for 30 minutes. Coat the pressure cooker with cooking spray. Add onion and carrot and cook until soft on Sauté. Add the pork chops along with the marinade. Whisk in the broth and starch. Seal the lid and cook for 40 minutes on Meat/Stew. Do a quick release and serve.

Pork Belly with Tamari Sauce

Serving Size: 6 | Total Time: 35 minutes

4 garlic cloves, sliced	½ cup onions, chopped
½ tsp ground cloves	¼ cup tamari sauce
1 tsp grated fresh ginger	1 tsp sugar maple syrup
1 ½ lb pork belly, sliced	4 cups white rice, cooked
2 ¼ cups water	Salt and pepper to taste
¼ cup white wine	

Brown pork belly for about 6 minutes per side on Sauté. Add garlic, cloves, ginger, water, wine, onions, tamari sauce, maple syrup, rice, salt, and pepper. Seal the lid and cook for 25 minutes on Pressure Cook. When ready, do a quick pressure release. Serve immediately.

Saucy Barbecue Baby Back Ribs

Serving Size: 4 | Total Time: 55 minutes

2 lb rack pork baby back ribs	1 tbsp Worcestershire sauce
	1 tsp cayenne pepper
2 tbsp olive oil	Salt and pepper to taste
½ tsp garlic powder	2 cups barbecue sauce
½ tsp onion powder	

Discard the membrane from the back of ribs and slice into individual bones. Mix the cayenne pepper, salt, pepper, garlic powder, and onion powder in a bowl. Sprinkle each rib with this mixture. Warm the olive oil in your Instant Pot on Sauté. Place in ribs and sear for 4-5 minutes on all sides. Add in Worcestershire sauce and barbecue sauce and seal the lid.

Select Manual and cook for 20 minutes on High. Once over, allow a natural release for 10 minutes, then perform a quick pressure release, and unlock the lid. Transfer ribs to a plate. Cook the sauce for 5-6 minutes on Sauté until it thickens. Serve the ribs topped with sauce.

Savory Pork Chops with Brussel Sprouts

Serving Size: 4 | Total Time: 30 minutes

4 pork chops	1 tbsp olive oil
½ lb Brussel sprouts	1 cup celery stalk, chopped
¼ cup sparkling wine	1 tbsp coriander
1 ½ cups beef stock	Salt and pepper to taste
2 shallots, chopped	

Heat olive oil on Sauté. Add the pork chops and cook until browned on all sides. Stir in sprouts, wine, stock, shallots, celery, coriander, salt, and pepper. Seal the lid and cook for 20 minutes on Meat/Stew on High. Release the pressure quickly. Serve.

Italian Sausage & Lentil Pot

Serving Size: 4 | Total Time: 40 minutes

1 cup canned tomatoes, diced	
1 red bell pepper, cut into strips	
1 lb Italian sausages, sliced	4 garlic cloves, minced
2 tbsp olive oil	1 tbsp basil, chopped
1 cup lentils, rinsed	Salt and pepper to taste
1 onion, chopped	1 tbsp Italian seasoning
1 tsp paprika	

Warm the olive oil in your Instant Pot on Sauté. Place in sausages and cook for 3-4 minutes. Add in onion, bell pepper, garlic, and and cook for another 4 minutes. Stir in paprika, Italian seasoning, salt, pepper, lentils, tomatoes, and 3 cups of water. Seal the lid, select Manual, and cook for 15 minutes on High. Once over, allow a natural release for 10 minutes. Top with basil and serve.

Merlot Pork Chops

Serving Size: 4 | Total Time: 50 minutes

4 pork chops	1 tsp dried oregano
3 carrots, chopped	2 tbsp olive oil
1 tomato, chopped	2 tbsp flour
1 onion, chopped	2 tbsp water
2 garlic cloves, minced	2 tbsp tomato paste
¼ cup merlot red wine	1 beef bouillon cube
½ cup beef broth	Salt and pepper to taste

Heat the oil on Sauté. In a bowl, mix in flour, pepper, and salt. Coat the pork chops. Place them in the pressure cooker and cook for a few minutes until browned on all sides. Add the carrots, onion, garlic, and oregano.

Cook for 2 more minutes. Stir in tomato, wine, broth, water, tomato paste, and bouillon cube and seal the lid. Cook on Soup/Broth and cook for 25 minutes on High. When ready, do a natural pressure release for 10 minutes, and serve immediately.

Broccoli & Cauliflower Pork Sausages

Serving Size: 6 | Total Time: 20 minutes

1 lb pork sausage, sliced	14 oz can mushroom soup
½ lb broccoli florets	10 oz evaporated milk
½ lb cauliflower florets	Salt and pepper to taste

Place ¼ of the sausage slices in your pressure cooker. In a bowl, whisk the soup, salt, pepper, and milk. Pour some of the mixtures over the sausages. Top the sausage slices with ¼ of the cauliflower and broccoli florets. Pour some of the soup mixtures again. Repeat the layers until you use up all ingredients. Seal the lid and cook on Pressure Cook for 10 minutes on High. When ready, do a quick release. Serve.

Friday Night BBQ Pork Butt

Serving Size: 6 | Total Time: 55 minutes

2 lb pork butt	¼ tsp cumin powder
Salt and pepper to taste	½ tsp onion powder
1 cup barbecue sauce	1 ½ cups beef broth

In a bowl, combine the barbecue sauce, cumin, onion powder, salt, and pepper. Brush the pork with the mixture. On Sauté, coat with cooking oil. Add the pork and sear on all sides for 6 minutes. Pour the beef broth around the meat. Seal the lid and cook for 40 minutes on Meat/Stew on High. Do the pressure quickly. Serve.

Cajun Pork Carnitas

Serving Size: 4 | Total Time: 65 minutes

1 lb pork shoulder, trimmed of excess fat	
3 tbsp olive oil	Salt and pepper to taste
1 onion, chopped	1 tsp cayenne pepper
1 cup chicken stock	1 tsp garlic powder
½ cup sour cream	1 tbsp Cajun seasoning
2 tbsp tomato paste	4 tortillas, warm
1 tbsp lemon juice	

Warm the olive oil in your Instant Pot on Sauté. Place in the pork and cook for 7-8 minutes on all sides. Stir in onion and cook for 1-2 more minutes. Pour in chicken stock, sour cream, tomato paste, lemon juice, salt, pepper, cayenne pepper, Cajun seasoning, and garlic powder. Seal the lid, select Manual, and cook for 25 minutes on High.

When ready, allow a natural release for 10 minutes and unlock the lid. Remove pork and shred it. Put shredded pork back to the pot and cook for 6-8 minutes on Sauté. Serve with warm tortillas.

Pork Chops & Mushrooms with Tomato Sauce

Serving Size: 4 | Total Time: 35 minutes

1 cup white button mushrooms, sliced	
4 large bone-in pork chops	1 tsp garlic, minced
1 cup tomato sauce	½ cup water
1 onion, chopped	1 tbsp oil

Heat oil on Sauté. Add garlic and onion and cook for 2 minutes until soft. Add pork and cook until browned, 6 minutes. Stir in mushrooms, tomato sauce, and water and seal the lid. Cook for 20 minutes on Meat/Stew. Do a quick pressure release. Carefully unlock the lid. Serve.

Garlic-Spicy Ground Pork with Peas

Serving Size: 6 | Total Time: 55 minutes

2 lb ground pork	1 cup beef broth
1 onion, diced	1 tsp ground ginger
1 can diced tomatoes	2 tsp ground coriander
1 can peas	Salt and pepper to taste
5 garlic cloves, minced	¾ tsp cumin
3 tbsp butter	¼ tsp cayenne pepper
1 serrano pepper, chopped	½ tsp turmeric

Melt butter on Sauté. Add onion and cook for 3 minutes until soft. Stir in ginger, coriander, salt, pepper, cumin, cayenne pepper, turmeric and garlic and cook for 2 more minutes. Add pork and cook until browned. Pour broth and add serrano pepper, peas, and tomatoes. Seal the lid and cook for 30 minutes on Meat/Stew on High. When ready, release the pressure naturally for 10 minutes. Carefully unlock the lid. Serve immediately.

Sweet Mustard Pork Chops with Piccalilli

Serving Size: 4 | Total Time: 30 minutes

1 lb pork chops, boneless	1 tbsp honey
2 tbsp olive oil	2 garlic cloves, minced
2 tbsp Dijon mustard	2 tbsp piccalilli
½ tbsp brown sugar	Salt and pepper to taste

Sprinkle pork chops with salt and pepper. Warm the olive oil in your Instant Pot on Sauté. Place the pork chops in the pot and brown for 6-8 minutes on both sides. Mix Dijon mustard, brown sugar, honey, garlic, and 1 cup of water in a bowl. Pour it into the pot and seal the lid. Select Manual and cook for 15 minutes on High pressure. Once done, perform a quick pressure release and unlock the lid. Top with piccalilli and serve.

Chili-Braised Pork Chops with Tomatoes

Serving Size: 4 | Total Time: 30 minutes

14 oz canned tomatoes with green chilies
4 pork chops   ½ cup beer
1 onion, chopped   ½ cup vegetable stock
2 tbsp chili powder   1 tsp olive oil
1 garlic clove, minced   Salt and pepper to taste

Heat oil on Sauté. Add onion, garlic, and chili powder and cook for 2 minutes. Add the pork chops and cook until browned on all sides. Stir in the tomatoes, stock, and beer. Season with salt and pepper. Seal the lid and cook for 20 minutes on Meat/Stew on High. When ready, quick Release the pressure and serve hot.

Chorizo with Macaroni & Cheddar Cheese

Serving Size: 6 | Total Time: 20 minutes

1 lb macaroni   2 tbsp minced garlic
3 oz chorizo, chopped   2 cups milk
3 cups water   2 cups cheddar, shredded
1 tbsp garlic powder   Salt to taste

On Sauté and stir-fry chorizo until crispy for about 6 minutes. Set aside. Wipe the pot with kitchen paper. Add in water, macaroni, garlic, and salt. Seal lid and cook for 5 minutes on High Pressure. Release the pressure quickly. Stir in cheese, garlic powder, and milk until the cheese melts. Top with chorizo and serve.

Baby Carrot & Onion Pork Chops

Serving Size: 4 | Total Time: 30 minutes

1 lb pork chops   1 tbsp butter
1 lb baby carrots   1 cup vegetable broth
1 onion, sliced   Salt and pepper to taste

Season the pork with salt and pepper. Melt butter on Sauté and brown the pork on all sides. Stir in carrots and onion and cook for 2 more minutes until soft. Pour in the broth. Seal the lid and cook for 20 minutes on Meat/Stew on High. When ready, release the pressure quickly.

Thai-Style Chili Pork

Serving Size: 4 | Total Time: 29 minutes

2 red Thai chili peppers, chopped
½ lb sugar snap peas, trimmed
1 lb ground pork   2 shallots, thinly sliced
2 tbsp olive oil   1 ½ cups coconut milk
2 garlic cloves, minced   1 tbsp soy sauce
1-inch piece ginger, grated   2 tbsp cilantro, chopped

Warm the olive oil in your Instant Pot on Sauté. Place in ground pork and brown for 5-6 minutes. Add in garlic, Thai chili, ginger, and shallots and cook for another 2-3 minutes. Stir in coconut milk, sugar snap peas, and soy sauce and seal the lid. Select Manual and cook for 10 minutes on High. When ready, perform a quick pressure release and unlock the lid. Top with cilantro and serve.

Sweet & Spicy Pork Ribs

Serving Size: 4 | Total Time: 50 minutes

3 lb pork baby back ribs   ½ cup orange marmalade
2 tbsp olive oil   2 tbsp ketchup
¼ tsp ground coriander   2 tbsp soy sauce
1 tsp garlic powder   Salt and pepper to taste
2 tsp cayenne pepper

Trim the ribs of excess fat and cut them into individual bones. In a bowl, combine olive oil, ground coriander, garlic powder, cayenne pepper, salt, and pepper and mix well. Add in the ribs and toss to coat. Transfer them to the Instant Pot and pour in 1 cup of water. Seal the lid, select Manual, and cook for 20 minutes on High.

When done, release the pressure naturally for 10 minutes. In a bowl, whisk together the ketchup, orange marmalade, and soy sauce until well combined. Transfer the ribs to a baking tray. Select Sauté and pour the marmalade mixture into the pot. Cook until the sauce has thickened to obtain a glaze texture, about 4-5 minutes. Brush the ribs with some glaze and place under a preheated broiler for 5 minutes or until charred and sticky. Serve the ribs with the remaining glaze.

BBQ Pork Lettuce Cups

Serving Size: 6 | Total Time: 60 minutes

1-2 little gem lettuces, leaves separated
3 lb pork roast, cut into chunks
2 tbsp olive oil   ½ cup BBQ sauce
Salt and pepper to taste   1 red onion, thinly sliced
1 cup chicken broth   2 tbsp cilantro, chopped

Sprinkle pork roast with salt and pepper. Place the roast, olive oil, chicken broth, and BBQ sauce in your Instant Pot and stir. Seal the lid, select Manual, and cook for 40 minutes on High. When ready, allow a natural release for 10 minutes, then perform a quick pressure release, and unlock the lid. Remove roast and shred it using two forks. Divide shredded pork between lettuce leaves. Scatter with onion and cilantro. Serve with the gravy.

Beer-Braised Pork

Serving Size: 4 | Total Time: 53 minutes

2 lb pork loin roast   1 tsp thyme
2 tbsp butter   1 bay leaf
1 onion, chopped   2 cups beer
2 garlic cloves, minced   Salt and pepper to taste

Melt butter in your Instant Pot on Sauté. Place the pork roast fatty-side down and cook on both sides. Add in onion and garlic and cook for 3 minutes. Put in thyme, salt, pepper, beer, bay leaf, and ½ cup of water and seal the lid. Select Manual and cook for 30 minutes on High.

When over, allow a natural release for 10 minutes and unlock the lid. Transfer roast to a bowl and cover it. Press Sauté and cook until the sauce thickens. Cut the roast and top with the sauce.

Hoisin Spare Pork Ribs

Serving Size: 4 | Total Time: 75 minutes

2 lb pork spare ribs	¼ cup Mirin rice wine
3 garlic cloves, minced	½ cup hoisin sauce
2 green onions, chopped	2 red chilies, sliced
3 ginger slices	1 tbsp honey
2 tbsp sesame oil	2 tbsp cilantro, chopped

Warm sesame oil in your Instant Pot on Sauté. Place in garlic, green onions, chilies, and ginger and cook for 2-3 minutes. Slice spare ribs into individual ribs, place it in the pot, and sauté for 4-5 minutes. Stir in rice wine, honey, 1 cup of water, and hoisin sauce and cook for 3-4 minutes. Seal the lid, select Manual, and cook for 40 minutes.

Once done, allow a natural release for 10 minutes, then perform a quick pressure release, and unlock the lid. Top the ribs with sauce and cilantro and serve.

Cinnamon BBQ Pork Ribs

Serving Size: 6 | Total Time: 60 minutes

3 lb pork ribs	1 tbsp brown sugar
½ cup apple jelly	1 tsp Worcestershire sauce
1 cup barbecue sauce	1 tsp ground cinnamon
1 onion, diced	Salt and pepper to taste
2 tbsp ground cloves	

Whisk together apple jelly, barbecue sauce, onion, cloves, sugar, Worcestershire sauce, cinnamon, salt, and pepper in your pressure cooker. Place the ribs inside and pour in ½ cup water. Seal the lid. Set the cooker to Meat/Stew and cook for 50 minutes. Release the pressure naturally.

Fruity Pork Steaks

Serving Size: 4 | Total Time: 30 minutes

4 pork steaks	¼ cup heavy cream
¼ cup milk	1 tbsp fruit jelly
8 prunes, pitted	½ tsp ground ginger
½ cup white wine	Salt and pepper to taste
2 apples, peeled, sliced	

Place pork, milk, prunes, wine, apples, heavy cream, and ginger in your pressure cooker. Stir and season with salt and pepper. Seal the lid and cook on High Pressure for 15 minutes. Once done, wait 5 minutes and do a quick pressure release. Stir in the jelly and serve.

Pork Sirloin Chili

Serving Size: 6 | Total Time: 45 minutes

3 lb sirloin pork roast	1 tbsp rosemary
1 tbsp honey	1 tbsp olive oil
1 tsp chili powder	Salt and pepper to taste

Combine chili powder, rosemary, salt, and pepper in a bowl and rub them onto the pork. Heat oil on Sauté and sear the pork on all sides. Stir in honey and seal the lid. Cook for 30 minutes on Meat/Stew. Do a natural pressure release for 10 minutes. Carefully unlock the lid.

Awesome Herby Pork Butt with Yams

Serving Size: 4 | Total Time: 35 minutes

1 lb pork butt, cut into 4	¼ tsp oregano
equal pieces	1 ½ tsp sage
1 lb yams, diced	1 ½ cups beef broth
2 tsp butter	Salt and pepper to taste
¼ tsp thyme	

Season the pork with thyme, sage, oregano, salt, and pepper. Melt butter on Sauté. Add pork and cook until brown, about 5 minutes. Add the yams and pour the broth. Seal the lid and cook for 20 minutes on Meat/Stew. Do a quick release. Serve hot.

Best Pork Chops with BBQ Sauce & Veggies

Serving Size: 4 | Total Time: 25 minutes

4 pork rib chops	1 cup onions, slice into rings
1 cup carrots, thinly sliced	1 ½ cups BBQ sauce
1 cup turnips, thinly sliced	2 cups water

Add the pork chops to your cooker. Pour in ½ cup of BBQ sauce and 2 cups of water. Select Meat/Stew. Stir in the onions, turnips, and carrots. Lock the lid and cook for 20 minutes on High. Once ready, Release the pressure quickly. Open the lid, drizzle with the remaining BBQ sauce and serve warm.

Chorizo & Tomato Pork Chops

Serving Size: 4 | Total Time: 40 minutes

4 pork chops, boneless	2 tbsp olive oil
2 oz chorizo sausage, sliced	1 yellow onion, sliced
1 tsp paprika	2 cups chopped tomatoes
2 garlic cloves, minced	

Place the pork chops in your Instant Pot and sear for 5 minutes on Sauté. Add in onion and garlic and cook for 3 more minutes. Stir in chorizo, paprika, tomatoes, and ½ cup of water. Seal the lid, select Manual, and cook for 15 minutes on High pressure. When done, allow a natural release for 10 minutes, then perform a quick pressure release, and unlock the lid. Serve right away.

Tarragon Apple Pork Chops

Serving Size: 4 | Total Time: 25 minutes

2 tbsp olive oil	2 Granny Smith apples, sliced
1 tsp nutmeg	4 pork chops
1 tsp Dijon mustard	Salt and pepper to taste
4 tbsp brown sugar	2 tbsp tarragon, chopped

Combine nutmeg, mustard, and brown sugar in a bowl. Add in apples and toss to coat. Warm oil in your Instant Pot on Sauté. Place the apples in the pot and cook for 2 minutes. Sprinkle pork chops with salt and pepper and put it over the apples. Seal the lid, select Manual, and cook for 15 minutes on High. Once done, perform a quick pressure release. Top with tarragon and serve.

Paprika Pulled Pork Fajitas

Serving Size: 4 | Total Time: 65 minutes

2 lb pork shoulder, cut into chunks
½ tsp garlic powder   1 ½ cups beef broth
½ tsp dried chili flakes   1 tsp smoked paprika
½ tsp brown sugar   Salt and pepper to taste
½ tsp cumin   4 tortillas
1 yellow onion, sliced

Combine garlic powder, smoked paprika, brown sugar, cumin, salt, and pepper in a bowl. Sprinkle pork shoulder with the spice mixture. Place onion slices in your Instant Pot and top with the pork shoulder. Pour in beef broth and seal the lid. Select Manual and cook for 40 on High.

Once done, allow a natural release for 10 minutes, then perform a quick pressure release, and unlock the lid. Remove pork and shred it. Warm each tortilla in a skillet over medium heat for 1 minute. To assemble, divide shredded pork between tortillas and top with chili flakes.

Mexican Pork Chili Verde

Serving Size: 4 | Total Time: 45 minutes

2 lb pork shoulder, cubed   ½ tsp oregano
½ lb tomatillos, quartered   ½ tsp ground coriander
2 serrano peppers, chopped   1 tsp cumin
2 jalapeño peppers, minced   1 cup chicken stock
1 onion, chopped   2 tbsp cilantro, chopped
4 garlic cloves, minced   Salt and pepper to taste
1 tsp cayenne pepper

Place pork shoulder, tomatillos, serrano peppers, jalapeño peppers, onion, garlic cloves, cayenne pepper, oregano, ground coriander, cumin, chicken stock, salt, and pepper in your Instant Pot and stir. Seal the lid, select Manual, and cook for 35 minutes on High pressure. Once done, perform a quick pressure release and unlock the lid. Transfer the pork to a plate. Put the cilantro in the pot and blend sauce using an immersion blender. Put the pork back in the pot and toss to coat. Serve immediately.

Pear & Cider Pork Tenderloin

Serving Size: 4 | Total Time: 55 minutes

1 lb pork loin   2 pears, cored and chopped
1 tbsp garlic powder   1 cup apple cider
2 tbsp olive oil   1 tbsp fennel seeds
1 yellow onion, chopped   Salt and pepper to taste

Sprinkle pork loin with salt, pepper, and garlic powder. Warm the olive oil in your Instant Pot on Sauté. Place the loin and sear for 8 minutes on all sides. Set aside. Add onion to the pot and cook for 3 minutes. Put in pears and apple cider and scrape any brown bits from the bottom. Put loin back to the pot along with fennel seeds.

Seal the lid. Select Manual and cook for 20 minutes on High pressure. When ready, allow a natural release for 10 minutes and unlock the lid. Slice the pork loin before serving and top with sauce.

Hot Pork Chops with Cheddar Cheese

Serving Size: 4 | Total Time: 30 minutes

4 boneless pork chops   2 tbsp butter
2 tbsp olive oil   1 cup cheddar, grated
1 cup water   Salt and pepper to taste
4 tbsp habanero pepper sauce   2 tbsp parsley, chopped

Warm the olive oil in your Instant Pot on Sauté. Sprinkle pork chops with salt and pepper. Place the chops in the pot and brown for 3 minutes on all sides. Add in 1 cup of water and habanero pepper sauce. Top each pork chop with butter and seal the lid. Select Manual and cook for 15 minutes on High pressure.

When done, perform a quick pressure release and unlock the lid. Scatter pork chops with cheddar cheese and broil in the oven for a few minutes. Top with parsley and serve.

Juicy Pork Butt Steaks

Serving Size: 4 | Total Time: 57 minutes

2 lb pork butt steaks   1 tsp ground bay leaf
2 tbsp olive oil   1 tsp oregano
1 tsp garlic powder   ½ cup red wine
1 onion, chopped   1 tbsp paprika
1 cup chicken broth   Salt and pepper to taste
1 cup tomato sauce

Warm the olive oil in your Instant Pot on Sauté. Place in pork steaks, salt, pepper, and garlic powder and cook for 4-5 minutes. Set aside. Put the onion in the pot and cook for 2 minutes. Pour in red wine and scrape any brown bits from the bottom. Put pork steaks back to the pot along with chicken stock, tomato sauce, bay leaf, oregano, and paprika.

Seal the lid, select Manual, and cook for 30 minutes on High pressure. When ready, allow a natural release for 10 minutes, then perform a quick pressure release, and unlock the lid. Serve right away.

Japanese-Style Pork Tenderloin

Serving Size: 4 | Total Time: 30 minutes

2 lb pork tenderloins   1 tbsp light soy sauce
2 tbsp peanut butter   Salt and pepper to taste
1 cup teriyaki sauce   4 green onions, chopped
¼ cup coconut milk   1 lime, zested
1 tbsp sesame seeds

Melt peanut butter in your Instant Pot on Sauté. Sprinkle pork tenderloins with salt and pepper, place it in the pot and brown for a few minutes on all sides. Put in teriyaki sauce, soy sauce, lime zest, coconut milk, and 1/2 cup of water and seal the lid. Select Manual. Cook for 15 minutes on High.

Once done, allow a natural release for 10 minutes, then perform a quick pressure release, and unlock the lid. Slice the tenderloin and garnish with toasted sesame seeds, green onions, and cooking juice. Serve immediately.

Pork Medallions with Porcini Sauce

Serving Size: 4 | Total Time: 60 minutes

1 oz dried porcini mushrooms
4 boneless pork loin chops
½ cup dry Marsala wine
1 garlic clove, minced
1 tbsp paprika
½ tsp rosemary

1 onion, sliced
2 tbsp butter
Salt and pepper to taste
2 tbsp chopped parsley

Cover the porcini mushrooms with 1 cup of boiling water in a bowl and let soak for 10-15 minutes. Sprinkle pork chops with paprika, salt, and pepper. Melt butter in your Instant Pot on Sauté. Place the pork chops in the pot and sear for 6 minutes on all sides. Set aside.

Add onion and garlic to the pot and cook for 3 minutes. Put pork on top along with Marsala wine, rosemary, and porcini mushrooms with the water. Seal the lid, select Manual, and cook for 15 minutes on High pressure. When over, allow a natural release for 10 minutes and unlock the lid. Garnish with parsley and serve.

Fennel & Rosemary Pork Belly

Serving Size: 2 | Total Time: 60 minutes

1 lb pork belly
2 tbsp olive oil
¼ tsp ground cinnamon
¼ tsp chili flakes
1 tsp fennel seeds

1 rosemary sprig
1 clove garlic, minced
1 cup red wine
Salt and pepper to taste
2 tbsp chopped chives

Warm the olive oil in your Instant Pot on Sauté. Place the pork belly and cook 4 minutes on both sides. Add in salt, pepper, garlic, fennel seeds, cinnamon, rosemary sprig, chili flakes, red wine, and 1 cup of water. Seal the lid, select Manual, and cook for 35 minutes on High.

Once over, allow a natural release for 10 minutes, then perform a quick pressure release, and unlock the lid. Cut the pork and scatter with chives. Serve warm.

Spicy Pork Sausage Ragu

Serving Size: 4 | Total Time: 25 minutes

1 lb pork sausage, casings removed
2 tbsp olive oil
2 garlic cloves, minced
1 onion, chopped
1 cup chopped tomatoes

½ tsp oregano
1 tsp red chili flakes
1 cup chicken stock
Salt and pepper to taste
2 tbsp parsley, chopped

Warm the olive oil in your Instant Pot on Sauté. Place in garlic and onion and cook until fragrant. Add and brown the sausage for 8 minutes. Stir constantly, breaking the meat with a wooden spatula. Stir in chicken stock, red chili flakes, oregano, and chopped tomatoes and seal the lid. Select Manual and cook for 10 minutes on High.

When over, perform a quick pressure release and unlock the lid. Adjust seasoning to taste. Cook on Sauté until the sauce thickens. Top with parsley and serve.

German Pork with Sauerkraut

Serving Size: 4 | Total Time: 40 minutes

2 lb pork belly, cut into 2-inch pieces
3 tbsp lard
2 garlic cloves, minced
1 onion, chopped
1 cup chicken broth
5 cups sauerkraut
1 tsp paprika

1 cup canned diced tomatoes
1 tsp cumin
2 tbsp parsley, chopped
Salt and pepper to taste

Sprinkle the pork with salt and pepper. Melt lard in your Instant Pot on Sauté. Place the pork, onion, and garlic and cook for 5-6 minutes. Stir in paprika and cumin. Put in sauerkraut, chicken broth, tomatoes, and 1/2 cup of water and seal the lid. Select Manual and cook for 30 minutes on High pressure. Once over, perform a quick pressure release and unlock the lid. Serve with parsley.

Tandoori Pork Butt

Serving Size: 4 | Total Time: 61 minutes

2 lb pork butt, boneless, trimmed of excess fat
1 tsp ground cumin
1 tsp ground coriander
1 tsp paprika
1 green chili, minced
1 tsp garam masala

2 tbsp ghee
1 onion, chopped
2 garlic cloves, minced
1-inch piece ginger, grated
1 can (14 oz) coconut milk
Salt and pepper to taste
Lime wedges for garnish

Mix the salt, pepper, ground coriander, paprika, cumin, and garam masala in a bowl. Sprinkle pork butt with this mixture. Melt ghee in your Instant Pot on Sauté. Place in green chili, ginger, onion, and garlic and cook for 2 minutes. Add in pork butt and cook for 3-4 minutes.

Pour in coconut milk and ½ cup of water and seal the lid. Select Manual and cook for 35 minutes on High pressure. Once ready, allow a natural release for 10 minutes, then perform a quick pressure release, and unlock the lid. Cut the butt into slices and serve with lemon wedges.

Prune & Shallot Pork Tenderloin

Serving Size: 6 | Total Time: 45 minutes

3 lb pork tenderloins, cut into large chunks
2 tbsp olive oil
2 shallots, chopped
Salt and pepper to taste
½ cup vegetable broth

½ cup balsamic vinegar
½ cup dried pitted prunes
1 carrot, sliced diagonally
2 garlic cloves, minced
2 tbsp rosemary, chopped

Warm the olive oil in your Instant Pot on Sauté. Sprinkle pork tenderloins with salt and pepper, place them in the pot, and brown for 2-3 minutes. Add in shallots, garlic, and carrots and cook for 3 minutes. Stir in vegetable broth, balsamic vinegar, prunes, and rosemary. Seal the lid, select Manual, and cook for 20 minutes on High pressure. When done, allow a natural release for 10 minutes, then perform a quick pressure release, and unlock the lid.

Quick Pork & Vegetable Rice

Serving Size: 4 | Total Time: 40 minutes

4 pork chops	1 carrot, chopped
2 tbsp olive oil	1 cup mushrooms, sliced
1 onion, finely chopped	1 red bell pepper, sliced
2 tbsp garlic cloves, minced	Salt and pepper to taste
1 cup white rice, rinsed	2 spring onions, sliced
1 ½ cups chicken broth	

Warm the olive oil in your Instant Pot on Sauté. Place in onion, garlic, carrot, bell pepper, and mushrooms and cook for 5 minutes. Add in rice, salt, and pepper.

Put pork chops over the rice and pour in chicken broth. Seal the lid, select Manual, and cook for 15 minutes on High pressure. Once done, allow a natural release for 10 minutes. Garnish with spring onions and serve.

Mushroom & Pork Stroganoff

Serving Size: 4 | Total Time: 35 minutes

1 cup button mushrooms, sliced	
1 lb pork loin, cut into strips	2 tsp Dijon mustard
2 tbsp olive oil	½ cup sour cream
1 leek, chopped	½ cup white wine
1 celery stalk, chopped	Salt and pepper to taste
2 cups vegetable broth	2 tbsp parsley, chopped

Warm the oil in your Instant Pot on Sauté. Sprinkle pork loin with salt and pepper, place it in the pot and brown on all sides. Set aside. Add leek, mushrooms, and celery to the pot and cook for 3 minutes. Pour in wine and scrape any brown bits from the bottom. Stir in vegetable broth and Dijon mustard. Put pork loin back to the pot.

Seal the lid. Select Manual and cook for 12 minutes on High. Once ready, allow a natural release for 10 minutes and unlock the lid. Mix in sour cream and simmer for 1 minute on Sauté. Top with parsley and serve.

Cilantro Pork with Avocado

Serving Size: 4 | Total Time: 45 minutes + marinating time

1 lb pork tenderloin, cut into strips	
3 garlic cloves, chopped	2 cups chicken stock
½ tsp oregano	Salt and pepper to taste
½ tsp ground cumin	1 avocado, sliced
1 tbsp Hungarian paprika	2 tbsp cilantro, chopped
2 tbsp olive oil	

Mix garlic, oregano, cumin, paprika, salt, and pepper in a bowl. Add in pork strips and toss to coat. Let marinate for 30 minutes in the fridge. Warm the olive oil in your Instant Pot on Sauté. Place the strips in the pot and sauté for 10 minutes. Stir in chicken stock and seal the lid. Select Manual and cook for 15 minutes on High pressure.

When done, allow a natural release for 10 minutes, then perform a quick pressure release, and unlock the lid. Scatter with cilantro. Serve topped with avocado slices.

Parsley Pork with Savoy Cabbage

Serving Size: 6 | Total Time: 35 minutes

2 lb pork roast, cut into chunks	
1 head Savoy cabbage, shredded	
3 tbsp canola oil	1 tsp mustard powder
2 garlic cloves, minced	1 cup chopped tomatoes
1 onion, chopped	Salt and pepper to taste
1 tsp cumin	2 tbsp parsley, chopped

Warm the canola oil in your Instant Pot on Sauté. Place in garlic and onion and cook for 3 minutes. Add in pork chunks and cook for 5 minutes on all sides. Stir in cumin, mustard powder, salt, pepper, tomatoes, cabbage, and 1 cup of water. Seal the lid, select Manual, and cook for 20 minutes on High pressure. Once ready, perform a quick pressure release. Top with parsley and serve.

Spiced Pork with Garbanzo Beans

Serving Size: 4 | Total Time: 60 minutes

1 ½ tbsp vegetable oil	2 tbsp fresh dill, chopped
1 ½ lb pork shoulder, diced	½ tsp ground mustard
1 red onion, sliced	½ tsp paprika
1 cup garbanzo beans, soaked	½ tsp dried thyme
3 cups chicken broth	½ tsp cayenne pepper
1 cup tomatoes, chopped	½ tsp garlic powder
2 garlic cloves, minced	Salt and pepper to taste

Mix the paprika, thyme, cayenne pepper, garlic powder, salt, and pepper in a bowl. Sprinkle pork with this mixture. Warm the vegetable oil in your Instant Pot on Sauté. Place in pork and brown for 4-5 minutes.

Remove to a bowl. Add red onion and garlic to the pot and cook for 2 minutes. Pour in chicken broth and scrape any brown bits from the bottom. Add in garbanzo beans, tomatoes, and mustard and seal the lid. Select Manual and cook for 30 minutes on High pressure. When over, allow a natural release for 10 minutes and unlock the lid. Garnish with dill and serve.

Smoky Shredded Pork with White Beans

Serving Size: 4 | Total Time: 65 minutes

2 lb pork shoulder, halved	2 tbsp liquid smoke
2 tbsp vegetable oil	Salt and pepper to taste
1 onion, chopped	1 cup cooked white beans
1 cup vegetable broth	2 tbsp parsley, chopped

Warm the vegetable oil in your Instant Pot on Sauté. Place in onion and cook for 3 minutes. Sprinkle pork shoulder with salt and pepper, add it to the pot and brown for 5 minutes on all sides. Pour in vegetable broth and liquid smoke and scrape any brown bits from the bottom. Seal the lid, select Manual, and cook for 35 minutes on High.

When ready, allow a natural release for 10 minutes, then perform a quick pressure release, and unlock the lid. Remove pork and shred it. Stir white beans in the pot and put shredded pork back. Top with parsley and serve.

Pulled Pork Tacos

Serving Size: 6 | Total Time: 55 minutes + marinating time

2 lb pork shoulder, trimmed of excess fat
3 garlic cloves, minced
1 cup onion, sliced
1 tsp ground cinnamon
1 tbsp cumin
1 tsp oregano
¼ tsp red chili flakes
½ cup pineapple juice
1 ½ cups tomatoes, diced
1 Iceberg lettuce, torn
1 red onion, thinly sliced
2 tbsp cilantro, chopped
Salt and pepper to taste
6 tortillas

Slice pork shoulder into 2-inch pieces. Place the garlic, onion, cinnamon, cumin, oregano, chili flakes, salt, and pepper in a bowl. Add in the pork pieces and toss to coat. Cover with cling film and let marinate for 30 minutes.

Transfer to your Instant Pot and pour in pineapple juice and tomatoes. Seal the lid, select Manual and cook for 30 minutes on High pressure. Once done, allow a natural release for 10 minutes and unlock the lid.

Shred the pork and simmer for 5 minutes on Sauté. To assemble, divide shredded pork between tortillas and top with lettuce, red onion, and cilantro. Serve right away.

Bacon & Potato Brussels Sprouts

Serving Size: 4 | Total Time: 20 minutes

4 bacon slices, chopped
1 lb Brussels sprouts, halved
1 cup potatoes, cubed
½ cup chicken stock
Salt and pepper to taste

Set to Sauté your Instant Pot and add the bacon. Cook for 5-6 minutes until crispy; remove to a paper-lined plate. Add potatoes, Brussels sprouts, chicken stock, salt, and pepper to the pot. Seal the lid, select Manual, and cook for 5 minutes on High. When done, perform a quick pressure release. Top with bacon. Serve warm.

Spiced Mexican Pork

Serving Size: 4 | Total Time: 55 minutes + marinating time

2 lb pork shoulder, cut into chunks
1 chipotle pepper in adobo sauce, chopped
3 garlic cloves, minced
1 red onion, chopped
½ tsp ground coriander
1 tsp ground cumin
1 tbsp lime juice
¼ cup chile enchilada sauce
1 tsp Mexican oregano
Salt and pepper to taste

Place garlic, onion, ground coriander, cumin, lime juice, Mexican oregano, chipotle pepper, enchilada sauce, salt, pepper, and ½ cup of water in a blender and pulse until smooth. Place the mixture in a large bowl and add in pork chunks; toss to coat. Cover with cling foil and let marinate in the fridge for 30 minutes.

Next, remove from the fridge and transfer to your Instant Pot. Pour in ½ cup of water and seal the lid. Select Manual and cook for 25 minutes on High pressure. When ready, allow a natural release for 15 minutes and unlock the lid. Cook for 5 minutes on Sauté until the sauce thickens. Serve warm.

Asian Pork & Noodle Soup

Serving Size: 4 | Total Time: 60 minutes

1 lb pork tenderloin, cut into strips
1 (1-inch) piece fresh ginger, halved lengthwise
2 tbsp olive oil
1 yellow onion, halved
2 tsp fennel seeds
1 tsp red pepper flakes
½ tsp coriander seeds
2-star anise
Salt and pepper to taste
8 oz rice noodles
1 lime, cut into wedges
2 tbsp cilantro, chopped

Warm oil on Sauté. Cook ginger and onion for 4 minutes. Add in flakes, fennel seeds, anise, and coriander seeds and cook for 1 minute as you stir. Add in 4 cups of water, salt, pepper, and pork. Seal the lid and cook on High Pressure for 30 minutes.

Soak the rice noodles in hot water for 8 minutes until softened and pliable. Stop the cooking process by draining and rinsing with cold water. Separate the noodles into 4 soup bowls.

Release the pressure naturally for 10 minutes. Remove the pork from the cooker and ladle among the bowls. Strain the broth to get rid of solids. Pour it over the pork and noodles. Season with red pepper flakes. Garnish with lime wedges and cilantro leaves and serve.

Awesome Pork & Celery Soup

Serving Size: 4 | Total Time: 45 minutes

1 ¼ lb pork ribs
1 leek, chopped
1 onion, chopped
1 cup celery root, diced
½ cup parsley, chopped
4 cups beef broth
1 tsp salt
1 tsp red chili flakes
2 bay leaves
A handful of basil, torn
2 tbsp olive oil

Heat oil on Sauté. Add the ribs in batches and brown on all sides for 5-6 minutes. Add leek, onion, celery, parsley, broth, salt, red chili flakes, bay leaves, and basil.

Seal the lid and cook on Meat/Stew on High for 30 minutes. Do a quick release. Serve.

Delicious Pork & Vegetables Soup

Serving Size: 4 | Total Time: 50 minutes

2 (8-oz) pork chops
1 tbsp cayenne pepper
1 tsp chili powder
½ tsp garlic powder
4 cups beef broth
2 tbsp olive oil
2 large carrots, chopped
2 celery stalks, diced
1 onion, diced
2 tbsp soy sauce

Warm the olive oil in your Instant Pot on Sauté and stir-fry the onion until translucent, 3 minutes. Add celery stalks, carrots, cayenne, and chili pepper. Give it a good stir and continue to cook for 6-7 minutes. Add in pork chops, garlic, and soy sauce.

Pour in the broth and seal the lid. Cook on Manual for 25 minutes on High. Do a quick release. Let chill for 5 minutes. Serve.

Cajun Orange Pork Shoulder

Serving Size: 6 | Total Time: 60 minutes + marinating time

3 lb pork shoulder, trimmed of excess fat
2 garlic cloves, sliced   ¼ cup orange juice
1 tsp cumin   Salt and pepper to taste
1 tsp Cajun seasoning   2 tbsp olive oil
1 large onion, sliced   2 tbsp cilantro, chopped
¼ cup lime juice

Mix the cumin, Cajun seasoning, garlic, onion, lime juice, orange juice, salt, and pepper in a bowl. Place in the pork shoulder and toss to coat. Let sit covered in the fridge for 30 minutes. Warm the olive oil in your Instant Pot on Sauté. Place in pork shoulder and cook for 10 minutes on all sides. Set aside.

Pour the remaining marinade into the pot and scrape any brown bits from the bottom. Pour in 1 cup of water and fit in a trivet. Place the pork inside the trivet and seal the lid. Select Manual and cook for 30 minutes on High.

When over, allow a natural release for 10 minutes, then perform a quick pressure release, and unlock the lid. Remove and slice the pork. Top with cilantro. Serve.

Garlic & Thyme Pork

Serving Size: 4 | Total Time: 58 minutes

1 lb pork brisket   1 ½ cups chicken broth
2 garlic cloves, minced   ½ cup red wine
2 tsp paprika   6 garlic cloves, minced
1 tsp ground cumin   1 tbsp thyme, chopped
1 tsp onion powder   1 tbsp butter
2 tbsp flour   1 cup mushrooms, sliced
2 tbsp olive oil   Salt and pepper to taste

Mix the onion powder, paprika, cumin, salt, pepper, and garlic in a bowl. Sprinkle pork brisket with this mixture. Cover all brisket with flour. Warm the oil in your Instant Pot on Sauté. Place in brisket and cook for 8 minutes on all sides. Pour in red wine and scrape any brown bits from the bottom. Add in garlic, thyme, and broth and seal the lid. Select Manual and cook for 30 minutes.

When ready, allow a natural release for 10 minutes, then perform a quick pressure release, and unlock the lid. Remove brisket to a plate and cooking liquid in a bowl. Melt butter in your Instant Pot on Sauté. Place in mushrooms and cook until they are soft. Pour in reserved liquid and cook for another minute. Cut brisket in slices and top with mushroom sauce. Serve warm.

German-Style Red Cabbage with Apples

Serving Size: 4 | Total Time: 20 minutes

1 cup Granny Smith apples, cubed
1 head red cabbage, shredded
2 tbsp olive oil   1 tbsp red wine vinegar
4 oz bacon, chopped   1 tsp ground cumin
1 sweet onion, chopped   Salt and pepper to taste
2 garlic cloves, chopped

Warm olive oil in your Instant Pot on Sauté. Place the bacon, onion, and garlic and cook for 5 minutes.

Put in cabbage, vinegar, apples, cumin, salt, pepper, and 1 cup of water and seal the lid. Select Manual and cook for 10 minutes on High pressure. When done, perform a quick pressure release. Carefully unlock the lid. Adjust the taste with salt and pepper and serve.

Gruyere Mushroom & Mortadella Cups

Serving Size: 4 | Total Time: 20 minutes

4 eggs, beaten   1 cup mortadella, chopped
1 tsp olive oil   1 tbsp parsley, minced
½ tsp paprika   Salt and pepper to taste
½ cup mushrooms, chopped   2 tbsp Gruyere, grated

Mix the eggs, olive oil, 1 tbsp of water, and paprika in a bowl. Add in mushrooms, parsley, salt, pepper, and mortadella. Divide the mixture between ramekins and top with Gruyere cheese.

Pour 1 cup of water into your Instant Pot and fit in a trivet. Place the ramekins on the trivet and seal the lid. Select Manual and cook for 12 minutes on High pressure. Once ready, perform a quick pressure release. Carefully unlock the lid. Serve warm.

Asparagus Wrapped in Parma Ham

Serving Size: 4 | Total Time: 15 minutes

1 lb asparagus, trimmed   2 tbsp Parmesan, grated
½ lb Parma ham, sliced

Pour 1 cup of water into your Instant Pot and fit in a trivet. Wrap each asparagus spear with a ham slice and place on the trivet. Seal the lid, select Manual, and cook for 3 minutes on High pressure.

When over, allow a natural release for 5 minutes, then perform a quick pressure release, and unlock the lid. Transfer the wraps to a greased baking dish and sprinkle with the Parmesan cheese. Place under preheated broiler for about 4 minutes until the cheese is melted. Serve.

Ranch Potatoes with Ham

Serving Size: 4 | Total Time: 20 minutes

1 lb Yukon gold potatoes, quartered
4 oz cooked ham, chopped   Salt to taste
1 tsp garlic powder   1/3 cup Ranch dressing
2 tsp chives, chopped

Cover potatoes with salted water in your Instant Pot and seal the lid. Select Manual and cook for 7 minutes on High pressure.

When done, perform a quick pressure release and unlock the lid. Drain the potatoes and transfer to a bowl. Stir in ranch dressing, garlic powder, and ham. Sprinkle with chives and serve.

BEEF & LAMB

Braised Beef Ribs with Mushrooms

Serving Size: 4 | Total Time: 1 hour

1 cup crimini mushrooms, chopped	1 small onion, chopped
2 lb beef short ribs	4 garlic cloves, smashed
1 tsp smoked paprika	1 cup beer
½ tsp cayenne pepper	1/3 cup beef broth
Salt and pepper to taste	1 tbsp soy sauce
1 tbsp olive oil	1 bell pepper, diced

In a bowl, combine pepper, paprika, cayenne, and salt. Rub the seasoning mixture on all sides of the short ribs. Warm oil the Instant Pot on Sauté. Add mushrooms and cook until browned, about 6-8 minutes. Set aside. Add short ribs in the pot and cook for 3 minutes for each side until browned; reserve. Throw garlic and onion in the oil and stir-fry for 2 minutes.

Add in beer to deglaze, scraping the pot's bottom to get rid of any browned bits of food. Bring to a simmer and cook for 2 minutes until reduced slightly. Stir in soy sauce, bell pepper, and broth. Dip short ribs into the liquid. Seal the lid, press Meat/Stew, and cook on High for 40 minutes. Release pressure quickly. Top the ribs and sauce fried mushrooms and serve.

Habanero Beef Brisket with Red Wine

Serving Size: 4 | Total Time: 1 hour 30 minutes

2 tsp smoked paprika	1 habanero pepper, minced
½ tsp dried oregano	¼ tsp cayenne pepper
Salt and pepper to taste	2 lb beef brisket
1 tbsp Worcestershire sauce	2 tbsp olive oil
½ tsp ground cumin	1 cup beef broth
½ tsp garlic powder	¼ cup red wine

In a bowl, combine oregano, cumin, cayenne, garlic powder, salt, paprika, pepper, and Worcestershire sauce. Rub the seasoning mixture on the beef to coat. Warm olive oil on Sauté. Add in beef and habanero pepper cook for 3-4 minutes on each side until browned completely. Pour in beef broth and red wine. Seal the lid and cook on High Pressure for 50 minutes.

Release the pressure naturally for about 10 minutes. Place the beef on a cutting board and allow to cool for 10 minutes before slicing. Arrange the beef slices on a serving platter, pour the cooking sauce over and serve.

Tasty Beef Cutlets with Vegetables

Serving Size: 4 | Total Time: 45 minutes

2 large beef cutlets	1 tbsp butter
4 whole potatoes, peeled	Salt and pepper to taste
1 whole onion, peeled	3 cups beef broth
1 whole carrot, peeled	
10 oz cauliflower florets	
3 tbsp olive oil	

Sprinkle the meat with salt and pepper and place it in your Instant Pot. Add in cauliflower, onion, carrot, and potatoes. Pour in broth, seal the lid, and cook on High Pressure for 25 minutes. Release the pressure naturally for about 10 minutes. Remove the meat and vegetables. Melt butter and oil on Sauté. Add the meat. Brown on both sides and serve with vegetables.

Italian Meatballs with Pomodoro Sauce

Serving Size: 6 | Total Time: 25 minutes

¾ cup grated Parmigiano-Reggiano cheese	
1 ½ lb ground beef	¼ tsp dried oregano
1/3 cup warm water	Salt and pepper to taste
½ cup bread crumbs	½ cup capers
1 egg	1 tsp olive oil
2 tbsp fresh parsley	3 cups marinara sauce
¼ tsp garlic powder	

In a bowl, mix ground beef, parsley, garlic powder, pepper, oregano, crumbs, egg, and salt; shape into meatballs. Warm oil on Sauté. Add meatballs to the oil and brown for 2-3 minutes and all sides. Pour in water and marinara and stir. Seal the lid and cook on High Pressure for 10 minutes. Release the pressure quickly. Serve topped with capers and cheese.

Thyme Beef with Mushrooms & Tomatoes

Serving Size: 4 | Total Time: 30 minutes

1 lb button mushrooms, chopped	
1 lb beef steaks	1 tbsp dried thyme
2 tbsp vegetable oil	6 oz cherry tomatoes
Salt and pepper to taste	

Rub steaks with salt, pepper, and thyme. Place in the Instant Pot. Pour in 3 cups of water and seal the lid. Cook on High Pressure for 13 minutes. Do a quick release and set the steaks aside. Heat oil on Sauté, and stir-fry mushrooms and tomatoes for 5 minutes. Add steaks and brown on both sides. Serve.

Beef Steaks with Onion Gravy

Serving Size: 4 | Total Time: 35 minutes

4 round beef steaks	1 tbsp oil
2 onions, sliced	½ tsp red pepper flakes
1 ½ cups beef broth	¼ cup half and half
1 tsp garlic, minced	2 tbsp flour
1 tbsp dried parsley	Salt and pepper to taste
½ tsp rosemary	

Heat the oil on Sauté. Add the beef and brown the steaks on all sides; set aside. Sauté the onions and garlic for 2 minutes until translucent and fragrant. Return the steaks to the pressure cooker. Stir in salt, pepper, pepper flakes, and rosemary. Pour in broth. Seal the lid.

Cook for 20 minutes on Meat/Stew on High. When ready, do a quick pressure release, and stir in the flour and half and half. Cook for 3 more minutes until thickened on Sauté. Serve topped with parsley.

Vietnamese-Style Rice Noodle Soup

Serving Size: 4 | Total Time: 1 hour 10 minutes

2 tbsp coconut oil	2 tbsp fish sauce
1 yellow onion, quartered	10 oz sirloin steak
¼ cup minced fresh ginger	2 tbsp cilantro, chopped
2 tsp coriander seeds	2 scallions, chopped
2 lb beef neck bones	2 jalapeño peppers, minced
Salt and pepper to taste	2 cups Swiss chard, chopped
8 oz rice noodles	1 red onion, chopped
¼ tbsp sugar	

Warm coconut oil on Sauté. Add ginger and yellow onion and cook for 4 minutes. Stir in coriander seeds for 1 minute. Add in beef meat, bones, 4 cups of water, and salt. Seal the lid and cook on High Pressure for 30 minutes. Release the pressure naturally for 10 minutes. Transfer the meat to a bowl to cool slightly. Pat the beef dry with paper towels and slice it.

In hot water, soak rice noodles for 8 minutes until softened and pliable. Drain and rinse with cold water. Drain the liquid from the cooker into a separate pot through a fine-mesh strainer; get rid of any solids.

Add fish sauce and sugar to the broth and pour in the cooker to heat on Sauté. Place the noodles in bowls. Top with beef slices, scallions, swiss chard, jalapeño, cilantro, red onion, and pepper. Spoon the broth over and serve.

Short Ribs with Red Wine & Cheese Sauce

Serving Size: 6 | Total Time: 1 hour

3 lb beef short ribs	14.5-oz can diced tomatoes
Salt and pepper to taste	½ cup dry red wine
2 tbsp olive oil	¼ cup red wine vinegar
1 onion, chopped	2 bay leaves
1 large carrot, chopped	¼ tsp red pepper flakes
1 celery stalk, chopped	2 tbsp chopped parsley
3 garlic cloves, chopped	½ cup cheese cream
2 cups beef broth	

Season short ribs with black pepper and salt. Warm olive oil on Sauté. Add in short ribs and sear for 3 minutes on each side until browned. Set aside on a bowl. Drain everything only to be left with 1 tbsp of the remaining fat from the pot. Stir-fry garlic, carrot, onion, and celery in the hot fat for 4-6 minutes until it was fragrant.

Stir in broth, wine, flakes, vinegar, tomatoes, bay leaves, and remaining pepper and salt. Set to Sauté and bring the mixture to a boil. With the bone-side up, lay short ribs into the braising liquid. Seal the lid and cook on High Pressure for 40 minutes.

Release the pressure quickly. Set the short ribs on a plate. Get rid of bay leaves. Skim and get rid of the fat from the surface of the braising liquid. Using an immersion blender, blitz the liquid for 1 minute. Add in cheese cream, pepper, and salt, and blend until smooth. Arrange the ribs onto a serving plate, pour the sauce over, and top with parsley. Serve.

Homemade Cuban Ropa Vieja

Serving Size: 6 | Total Time: 60 minutes

2 lb beef skirt steak	1 tsp dried oregano
3 ½ cups beef stock	1 tsp ground cumin
2 bay leaves	1 cup tomato sauce
¼ cup olive oil	1 cup dry red wine
1 red onion, chopped	1 tbsp vinegar
1 green bell pepper, chopped	Salt and pepper to taste
1 red bell pepper, chopped	¼ cup cheddar, shredded
¼ cup minced garlic	

Season the skirt steak with pepper and salt. Add beef stock to the cooker; mix in bay leaves and skirt steak. Seal the lid and cook on High Pressure for 25 minutes. Release the pressure quickly. Remove skirt steak to a cutting board and allow to sit for about 5 minutes. Shred it with two forks. Empty the pressure cooker and reserve the bay leaves and 1 cup liquid.

Warm oil on Sauté. Add onion, bell peppers, cumin, garlic, and oregano and cook for 5 minutes until vegetables are softened. Stir in reserved liquid, tomato sauce, bay leaves, vinegar, and wine. Return the beef to the pot and season with pepper and salt. Bring to a boil and simmer for 15 minutes. Serve topped with cheese.

Savory Pot Beef Roast with Pancetta

Serving Size: 4 | Total Time: 80 minutes

1 ½ lb beef brisket, trimmed	2 fresh thyme sprigs
Salt and pepper to taste	2 fresh rosemary sprigs
2 tbsp olive oil	4 oz pancetta, chopped
1 onion, chopped	1 carrot, chopped
1 cup beef broth	1 bay leaf
¾ cup dry red wine	2 tbsp parsley, chopped

Warm oil on Sauté. Fry the pancetta for 4-5 minutes until crispy. Set aside. Season the beef with pepper and salt and brown for 5-7 minutes; reserve. In the same oil, fry onion for 3 minutes until softened. Pour in red wine and beef broth to deglaze the bottom, scrape the bottom of the pot to get rid of any browned bits of food. Return the beef and pancetta to the pot.

Add in rosemary sprigs and thyme. Seal the lid and cook for 50 minutes on High Pressure. Release the pressure quickly. Add carrots and bay leaf to the pot. Seal the lid and cook for an additional 4 minutes on High Pressure. Release the pressure quickly. Get rid of the thyme, bay leaf, and rosemary sprigs. Place beef on a serving plate and sprinkle with parsley to serve.

Meatloaf with Potatoes & Ricotta Mash

Serving Size: 6 | Total Time: 35 minutes

1 ½ lb ground beef	Salt and pepper to taste
1 onion, diced	4 potatoes, chopped
1 egg	½ cup milk
1 potato, grated	2 tbsp butter
¼ cup tomato puree	1 cup ricotta cheese
1 tsp garlic powder	

In a bowl, combine ground beef, egg, pepper, garlic powder, grated potato, onion, tomato puree, and salt to obtain a consistent texture. Shape the mixture into a meatloaf and place it onto an aluminum foil. Place the chopped potatoes in the pot and cover with water. Place a trivet onto potatoes and set the foil sheet with meatloaf onto the trivet. Seal the lid.

Cook on High Pressure for 20 minutes. Release the pressure quickly. Take the meatloaf from the pot and set on a cutting board to cool before slicing. Drain the liquid out of the pot. Mash potatoes in the pot and stir in pepper, milk, ricotta cheese, salt, and butter until smooth. Divide potatoes between plates and lean a meatloaf slice to one side of the potato pile to serve.

Awesome Beef Chili with Bacon

Serving Size: 6 | Total Time: 1 hour 30 minutes

4 oz smoked bacon, cut into strips
1 chipotle in adobo sauce, chopped

2 lb stewing beef, trimmed	1 tbsp ground cumin
Salt and pepper to taste	1 tsp chili powder
2 tsp olive oil	½ tsp cayenne pepper
1 onion, diced	2 cups beef broth
2 bell peppers, diced	29 oz canned tomatoes
3 garlic cloves, minced	15 oz canned kidney beans

Set to Sauté and fry the bacon until crispy, about 5 minutes. Set aside. Rub the beef with pepper and salt. In the bacon fat, brown beef for 5-6 minutes. Transfer to a plate. Warm the oil. Add in garlic, peppers, and onion and sauté for 3 minutes. Stir in cumin, cayenne pepper, chipotle, chili powder, and cook for 30 seconds.

Return beef and bacon to the pot with vegetables and spices. Add in tomatoes and broth. Seal the lid and cook on High Pressure for 45 minutes. Release the pressure quickly. Stir in beans. Simmer on Sauté for 10 minutes.

Sticky Baby Back BBQ Ribs

Serving Size: 6 | Total Time: 50 minutes

1 rack baby back ribs, cut into bones

2 tbsp olive oil	Salt and pepper to taste
1 tbsp mustard powder	1/3 cup ketchup
1 tbsp smoked paprika	1 cup barbecue sauce
1 tbsp dried oregano	½ cup apple cider

In a bowl, thoroughly combine salt, mustard, paprika, oregano, and black pepper. Rub the mixture over the ribs. Warm oil on Sauté. Add in the ribs and sear for 1 to 2 minutes for each side until browned.

Pour apple cider, ketchup, and barbecue sauce into the pot. Turn the ribs to coat. Seal the lid, press Meat/Stew, and cook on High Pressure for 30 minutes. Release the pressure quickly. Preheat a broiler. Cook the ribs and sauce under the broiler for 7 minutes until the ribs become sticky and have a dark brown color. Transfer the ribs to a serving plate. Baste with the sauce.

Swedish Meatballs with Cauliflower Mash

Serving Size: 6 | Total Time: 35 minutes

¾ lb ground beef	3 tbsp flour
¾ lb ground pork	½ tsp red wine vinegar
1 large egg, beaten	1 ¾ cups heavy cream
½ onion, minced	4 tbsp blue cheese, crumbled
¼ cup bread crumbs	10 oz cauliflower florets
Salt and pepper to taste	¼ cup sour cream
4 tbsp butter	¼ cup chopped parsley
2 cups beef stock	

In a bowl, mix beef, onion, salt, bread crumbs, pork, egg, 1 tbsp water, and pepper; shape meatballs.

Warm 2 tbsp of butter on Sauté. Add meatballs and cook until browned, about 5-6 minutes. Set aside to a plate.

Pour beef stock in the pot to deglaze, scrape the pan to get rid of browned bits of food. Stir vinegar and flour with the liquid in the pot until smooth.

Bring to a boil. Stir ¾ cup heavy cream into the liquid. Arrange meatballs into the gravy. Place trivet onto meatballs.

Arrange cauliflower florets onto the trivet. Seal the lid and cook on High Pressure for 8 minutes. Release the pressure quickly.

Set the cauliflower in a mixing bowl. Add in the remaining 1 cup heavy cream, pepper, sour cream, salt, and 2 tbsp butter and use a potato masher to mash the mixture. Add the blue cheese and mix well.

Spoon the mashed cauliflower onto serving bowls; top with gravy and meatballs. Garnish with parsley and serve.

Southern Pot Roast with Pepperoncini

Serving Size: 6 | Total Time: 1 hour 30 minutes

3 tbsp canola oil	½ tsp dried thyme
2 lb chuck roast	½ tsp dried parsley
Salt and pepper to taste	6 cups beef broth
¼ cup butter	½ cup pepperoncini juice
1 onion, finely chopped	10 pepperoncini
1 tsp onion powder	5 potatoes, peeled, chopped
1 tsp garlic powder	2 bay leaves

Warm oil on Sauté. Season chuck roast with pepper and salt, then sear in hot oil for 2 to 4 minutes per side until browned. Set aside.

Melt butter and cook the onion for 3 minutes until fragrant. Sprinkle with dried parsley, onion powder, dried thyme, and garlic powder and stir for 30 seconds. Stir in bay leaves, broth, pepperoncini juice, potatoes, and pepperoncini.

Nestle chuck roast down into the liquid. Seal the lid and cook on High for 60 minutes. Release pressure naturally for about 10 minutes. Set the chuck roast to a cutting board and use two forks to shred. Serve immediately.

Stuffed Onions with Beef & Rice

Serving Size: 4 | Total Time: 30 minutes

10 sweet onions, peeled	½ tsp cumin, ground
1 lb of lean ground beef	1 tsp salt
½ tbsp rice	½ tbsp sour cream
3 tbsp olive oil	½ cup bread crumbs
1 tbsp dry mint, ground	2 tbsp parsley, chopped
1 tsp cayenne pepper	

Cut a ¼-inch slice from the top of each onion and trim a small amount from the bottom end; this will make the onions stand upright. Place onions in a microwave-safe dish, and Pour one cup of water. Cover with a tight lid and microwave for 10-12 minutes. Remove and cool slightly. Remove inner layers of onions with a paring knife, leaving about a ¼-inch onion shell.

In a bowl, combine beef, rice, oil, mint, cayenne pepper, cumin, salt, and bread crumbs. Use one tablespoon of the mixture to fill the onions. Grease the inner pot with oil. Add onions and pour 2 ½ cups of water. Seal the lid and cook on Manual/Pressure Cook for 10 minutes on High. Do a quick release. Top with parsley and serve with sour cream and pide bread.

Traditional French Beef Stew

Serving Size: 5 | Total Time: 55 minutes

1 lb boneless chuck steak, cut into chunks	
2 cups portobello mushrooms, quartered	
¼ cup flour	1 carrot, diced
Salt and pepper to taste	4 shallots, chopped
1 cup pancetta, chopped	3 garlic cloves, crushed
½ cup red burgundy wine	2 tbsp parsley, chopped
1 ¼ cups beef broth	

Toss beef with black pepper, salt, and flour in a large bowl to coat. Set the Instant Pot to Sauté. Cook pancetta for 5 minutes until brown and crispy. Pour in approximately half the beef and cook for 5 minutes on each side until browned all over. Transfer the pancetta and beef to a plate. Sear remaining beef and transfer to the plate.

Add beef broth and wine to the cooker to deglaze the pan, scrape the pan's bottom to get rid of any browned bits of food. Return beef and pancetta to cooker and stir in garlic, carrot, shallots, and mushrooms. Seal the lid and cook on High Pressure for 32 minutes. Release the pressure quickly. Garnish with parsley and serve.

Beef Short Ribs with Asparagus Sauce

Serving Size: 6 | Total Time: 1 hour 15 minutes

3 lb boneless beef short ribs, cut into pieces	
Salt and pepper to taste	5 sprigs parsley, chopped
3 tbsp olive oil	2 sprigs rosemary, chopped
1 onion, diced	3 sprigs oregano, chopped
1 cup dry red wine	4 cups beef stock
1 tbsp tomato puree	10 oz mushrooms, quartered
2 carrots, chopped	1 bunch asparagus, chopped
2 garlic cloves, minced	1 tbsp cornstarch

Season the ribs with black pepper and salt. Warm oil on Sauté. In batches, add the short ribs to the oil and cook for 3 to 5 minutes on each side until browned. Set aside. Add onion and Sauté for 4 minutes until soft. Add tomato puree and red wine into the pot to deglaze, scrape the bottom to get rid of any browned beef bits. Cook for 2 minutes until wine reduces slightly. Return the ribs to the pot and top with carrots, oregano, rosemary, and garlic. Add in stock and press Cancel.

Seal the lid, press Meat/Stew, and cook on High for 35 minutes. Release pressure naturally for 10 minutes. Transfer ribs to a plate. Strain and get rid of herbs and vegetables, and return cooking stock to the inner pot. Add mushrooms and asparagus to the broth. Press Sauté and cook for 2 to 4 minutes until soft.

In a bowl, mix ¼ cup cold water and cornstarch until cornstarch dissolves completely. Add the cornstarch mixture into the broth as you stir for 1-3 minutes until the broth thickens slightly. Season the sauce with black pepper and salt. Pour the sauce over ribs, add chopped parsley for garnish before serving.

Mushroom Beef Stroganoff

Serving Size: 6 | Total Time: 1 hour

¼ cup flour	1 cup beef broth
Salt and pepper to taste	3 cups mushrooms, chopped
2 lb beef stew meat	8 oz sour cream
2 tbsp olive oil	1 tbsp chopped parsley
1 onion, chopped	1 cup rice, cooked
2 garlic cloves, minced	

In a large bowl, combine salt, pepper, and flour. Add beef and massage to coat beef in flour mixture. Warm oil on Sauté. Brown the beef for 4 to 5 minutes. Add garlic and onion and cook for 3 minutes until fragrant. Add beef broth to the pot.

Seal the lid and cook on High Pressure for 35 minutes. Release the pressure quickly. Open the lid and stir mushrooms and sour cream into the beef mixture. Seal the lid and cook on High Pressure for 2 minutes. Release the pressure quickly. Scoop over cooked rice. Season the stroganoff with pepper, parsley, and salt. Serve warm.

Dijon & Lemon Beef Steak

Serving Size: 4 | Total Time: 50 minutes

4 rib-eye steaks, boneless	3 tbsp Dijon mustard
2 tbsp lemon juice	Salt and pepper to taste
3 tbsp canola oil	3 cups beef broth

In a bowl, mix lemon juice, oil, mustard, salt, and pepper. Brush the steaks with this mixture and set aside. Pour the beef broth into the Instant Pot. Place the steamer tray and arrange the steaks on top. Seal the lid and cook on High Pressure for 35 minutes. Do a quick release and remove the broth. Press Sauté and brown steaks on both sides for 3-4 minutes. Serve warm.

Hearty Beef Stew with Vegetables

Serving Size: 4 | Total Time: 40 minutes

1 lb beef stew meat, cubed	1 tsp cayenne pepper
2 onions, peeled, chopped	1 tbsp apple cider vinegar
3 potatoes, peeled, chopped	3 tbsp olive oil
1 cup green peas	3 cups beef broth
1 tsp salt	

Heat oil on Sauté. Stir-fry the onions until translucent. Add the meat and potatoes, and brown for about 10 minutes. Add peas, and season with salt and cayenne pepper. Pour in broth and apple cider. Seal the lid and Set to Meat/Stew for 25 minutes on High. Do a quick release. Carefully unlock the lid. Serve.

Friday Night Chili Con Carne

Serving Size: 6 | Total Time: 1 hour

14 oz canned black beans	½ tsp onion powder
Salt and pepper to taste	1 (4-pound) beef brisket
1 tsp sweet paprika	1 cup beef broth
1 tsp chili powder	2 tbsp Worcestershire sauce

In a bowl, combine pepper, paprika, chili powder, salt, onion powder, and garlic salt. Rub onto brisket pieces to coat. Add the brisket to your Instant Pot. Cover with Worcestershire sauce and broth. Seal the lid and cook on High Pressure for 50 minutes. Release the pressure naturally. Transfer the brisket to a cutting board.

Drain any liquid present in the pot using a fine-mesh strainer; get rid of any solids and fat. Slice brisket, arrange the slices onto a platter, add the black beans on the side and spoon the cooking liquid over the slices and beans to serve.

Easy Roast Beef with Bearnaise Sauce

Serving Size: 6 | Total Time: 40 minutes

2 lb beef scotch fillets	4 egg yolks
6 tbsp butter	2 tbsp lemon juice
1 cup white wine	2 cups beef broth
1 onion, chopped	Salt and pepper to taste
1 tsp basil, chopped	

Melt butter on Sauté and stir-fry the onion until translucent for about 3 minutes. Add in wine, basil, salt, pepper, and lemon juice. Stir well and seal the lid. Cook on High Pressure for 3 minutes. Do a quick pressure release and stir in egg yolks. Add in beef and broth and seal the lid. Cook on Meat/Stew for 25 minutes on High Pressure. Do a quick release. Serve.

Beef & Jasmine Rice Porridge

Serving Size: 6 | Total Time: 50 minutes

1 cup jasmine rice	1 cup water
2 cloves garlic, minced	2 lb ground beef
1-inch piece ginger, minced	Salt and pepper to taste
6 cups beef stock	Fresh cilantro, chopped
1 cup kale, chopped	

Run cold water and rinse rice. Add garlic, rice, and ginger into the pot. Pour water and stock into the pot and Spread the beef on top of rice. Seal the lid and cook on High Pressure for 30 minutes. Release pressure naturally for 10 minutes. Stir in kale to obtain the desired consistency. Season with pepper and salt. Top with cilantro to serve.

Butternut Squash & Beef Stew

Serving Size: 6 | Total Time: 40 minutes

2 lb stew beef, cut into 1-inch chunks	
½ butternut pumpkin, chopped	
2 tbsp canola oil	3 whole cloves
1 cup red wine	1 bay leaf
1 onion, chopped	3 carrots, chopped
1 tsp garlic powder	2 tbsp cornstarch
1 tsp salt	3 tbsp water

Warm oil on Sauté. Brown the beef for 5 minutes on each side. Deglaze the pot with wine, scrape the bottom to get rid of any browned beef bits. Add in onion, salt, bay leaf, cloves, and garlic powder. Seal the lid, press Meat/Stew, and cook on High for 15 minutes. Release the pressure quickly. Add in pumpkin and carrots without stirring.

Seal the lid.Cook on High Pressure for 5 minutes. Release the pressure quickly. In a bowl, mix water and cornstarch until cornstarch dissolves completely and mix into the stew. Allow to simmer on Sauté for 5 minutes until you attain the desired thickness.

Beef Fillets with Onions

Serving Size: 6 | Total Time: 50 minutes

2 lb beef fillets, cut into bite-sized pieces	
4 onions, chopped	1 tbsp butter, melted
3 tbsp tomato paste	Salt and pepper to taste
2 tbsp oil	

Grease your Instant Pot with 2 tbsp of oil. Make the first layer of meat. Add onions, tomato paste, salt, and pepper. Stir and Pour 2 cups of water. Seal the lid and cook on Meat/Stew for 30 minutes on High. Release the steam naturally for about 10 minutes. Stir in 1 tbsp of butter and serve warm.

Beef Gyros with Yogurt & Dill

Serving Size: 4 | Total Time: 55 minutes

1 lb beef sirloin, cut into thin strips	
1 onion, chopped	1 clove garlic, minced
1/3 cup beef broth	Salt and pepper to taste
2 tbsp fresh lemon juice	4 slices pita bread
2 tbsp olive oil	1 cup Greek yogurt
2 tsp dry oregano	2 tbsp fresh dill, chopped

In your Instant Pot, mix beef, beef broth, oregano, garlic, lemon juice, pepper, onion, olive oil, and salt. Seal the lid and cook on High Pressure for 30 minutes. Release pressure naturally for 15 minutes. Carefully unlock the lid. Divide the beef mixture between the pita bread. Top with yogurt and dill and roll up to serve.

Ground Beef & Eggplant Casserole

Serving Size: 2 | Total Time: 40 minutes

2 eggplants, peeled, cut lengthwise
Salt and pepper to taste   1 tsp olive oil
1 cup lean ground beef   2 tomatoes
1 onion, chopped

Place eggplants in a bowl and season with salt. Let sit for 10 minutes. Rinse well and drain. Grease the inner pot with oil. Stir-fry onion for 2 minutes until soft. Add ground beef, tomatoes, and cook for 5 minutes. Remove to a deep bowl.

Make a layer with eggplant slices in the pot. Spread the ground beef mixture over and sprinkle with black pepper and salt. Make another layer with eggplants and repeat until you've used up all ingredients. Seal the lid and cook on High Pressure for 12 minutes. Do a quick release. Serve.

Sirloin Steaks with Red Wine

Serving Size: 4 | Total Time: 1 hour 25 minutes

2 lb beef sirloin   1 large onion, chopped
1 cup red wine   1 stalk celery, diced
2 cups beef consomme   1 tbsp tomato puree
2 bay leaves   2 cloves garlic, minced
2 tbsp olive oil   2 sprigs fresh parsley
Salt and pepper to taste

Rub the meat with salt and pepper on all sides. Heat oil on Sauté and sear the beef for 4-5 minutes. Set aside. In the same oil, add onion, celery, garlic, and tomato puree. Cook for 4-5 minutes until soft. Pour in wine to deglaze.

Bring the meat back to the pot, add consomme, parsley, and bay leaf. Seal the lid and cook on High Pressure for 50 minutes. Do a natural pressure release. Slice the sirloin and spoon over the cooking sauce to serve.

Chili Beef & Turnip Stew

Serving Size: 6 | Total Time: 30 minutes

3 tbsp olive oil   ½ tsp ground turmeric
1 onion, chopped   1 lb ground beef meat
Salt to taste   28-oz can whole tomatoes
4 garlic cloves, minced   2 cups beef stock
2 tbsp tomato puree   1 lb turnips, cubed
1 tbsp chili powder   2 tomatoes, chopped
2 tsp ground cumin   1 bell pepper, chopped
1 tsp dried oregano

Warm oil on Sauté. Add in onion and salt and cook for 3 minutes until softened. Stir in garlic, chili powder, turmeric, cumin, tomato paste, and oregano.

Cook for 2-3 minutes as you stir until very soft and sticks to the pot's bottom. Add beef and cook for 5 minutes until completely browned. Stir in tomatoes, turnips, bell pepper, and stock. Seal the lid and cook on High Pressure for 15 minutes. Release the pressure quickly. Serve.

Penne with Beef & Tomato Sauce

Serving Size: 5 | Total Time: 30 minutes

6 oz beef, braising steak cut into chunks
16 oz penne   3 tbsp butter, unsalted
1 onion, chopped   Salt and pepper to taste
1 tomato peeled, diced   1 tsp cayenne pepper
1 tbsp tomato paste   1 tbsp vegetable oil

Heat oil on Sauté and stir-fry the onion until translucent. Add tomato, tomato paste, butter, salt, black pepper, and cayenne pepper. Cook until tomato softens. Add beef chunks and 1 cup of water. Give it a good stir.

Seal the lid. Cook for 14 minutes on High Pressure. Do a quick release and set the meat aside. Add in penne and 2 cups of water. Seal the lid and cook on High Pressure for 4 minutes. Do a quick release. Transfer macaroni to a bowl, stir in beef sauce, and serve.

Moroccan Beef & Cherry Stew

Serving Size: 4 | Total Time: 1 hour 20 minutes

1 ½ lb stewing beef, trimmed
¼ cup toasted almonds, slivered
2 tbsp olive oil   ¼ tsp ground ginger
1 onion, chopped   ¼ tsp ground allspice
1 tsp ground cinnamon   1-star anise
½ tsp paprika   1 cup water
½ tsp turmeric   1 tbsp honey
½ tsp salt   1 cup dried cherries, halved

Set the Instant Pot to Sauté and warm olive oil. Add in onion and cook for 3 minutes. Mix in beef and cook for 2 minutes each side until browned. Stir in anise, cinnamon, turmeric, allspice, salt, paprika, and ginger; cook for 2 minutes until aromatic. Add in honey and water. Seal the lid, press Meat/Stew, and cook on High for 50 minutes.

In a bowl, soak dried cherries in hot water until softened. Once ready, release pressure naturally for 15 minutes. Drain cherries and stir into the tagine. Top with toasted almonds before serving.

Traditional Turkish Dolma (Stuffed Peppers)

Serving Size: 4 | Total Time: 35 minutes

2 lb red bell peppers   1 tomato, sliced
1 onion, finely chopped   ½ tsp salt
1 lb lean ground beef   1 tsp cayenne pepper
¼ cup rice   1 tbsp olive oil
½ cup tomatoes, chopped

In a bowl, combine meat, onion, rice, tomatoes, salt, and cayenne. Stir well to combine. Remove the stems and seeds from the peppers. Fill each pepper with 2 tbsp of the meat mixture. Make sure to leave at least ½ inch of headspace. Grease the bottom of your Instant Pot with olive oil. Make the first layer with tomato slices and arrange the peppers on top of them. Add 2 cups of water. Seal the lid and cook on High Pressure for 15 minutes. Do a natural pressure release for 10 minutes.

Easy Wax Beans with Ground Beef

Serving Size: 4 | Total Time: 20 minutes

1 lb ground beef	2 tbsp olive oil
1 lb wax beans	2 tbsp parsley, chopped
1 small onion, chopped	1 tsp salt
1 tbsp tomato paste	½ tsp paprika
2 cups beef broth	1 tbsp Parmesan, grated
2 garlic cloves, crushed	

Grease the pot with olive oil. Stir-fry the onion and garlic for a few minutes until translucent on Sauté. Add beef, tomato paste, parsley, salt, and paprika. Cook for 5 more minutes, stirring constantly. Add wax beans and beef broth. Press Cancel and seal the lid. Cook on High Pressure for 4 minutes. Do a natural release. Carefully unlock the lid. Top with Parmesan and serve hot.

Pesto Beef Sandwiches with Pepperoncini

Serving Size: 4 | Total Time: 50 minutes

1 ½ lb beef steak, cut into strips
½ cup pepperoncini peppers, chopped

Salt and pepper to taste	1 tsp onion powder
1 tbsp olive oil	1 tsp garlic powder
¼ cup dry red wine	4 hoagie rolls, halved
1 cup beef broth	8 slices mozzarella cheese
1 tbsp oregano	4 tbsp pesto

Season the beef strips with salt and pepper. Warm oil on Sauté and sear the beef for 2-3 minutes for each side until browned. Add wine into the pot to deglaze and scrape the bottom to eliminate any browned beef bits. Stir garlic powder, beef broth, onion powder, and oregano into the pot. Seal the lid, press Meat/Stew, and cook for 25 minutes on High. Release pressure naturally for 10 minutes. Spread each bread half with pesto, put beef on top, place pepperoncini over, add mozzarella cheese slices, and cover with the second half of bread.

Creamy Beef & Cauliflower Chili

Serving Size: 6 | Total Time: 20 minutes

1 lb beef stew meat	2 cups heavy cream
4 oz cauliflower, chopped	1 tsp Italian seasoning
1 onion, chopped	1 tsp salt
2 cups beef broth	½ tsp chili pepper

Add beef, cauliflower, onion, broth, heavy cream, Italian seasoning, salt, and chili pepper to your Instant Pot. Pour in 1 cup water. Seal the lid and cook on High Pressure for 15 minutes. When ready, do a quick release and serve.

Gingered Beef Pot Roast

Serving Size: 6 | Total Time: 45 minutes

2 lb beef chuck roast, cubed	3 minced garlic cloves
2 tbsp olive oil	1 tbsp grated ginger
Salt and pepper to taste	2-star anise
1 cup beef broth	1 jalapeño pepper, minced
½ cup soy sauce	

Warm the olive oil in your Instant Pot on Sauté. Sprinkle beef with salt and pepper and place it in the pot and garlic, ginger, and jalapeño pepper and cook until browned. Remove to a plate.

Pour beef broth in the pot and scrape any brown bits from the bottom. Stir in soy sauce and star anise. Put the beef back in the pot and seal the lid. Select Manual and cook for 35 minutes on High pressure. Once ready, perform a quick pressure release and unlock the lid.

Beef Lasagna with Eggplant & Almonds

Serving Size: 4 | Total Time: 25 minutes

2 lb stewed beef, boneless, sliced
3 oz toasted almonds, chopped

3 eggplants, halved	2 tbsp parsley, chopped
2 tomatoes, chopped	2 tbsp capers
2 red bell peppers, sliced	¼ cup olive oil
¼ tbsp tomato paste	

Grease the Instant Pot with 2 tbsp of olive oil. Make the first layer with halved eggplants tucking the ends gently to fit in. Make the second layer with beef slices, tomatoes, and red bell peppers. Spread the tomato paste evenly over, sprinkle with almonds and capers. Add in the remaining olive oil. Pour 1 ½ cups of water and seal the lid. Cook on High Pressure for 13 minutes. Do a quick release. Serve with fresh parsley.

T-Bone Steaks with Basil & Mustard

Serving Size: 4 | Total Time: 40 minutes + marinating time

1 lb T-bone steak	¼ cup oil
Salt and pepper to taste	½ tsp dried basil, crushed
2 tbsp Dijon mustard	

Whisk together oil, mustard, salt, pepper, and basil. Brush each steak and Refrigerate for 1 hour. Then, insert a steamer tray in the Instant Pot. Pour in 1 cup of water and arrange the steaks on the tray. Seal the lid and cook on Manual for 25 minutes on High. Do a quick release. Discard the liquid, remove the tray, and hit Sauté. Brown the steaks for 5 minutes, turning once.

Stewed Beef with Potatoes

Serving Size: 4 | Total Time: 60 minutes

1 lb russet potatoes, cut into chunks

1 lb beef shoulder	4 cups beef broth
2 carrots, chopped	1 celery stalk, chopped
1 onion, finely chopped	1 tbsp parsley, chopped
4 tbsp olive oil	1 cayenne pepper, chopped
2 tbsp tomato paste	Salt and pepper to taste
1 tbsp flour	

Warm oil on Sauté. Stir-fry onion, carrots, and potatoes for 7-8 minutes. Stir in flour and press Cancel. Add beef, tomato paste, broth, celery, parsley, cayenne pepper, salt, and pepper Seal the lid and cook on High Pressure for 40 minutes. Do a quick release.

Carrot Casserole with Beef & Potato

Serving Size: 3 | Total Time: 20 minutes

1 lb lean beef, with bones	3 tbsp olive oil
2 carrots	½ tsp salt
1 potato, sliced	

Mix beef, carrots, potato, olive oil, and salt in the Instant Pot. Pour enough water to cover and seal the lid. Cook on High Pressure for 15 minutes. Do a quick release and serve hot.

Beef Goulash with Cabbage & Potatoes

Serving Size: 6 | Total Time: 45 minutes

1 cup sun-dried tomatoes, diced	
2 lb beef stew meat	4 cups beef broth
3 potatoes, cut into chunks	3 tbsp tomato paste
1 onion, chopped	1 tsp tabasco sauce
1 carrot, chopped	Salt and pepper to taste
1 cabbage head, shredded	3 tbsp butter

Melt the butter oil in your Instant Pot on Sauté and cook the onion until translucent for 2 minutes. Add the tomato paste and stir. Add the beef, tomatoes, potatoes, carrot, cabbage, broth, tabasco sauce, salt, and pepper and seal the lid. Cook on High Pressure for 35 minutes. Do a quick release.

Beef Arancini with Potatoes

Serving Size: 4 | Total Time: 40 minutes

1 lb lean ground beef	1 egg, beaten
6 oz rice	1 potato peeled, chopped
2 onions, peeled, chopped	3 tbsp olive oil
2 garlic cloves, crushed	1 tsp salt

In a bowl, combine beef, rice, onions, garlic, egg, and salt. Shape the mixture into 15-16 meatballs. Grease the inner pot with 1 tbsp of olive oil. Press Sauté and cook the meatballs for 3-4 minutes, or until slightly brown.

Remove the meatballs. Add the remaining oil and make a layer of potato. Top with meatballs, cover with water, and seal the lid. Adjust the release steam handle. Cook on Meat/Stew for 15 minutes on High. Do a quick release.

Green Pea & Beef Ragout

Serving Size: 4 | Total Time: 25 minutes

2 lb beef, tender cuts, cut into bits	
2 cups green peas	1 tsp cayenne pepper
1 onion, diced	1 tbsp flour
1 tomato, diced	1 tsp salt
3 cups beef broth	½ tsp dried thyme
½ cup tomato paste	½ tsp red pepper flakes

Add beef, green peas, onion, tomato, broth, tomato paste, cayenne pepper, flour, salt, thyme, and red pepper flakes to the Instant Pot. Seal the lid, press Manual/Pressure Cook and cook for 10 minutes on High Pressure. When done, release the steam naturally for 10 minutes. Serve.

Classic Mushroom Beef Stroganoff

Serving Size: 6 | Total Time: 45 minutes

1 lb beef steak, cut into bite-sized pieces	
1 cup button mushrooms, chopped	
1 cup sour cream	1 tbsp flour
2 cups beef broth	1 onion, chopped
3 tbsp Worcestershire sauce	Salt and pepper to taste
3 tbsp olive oil	

In a bowl, mix flour, salt, and pepper. Coat steaks with the mixture. Place the meat and broth in the inner pot. Seal the lid and cook for 10 minutes on High Pressure. Do a quick release. Add mushrooms, onion, and Worcestershire sauce. Seal the lid and cook on High Pressure for 15 minutes. Do a quick release. Stir in sour cream. Let simmer for 10 minutes and serve.

Eggplant & Beef Stew with Parmesan

Serving Size: 6 | Total Time: 70 minutes

9 oz beef neck, cut into bite-sized pieces	
2 cups fire-roasted tomatoes	
1 eggplant, chopped	2 tbsp tomato paste
½ tbsp fresh green peas	1 tbsp ground chili pepper
1 tbsp cayenne pepper	½ tsp salt
1 tbsp beef broth	Parmesan, for garnish
4 tbsp olive oil	

Rub the meat with salt, cayenne, and chili pepper. Grease the Instant Pot with oil and brown the meat for 5-7 minutes or until golden on Sauté. Add tomatoes, eggplant, green peas, broth, and tomato paste and seal the lid. Cook on Meat/Stew for 40 minutes on High. Do a natural release for 10 minutes. Carefully unlock the lid. Serve warm sprinkled with grated Parmesan cheese.

Tasty Spicy Beef

Serving Size: 6 | Total Time: 33 minutes

2 lb lean beef, cut into bite-sized pieces	
5 onions, chopped	1 tsp cayenne pepper
5 garlic cloves, minced	2 tbsp tomato sauce
1 jalapeño pepper, chopped	2 tbsp vegetable oil
Salt and pepper to taste	

Heat oil on Sauté. Stir-fry onions and garlic for 3 minutes. Add in the meat, salt, pepper, cayenne pepper, jalapeño pepper, and tomato sauce. Mix and cover with water. Seal the lid. Cook for 20 minutes on High Pressure. Do a quick pressure release. Carefully unlock the lid. Serve.

Red Wine Beef & Vegetable Hotpot

Serving Size: 6 | Total Time: 40 minutes

2 sweet potatoes, cut into chunks	
2 lb stewing beef meat	½ tsp salt
¾ cup red wine	4 cups beef broth
1 tbsp ghee	½ cup green peas
6 oz tomato paste	1 tsp dried thyme
6 oz baby carrots, chopped	3 garlic cloves, crushed
1 onion, finely chopped	

Heat ghee on Sauté. Add beef and brown for 5-6 minutes. Add onion and garlic, and keep stirring for 3 more minutes. Add the sweet potatoes, wine, tomato paste, carrots, salt, broth, green peas, and thyme and seal the lid. Cook on Meat/Stew for 20 minutes on High Pressure. Do a quick release. Serve.

Beef Bones with Beans & Chili Pepper

Serving Size: 4 | Total Time: 30 minutes

14.5 oz canned beans	1 tbsp parsley, chopped
12 oz beef bones	1 bay leaf
1 onion, chopped	Salt and pepper to taste
3 garlic cloves	1 chili pepper, minced
1 carrot, chopped	3 tbsp vegetable oil

Place beans, beef bones, onion, garlic, carrot, parsley, bay leaf, salt, pepper, chili pepper, and oil in the Instant Pot. Pour water enough to cover. Seal the lid. Cook on High Pressure for 15 minutes. Release the steam naturally for 10 minutes. Let it chill for a while before serving.

Beef & Potatoes Moussaka

Serving Size: 4 | Total Time: 35 minutes

2 lb potatoes, chopped	½ cup milk
1 lb lean ground beef	2 eggs, beaten
1 onion, chopped	1 tbsp vegetable oil
Salt and pepper to taste	Sour cream for serving

Grease the pot with vegetable oil. Make 1 layer of potatoes and brush with milk. Spread the beef on top and make another layer of potatoes. Brush with the remaining milk. Seal the lid and cook for 15 minutes on High Pressure. Do a quick release. Sprinkle with salt and pepper and top with the eggs and onion. Seal the lid and let it stand for about 10 minutes. Top with sour cream.

Beef with Potatoes & Mushrooms

Serving Size: 6 | Total Time: 40 minutes

2 lb round roast	Salt and pepper to taste
2 tbsp olive oil	1 tsp oregano
2 cups vegetable broth	2 cups sliced mushrooms
2 garlic cloves, minced	1 large white onion, diced
1 celery stalk, chopped	1 lb potatoes, quartered

Place the olive oil, vegetable broth, garlic, salt, pepper, and oregano in your Instant Pot and stir. Mix in the round roast, mushrooms, potatoes, celery, and onion. Seal the lid, select Manual, and cook for 25 minutes on High pressure. When done, perform a quick pressure release and unlock the lid. Serve immediately.

Chinese Beef with Bok Choy

Serving Size: 4 | Total Time: 45 minutes

1 lb stew beef meat, cubed	1 tbsp rice wine
1 onion, quartered	1 (12 oz) bok choy, sliced
1 garlic clove, minced	12 oz broccoli florets
2 tbsp sesame oil	1 red chili, sliced
1 carrot, thinly chopped	1 tsp ground ginger

1 cup beef broth	2 tbsp fish sauce
¼ cup soy sauce	

Warm the sesame oil in your Instant Pot on Sauté. Add in beef meat, onion, garlic, carrot, ginger, and red chili and cook for 5-6 minutes. Stir in beef broth, rice wine, soy sauce, and fish sauce and seal the lid. Select Manual and cook for 30 minutes on High pressure. When done, perform a quick pressure release. Put in broccoli and bok choy and cook for 4-5 minutes on Sauté. Serve.

Simple Beef with Rice & Cheese

Serving Size: 4 | Total Time: 65 minutes

2 lb beef shoulder	3 tbsp butter
1 cup rice	¼ cup Parmesan, grated
2 cups beef broth	Salt and pepper to taste

Rub the beef with salt and pepper. Place it in the pot and pour in broth. Seal the lid and cook on Meat/Stew for 25 minutes on High. Do a quick release. Unlock the lid and remove the meat but keep the broth. Add rice and stir in 1 tbsp butter. Season with pepper and salt. Seal the lid. Cook on Manual for 20 minutes on High. Do a quick release. Remove the rice and wipe the pot clean. Melt 2 tbsp of butter on Sauté. Add meat and lightly brown for 10 minutes. Serve with rice topped with Parmesan.

Fall Beef Steak with Vegetables

Serving Size: 4 | Total Time: 51 minutes

1 lb beef chuck roast, cut into chunks	
2 tbsp olive oil	1 cup mushrooms, sliced
1 leek, sliced	1 carrot, chopped
2 garlic cloves, minced	1 celery stalk, chopped
1 tsp thyme	1 cup beef stock
1 tsp steak seasoning	Salt and pepper to taste
2 green bell peppers, sliced	

Warm the olive oil in your Instant Pot on Sauté. Place in garlic and leek and cook for 3-4 minutes. Stir in beef chunks and brown for 6-7 minutes, stirring occasionally. Mix in steak seasoning, bell peppers, celery, carrot, mushrooms, beef stock, thyme, salt, and pepper. Seal the lid, select Manual, and cook for 30 minutes on High pressure. When done, perform a quick pressure release and unlock the lid. Serve right away.

Calf's Liver Venetian-Style

Serving Size: 2 | Total Time: 55 minutes

1 lb calf's liver, rinsed	1 tbsp mint, chopped
3 tbsp olive oil	½ tsp cayenne pepper
2 garlic cloves, crushed	½ tsp Italian seasoning

In a bowl, mix oil, garlic, mint, cayenne, and Italian seasoning. Brush the liver and chill for 30 minutes. Remove from the fridge and pat dry with paper. Place the liver into the inner pot. Seal the lid and cook on High Pressure for 5 minutes. When ready, release the steam naturally for about 10 minutes.

Thyme Ground Beef Roll

Serving Size: 6 | Total Time: 50 minutes

2 lb ground beef	1 tsp dried thyme
2 large eggs	3 tbsp olive oil
½ tsp minced garlic	½ tsp salt
1 cup all-purpose flour	

In a bowl, combine the meat, garlic, flour, and eggs. Sprinkle with thyme and salt. Mix with hands and set aside. Grease a baking dish with olive oil. Form the meatloaf at the bottom. Add 1 cup water and place a trivet in your cooker. Lay the baking dish on the trivet. Seal the lid, press Meat/Stew, and cook for 40 minutes on High. Do a quick release. Carefully transfer the meatloaf to a serving dish. Garnish with salad and serve.

Pino Noir Beef Pot Roast

Serving Size: 6 | Total Time: 61 minutes

3 lb beef chuck roast	3 garlic cloves, peeled
2 tbsp olive oil	1 cup Pino Noir red wine
1 cup beef broth	1 onion, sliced
4 carrots, julienned	2 sprigs rosemary
1 lb potatoes, chopped	2 tbsp tomato puree
2 celery stalks, chopped	Salt and pepper to taste

Warm the olive oil in your Instant Pot on Sauté. Add in the beef roast and brown for 5-6 minutes on all sides. Remove to a plate. Pour in the red wine and scrape any brown bits from the bottom. Stir in onion, garlic, carrots, potatoes, celery, tomato puree, rosemary sprigs, salt, and pepper. Put the beef back on the vegetables and add in the beef broth.

Seal the lid. Select Manual and cook for 35 minutes on High. When over, allow a natural release for 10 minutes and unlock the lid. Discard rosemary sprigs and remove beef to a plate. Serve with gravy and vegetables.

Beer-Braised Beef Short Ribs

Serving Size: 6 | Total Time: 70 minutes

3 lb beef short ribs	1 onion, diced
Salt and pepper to taste	1 tsp dried thyme
2 tbsp olive oil	1 ½ cups beef broth
3 garlic cloves, minced	1 cup pilsner beer
4 carrots, chopped	

Sprinkle beef ribs with salt and pepper. Warm the olive oil in your Instant Pot on Sauté. Add in the ribs and cook for 10 minutes on all sides until browned; set aside. Add carrot, onion, garlic, and thyme to the pot and cook for 5 more minutes. Pour in beef broth and scrape any brown bits from the bottom. Mix in beer and return the ribs.

Maple Beef Teriyaki

Serving Size: 4 | Total Time: 50 minutes

2 lb flank steak, cut into strips	¼ cup maple syrup
2 garlic cloves, minced	¼ cup tamari sauce
¼ cup soy sauce	1-inch piece grated ginger

Place the soy sauce, garlic, maple syrup, tamari sauce, ginger, and ½ cup of water in your Instant Pot and cook for 5 minutes on Sauté. Stir in steak strips.

Seal the lid. Select Manual and cook for 25 minutes on High pressure. Once over, allow a natural release for 10 minutes, then perform a quick pressure release. Carefully unlock the lid. Serve immediately.

Beef with Snow Peas

Serving Size: 4 | Total Time: 46 minutes

1 lb beef brisket, cubed	8 oz bag snow peas, trimmed
Salt and pepper to taste	1 carrot, chopped
2 tbsp olive oil	1 turnip, chopped
1 onion, chopped	1 lb potatoes, cut into quarters
2 garlic cloves, minced	Bearnaise sauce for serving
2 bay leaves	

Warm the olive oil in your Instant Pot on Sauté. Place in beef brisket, onion, garlic, carrot, and turnip and cook for 5 minutes. Add in 2 cups of water, potatoes, bay leaves, salt, and pepper and seal the lid. Select Manual and cook for 25 minutes on High pressure. When ready, perform a quick pressure release and unlock the lid. Discard bay leaves and put in snow peas, and cook for 6 minutes on Sauté. Serve with bearnaise sauce.

Italian Roast Beef

Serving Size: 4 | Total Time: 75 minutes

1 lb boneless beef chuck roast	
2 oz dried porcini mushrooms	
4 oz pancetta, diced	½ cup Chianti red wine
1 onion, chopped	1 tsp dried oregano
2 garlic cloves, minced	2 bay leaves
1 cup chicken broth	½ tsp Italian seasonings
1 tsp tomato paste	Salt and pepper to taste
14 oz can crushed tomatoes	2 tbsp parsley, chopped

In a bowl, place porcini mushrooms and pour in ½ cup of boiling water to cover. Let sit for 10 minutes. Set your Instant Pot to Sauté. Place in pancetta and cook for 5 minutes until crispy; set aside. Add in onion and garlic and cook for 3 minutes until fragrant. Stir in the beef roast, pancetta, soaked mushrooms with their water, chicken broth, tomato paste, tomatoes, red wine, oregano, bay leaves, Italian seasonings, salt, and pepper.

Seal the lid, select Meat/Stew, and cook for 35 minutes on High pressure. Once over, allow a natural release for 10 minutes, then perform a quick pressure release, and unlock the lid. Serve topped with parsley.

Classic Beef Stroganoff

Serving Size: 6 | Total Time: 45 minutes

2 lb chuck roast, thin slices	1 cup mushrooms, sliced
2 tbsp butter	2 garlic cloves, minced
1 tbsp olive oil	1 ¼ cups beef broth
1 onion, sliced	½ cup crème fraiche
Salt and pepper to taste	2 cup cooked rice

Warm the olive oil and butter in your Instant Pot on Sauté. Place in onion and cook for 3 minutes. Sprinkle chuck roast with salt and pepper and place it in the pot and brown for 2 minutes on all sides. Add in mushrooms and garlic and cook for another 3 minutes. Stir in beef broth and seal the lid.

Select Manual and cook for 20 minutes on High pressure. Once ready, perform a quick pressure release and unlock the lid. Mix in créme fraiche and lock the lid. Let sit for 5 minutes. Serve with rice.

Sambal Beef Noodles

Serving Size: 4 | Total Time: 65 minutes

1 lb beef chuck roast, cubed	3 tbsp sambal oelek chili paste
2 tbsp sesame oil	
Salt and pepper to taste	2 cups water
1 chopped onion	8 oz egg noodles
2 minced garlic cloves	

Warm the sesame oil in your Instant Pot on Sauté. Place in the beef roast and cook for 6-7 minutes, stirring often. Add in salt, pepper, onion, sambal oelek chili paste, garlic, and 1 cup of water. Seal the lid, select Manual, and cook for 30 minutes on High pressure.

Once done, allow a natural release for 10 minutes, then perform a quick pressure release. Transfer beef roast to a plate. Pour in 1 cup of water in the pot and bring to a boil on Sauté. Add in noodles and cook for 4-5 minutes. Put the beef back to the pot and stir. Serve warm.

Beef Tikka Masala

Serving Size: 4 | Total Time: 50 minutes

2 tbsp tikka masala powder	1 onion, chopped
1 lb beef chuck steak, cubed	1 cup beef broth
2 tbsp olive oil	1 (14 oz) diced tomatoes
1 green chili, chopped	½ cup coconut cream
2 tsp ginger purée	Salt and pepper to taste
2 tsp garlic purée	3 tbsp chopped cilantro

Warm the olive oil in your Instant Pot on Sauté. Sprinkle beef steak with salt and pepper. Place it in the pot and sauté for 4-5 minutes, stirring periodically; set aside. Add onion, ginger puree, garlic puree, green chili, tikka masala powder, salt, and pepper in the pot.

Cook for 3 minutes. Pour in beef broth and scrape any brown bits from the bottom. Put back beef to the pot and diced tomatoes and seal the lid. Select Manual and cook for 25 minutes on High pressure.

Once done, perform a quick pressure release and unlock the lid. Mix in coconut cream for 4-5 minutes. Scatter cilantro on top and serve.

Traditional American Beef Meatloaf

Serving Size: 6 | Total Time: 45 minutes

2 lb ground beef	½ cup breadcrumbs
½ cup milk	1 onion, grated

1 egg, beaten	½ garlic powder
1 tsp allspice	½ tsp brown sugar
Salt and pepper to taste	2 tbsp tomato paste
¼ cup ketchup	

I a bowl, add ground beef, beaten egg, onion, milk, breadcrumbs, allspice, salt, and pepper and stir with your hands. Pour 1 cup of water into your Instant Pot and fit in a trivet. Place the meatloaf on an aluminum sheet and shape a loaf. Combine ketchup, garlic powder, brown sugar, and tomato paste in a bowl.

Spread the ketchup mixture on top of the meatloaf and place it on the trivet. Seal the lid, select Manual, and cook for 25 minutes on High pressure. Once over, allow a natural release for 10 minutes and unlock the lid. Cut into slices and serve with rice or cooked potatoes.

Savory Herb Meatloaf

Serving Size: 4 | Total Time: 45 minutes

1 lb ground beef	½ tsp rosemary
1 egg, beaten	½ tsp thyme
1 tsp garlic powder	1 ½ tsp parsley
1 tsp onion powder	Salt and pepper to taste
1 shredded potato	Dill pickles, to serve

Add the ground beef, egg, onion powder, garlic powder, shredded potato, rosemary, thyme, parsley, salt, and pepper to a bowl and combine them until everything is well mixed. Press the meatloaf mixture to a greased cooking pan. Pour 1 cup of water into your Instant Pot and fit in a trivet. Place the pan on the trivet and seal the lid. Select Manual and cook for 25 minutes on High.

When ready, allow a natural release for 10 minutes, then perform a quick pressure release, and unlock the lid. Remove the meatloaf to a plate and let cool before slicing. Serve with dill pickles.

Beef Steak with Mustard Sauce

Serving Size: 4 | Total Time: 55 minutes

1 lb flank steak, sliced	1 tbsp onion powder
2 tbsp olive oil	1 tbsp Worcestershire sauce
Salt and pepper to taste	1 cup heavy cream
½ cup beef broth	1 tbsp yellow mustard
¼ cup apple cider vinegar	

Warm 1 tbsp of olive oil in your Instant Pot on Sauté. Season the flank steak with onion powder, salt, and pepper and place in the pot; brown for 4-5 minutes on both sides. Stir in beef broth, vinegar, and Worcestershire sauce and seal the lid. Cook on Meat/Stew for 30 minutes.

Once ready, allow a natural release for 10 minutes, then perform a quick pressure release, and unlock the lid. Mix in heavy cream and mustard. Serve immediately.

Seal the lid, select Manual, and cook for 35 minutes on High pressure. Once done, allow a natural release for 10 minutes, then perform a quick pressure release, and unlock the lid. Serve with vegetables or potatoes.

Thai Beef Short Ribs

Serving Size: 6 | Total Time: 55 minutes

3 tbsp Thai yellow curry paste
12 beef short ribs
2 tbsp olive oil | 2 tbsp apple cider vinegar
Salt to taste | 4 garlic cloves, minced
½ cup soy sauce | 1 tbsp ginger root, grated
2 tbsp tomato paste | 2 tbsp sriracha sauce
| ¼ cup raw honey

Warm the olive oil in your Instant Pot on Sauté. Sprinkle beef ribs with salt and place them in the pot. Sear until browned on all sides; set aside. Place the soy sauce, curry paste, tomato paste, vinegar, garlic, ginger, sriracha, and honey in the pot. Stir well and scrape any bits from the bottom. Put ribs back to the pot. Pour in 1 cup of water.

Seal the lid, select Manual, and cook for 35 minutes on High pressure. When over, allow a natural release for 10 minutes and unlock the lid. Serve with gravy.

Mediterranean Beef Stew with Olives

Serving Size: 6 | Total Time: 50 minutes

2 cups canned spicy diced tomatoes with juice
2 lb beef stew meat, cubed | ½ cup dry white wine
3 tbsp olive oil | 1 red pepper, sliced
1 onion, sliced | 20 kalamata olives, pitted
2 garlic cloves, minced | Salt and pepper to taste

Warm the oil in your Instant Pot on Sauté. Place in the beef cubes and cook for 4-5 minutes or until no longer pink, stirring often. Add in onion, garlic, red pepper, salt, and pepper and cook for another 3 minutes. Pour in white wine and scrape any brown bits from the bottom. Stir in tomatoes, kalamata olives, and 1 cup of water.

Seal the lid. Select Manual and cook for 30 minutes on High pressure. Once done, perform a quick pressure release and unlock the lid. Adjust the seasoning with salt and pepper. Serve with potatoes or cooked rice.

Smoky Chipotle Beef Brisket

Serving Size: 4 | Total Time: 60 minutes + marinating time

1 tsp seasoned meat tenderizer
2 lb beef brisket, flat cut | 1 tbsp Worcestershire sauce
¼ tsp garlic salt | 1 cup smoky chipotle sauce
1 tbsp smoked paprika

Combine garlic salt, smoked paprika, Worcestershire sauce, and seasoned meat tenderizer in a bowl. Rub the brisket with the mixture. Cover with cling film and allow to marinate for 30 minutes in the fridge.

Place 1 cup of water, smoky chipotle, and brisket with its marinate in your Instant Pot and seal the lid. Select Manual and cook for 40 minutes on High pressure.

Once done, allow a natural release for 10 minutes, then perform a quick pressure release, and unlock the lid. Remove brisket to a plate. Slice before serving with sauce.

Beef Ragù Bolognese

Serving Size: 4 | Total Time: 40 minutes

½ cup Pecorino Romano cheese, shredded
1 lb ground beef | 2 tbsp basil, chopped
2 tbsp butter | 1 tbsp red wine
1 onion, chopped | 16 oz tomato sauce
1 carrot, chopped | 2 tbsp passata
1 celery stalk, chopped | 16 oz fettuccine pasta
Salt and pepper to taste

In the Instant Pot, add the pasta and cover with salted water. Seal the lid, press Manual, and cook for 4 minutes on High. Once ready, do a quick pressure release. Drain the pasta and remove to a bowl; cover with foil to keep warm.

Melt the butter on Sauté. Add in onion, carrot, and celery. Cook for 3-4 minutes. Mix in the ground beef and brown for 8-10 minutes, stirring occasionally. Pour in red wine, tomato sauce, and passata, and season with salt and black pepper. Seal the lid and select Manual.

Cook for 10 minutes on High. When ready, do a quick pressure release. Carefully unlock the lid. Pour the Bolognese sauce over the pasta, sprinkle with Pecorino Romano cheese, and top with basil to serve.

Leftover Beef Sandwiches

Serving Size: 4 | Total Time: 30 minutes

1 lb leftover roast beef | 2 tsp onion flakes
4 ciabatta rolls | 2 cups beef stock
Salt and pepper to taste | 2 tbsp Worcestershire sauce
1 tsp brown sugar | 1 tbsp balsamic vinegar
½ tsp garlic powder | 4 tsp butter, softened
1 tsp mustard powder | 4 cheddar cheese slices
1 tsp paprika

In a bowl, mix salt, pepper, sugar, garlic powder, mustard powder, paprika, and onion flakes and rub the beef roast with the mixture. Transfer to your Instant Pot and add beef stock, Worcestershire sauce, and balsamic vinegar.

Seal the lid, select Manual, and cook for 10 minutes on High pressure. When over, allow a natural release for 10 minutes, then perform a quick pressure release, and unlock the lid. Remove beef roast and shred it.

Discard sauce and reserve 1 cup for serving. Brush ciabatta rolls with butter and top with cheddar cheese. Stuff the rolls with some shredded beef. Serve sandwiches with sauce.

Rich Beef & Vegetable Casserole

Serving Size: 4 | Total Time: 40 minutes

1 cup mixed mushrooms, sliced
1 lb stewing steak, cubed | 1 red bell pepper, chopped
2 tbsp olive oil | 2 tbsp tomato paste
1 onion, chopped | 1 lb tomatoes, chopped
2 garlic cloves, minced | ½ cup red wine
1 celery stalk, chopped | ½ cup green olives
Salt and pepper to taste | 2 tbsp oregano, chopped

Warm the olive oil in your Instant Pot on Sauté. Add in the steak and cook for 5 minutes until browned, stirring often. Add in onion, bell pepper, garlic, celery, mushrooms, salt, and pepper and sauté for 3-4 minutes. Stir in tomato paste, tomatoes, red wine, 1 cup of water, and green olives and seal the lid. Select Manual and cook for 20 minutes on High pressure. Once ready, perform a quick pressure release and unlock the lid. Serve topped with fresh oregano.

Rosemary Braised Beef in Red Wine

Serving Size: 6 | Total Time: 75 minutes

3 lb diced braising steak
3 tbsp olive oil
Salt and pepper to taste
10 pearl onions, peeled
1 tsp Worcestershire sauce
4 baby carrot, chopped
1 celery stalk, diced

1 tbsp tomato paste
2 garlic cloves, minced
1 cup beef broth
1 cup red wine
2 sprigs fresh rosemary
1 bay leaf
1 tbsp cornstarch

Warm the olive oil in your Instant Pot on Sauté. Sprinkle beef with salt and pepper and place it in the pot. Cook for 8-10 minutes on all sides; reserve. Add pearl onions, garlic, baby carrot, celery, and tomato paste to the pot and cook for 4-5 minutes. Pour in red wine and scrape any brown bits from the bottom. Put meat back to the pot and thyme, Worcestershire sauce, beef broth, rosemary sprigs, and bay leaf.

Seal the lid, select Manual, and cook for 40 minutes on High pressure. When over, allow a natural release for 10 minutes, then perform a quick pressure release, and unlock the lid. Remove meat to a plate and let cool before slicing. Discard the rosemary and bay leaf. Combine cornstarch with 1 cup of cooking liquid and pour in the pot, and simmer on Sauté until the sauce thickens. Serve brisket with the sauce.

Beef & Bean Chili

Serving Size: 4 | Total Time: 70 minutes

1 lb ground beef
2 tbsp olive oil
½ lb white beans, soaked
14 oz can diced tomatoes
1 tbsp tomato paste
1 white onion, diced
2 garlic cloves, chopped

1 green bell pepper, diced
1 cup beef broth
Salt and pepper to taste
½ tsp oregano
1 jalapeño pepper, minced
1 tsp ground cumin

Heat olive oil on Sauté. Add onion, garlic, green pepper, and jalapeño pepper, and sauté for 3-5 minutes until tender. Stir in beef and cook for another 6 minutes. Season with oregano, cumin, salt, and pepper, and pour in tomato paste, tomatoes, beef broth, and white beans.

Seal the lid, select the Bean/Chili and cook for 25 minutes on High. When the timer is over, let the pressure release naturally for 10 minutes. Unlock the lid. Select Sauté to cook for another 8-10 minutes until the desired texture and thickness is reached. Ladle into bowls and serve.

Garlicky Herb-Rubbed Beef Brisket

Serving Size: 4 | Total Time: 60 minutes + marinating time

2 lb beef brisket, flat cut
2 garlic cloves, minced
Salt and pepper to taste
½ tsp oregano

½ tsp marjoram
½ tsp ground cumin
½ tsp dried rosemary
1 ½ cups beef stock

Combine garlic, salt, pepper, marjoram, oregano, cumin, and rosemary in a bowl. Add in the brisket, toss to coat, and marinate for 30 minutes in the fridge. Place the brisket and beef stock in your Instant Pot and seal the lid. Select Manual and cook for 40 minutes on High pressure. When done, allow a natural release for 10 minutes, then perform a quick pressure release, and unlock the lid. Slice before serving.

Beef & Lentil Stew

Serving Size: 4 | Total Time: 45 minutes

2 lb beef shoulder, cut into chunks
2 tbsp olive oil
Salt and pepper to taste
1 cup lentils
1 cup beef broth
½ cup sun-dried tomatoes

1 onion, sliced
2 garlic cloves, minced
½ tsp oregano
½ tsp marjoram

Combine the beef shoulder, olive oil, salt, pepper, lentils, beef broth, sun-dried tomatoes, onion, garlic cloves, oregano, and marjoram in your Instant Pot and stir. Seal the lid, select Manual, and cook for 25 minutes on High pressure. Once ready, allow a natural release for 10 minute and unlock the lid. Serve.

Beef & Vegetable Stew

Serving Size: 6 | Total Time: 55 minutes

2 lb beef stew meat, cubed
Salt and pepper to taste
½ tsp onion powder
1/3 cup flour
1 tsp Italian seasoning
2 tbsp olive oil
1 onion, chopped
3 garlic cloves, minced
1 tbsp red wine
1 tbsp tomato paste

4 potatoes, peeled, chopped
1 cup green beans, trimmed
1 tsp paprika
1 cup tomatoes, chopped
1 celery rib, chopped
2 carrots, sliced
3 cups beef broth
1 bay leaf
2 tbsp parsley, chopped

Combine salt, pepper, onion powder, flour, and Italian seasoning in a bowl. Add in beef meat and toss to coat. Warm the olive oil in your Instant Pot on Sauté. Place the meat in the pot and cook for 5-6 minutes, stirring occasionally; set aside. Place the onion, garlic, celery, carrot, and paprika in the pot and cook for 3-4 minutes.

Pour in wine and scrape any brown bits from the bottom. Put the meat back to the pot and tomato paste, tomatoes, potatoes, green beans, broth, bay leaf, salt, and pepper and stir. Seal the lid, select Manual, and cook for 25 minutes on High. When ready, allow a natural release for 10 minutes. Serve topped with parsley.

Beef & Root Vegetable Pot

Serving Size: 4 | Total Time: 65 minutes

1 lb beef stew meat, cubed	1 cup dry red wine
2 tbsp olive oil	2 cups chopped tomatoes
Salt and pepper to taste	1 turnip, chopped
1 leek, chopped	1 lb sweet potatoes, sliced
2 garlic cloves, minced	2 carrots, chopped
1 tsp dried thyme	2 cups beef broth
2 tbsp flour	¼ cup parsley, chopped

Warm the olive oil in your Instant Pot on Sauté. Sprinkle beef meat with salt and pepper and place it in the pot. Sauté for 6-7 minutes on all sides until browned; set aside. Add leek and garlic to the pot and cook for 3 minutes. Stir in thyme and flour and cook for 1 minute. Pour in red wine and scrape any brown bits from the bottom.

Add in turnip, carrots, sweet potatoes, tomatoes, and beef broth. Put the meat back to the pot and seal the lid. Select Manual and cook for 30 minutes on High pressure. Once over, allow a natural release for 10 minutes and unlock the lid. Serve topped with parsley.

Beef & Butternut Squash Chili

Serving Size: 4 | Total Time: 65 minutes

2 tbsp olive oil	2 cups beef broth
1 lb stewed beef meat, cubed	Salt and pepper to taste
1 lb butternut squash, cubed	2 tbsp tomato paste
1 cup canned tomatoes, diced	1 tsp chili powder
	1 tsp ground cumin
1 onion, diced	1 tsp oregano
2 garlic cloves	1 tsp cayenne pepper

Warm the olive oil in your Instant Pot on Sauté. Place in beef meat and cook for 7-8 minutes on all sides; reserve. Add onion, garlic, chili powder, cumin, oregano, cayenne pepper, salt, and pepper to the pot and cook for 5 minutes. Put in butternut squash, tomato paste, tomatoes, and beef broth and return the beef.

Seal the lid, select Manual, and cook for 30 minutes on High pressure. When ready, allow a natural release for 10 minutes, then perform a quick pressure release, and unlock the lid. Serve warm.

Beef Neapolitan Ragù

Serving Size: 4 | Total Time: 53 minutes

1 ½ lb beef steak, cut into strips	1 celery stalk, chopped
	1 cup beef broth
2 tbsp lard	½ cup red wine
1 onion, chopped	1 tbsp passata
2 cups crushed tomatoes	Salt and pepper to taste
1 carrot, chopped	

Melt lard in your Instant Pot on Sauté. Place in onion, carrot, and celery and sauté until fragrant. Add in beef steak and cook for 3 minutes, stirring often. Pour in tomatoes, beef broth, red wine, passata, salt, and pepper and seal the lid. Select Meat/Stew.

Cook for 30 minutes on High pressure. When over, allow a natural release for 10 minutes, then perform a quick pressure release, and unlock the lid. Serve immediately.

Boeuf Bourguignon

Serving Size: 4 | Total Time: 63 minutes

1 lb flank steak	4 oz bacon, chopped
2 tbsp olive oil	1 cup beef broth
1 cup pearl onions	1 cup Burgundy red wine
2 garlic cloves, minced	Salt and pepper to taste
1 cups crimini mushrooms	1 bay leaf
1 carrot, sliced	2 tbsp thyme, chopped

Warm the oil in your Instant Pot on Sauté. Place in the steak and cook for 6-8 minutes in total. Set aside. Add onions, garlic, mushrooms, carrots, and bacon to the pot and cook for 4-5 minutes. Stir in beef broth and wine.

Put the meat back to the pot and salt, pepper, and bay leaf and seal the lid. Select Manual and cook for 30 minutes on High. When over, allow a natural release for 10 minutes, then perform a quick pressure release, and unlock the lid. Discard bay leaf. Top with thyme.

Pulled BBQ Beef

Serving Size: 6 | Total Time: 65 minutes

3 lb beef chuck roast	1 tsp smoked paprika
2 tbsp olive oil	Salt and pepper to taste
1 cup BBQ sauce	2 cups beef broth
1 tbsp Dijon mustard	3 tbsp cilantro, chopped

Warm the olive oil in your Instant Pot on Sauté. Sprinkle beef with salt and pepper and place it in the pot and cook for 8-10 minutes on all sides. Add in BBQ sauce, Dijon mustard, smoked paprika, salt, pepper, and beef broth and seal the lid. Select Manual and cook for 35 minutes on High pressure.

Once ready, allow a natural release for 10 minutes, then perform a quick pressure release, and unlock the lid. Remove beef and shred it using 2 forks. Put it back to the pot and mix with the remaining liquid. Top with cilantro and serve.

Beef Meatballs with Tomato-Basil Sauce

Serving Size: 4 | Total Time: 30 minutes

2 cups tomato and basil pasta sauce	
1 ¼ lb ground beef	2 tbsp breadcrumbs
1 tsp garlic powder	Salt and pepper to taste
1 tsp onion powder	2 tbsp olive oil
1 tsp oregano	

Combine ground beef, garlic powder, onion powder, oregano, breadcrumbs, salt, and pepper in a bowl. Make 2-inch meatballs of the mixture. Warm the olive oil in your Instant Pot on Sauté. Add in the meatballs and cook for 4-5 minutes on all sides until browned. Stir in tomato and basil pasta sauce and ¼ cup of water.

Seal the lid, select Manual, and cook for 10 minutes on High pressure. When done, allow a natural release for 10 minutes, then perform a quick pressure release, and unlock the lid. Serve immediately.

Vietnamese Beef

Serving Size: 6 | Total Time: 60 minutes

2 lb beef steak, sliced	3 tbsp fish sauce
3 tbsp olive oil	1 tbsp brown sugar
Salt and pepper to taste	2 tbsp cornflour
4 garlic cloves, minced	2 tbsp mint leaves, chopped
1 tsp minced ginger	1 red chili pepper, minced
3 white onions, chopped	

Sprinkle beef steak with salt and pepper. Warm the olive oil in your Instant Pot on Sauté. Place in the steak and sauté for 10-12 minutes on all sides. Set aside.

Add garlic, ginger, red chili pepper, and onions to the pot and cook for 2-3 minutes. Stir in fish sauce, brown sugar, and 1 ¼ cups of water. Put the steak back to the pot.

Seal the lid. Select Manual and cook for 25 minutes on High pressure. When done, allow a natural release for 10 minutes, then perform a quick pressure release, and unlock the lid. Combine ½ cup of water and cornflour in a bowl and pour it into the pot. Simmer on Sauté until the liquid thickens. Serve topped with mint leaves.

Greek-Style Stuffed Peppers

Serving Size: 4 | Total Time: 39 minutes

¼ cup Halloumi cheese, grated	
2 tbsp olive oil	1 tsp oregano
1 lb ground beef	1 tsp paprika
2 onions, chopped	½ tsp ground cinnamon
Salt and pepper to taste	1 cup canned tomato sauce
4 bell peppers, tops removed	1 tbsp flour

Mix the cheese, ground beef, onions, paprika, cinnamon, salt, and pepper in a bowl. Stuff each bell pepper with the mixture. Pour the tomato sauce and ½ of water in your Instant Pot and fit in a trivet. Place the peppers on the trivet and seal the lid. Select Manual and cook for 15 minutes on High pressure.

When over, allow a natural release for 10 minutes and unlock the lid. Remove peppers to a plate. Whisk the flour and oregano with some cooking sauce in a bowl. Pour it in the pot and select Sauté; cook until the sauce thickens, about 3-4 minutes. Adjust the seasoning before pouring it over the peppers.

Chipotle Shredded Beef

Serving Size: 4 | Total Time: 45 minutes

2 lb beef shoulder roast	2 tbsp tomato salsa
2 tbsp vegetable oil	1 tsp chipotle chili pepper
1 onion, chopped	Salt and pepper to taste
3 garlic cloves, minced	4 tbsp sour cream
3 cups beef broth	2 tbsp cilantro, chopped

Rub the beef roast with chipotle chili pepper, salt, and pepper on all sides. Warm the vegetable oil in your Instant Pot on Sauté. Place the onion and garlic and cook for 2-3 minutes. Add in the beef roast and beef broth and seal the lid.

Select Manual and cook for 30 minutes on High pressure. Once ready, perform a quick pressure release and unlock the lid. Remove meat and shred it. Pour tomato salsa in the pot and cook until the sauce thickens on Sauté. Stir in shredded beef. Top with cilantro and serve with a dollop of sour cream on the side.

Veal Chops with Greek Yogurt

Serving Size: 4 | Total Time: 60 minutes

2 lb boneless veal shoulder, cubed	
3 tomatoes, chopped	1 tsp salt
2 tbsp flour	1 tbsp parsley, chopped
3 tbsp butter	1 cup Greek yogurt
1 tbsp cayenne pepper	1 pide bread

Grease the bottom of the inner pot with 1 tbsp of butter. Make a layer with veal pieces and Pour water to cover. Season with salt and seal the lid. Cook on High Pressure for 45 minutes. Do a quick release.

Melt the remaining butter in a skillet. Add the cayenne pepper and flour and briefly stir-fry, about 2 minutes. Slice pide bread and arrange on a serving plate. Place the meat and tomatoes on top. Drizzle with cayenne pepper, Top with yogurt and sprinkle with parsley to serve.

Easy Lamb & Spinach Soup

Serving Size: 5 | Total Time: 45 minutes

1 lb lamb shoulder, cubed	5 cups vegetable broth
10 oz spinach, chopped	3 tbsp olive oil
3 eggs, beaten	1 tsp salt

Place in your Instant Pot the lamb, spinach, eggs, broth, olive oil, and salt. Seal the lid, press Soup/Broth, and cook for 30 minutes on High Pressure. Do a natural pressure release for about 10 minutes. Serve warm.

Roast Lamb Leg with Potatoes

Serving Size: 6 | Total Time: 35 minutes

2 lb lamb leg	3 tbsp oil
2 garlic cloves	¼ cup red wine vinegar
1 tbsp thyme, chopped	1 tsp brown sugar
1 lb potatoes	1 tsp salt
1 lemon, chopped	

Place the potatoes in the pot, and pour enough water to cover. Season with salt, add garlic, and seal the lid. Set to Meat/Stew. Cook for 20 minutes on High Pressure. Do a quick release and remove potatoes; reserve the liquid.

Rub the meat with oil and thyme. Place in the pot. Pour in red wine vinegar, sugar, and add lemon. Add 1 cup of the reserved liquid and seal the lid. Cook on High Pressure for 7 minutes. Do a quick release.

Lamb Shanks with Garlic & Thyme

Serving Size: 4 | Total Time: 65 minutes

2 ½ lb lamb shanks, trimmed of excess fat
Salt and pepper to taste   2 tbsp tomato paste
10 whole garlic cloves, peeled   ½ cup red wine
1 cup vegetable broth   2 tbsp fresh thyme, chopped
1 (14-oz) can diced tomatoes   2 tbsp butter
1 onion, sliced   2 tsp balsamic vinegar

Sprinkle lamb shanks with salt and pepper. Warm the butter in your Instant Pot on Sauté. Place in lamb shanks and cook for 4-5 minutes on all sides until browned. Add in onion and garlic and sauté for 2 more minutes. Stir in vegetable broth, tomato paste, red wine, tomatoes, and thyme and seal the lid. Select Manual and cook for 35 minutes on High.

Once done, allow a natural release for 10 minutes and unlock the lid. Remove lamb to a plate. Stir the butter and balsamic vinegar in the pot and select Sauté; cook until the sauce thickens. Serve the lamb with sauce.

Lamb with Tomato & Green Peas

Serving Size: 4 | Total Time: 65 minutes

1 cup green peas   2 tbsp parsley, chopped
1 lb lamb, cubed   2 garlic cloves, crushed
1 tomato, roughly chopped   4 tbsp tomato sauce
1 onion, peeled, chopped   2 tbsp olive oil
2 carrots, peeled, chopped   4 cups vegetable stock
1 celery stalk, chopped   Salt and pepper to taste

Warm the olive oil in your Instant Pot on Sauté. Cook the onion, carrots, celery, and garlic for 8 minutes until tender. Add in the lamb and sauté for another 5-6 minutes. Season with salt and black pepper. Add in green peas, tomato, tomato sauce, and stock and seal the lid. Cook on High Pressure for 30 minutes. Do a natural pressure release for about 10 minutes. Carefully fully unlock the lid. Top with parsley to serve.

Minty Lamb

Serving Size: 6 | Total Time: 55 minutes

3 lb lamb, boneless and cubed
2 tbsp butter   3 tbsp flour
4 garlic cloves, minced   1 ½ cups vegetable stock
4 green onions, chopped   1 cup carrots, sliced
1 tsp cumin seeds   4 mint sprigs
1 tsp coriander seeds   Salt and pepper to taste

Sprinkle the lamb with salt and pepper and coat in flour. Melt butter in your Instant Pot on Sauté. Add in onion and garlic and cook for 3 minutes. Put in lamb and cook for 5-6 minutes until browned. Stir in stock, carrots, cumin and coriander seeds, and mint sprigs and seal the lid. Select Manual and cook for 25 minutes on High.

When ready, allow a natural release for 10 minutes. Carefully unlock the lid. Discard the mint sprigs. Top the lamb with sauce and serve warm.

Hot Paprika & Oregano Lamb

Serving Size: 4 | Total Time: 70 minutes + marinating time

1 lb lamb shoulder   ¼ cup red wine
1 tsp hot paprika   ¼ cup chicken stock
1 tsp oregano   1 tbsp olive oil
1 tsp cumin   ½ cup water
¼ tsp ground cinnamon   2 tbsp butter
2 tbsp tomato puree   Salt and pepper to taste

Mix the oregano, hot paprika, salt, black pepper, cumin, and cinnamon in a bowl. Add in lamb and toss to coat. Cover and let marinate for 20-30 minutes. Warm the olive oil in your Instant Pot on Sauté. Place in lamb shoulder and brown for 5 minutes on all sides. Pour in red wine, chicken stock, tomato puree, butter, and ½ cup of water.

Seal the lid, select Manual, and cook for 45 minutes on High pressure. Once over, allow a natural release for 10 minutes, then perform a quick pressure release, and unlock the lid. Remove the lamb to a cutting board shred it. Return to the pot and stir. Serve warm.

Mediterranean Lamb

Serving Size: 4 | Total Time: 55 minutes

1 lb lamb meat, cut into strips
1 tsp vegetable oil   1 carrot, sliced
4 tomatoes, chopped   2 thyme sprigs
2 tbsp tomato paste   ½ cup dry white wine
1 red bell pepper, sliced   10 black olives, sliced
2 garlic cloves, minced   Salt and pepper to taste
1 yellow onion, chopped   2 tbsp parsley, chopped

Warm oil in your Instant Pot on Sauté. Add in lamb and cook for 8 minutes on all sides. Stir in tomatoes, tomato paste, bell pepper, garlic, onion, carrots, salt, pepper and sauté for 5 more minutes. Pour in wine and enough water to cover everything. Add in thyme sprigs and olives. Seal the lid, select Manual, and cook for 30 minutes on High.

Once done, perform a quick pressure release and unlock the lid. Remove the lamb to a plate, discard bones and shred it. Put the shredded lamb back to the pot and stir parsley. Serve immediately.

Quick French-Style Lamb with Sesame

Serving Size: 4 | Total Time: 45 minutes

12 oz lamb, tender cuts, ½-inch thick
1 cup rice   1 tsp salt
1 cup green peas   ½ tsp dried thyme
3 tbsp sesame seeds   3 tbsp butter
4 cups beef broth

Mix the meat in the pot with broth. Seal the lid and cook on High Pressure for 15 minutes. Do a quick release. Remove the meat but keep the liquid. Add rice and green peas. Season with salt and thyme. Stir well and top with the meat. Seal the lid and cook on Manual for 18 minutes on High. Do a quick release. Carefully unlock the lid. Stir in butter and sesame seeds. Serve immediately.

Lamb Stew with Lemon & Parsley

Serving Size: 4 | Total Time: 60 minutes

2 potatoes, cut into bite-sized pieces
1 lb lamb neck, boneless   1 garlic head, whole
2 large carrots, chopped   2 tbsp parsley, chopped
1 tomato, diced   ¼ cup lemon juice
1 red bell pepper, chopped   Salt and pepper to taste

Add the meat and season with salt. Add in potatoes, carrots, tomato, bell pepper, lemon juice, and pepper, tuck in one garlic head in the middle of the pot and add 2 cups water. Add parsley and seal the lid. Cook on High Pressure for 45 minutes. When ready, do a quick release. Carefully unlock the lid. Serve.

Simple Roast Lamb

Serving Size: 4 | Total Time: 40 minutes

2 lb lamb leg   Salt and pepper to taste
1 tbsp garlic powder   4 rosemary sprigs, chopped
3 tbsp extra virgin olive oil

Grease the inner pot with oil. Rub the meat with salt, pepper, and garlic powder, and place in the Instant Pot. Pour enough water to cover and seal the lid. Cook on Meat/Stew for 30 minutes on High. Do a quick release. Make sure the meat is tender and falls off the bones. Top with cooking juices and rosemary. Serve.

Traditional Lamb with Vegetables

Serving Size: 6 | Total Time: 30 minutes

1 lb lamb chops, 1-inch thick
1 cup green peas, rinsed   1 tomato, chopped
3 carrots, chopped   3 tbsp olive oil
3 onions, chopped   1 tbsp paprika
1 potato, chopped   Salt and pepper to taste

Grease the Instant Pot with olive oil. Rub salt onto the lamb and make a bottom layer. Add peas, carrots, onions, potato, and tomato. Season with paprika. Add olive oil, 1 cup of water, salt, and pepper. Give it a good stir and seal the lid. Cook on Meat/Stew for 20 minutes on High Pressure. When ready, do a natural pressure release. Carefully unlock the lid. Serve hot.

Garlic Lamb with Thyme

Serving Size: 4 | Total Time: 60 minutes

2 lb lamb, cubed   2 tbsp butter, softened
2 garlic cloves, minced   2 celery stalks, chopped
1 cup onions, chopped   1 tbsp fresh thyme
1 cup red wine   2 tbsp flour
2 cups beef stock   Salt and pepper to taste

Rub the lamb with salt and pepper. Melt butter on Sauté and cook onions, celery, and garlic for 5 minutes. Add lamb and fry until browned for about 5-6 minutes. Dust the flour and stir. Pour in the stock and red wine. Seal the lid, and cook on High Pressure for 30 minutes. Do a natural release for 10 minutes. Serve with thyme.

Leg of Lamb with Garlic and Pancetta

Serving Size: 6 | Total Time: 40 minutes

2 lb lamb leg   1 tsp rosemary
6 garlic cloves   Salt and pepper to taste
1 large onion, chopped   2 tbsp oil
6 pancetta slices   3 cups beef broth

Heat the oil in your Instant Pot on Sauté. Add the pancetta and onion, making two layers. Season with salt and pepper and cook for 3 minutes until lightly browned.

Place the lamb on a separate dish. Using a sharp knife, make 6 incisions into the meat and place a garlic clove in each. Rub the meat with rosemary and transfer to the pot. Press Cancel and pour in the beef broth. Seal the lid and cook on High Pressure for 25 minutes. When done, do a natural pressure release. Serve.

Savory Irish Lamb Stew

Serving Size: 4 | Total Time: 36 minutes

1 lb lamb, cut into pieces   2 carrots, chopped
1 ½ tbsp canola oil   2 ½ cups beef broth
1 onion, sliced   ½ tsp dried oregano
2 tbsp cornstarch   Salt and pepper to taste
2 potatoes, cubed

Season the lamb with salt and pepper. Heat the canola oil in your Instant Pot on Sauté. Sear the lamb until browned on all sides, about 4-5 minutes. Add onion, potatoes, carrots, broth, and oregano, and stir. Seal the lid and cook on High Pressure for 18 minutes. When ready, do a quick pressure release. Whisk the cornstarch with a little bit of water and stir it into the stew. Cook on Sauté for 3 more minutes. Serve hot.

Asian-Style Lamb Curry

Serving Size: 4 | Total Time: 55 minutes + marinating time

1 ½ lb lamb stew meat, cubed
½ cup coconut milk   1 tbsp soy sauce
4 garlic cloves, minced   14 oz canned tomatoes, diced
Juice of ½ lime   3 carrots, sliced
1-inch piece ginger, grated   1 onion, diced
Salt and pepper to taste   1 eggplant, diced
2 tbsp yellow curry paste   2 tbsp cilantro, chopped
½ tsp turmeric   2 cups basmati rice, cooked
2 tbsp butter

Mix coconut milk, garlic, lime juice, ginger, salt, and pepper in a bowl. Add in lamb cubes and toss to coat. Let marinate for 30 minutes. Set your Instant Pot to Sauté. Melt butter and add onion, curry paste, turmeric, eggplant, and carrots and cook for 3-4 minutes. Stir in tomatoes, soy sauce, and 1 cup water.

Add in the marinated lamb with their juice and seal the lid. Select Manual and cook for 30 minutes on High pressure. Once ready, allow a natural release for 10 minutes, then perform a quick pressure release, and unlock the lid. Serve with the rice topped with cilantro.

Spicy Lamb & Bean Chili

Serving Size: 4 | Total Time: 53 minutes

1 cup chopped green chilies
1 cup cannellini beans, soaked
1 lb ground lamb
2 tbsp olive oil
1 onion, chopped
½ tbsp chili powder
½ tsp cayenne pepper
1 tsp cumin

1 tsp fennel seeds
1 (14-oz) can diced tomatoes
1 tbsp tomato paste
3 cups chicken broth
Salt and pepper to taste

Warm the olive oil in your Instant Pot on Sauté. Add in ground lamb and cook for 5 minutes until mostly brown. Stir in onion, chili powder, cayenne pepper, cumin, fennel seeds, salt, and pepper and sauté for 3 minutes.

Pour in tomatoes, tomato paste, green chilies, cannellini beans, and chicken broth and seal the lid. Select Manual and cook for 25 minutes on High.

When ready, allow a natural release for 10 minutes and unlock the lid. Serve with sour cream.

Fennel Lamb Ribs

Serving Size: 4 | Total Time: 47 minutes

3 lb lamb ribs
2 tbsp olive oil
4 garlic cloves, chopped
3 tbsp all-purpose flour
1 ½ cups vegetable stock

½ tsp cumin
½ fennel bulb, sliced
2 carrots, chopped
4 rosemary sprigs
Salt and pepper to taste

Warm olive oil in your Instant Pot on Sauté. Sprinkle lamb ribs with salt and pepper and add them to the pot. Cook for 6-7 minutes on all sides. Add in garlic, cumin and fennel and cook for 3 more minutes. Stir in flour, stock, rosemary, and carrots and seal the lid. Select Manual and cook for 22 minutes on High. When ready, allow a natural release for 5 minutes and unlock the lid. Remove rosemary sprigs. Serve the ribs with sauce.

Lamb Chops with Mashed Potatoes

Serving Size: 6 | Total Time: 20 minutes

8 lamb chops
Salt to taste
3 sprigs rosemary, chopped
3 tbsp butter, softened
2 tbsp olive oil
1 tbsp tomato puree

1 green onion, chopped
1 cup beef stock
5 potatoes, peeled, chopped
1/3 cup milk
2 tbsp cilantro, chopped

Rub rosemary leaves and salt to the lamb chops. Warm oil and 2 tbsp of butter on Sauté. Brown lamb chops for 1 minute per each side; set aside. In the pot, mix tomato puree and green onion and cook for 2-3 minutes. Add the stock into the pot to deglaze and scrape the bottom to get rid of any browned food bits. Return the lamb chops to the pot. Set a steamer rack on lamb chops. Place the steamer basket on the rack. Pour in the potatoes.

Seal the lid and cook on High Pressure for 4 minutes. Release the pressure quickly. Remove trivet and steamer basket.

In a blender, add potatoes, milk, salt, and remaining butter. Blend well until you obtain a smooth consistency. Place the potato mash on a serving dish. Lay lamb chops on the mash. Drizzle with cooking liquid and top with cilantro.

Vegetable & Lamb Casserole

Serving Size: 4 | Total Time: 50 minutes

1 lb lamb stew meat, cubed
2 tbsp olive oil
1 onion, chopped
3 garlic cloves, minced
2 tomatoes, chopped
½ lb baby potatoes
½ lb green beans, chopped
1 carrot, chopped
1 onion, chopped

1 celery stalk, chopped
2 tbsp white wine
2 cups lamb stock
1 tsp Hungarian paprika
1 tsp cumin, ground
¼ tsp oregano, dried
¼ tsp rosemary, dried
Salt and pepper to taste

Warm the olive oil in your Instant Pot on Sauté. Add in lamb cubes and cook for 5-6 minutes until no longer pink. Stir in onion and garlic and sauté for another 3 minutes. Pour in tomatoes, potatoes, green beans, carrot, onion, celery, white wine, lamb stock, paprika, cumin, oregano, rosemary, salt, and pepper and seal the lid. Select Manual and cook for 20 minutes on High pressure. When over, allow a natural release for 10 minutes and unlock the lid.

Balsamic Lamb

Serving Size: 4 | Total Time: 45 minutes

2 lb lamb shanks
2 tbsp sesame oil
2 garlic cloves, peeled
1 onion, chopped
1 cup vegetable broth

1 tbsp tomato paste
½ tsp thyme
¼ tsp dried dill weed
1 tbsp balsamic vinegar
1 tbsp butter

Warm sesame oil in your Instant Pot on Sauté. Place in onion and garlic and sauté for 3 minutes. Stir in broth, tomato paste, dill, and thyme. Add in the lamb and seal the lid. Select Manual and cook for 25 minutes on High.

When ready, allow a natural release for 5 minutes and unlock the lid. Remove the lamb to a bowl. Stir the balsamic vinegar and butter in the pot for 1-2 minutes until the butter melts. Serve the lamb with sauce.

Lamb Chorba

Serving Size: 4 | Total Time: 35 minutes

2 lb lamb shanks
2 tbsp olive oil
2 garlic cloves, peeled
1 onion, chopped
1 celery stalk, chopped
1 tomato, chopped

1 carrot, chopped
2 tbsp oregano, chopped
Salt and pepper to taste
4 cups vegetable broth
1 tbsp white wine vinegar

Warm the olive oil in your Instant Pot on Sauté. Place in the lamb, celery, onion, carrot, and garlic and sauté for 6 minutes. Stir in vegetable broth, tomato, salt, and pepper. Seal the lid. Select Manual and cook for 20 minutes. Release the pressure quickly. Drizzle with vinegar and sprinkle with oregano to serve.

FISH & SEAFOOD

Salmon Steaks with Garlic & Lemon

Serving Size: 3 | Total Time: 60 minutes

1 lb salmon steaks
1 tsp garlic powder
2 tbsp olive oil

Salt and pepper to taste
¼ cup lemon juice

In a bowl, mix garlic powder, olive oil, salt, lemon juice, and pepper. Pour the mixture into a Ziploc bag along with the salmon. Seal the bag and shake to coat well. Refrigerate for 30 minutes. Pour in 1 cup of water in the Instant Pot and insert the trivet. Remove the fish from the Ziploc bag and place it on top. Reserve the marinade. Seal the lid and select Steam.

Cook for 15 minutes on High. When ready, do a quick release and remove the steaks. Discard the liquid. Wipe clean the pot. Pour in the marinade and hit Sauté. Cook for 3-4 minutes. Serve the salmon drizzled with the sauce.

Salmon with Green Beans & Rice

Serving Size: 4 | Total Time: 20 minutes

1 cup rice
2 cups vegetable stock
4 skinless salmon fillets
1 cup green beans, chopped
3 tbsp olive oil
Salt and pepper to taste

2 limes, juiced
1 tsp sweet paprika
2 jalapeño peppers, diced
2 garlic cloves, minced
½ cup corn kernels
2 tbsp chopped fresh dill

Add rice, stock, and salt to your Instant Pot. Place a trivet over the rice. In a bowl, mix oil, lime juice, paprika, jalapeño, garlic, and dill. Coat the fish with the dill sauce while reserving a little for garnishing. Lay the salmon fillets on the trivet. Seal the lid and cook on High Pressure for 8 minutes. Do a quick release. Fluff the rice with a fork and mix in the green beans and corn kernels. Transfer to a serving plate and top with the salmon. Drizzle with the remaining dill sauce and serve.

Herbed Poached Salmon

Serving Size: 2 | Total Time: 20 minutes

2 salmon fillets, skin-on
1 cup chicken broth
¼ cup dry white wine
1 tsp lemon zest
¼ tsp basil
¼ tsp oregano

¼ tsp thyme
¼ tsp marjoram
1 tbsp garlic oil
4 scallions, chopped
Salt and pepper to taste

Pour chicken broth and white wine in your Instant Pot and fit in a trivet. In a bowl, combine basil, oregano, thyme, marjoram, lemon zest, garlic oil, salt, and pepper. Spread the rub evenly onto the salmon and place it on the trivet. Seal the lid, select Manual, and cook for 5 minutes on High pressure. Once over, allow a natural release for 5 minutes, perform a quick pressure release, and unlock the lid. Sprinkle with scallions and serve.

Dilled Salmon Fillets

Serving Size: 4 | Total Time: 25 minutes

4 salmon fillets
1 cup lemon juice
2 tbsp butter, softened

2 tbsp dill
Salt and pepper to taste

Sprinkle the fillets with salt and pepper. Insert the steamer tray and place the salmon on top. Pour in the lemon juice and 2 cups of water. Seal the lid. Cook on Steam for 5 minutes on High.

Release the pressure naturally for 10 minutes. Set aside the salmon and discard the liquid. Wipe the pot clean and press Sauté. Add butter and briefly brown the fillets on both sides, about 3-4 minutes. Sprinkle with dill.

Steamed Salmon over Creamy Polenta

Serving Size: 4 | Total Time: 30 minutes

4 salmon fillets, skin removed
1 cup corn grits polenta
½ cup coconut milk
3 cups chicken stock
3 tbsp butter

Salt to taste
3 tbsp Cajun seasoning
1 tbsp sugar

Combine polenta, milk, chicken stock, butter, and salt in the pot. In a bowl, mix Cajun seasoning, sugar, and salt. Oil the fillets with cooking spray and brush with the spice mixture. Insert a trivet in the pot and arrange the fillets on top. Seal the lid and cook on High Pressure for 9 minutes. Do a natural pressure release for 10 minutes.

Mint Salmon on Spinach Bed

Serving Size: 4 | Total Time: 15 minutes

1 lb salmon fillets, boneless
1 lb fresh spinach, torn
2 tbsp olive oil

2 garlic cloves, chopped
2 tbsp lemon juice
1 tbsp fresh mint, chopped

Place spinach in the pot, cover with water, and lay the trivet on top. Rub the salmon fillets with half of the olive oil, mint, and garlic. Lay on the trivet. Seal the lid and cook on Steam for 5 minutes on High. Do a quick release. Remove salmon to a serving plate. Drain the spinach. Serve the fish on a bed of spinach. Season with salt and drizzle with lemon juice.

Mustard Salmon

Serving Size: 2 | Total Time: 15 minutes

2 salmon fillets
Salt and pepper to taste
1 rosemary sprig
1 thyme sprig

1 tbsp parsley, chopped
1 tbsp olive oil
2 tsp Dijon mustard

Pour 1 cup of water into your Instant Pot and fit in a trivet. Brush the salmon fillets with mustard and place it skin-side down on the rack. Top with olive oil, rosemary, thyme, and parsley. Season with salt and pepper. Seal the lid, select Manual, and cook for 5 minutes on High. Once done, perform a quick pressure release. Serve.

Salmon Fillets With Orange Sauce

Serving Size: 4 | Total Time: 30 minutes

1 lb salmon fillets	Salt and pepper to taste
1 cup orange juice	1 garlic clove, minced
2 tbsp cornstarch	1 tsp orange zest

Combine orange juice, cornstarch, salt, pepper, garlic, orange zest, and salmon in a large bowl. Cover and let to marinate for 10-15 minutes. Then, add to the pot and seal the lid. Cook on High pressure for 10 minutes. Do a quick pressure release. Serve.

Basil Salmon with Artichokes & Potatoes

Serving Size: 4 | Total Time: 25 minutes

1 cup artichoke hearts, halved	
4 salmon fillets	Salt and pepper to taste
1 lb new potatoes	2 tbsp basil, chopped
2 tbsp butter	

Season the potatoes with salt and pepper. Pour 1 cup of water into your Instant Pot and fit in a trivet. Place the potatoes on the trivet and seal the lid. Select Manual and cook for 2 minutes on High pressure. Once over, perform a quick pressure release and unlock the lid. Sprinkle the salmon and artichokes with salt and pepper. Put them on the trivet with the potatoes, sprinkle with basil, and seal the lid. Select Manual and cook for another 5 minutes on High pressure. Once done, allow a natural release for 10 minutes. Remove potatoes to a bowl and stir in butter. Serve the salmon with artichokes and potatoes.

Spicy Salmon with Oregano & Sea Salt

Serving Size: 4 | Total Time: 50 minutes

1 lb fresh salmon fillets, skin on	
¼ cup olive oil	1 tsp sea salt
½ cup lemon juice	¼ tsp chili flakes
2 garlic cloves, crushed	2 cups fish stock
1 tbsp oregano, chopped	

In a bowl, mix oil, lemon juice, garlic, oregano leaves, salt, and flakes. Brush the fillets with the mixture and refrigerate for 30 minutes. Pour the stock in, and insert the trivet. Pat dry the salmon and place it on the steamer rack. Seal the lid, and cook on Steam for 10 minutes on High. Do a quick release and serve.

Salmon & Broccoli Salad

Serving Size: 2 | Total Time: 15 minutes

2 salmon fillet	½ lemon, juiced
8 oz broccoli	2 tbsp olive oil
2 mini bell peppers, chopped	1 gem lettuce, torn
Salt and pepper to taste	

Pour 1 cup of water into your Instant Pot and fit in a trivet. Chop broccoli into florets and transfer to a greased baking dish with the peppers. Add in the salmon and place the dish on the trivet; sprinkle with salt and pepper.

Seal the lid and cook for 5 minutes on Steam. When ready, perform a quick pressure release. Place the lettuce in a serving bowl, add in broccoli, peppers, olive oil, lemon juice, and salt. Top with the salmon and serve.

Paprika Salmon with Dill Sauce

Serving Size: 2 | Total Time: 15 minutes

2 salmon fillets	Juice from ½ lemon
¼ tsp paprika	Sea salt to taste
Salt and pepper to taste	¼ cup olive oil
¼ cup fresh dill	

In a food processor, blend the olive oil, lemon juice, dill, and seas salt until creamy; reserve. To the cooker, add 1 cup water and place a steamer basket. Arrange salmon fillets skin-side down on the steamer basket. Sprinkle the salmon with paprika, salt, and pepper. Seal the lid and cook for 3 minutes on High Pressure. Release the pressure quickly. Top the fillets with dill sauce to serve.

Chili Steamed Salmon

Serving Size: 2 | Total Time: 25 minutes

2 salmon fillets	1 tsp sesame oil
1 red chili, chopped	Salt and pepper to taste

Pour 1 cup of water into your Instant Pot and fit in a trivet. Sprinkle salmon with salt and pepper and place it on the trivet. Seal the lid and cook for 6 minutes on Steam. Once ready, allow a natural release for 10 minutes and unlock the lid. Drizzle with sesame oil and top with red chili. Serve with lemon wedges.

Salmon with Coconut Rice

Serving Size: 2 | Total Time: 20 minutes

1 oz vegetable soup mix, dried	
2 salmon fillets	½ oz grated ginger
½ cup jasmine rice	1 spring onion, chopped
1 cup coconut milk	Salt and pepper to taste
1 tbsp ghee	

Stir the rice, coconut milk, ghee, ginger, and soup mix in your Instant Pot and fit in a trivet. Season salmon with salt and pepper and place it on the trivet. Seal the lid, select Manual, and cook for 5 minutes on High pressure. Once done, allow a natural release for 10 minutes and unlock the lid. Serve topped with spring onion.

Creamy Wild Salmon

Serving Size: 4 | Total Time: 20 minutes

4 wild sockeye salmon fillets	1 cup heavy cream
1 tsp dill	¼ cup capers
¼ cup lemon juice	2 tbsp butter
4 green onions, sliced	Salt and pepper to taste

Sprinkle salmon fillets with dill, salt, pepper, and lemon juice. Pour 1 cup of water into your Instant Pot and fir in a trivet. Place the fillets on the trivet and seal the lid. Select Manual and cook for 5 minutes on High pressure.

Once done, perform a quick pressure release and unlock the lid. Remove the salmon and discard the water. Set the pot to Sauté and add in the butter to melt it. Cook the green onions for 3-4 minutes and stir in heavy cream and capers; cook for 2-3 minutes. Taste and adjust the seasoning. Pour the sauce over the salmon and serve.

Lemon Salmon with Blue Cheese

Serving Size: 4 | Total Time: 15 minutes

1 lb salmon fillets	1 tbsp blue cheese, crumbled
2 tbsp olive oil	1 lemon, sliced
1 garlic clove, minced	2 sprigs fresh rosemary
1 tbsp lemon juice	Salt and pepper to taste
¼ tsp thyme	

Mix the olive oil, garlic, lemon juice, thyme, salt, pepper, and blue cheese in a bowl. Pour 1 cup of water into your Instant Pot and fit in a trivet. Place salmon on the trivet and top with cheese mixture, lemon slices, and rosemary sprigs. Seal the lid, select Manual, and cook for 5 minutes on High pressure. When done, perform a quick pressure release and unlock the lid. Discard the rosemary sprigs and serve.

Almond-Crusted Salmon Fillets

Serving Size: 2 | Total Time: 25 minutes

2 salmon fillets	1 egg, beaten
½ cup olive oil	¼ cup almonds, ground
Salt to taste	2 tbsp dill, chopped
¼ cup flour	

Warm the olive oil in your Instant Pot on Sauté. Sprinkle salmon with salt. Dip it in the flour, then in beaten eggs, and finally in almonds. Put them in the pot and cook on both sides until browned. Set aside. Pour 1 cup of water into your Instant Pot; fit in a trivet. Place the salmon on the trivet and seal the lid. Select Manual and cook for 4 minutes on High. When done, allow a natural release for 10 minutes and unlock the lid. Serve sprinkled with dill.

Herby Trout with Farro & Green Beans

Serving Size: 4 | Total Time: 20 minutes

1 cup farro	4 tbsp melted butter
2 cups water	½ tbsp sugar
4 skinless trout fillets	½ tbsp lemon juice
8 oz green beans	½ tsp dried rosemary
1 tbsp olive oil	2 garlic cloves, minced
Salt and pepper to taste	½ tsp dried thyme

Pour the farro and water into the pot and mix with green beans and olive oil. Season with salt and black pepper. In another bowl, mix the remaining black pepper and salt, butter, sugar, lemon juice, rosemary, garlic, and thyme.

Coat the trout with the buttery herb sauce. Insert a trivet in the pot and lay the trout fillets on the trivet. Seal the lid and cook on High Pressure for 12 minutes. Do a quick release and serve immediately.

Smoky Salmon with Garlic Mayo Sauce

Serving Size: 6 | Total Time: 25 minutes

2 lb salmon fillets	1 tsp smoked paprika
½ cup mayonnaise	2 tbsp olive oil
1 tbsp lemon juice	2 tbsp chives, chopped
2 garlic cloves, minced	Salt and pepper to taste
1 tsp dill	

Mix the mayonnaise, smoked paprika, lemon juice, garlic, and dill in a bowl. Set aside. Sprinkle salmon with salt and pepper. Warm the olive oil in your Instant Pot on Sauté. Place in salmon and cook for 3-4 minutes per side. Spread the mayonnaise mixture on the salmon and cook for 5 minutes, turning once. Serve topped with chives.

Red Onion Trout Fillets with Olives

Serving Size: 6 | Total Time: 15 minutes+ marinating time

2 lb trout fillets, skin on	2 garlic cloves, crushed
½ cup olive oil	1 tbsp rosemary, chopped
¼ cup apple cider vinegar	Salt and pepper to taste
1 red onion, chopped	3 cups fish stock
1 lemon, sliced	12 black olives

In a bowl, mix oil, apple cider, onion, garlic, rosemary, sea salt, and pepper. Submerge the fillets into this mixture and refrigerate for 1 hour. Pour 4 tbsp of the marinade into your Instant Pot and add in the stock. Add the fish, seal the lid, and cook on High pressure for 4 minutes. Do a quick release. Serve with lemon and olives.

Steamed Trout with Garlic & Fresh Herbs

Serving Size: 2 | Total Time: 25 minutes

2 fresh trout pieces	3 tbsp olive oil
1 tbsp fresh mint, chopped	2 tbsp fresh lemon juice
¼ tsp fresh thyme, chopped	1 tsp sea salt
3 garlic cloves, chopped	1 tbsp chili

In a bowl, mix mint, thyme, garlic, olive oil, lemon juice, chili, and salt. Stir to combine. Spread the abdominal cavity of the fish and brush with the marinade. Brush the fish from the outside and set aside. Insert the trivet in Instant Pot. Pour in 1 cup of water and place the trout on top. Seal the lid and cook on Steam for 15 minutes on High Pressure. Do a quick release. Serve.

Savory Cod Fillets in Maple-Lemon Sauce

Serving Size: 4 | Total Time: 15 minutes

1 lb cod fillets, skinless and boneless	
1 cup maple syrup	1 lemon, juiced
½ cup soy sauce	1 tbsp butter
3 garlic cloves, chopped	

In a bowl, mix maple syrup, soy sauce, garlic, and lemon juice. Stir until combined and set aside. Grease the pot with butter. Place the fillets at the bottom and pour over the maple mixture. Seal the lid and cook on Steam for 8 minutes on High. Release the pressure naturally. Serve.

Trout Fillets with Tri-Color Pasta & Capers

Serving Size: 5 | Total Time: 50 minutes

16 oz tri-color rotini pasta	3 garlic cloves, crushed
6 oz trout fillets	Salt and pepper to taste
1 cup olive oil	2 tbsp parsley, chopped
½ cup lemon juice	Olives, capers for serving
1 tsp rosemary, chopped	

In a bowl, mix oil, lemon juice, rosemary, 2 garlic cloves, black pepper, and salt. Stir well and submerge fillets in this mixture. Refrigerate for 30 minutes. Remove from the fridge. Place the fillets and marinade in the pot. Add in 1 cup of water. Seal the lid and cook on High pressure for 4 minutes. Do a quick release. Add in the pasta and 1 cup of water. Seal the lid and cook for 3 minutes on High. Do a quick release. Serve with capers and parsley.

Lime Trout with Spinach & Tomatoes

Serving Size: 3 | Total Time: 50 minutes

1 lb trout fillets	¼ cup olive oil
6 oz spinach, torn	¼ cup lime juice
2 tomatoes, peeled, diced	Sea salt to taste
3 cups fish stock	2 garlic cloves, crushed

Sprinkle the fillets with sea salt. In a bowl, mix olive oil and lime juice. Stir well and submerge fillets in this mixture. Refrigerate for 30 minutes; then drain the fillets. Reserve the marinade, grease the pot with 3 tbsp of the marinade, and add the fillets and stock. Seal the lid and cook on Steam for 8 minutes on High Pressure. Do a quick release. Remove the fish and set aside.

Add the remaining marinade to the pot. Hit Sauté and add the tomatoes and spinach. Cook until soft. Give it a good stir and remove it to a plate. Add fish, drizzle with tomato sauce and serve warm.

Mediterranean Cod with Cherry Tomatoes

Serving Size: 4 | Total Time: 20 minutes

1 lb cherry tomatoes, halved	Salt and pepper to taste
1 bunch fresh thyme sprigs	1 cup white rice
4 fillets cod	1 cup kalamata olives
2 tbsp olive oil	2 tbsp pickled capers
1 clove garlic, pressed	

Line a parchment paper on the basket of the pot. Place about half the tomatoes in a single layer on the paper. Sprinkle with thyme, reserving some for garnish. Arrange cod fillets on top. Sprinkle with some olive oil. Spread the garlic, pepper, salt, and remaining tomatoes over the fish. In the pot, mix rice and 2 cups of water. Lay a trivet over the rice and water.

Lower steamer basket onto the trivet. Seal the lid, and cook for 7 minutes on Low Pressure. Release the pressure quickly. Remove the steamer basket and trivet from the pot. Use a fork to fluff the rice. Plate the fish fillets and apply a garnish of olives, reserved thyme, remaining olive oil, and capers. Serve with rice.

Buttery Cod with Scallions

Serving Size: 4 | Total Time: 15 minutes

4 cod fillets	1 lemon, cut into wedges
1 fennel bulb, sliced	1 tbsp garlic powder
Salt and pepper to taste	2 tbsp butter, melted
2 tbsp scallions, chopped	

Pour 1 cup of water into your Instant Pot; fit in a trivet. Brush the cod fillets with butter and season with garlic, salt, and pepper. Place them on the trivet and top with fennel slices. Seal the lid, Select Manual, and cook for 5 minutes on High. Once ready, perform a quick pressure release. Sprinkle with scallions and serve with lemon wedges.

Cilantro Cod on Millet with Peppers

Serving Size: 4 | Total Time: 15 minutes

2 tbsp olive oil	1 cup breadcrumbs
1 cup millet	4 tbsp melted butter
1 yellow bell pepper, diced	¼ cup minced fresh cilantro
1 red bell pepper, diced	4 cod fillets
2 cups chicken broth	1 lemon, zested and juiced

Combine oil, millet, yellow and red bell peppers in the pot, and cook for 1 minute on Sauté. Mix in the chicken broth. Place a trivet on to. In a bowl, mix crumbs, butter, cilantro, lemon zest, and juice. Spoon the bread crumb mixture evenly on the cod fillet. Lay the fish on the trivet. Seal the lid and cook on High for 6 minutes. Do a quick release and serve immediately.

Paprika Cod with Orange Sauce

Serving Size: 4 | Total Time: 20 minutes

4 cod fillets	¼ cup dry white wine
2 tsp ginger, grated	½ tsp paprika
1 orange, juiced and zested	½ jalapeno pepper, minced
1 cup fish stock	1 tbsp arrowroot powder
2 tbsp olive oil	Salt and pepper to taste

Sprinkle fish fillets with olive oil, paprika, salt, and pepper. Mix the ginger, orange juice, orange zest, jalapeño pepper, fish stock, and white wine in your Instant Pot. Fit in a trivet. Place the fillets on the trivet and seal the lid. Select Manual and cook for 6 minutes on High.

When done, perform a quick pressure release and unlock the lid. Remove the cod. In a bowl, mix the arrowroot powder with 1 cup of the cooking liquid and pour into the pot. Press Sauté and cook for 4-5 minutes until thickened. Top the fillets with sauce and serve.

Mediterranean Cod with Capers

Serving Size: 4 | Total Time: 15 minutes

4 cod fillets, boneless	Salt and pepper to taste
½ cup white wine	¼ cup capers
1 tsp oregano	

Pour the white wine and ½ cup of water in your Instant Pot and fit in a trivet. Place cod fillets on the trivet.

Sprinkle with oregano, salt, and pepper. Seal the lid, select Steam, and cook for 3 minutes on Low. Once ready, perform a quick pressure release. Top the cod with capers and drizzle with the sauce to serve.

Rosemary Cod with Cherry Tomatoes

Serving Size: 4 | Total Time: 25 minutes

1 ½ lb cod fillets	1 lemon juice
3 tbsp butter	Salt and pepper to taste
1 onion, sliced	2 tbsp rosemary, chopped
2 garlic cloves, minced	1 cup vegetable broth
½ lb cherry tomatoes, halved	

Melt the butter in your Instant Pot on Sauté. Add in the onion, garlic, and rosemary and sauté for 3 minutes, stirring often. Add in the cod fillets and cook for 3-4 minutes on both sides. Sprinkle with salt and pepper, and cook for 3-4 minutes. Pour in vegetable broth and top with cherry tomatoes. Seal the lid, select Manual. Cook for 3 minutes on High pressure. When ready, perform a quick pressure release and unlock the lid. Top the cod with lemon juice and serve with sauce.

Citrus Smelt with Okra & Cherry Tomatoes

Serving Size: 4 | Total Time: 30 minutes + cooling time

1 lb fresh smelt, cleaned, heads removed	
1 cup extra virgin olive oil	1 tsp sea salt
½ cup lemon juice	5 oz okra
¼ cup orange juice	1 carrot, chopped
1 tbsp Dijon mustard	¼ cup green peas
1 tsp rosemary, chopped	5 oz cherry tomatoes, halved
4 tbsp vegetable oil	1 cup fish stock
2 garlic cloves, crushed	

In a bowl, mix olive oil, lemon and orange juices, Dijon mustard, garlic, salt, and rosemary. Stir well and submerge fish in this mixture. Refrigerate for 1 hour. Heat the vegetable oil on Sauté and stir-fry carrot, peas, cherry tomatoes, and okra for 10 minutes. Add in the fish stock.

Place a trivet over the mixture and lower the fish onto the trivet. Pour in the marinade. Seal the lid and cook on Manual for 8 minutes on High. When done, do a quick release. Serve the smelt drizzled with the cooking sauce.

Tuna & Veggie Egg Mix

Serving Size: 4 | Total Time: 25 minutes

2 (5-oz) cans tuna, drained	½ cup vegetable broth
1 carrot, chopped	¾ cup milk
10 oz broccoli, chopped	2 tbsp butter
1 diced onion	½ tsp oregano
2 eggs, beaten	½ rosemary
1 can cream of celery soup	Salt and pepper to taste

Stir the tuna, carrot, broccoli, onion, eggs, celery soup, vegetable broth, milk, butter, oregano, rosemary, salt, and pepper in your Instant Pot and seal the lid. Select Manual and cook for 15 minutes on High. Perform a quick pressure release.

Pizza with Tuna & Goat Cheese

Serving Size: 4 | Total Time: 25 minutes

1 cup canned tuna, oil-free	1 tbsp tomato paste
½ cup mozzarella, shredded	½ tsp dried rosemary
¼ cup goat's cheese	14 oz pizza crust
3 tbsp olive oil	1 cup olives

Grease the bottom of a baking dish with some olive oil. Line with parchment paper. Flour the working surface and roll out the pizza dough to the approximate size of your Instant Pot. Gently fit the dough in the previously prepared baking dish.

In a bowl, combine olive oil, tomato paste, and rosemary. Whisk together and Spread the mixture over the crust. Sprinkle with goat cheese, mozzarella, olives, and tuna.

Place a trivet inside the pot and pour in 1 cup of water. Seal the lid, and cook for 15 minutes on High Pressure. Do a quick release. Cut and serve.

Tuna & Pasta Bake

Serving Size: 4 | Total Time: 25 minutes

28 oz canned cream of mushroom soup	
14 oz canned tuna, drained	Salt and pepper to taste
16 oz penne pasta	4 oz colby cheese, grated
1 cup green beans, frozen	¼ cup breadcrumbs

Mix 3 cups of water with mushroom soup in your Instant Pot. Add in penne and seal the lid. Select Manual and cook for 4 minutes on High pressure.

When ready, perform a quick pressure release and unlock the lid. Press Sauté and stir in tuna, green beans, salt, and pepper. Cook an additional 3 minutes or until everything is heated through and transfer to a baking dish.

Sprinkle with colby cheese and breadcrumbs on top and place under the broiler for 5 minutes until the cheese melts. Plate and serve immediately.

Cheesy Tuna

Serving Size: 4 | Total Time: 20 minutes

1 lb tuna fillets	Salt and pepper to taste
2 tbsp butter	½ cup milk
1 tbsp flour	1 cup mozzarella, grated

Melt the butter in your Instant Pot on Sauté. Place in flour, salt, and pepper and cook for 1 minute. Pour in milk and cook for 3-5 minutes, stirring often.

Stir in mozzarella cheese. Place the tuna fillets in a greased baking pan and pour the cheese sauce over the fish. Cover with aluminum foil.

Clean the pot and add 1 cup of water. Fit in a trivet. Place the pan on the trivet and seal the lid. Select Manual and cook for 5 minutes on High pressure. When ready, perform a quick pressure release and unlock the lid.

Spicy Haddock with Beer & Potatoes

Serving Size: 4 | Total Time: 25 minutes

4 potatoes, cut into matchsticks

8 oz beer	1 tbsp cumin powder
2 eggs	Salt and pepper to taste
1 cup flour	4 haddock fillets
½ tbsp cayenne powder	2 tbsp olive oil

In a bowl, whisk beer and eggs. In another bowl, combine flour, cayenne, cumin, pepper, and salt. Coat each fish piece in the egg mixture, then dredge in the flour mixture, coating all sides. Grease a baking dish with cooking spray.

Place in the fish fillets, pour ¼ cup of water, and grease with cooking spray. Place the potatoes in the pot and cover with water and place a trivet over the potatoes. Lay the baking dish on top and seal the lid. Cook on High Pressure for 15 minutes. Do a quick release. Drain and crush the potatoes with olive oil and serve with the fish.

Haddock with Edamame Soybeans

Serving Size: 4 | Total Time: 25 minutes

1 pack (12-oz) edamame soybeans

1 lb haddock fillets	1 tbsp honey
1 clove garlic, minced	2 tbsp soy sauce
2 tsp grated ginger	Salt and pepper to taste
¼ red chili, sliced	

Pour 1 cup of water into your Instant Pot and fit in a trivet. Mix garlic, ginger, red chili, honey, soy sauce, salt, and pepper in a bowl. Add in the haddock fillets and toss to coat. Spread the fillets on a greased baking pan; scatter edamame soybeans around. Place the pan on the trivet.

Seal the lid. Cook on Steam for 6 minutes on High pressure. When done, allow a natural release for 10 minutes, then perform a quick pressure release. Serve.

Italian Steamed Sea Bream with Lemon

Serving Size: 4 | Total Time: 50 minutes

2 pieces sea bream (2 lb), cleaned

¼ cup olive oil	½ tsp sea salt
¼ cup lemon juice	1 tsp garlic powder
1 tbsp fresh thyme sprigs	4 cups fish stock
1 tbsp Italian seasoning	

In a bowl, mix oil, lemon juice, thyme, Italian seasoning, sea salt, and garlic powder. Brush onto fish and wrap tightly with a plastic foil. Refrigerate for 30 minutes. Pour fish stock into the pot. Set the steamer rack and place the fish on top. Seal the lid. Cook on Steam for 8 minutes on High. Do a quick release. Unwrap the fish. Serve immediately with steam vegetables.

Tilapia with Basil Pesto & Rice

Serving Size: 2 | Total Time: 15 minutes

2 tilapia fillets	½ cup basmati rice
2 tbsp basil pesto	Salt and pepper to taste

Place the rice and 1 cup of water in your Instant Pot and season with salt and pepper; fit in a trivet. Place tilapia fillets in the middle of a parchment paper sheet. Top each fillet with pesto and roll all the edges to form a packet. Place it on the trivet and seal the lid.

Select Manual and cook for 6 minutes on Low pressure. Once ready, perform a quick pressure release. Carefully unlock the lid. Fluff the rice with a fork and transfer to a plate. Top with tilapia and serve.

Tilapia Fillets with Hazelnut Crust

Serving Size: 4 | Total Time: 15 minutes

4 tilapia fillets	½ cup chopped hazelnuts
2 tsp olive oil	2 tbsp parsley, chopped
¼ tsp lemon pepper	Salt and pepper to taste
2 tbsp Dijon mustard	

Pour 1 cup of water into your Instant Pot and fit in a trivet. Mix the olive oil, lemon pepper, and Dijon mustard in a bowl. Rub each fillet with mustard mixture, then roll them in the hazelnuts to coat.

Place the fillets on the trivet, sprinkle with salt and pepper, and seal the lid. Select Manual, and cook for 5 minutes on High. When done, perform a quick pressure release. Unlock the lid. Serve scattered with parsley.

Lemon & Leek Tilapia

Serving Size: 2 | Total Time: 15 minutes

2 tilapia fillets	1 leek, white part, sliced
¼ tsp garlic powder	1 tbsp cold butter, sliced
2 sprigs fresh dill	Salt and pepper to taste
4 slices lemon	

Pour 1 cup of water into your Instant Pot and fit in a trivet. Season the tilapia fillets with salt, pepper, and garlic and place on the trivet. Top each fillet with 1 sprig of dill, 2 lemon slices, leek slices, and butter and seal the lid. Select Manual and cook for 5 minutes on High pressure. When done, perform a quick pressure release.

Thyme Sea Bass with Turnips

Serving Size: 4 | Total Time: 15 minutes

1 white onion, chopped into thin rings

1 lemon, chopped	2 turnips, sliced
4 sea bass fillets	Salt and pepper to taste
4 sprigs thyme	2 tsp olive oil

Add 1 cup water and set a rack into the pot. Line a parchment paper to the bottom of the steamer basket.

Place lemon slices in a single layer on the basket. Arrange fillets on the top of the lemons, cover with onion and thyme sprigs. Top with turnips. Sprinkle pepper, salt, and oil over the mixture. Put a steamer basket onto the rack.

Seal lid and cook on High Pressure for 8 minutes. Release the pressure quickly. Carefully unlock the lid. Serve over the delicate onion rings and thinly turnips.

Stuffed Tench with Herbs & Lemon

Serving Size: 2 | Total Time: 20 minutes

1 tench, cleaned, gutted	1 tsp rosemary, chopped
1 lemon, quartered	¼ tsp dried thyme
2 tbsp olive oil	2 garlic cloves, crushed

In a bowl, mix olive oil, garlic, rosemary, and thyme. Stir to combine. Brush the fish with the previously prepared mixture and stuff with lemon. Pour 4 cups of water into the Instant Pot, set the steamer tray, and place the fish on top. Seal the lid and cook on Steam for 15 minutes on High Pressure. Do a quick release. Unlock the lid. For a crispier taste, briefly brown the fish in a grill pan.

Pollock & Tomato Stew

Serving Size: 4 | Total Time: 30 minutes

1 lb pollock fillets	2 cups fish stock
4 cloves, crushed	Salt and pepper to taste
1 lb tomatoes, chopped	1 onion, finely chopped
2 bay leaves, whole	½ cup olive oil

Heat 2 tbsp olive oil on Sauté. Add onion and sauté for 3 minutes. Add tomatoes and cook until soft. Press Cancel. Add pollock fillets, cloves, bay leaves, stock, salt, and pepper and seal the lid. Cook on High pressure for 15 minutes. When ready, do a quick release. Serve warm.

Dijon Catfish Fillets with White Wine

Serving Size: 3 | Total Time: 15 minutes + cooling time

1 lb catfish fillets	1 tbsp dill, chopped
1 lemon, juiced	1 tbsp rosemary, chopped
½ cup parsley, chopped	2 cups white wine
2 garlic cloves, crushed	2 tbsp Dijon mustard
1 onion, finely chopped	1 cup extra virgin olive oil

In a bowl, mix lemon juice, parsley, garlic, onion, dill, rosemary, wine, mustard, and oil. Stir well. Submerge the fillets and cover with a tight lid. Refrigerate for 1 hour. Insert a trivet in the Instant Pot. Remove the fish from the fridge and place it on the rack. Pour in 1 cup of water and marinade. Seal the lid. Cook on Steam for 8 minutes on High. Release the pressure quickly. Serve immediately.

Chili Steamed Catfish

Serving Size: 4 | Total Time: 70 minutes

1 lb flathead catfish	1 tbsp dried thyme
1 cup orange juice	1 tbsp dried rosemary
¼ cup lemon juice	1 tsp chili flakes
½ cup olive oil	1 tsp sea salt

In a bowl, mix orange juice, lemon juice, olive oil, thyme, rosemary, chili flakes, and salt. Brush the fish with the mixture and refrigerate for 30 minutes. Remove from the fridge, drain, and reserve the marinade. Insert a trivet in the pot. Pour in 1 cup of water and marinade. Place the fish onto the top. Seal the lid and cook on High Pressure for 10 minutes. Do a quick release. Serve immediately.

Mackerel with Potatoes & Spinach

Serving Size: 4 | Total Time: 20 minutes

4 mackerels, skin on	2 garlic cloves, crushed
1 lb spinach, torn	2 tbsp mint leaves, chopped
5 potatoes, peeled, chopped	1 lemon, juiced
3 tbsp olive oil	Sea salt to taste

Heat 2 tbsp of the olive oil on Sauté. Stir-fry garlic for 1 minute. Stir in spinach and salt and cook for 4-5 minutes until wilted; set aside. Make a layer of potatoes in the pot. Top with fish and drizzle with lemon juice, remaining olive oil, and salt. Pour in 1 cup of water, seal the lid, and cook on Steam for 7 minutes on High. When ready, do a quick release. Carefully unlock the lid. Plate the fish and potatoes with spinach and serve topped with mint leaves.

Corn & Mackerel Chowder

Serving Size: 4 | Total Time: 45 minutes

6 oz mackerel fillets	1 lb tomatoes, chopped
½ cup wheat groats, soaked	4 cups fish stock
½ cup kidney beans, soaked	4 tbsp olive oil
¼ cup sweet corn	2 garlic cloves, crushed

Heat olive oil on Sauté. Stir-fry tomatoes and garlic for 5 minutes. Add in stock, corn, kidney beans, and wheat groats. Seal the lid and cook on High Pressure for 25 minutes. Do a quick release. Add mackerel fillets. Seal the lid and cook on Steam for 8 minutes on High. Do a quick release. Serve.

Steamed Halibut Packets

Serving Size: 4 | Total Time: 20 minutes

4 halibut fillets	1 garlic clove, minced
1 lb cherry tomatoes, halved	½ tsp thyme
1 cup olives, chopped	Salt and pepper to taste
2 tbsp olive oil	Arugula for garnish

Pour 1 cup of water into your Instant Pot and insert a trivet. Divide the halibut fillets, cherry tomatoes, and olives between 4 sheets of aluminum foil. Drizzle with olive oil and season with salt, pepper, garlic, and thyme. Close the packets and seal the edges. Place them on the trivet. Secure the lid, select Steam, and cook for 4 minutes on Low. When done, allow a natural release for 10 minutes. Serve scattered with arugula.

Seafood & Fish Stew

Serving Size: 6 | Total Time: 25 minutes

2 lb different fish and seafood	2 tbsp parsley, chopped
3 tbsp olive oil	2 garlic cloves, crushed
2 onions, peeled, chopped	3 cups water
2 carrots, grated	1 tsp sea salt

Heat olive oil on Sauté. Stir-fry onions and garlic for 3-4 minutes, or until translucent. Add carrots, fish and seafood, parsley, water, and salt. Seal the lid, and cook on High Pressure for 10 minutes. Do a quick release. Serve.

Vietnamese Fish & Noodle Soup

Serving Size: 6 | Total Time: 32 minutes

2 tbsp sesame oil	½ tbsp cilantro, chopped
1 lb snapper fillets, chopped	1 tsp chili flakes
12 oz squid	1 garlic clove, sliced
5 oz rice noodles	1 onion, thinly sliced
¼ cup soy sauce	Salt and pepper to taste
¼ tsp thyme	

Heat the sesame oil in your Instant Pot on Sauté. Add in onion, garlic, salt, and pepper and cook for 2 minutes. Stir in fish, squid, chili flakes, and thyme and sauté for 5-6 minutes. Pour in soy sauce and 5 cups of water and seal the lid. Select Manual and cook for 10 minutes.

Once ready, perform a quick pressure release. Press Sauté and add in the rice noodles. Cook for 3-4 minutes until just tender. Ladle into bowls and serve scattered cilantro.

Seafood Medley with Rosemary Rice

Serving Size: 4 | Total Time: 45 minutes

1 lb frozen seafood mix	1 tbsp chopped rosemary
1 cup brown rice	½ tsp salt
1 tbsp calamari ink	3 cups fish stock
2 tbsp extra virgin olive oil	½ lemon
2 garlic cloves, crushed	

Add in seafood mix, rice, calamari ink, olive oil, garlic, rosemary, salt, stock, and lemon, seal the lid and cook on Manual for 25 minutes on High. Release the pressure naturally for 10 minutes. Squeeze lemon juice and serve.

Seafood Chowder with Oyster Crackers

Serving Size: 4 | Total Time: 40 minutes

20 oz canned mussels, drained, liquid reserved
¼ cup grated Pecorino Romano cheese
1 lb potatoes, peeled and cut chunks

2 cups oyster crackers	
2 tbsp olive oil	1 tbsp flour
½ tsp garlic powder	¼ cup white wine
Salt and pepper to taste	1 tsp dried rosemary
2 pancetta slices, chopped	1 bay leaf
2 celery stalks, chopped	1 ½ cups heavy cream
1 medium onion, chopped	2 tbsp chopped fresh chervil

Fry pancetta on Sauté for 5 minutes until crispy. Remove to a paper towel-lined plate and set aside. Sauté the celery and onion in the same fat for 1 minute, stirring until the vegetables soften. Mix in the flour to coat the vegetables. Pour in the wine simmer. Cook for about 1 minute or until reduced by about one-third.

Pour in 1 cup water, the reserved mussel liquid, potatoes, salt, rosemary, and bay leaf. Seal the lid and cook on High Pressure for 4 minutes. Do a natural pressure release for 10 minutes. Stir in mussels and heavy cream.

Press Sauté and bring the soup to a simmer to heat the mussels through. Discard the bay leaf. Top with pancetta, chervil, cheese, and crackers and serve.

Seafood Traditional Spanish Paella

Serving Size: 4 | Total Time: 30 minutes

2 tbsp olive oil	1 ½ tsp sweet paprika
1 onion, chopped	1 tsp turmeric powder
4 garlic cloves, minced	1 lb small clams, scrubbed
½ cup dry white wine	1 lb prawns, deveined
1 cup rice	1 red bell pepper, diced
1 ½ cups chicken stock	1 lemon, cut into wedges

Cook onion and garlic in 1 tbsp of oil on Sauté for 3 minutes. Pour in wine to deglaze, scraping the bottom of the pot of any brown. Cook for 2 minutes until the wine is reduced by half. Add in rice and broth. Stir in paprika, turmeric, and bell pepper. Seal the lid and cook on High Pressure for 10 minutes. Do a quick release. Remove to a plate and wipe the pot clean. Heat the remaining oil on Sauté. Cook clams and prawns for 6 minutes until the shrimp are pink. Discard unopened clams. Arrange seafood and lemon wedges over paella to serve.

Easy Seafood Paella

Serving Size: 4 | Total Time: 20 minutes

1 cup tiger prawns, peeled and deveined
1 lb mussels, cleaned and debearded
½ tsp guindilla (cayenne pepper)

½ lb clams	2 cups clam juice
2 tbsp olive oil	¾ cup green peas, frozen
1 onion, chopped	1 tbsp parsley, chopped
2 garlic cloves, minced	1 tbsp turmeric
1 red bell pepper, chopped	1 whole lemon, quartered
1 cup rice	

Warm the olive oil in your Instant Pot on Sauté. Add in prawns, red pepper, onion, and garlic and cook for 3 minutes. Stir in rice for 1 minute and pour in clam juice, turmeric, mussels, and clams. Seal the lid, select Manual, and cook for 5 minutes on High pressure. When ready, perform a quick pressure release and unlock the lid. Stir in green peas and guindilla for 3-4 minutes. Top with lemon quarters and parsley. Serve immediately.

Seafood Pilaf

Serving Size: 6 | Total Time: 35 minutes

1 lb chopped catfish fillets	½ tsp oregano
2 cups mussels and shrimp	1 red bell pepper, diced
4 tbsp olive oil	1 green bell pepper, diced
1 onion, diced	2 cups Jasmine rice
2 garlic cloves, minced	A few saffron threads
½ tsp cayenne pepper	3 cups fish stock
½ tsp basil	Salt and pepper to taste

Warm the olive oil in your Instant Pot on Sauté. Add in onion, garlic, and bell peppers and cook for 4 minutes. Add in catfish, rice, and saffron and cook for another 2 minutes. Add mussels, shrimps, cayenne pepper, basil, oregano, stock, salt, and pepper, stir, and seal the lid. Select Manual and cook for 6 minutes. When done, allow a natural release for 10 minutes. Serve.

Seafood Hot Pot with Rice

Serving Size: 4 | Total Time: 20 minutes

½ lb shrimp, deveined	1 carrot, shredded
½ lb scallops	1 cup basmati rice
2 tbsp butter	Salt and pepper to taste
1 onion, chopped	2 cups fish broth
1 bell pepper, sliced	1 lemon, sliced

Melt the butter in your Instant Pot on Sauté. Add in onion, bell pepper, and carrot and cook for 3-4 minutes. Stir in rice, shrimp, scallops, salt, pepper, and fish broth and seal the lid. Press Manual and cook for 6 minutes on High pressure. Once done, use a quick pressure release and unlock the lid. Top with lemon slices and serve.

Spicy Pasta with Seafood

Serving Size: 4 | Total Time: 20 minutes

2 tbsp olive oil	Salt and pepper to taste
1 onion, diced	16 oz scallops
16 oz penne	¼ cup Parmesan, grated
24 oz arrabbiata sauce	Basil leaves for garnish
3 cups chicken broth	

Heat oil on Sauté. Stir-fry onion for 3 minutes. Stir in penne, arrabbiata sauce, salt, pepper, and 2 cups of broth. Seal the lid and cook for 6 minutes on High Pressure. Do a quick release. Remove to a plate. Pour the remaining broth and add scallops. Press Sauté and cook for 4 minutes. Mix in the pasta and serve topped with Parmesan cheese and basil leaves.

Creole Seafood Gumbo

Serving Size: 4 | Total Time: 20 minutes

12 oz pollock filets, cut into chunks	
1 lb medium raw shrimp, deveined	
Salt and pepper to taste	1 cup chicken broth
1 tbsp creole seasoning	14 oz diced tomatoes
1 olive oil	¼ cup tomato paste
1 yellow onion, diced	2 bay leaves
2 celery ribs, diced	6 oz okra, trimmed

Sprinkle the pollock with salt, pepper, and creole seasoning. Warm the olive oil in your Instant Pot on Sauté. Add in the fish and cook for 4 minutes. Set aside. Add onions and celery to the pot and cook for 2 minutes.

Put in chicken broth, tomatoes, tomato paste, bay leaves, okra, shrimp, and cooked fish and seal the lid. Select Manual and cook for 5 minutes on High pressure. When ready, perform a quick pressure release. Serve.

Shrimp with Chickpeas & Olives

Serving Size: 6 | Total Time: 25 minutes

2 lb shrimp, deveined	½ cup olives, pitted
2 garlic cloves, minced	Salt and pepper to taste
1 carrot, chopped	1 cup tomatoes, chopped
1 cup chickpeas, soaked	2 tbsp olive oil
3 cups fish broth	1 onion, chopped

Warm the olive oil in your Instant Pot on Sauté. Add in onion, garlic, carrot, salt, and pepper and cook for 4 minutes until soft. Add tomatoes, chickpeas, olives and broth. Simmer for 5 minutes. Add the shrimp and toss to coat in the sauce. Seal the lid and cook on High Pressure for 4 minutes. Release the pressure naturally. Serve warm.

Shrimp Boil with Chorizo Sausages

Serving Size: 4 | Total Time: 15 minutes

3 red potatoes	2 tbsp of seafood seasoning
3 ears corn, cut into rounds	Salt to taste
1 cup white wine	1 lemon, cut into wedges
4 chorizo sausages, chopped	¼ cup butter, melted
1 lb shrimp, deveined	

Add potatoes, corn, wine, chorizo, shrimp, seafood seasoning, and salt. Do not stir. Add in 2 cups of water. Seal the lid and cook for 2 minutes on High Pressure. Release the pressure quickly. Drain the mixture through a colander. Transfer to a plate. Serve with melted butter and lemon wedges.

Party Shrimp with & Rice Veggies

Serving Size: 4 | Total Time: 36 minutes

¼ cup olive oil	1 cup rice
1 onion, chopped	¼ cup green peas
1 red bell pepper, diced	2 cups fish broth
2 garlic cloves, minced	1 lb shrimp, deveined
1 tsp turmeric	Chopped fresh parsley
Salt and pepper to taste	1 lemon, cut into wedges

Warm oil on Sauté. Add in bell pepper and onion and garlic and cook for 5 minutes until fragrant. Season with pepper, salt, and turmeric and cook for 1 minute. Stir in fish broth and rice. Seal the lid and cook on High Pressure for 15 minutes. Release the pressure quickly. Stir in green peas and shrimp and cook for 5 minutes on Sauté. Serve with parsley and lemon.

Quick Shrimp Gumbo with Sausage

Serving Size: 4 | Total Time: 30 minutes

1 lb jumbo shrimp	2 garlic cloves, minced
2 tbsp olive oil	1 serrano pepper, minced
1/3 cup flour	2 ½ cups chicken broth
1 ½ tsp Cajun seasoning	6 oz andouille sausage, sliced
1 onion, chopped	2 green onions, finely sliced
1 red bell pepper, chopped	Salt and pepper to taste
2 celery stalks, chopped	

Heat olive oil on Sauté. Whisk in the flour with a wooden spoon and cook 3 minutes, stirring constantly. Stir in Cajun seasoning, onion, bell pepper, celery, garlic, and serrano pepper for about 5 minutes. Pour in the chicken broth, ¾ cup water, and andouille sausage. Seal and cook for 6 minutes on High Pressure. Do a natural pressure for 5 minutes. Stir the shrimp into the gumbo to eat it up for 3 minutes. Adjust the seasoning. Ladle the gumbo into bowls and garnish with the green onions.

Hot Shrimp & Potato Chowder

Serving Size: 4 | Total Time: 35 minutes

4 slices pancetta, chopped	1 tsp dried rosemary
4 tbsp minced garlic	Salt and pepper to taste
1 onion, chopped	1 lb jumbo shrimp, deveined
2 potatoes, chopped	1 tbsp olive oil
16 oz canned corn kernels	½ tsp red chili flakes
4 cups vegetable stock	¾ cup heavy cream

Fry pancetta for 5 minutes until crispy on Sauté and set aside. Add in onion and stir-fry for 3 minutes. Pour in the potatoes, corn, stock, rosemary, salt, and pepper. Seal the lid and cook on High Pressure for 10 minutes. Do a quick pressure release. Carefully unlock the lid.

In a bowl, toss the shrimp in the garlic, salt, olive oil, and flakes. Remove the chowder from the pot to a serving bowl. Wipe the pot clean and fry shrimp for 3-4 minutes until pink. Mix in the heavy cream and cook for 2 minutes. Add shrimp to chowder and garnish with the reserved pancetta. Ladle into bowls and serve.

Shrimp with Okra & Brussels Sprouts

Serving Size: 4 | Total Time: 40 minutes

1 lb large shrimp, cleaned, rinsed	
6 oz Brussels sprouts	½ tsp cayenne pepper
4 oz okra, whole	Salt and pepper to taste
2 carrots, chopped	2 tbsp olive oil
2 cups vegetable broth	¼ cup balsamic vinegar
2 tomatoes, diced	1 tbsp rosemary, chopped
2 tbsp tomato paste	2 tbsp sour cream

Mix olive oil, vinegar, rosemary, salt, and pepper in a large bowl. Stir the shrimp into the mixture. Toss well to coat. Mix tomatoes, tomato paste, and cayenne pepper in the pressure cooker. Cook on Sauté for 5 minutes, stirring constantly. Set aside. Pour broth, Brussels sprouts, carrots, and okra into the pot. Cook on High pressure for 15 minutes. Do a quick release.

Remove the vegetables and add the shrimp to the remaining broth in the pot. Press Sauté and cook for 5 minutes. Add in the cooked vegetables. Cook for 2-3 minutes, stirring constantly. Stir in sour cream and serve.

Spinach & Shrimp Fusilli

Serving Size: 4 | Total Time: 15 minutes

1 ¼ lb shrimp, deveined	1/3 cup tomato puree
2 tbsp melted butter	½ tsp red chili flakes
2 garlic cloves, minced	1 tsp lemon zest
¼ cup white wine	1 tbsp lemon juice
10 oz fusilli pasta	6 cups spinach

On Sauté, pour the white wine and bring to simmer for 2 minutes to reduce the liquid by half. Stir in the fusilli pasta, 2 ½ cups water, garlic, puréed tomato, shrimp, melted butter, and chili flakes. Seal the lid. Cook for 5 minutes on High pressure. Do a quick release. Stir in lemon zest, juice, and spinach until wilted and soft. Serve.

Jalapeño Shrimp with Herbs & Lemon

Serving Size: 4 | Total Time: 25 minutes

1 lb shrimp, deveined	½ tsp basil, chopped
½ cup olive oil	½ tsp sage, chopped
1 tsp garlic powder	½ tsp salt
1 tsp rosemary, chopped	1 tsp jalapeño pepper
1 tsp thyme, chopped	

Pour 1 cup of water into the inner pot. In a bowl, mix oil, garlic, rosemary, thyme, basil, sage, salt, and jalapeño pepper. Brush the marinade over the shrimp. Insert a steamer rack in the pot and arrange the shrimp on top.

Seal the lid and cook on Steam for 3 minutes on High. Release the steam naturally for 10 minutes. Press Sauté and stir-fry for 2 more minutes or until golden brown.

Creole Shrimp with Okra

Serving Size: 2 | Total Time: 10 minutes

1 lb shrimp, deveined	½ tsp cayenne pepper
6 oz okra, trimmed	½ tbsp Creole seasoning
2 tbsp olive oil	Salt and pepper to taste
1 tsp garlic powder	

Pour 1 cup water into your Instant Pot and fit in a trivet. In a baking dish, combine shrimp, okra, olive oil, garlic powder, cayenne pepper, Creole seasoning, salt, and pepper and mix to combine. Place the dish on the trivet. Seal the lid and cook for 2 minutes on Steam on High. When ready, perform a quick pressure release. Serve.

Rich Shrimp Risotto

Serving Size: 4 | Total Time: 30 minutes

¾ cup Pecorino Romano cheese, grated	
1 lb shrimp, deveined	2 tbsp dry white wine
4 tbsp butter	4 cups fish broth
2 garlic cloves, minced	½ tsp Italian seasoning
1 yellow onion, chopped	2 tbsp heavy cream
1 ½ cups Arborio rice	Salt and pepper to taste

Melt half of the butter in your Instant Pot. Add in garlic and onion and cook for 4 minutes. Stir in rice and cook for another minute. Mix in white wine and cook for 3 minutes until the wine evaporates. Pour in 3 cups of fish broth and Italian seasoning and seal the lid. Select Manual and cook for 10 minutes on High pressure.

When ready, perform a quick pressure release and unlock the lid. Add in shrimp and the remaining broth and cook for 4-5 minutes on Sauté. Stir in Pecorino Romano cheese, heavy cream, and the remaining butter.

Tangy Shrimp Curry

Serving Size: 4 | Total Time: 15 minutes

1 lb shrimp, deveined	1 tsp cayenne pepper
2 tbsp sesame oil	1 tbsp lime juice
1 onion, chopped	1 cup coconut milk
½ tsp fresh ginger, grated	1 tbsp curry powder
1 garlic clove, minced	Salt and pepper to taste

Heat the sesame oil in your Instant Pot on Sauté and cook the onion, garlic, and ginger for 3-4 minutes. Stir in curry powder, cayenne pepper, salt, and pepper and cook for 3 minutes. Pour in coconut milk, shrimp, and 1 cup of water and seal the lid. Select Manual and cook for 4 minutes on Low pressure. Once done, perform a quick pressure release. Drizzle with lime juice and serve.

Chinese Shrimp with Green Beans

Serving Size: 2 | Total Time: 20 minutes

1 tbsp sesame oil	2 cups vegetable stock
1 lb shrimp, deveined	3 tbsp soy sauce
½ cup diced onion	2 tbsp rice wine vinegar
2 cloves garlic, minced	10 oz lo mein egg noodles
1 carrot, cut into strips	½ tsp toasted sesame seeds
½ lb green beans, chopped	Sea Salt and pepper to taste

Warm oil on Sauté. Stir-fry the shrimp for 5 minutes; set aside. Add in garlic and onion and cook for 3 minutes until fragrant. Mix in soy sauce, carrot, stock, beans, and rice wine vinegar. Add in noodles and ensure they are covered. Season with pepper and salt. Seal the lid and cook on High Pressure for 5 minutes. Release the pressure quickly. Place the main in 2 plates. Add the reserved shrimp, sprinkle with sesame seeds, and serve.

Cheesy Shrimp Scampi

Serving Size: 4 | Total Time: 10 minutes

1 lb shrimp, deveined	½ cup dry white wine
2 tbsp olive oil	1 tsp red chili pepper
1 clove garlic, minced	1 tbsp parsley, chopped
1 tbsp tomato paste	Salt and pepper to taste
10 oz canned tomatoes, diced	1 cup Grana Padano, grated

Warm the olive oil in your Instant Pot on Sauté. Add in garlic and cook for 1 minute. Stir in shrimp, tomato paste, tomatoes, white wine, chili pepper, parsley, salt, pepper, and ¼ cup of water and seal the lid. Select Manual and cook for 3 minutes on High pressure. Once done, perform a quick pressure release and unlock the lid. Serve garnished with Grana Padano cheese.

Indian Prawn Curry

Serving Size: 4 | Total Time: 30 minutes

1 ½ lb prawns, deveined	2 tsp ground coriander
2 tbsp ghee	2 tbsp curry paste
2 garlic cloves, minced	2 cups coconut milk
1 onion, chopped	1 cup tomatoes, chopped
1 tsp ginger, grated	2 habanero peppers, minced
½ tsp ground turmeric	Salt and pepper to taste
1 tsp red chili powder	1 tbsp fresh lemon juice
2 tsp ground cumin	

Melt the ghee in your Instant Pot on Sauté. Add in garlic, onion, and ginger and cook for 4 minutes. Stir in the turmeric, chili powder, cumin, coriander, and curry paste and cook for 1 more minute. Stir in coconut milk, prawns, tomatoes, habanero peppers, salt, and pepper.

Seal the lid. Select Manual and cook for 5 minutes on Low. Once ready, allow a natural release for 10 minutes, then perform a quick pressure release, and unlock the lid. Top with lemon juice and serve.

Butter & Wine Lobster Tails

Serving Size: 4 | Total Time: 10 minutes

1 lb lobster tails, cut in half	½ cup butter, melted
½ cup white wine	1 tsp red pepper flakes

Pour ½ cup of water and white wine in your Instant Pot and fit in a trivet. Place lobster tails on the trivet and seal the lid. Select Steam and cook for 5 minutes on Low. When ready, perform a quick pressure release. Drizzle with butter and top with red pepper flakes to serve.

Ginger & Garlic Crab

Serving Size: 4 | Total Time: 15 minutes

1 lb crabs, halved	1-inch ginger, sliced
2 tbsp butter	1 lemongrass stalk
1 shallot, chopped	Salt and pepper to taste
1 garlic cloves, minced	1 lemon, sliced
1 cup coconut milk	

Melt the butter in your Instant Pot on Sauté. Place in shallot, garlic, and ginger and cook for 3 minutes. Pour in coconut milk, crabs, lemongrass, salt, and pepper and seal the lid. Select Manual and cook for 6 minutes on High pressure. Once ready, perform a quick pressure release and unlock the lid. Serve with lemon slices.

Herby Crab Legs with Lemon

Serving Size: 4 | Total Time: 10 minutes

3 lb king crab legs, broken in half	
1 tsp rosemary	¼ cup butter, melted
1 tsp thyme	Salt and pepper to taste
1 tsp dill	1 lemon, cut into wedges

Pour 1 cup of water into your Instant Pot and fit in a trivet. Season the crab legs with rosemary, thyme, dill, salt, and pepper; place on the trivet. Seal the lid, select Manual, and cook for 3 minutes. When ready, perform a quick pressure release. Remove crab legs to a bowl and drizzle with melted butter. Serve with lemon wedges.

Black Squid Ink Tagliatelle

Serving Size: 4 | Total Time: 25 minutes

18 oz squid ink tagliatelle, cooked	
1 lb fresh seafood mix	1 tbsp parsley, chopped
¼ cup olive oil	1 tsp rosemary, chopped
4 garlic cloves, crushed	½ tbsp white wine

Heat 3 tbsp olive oil on Sauté and stir-fry the garlic for 1-2 minutes until fragrant. Add seafood, parsley, and rosemary and stir. Add the remaining oil, wine, and ½ cup of water. Seal the lid and cook on High Pressure for 4 minutes. Do a quick release and set aside. Open the lid, add the pasta, and stir. Serve hot.

Crab Pilaf with Broccoli & Asparagus

Serving Size: 4 | Total Time: 30 minutes

½ lb asparagus, trimmed and cut into 1-inch pieces
½ lb broccoli florets
1 cup rice
Salt to taste
1/3 cup white wine
2 tbsp olive oil
2 cups vegetable stock
1 small onion, chopped
8 oz lump crabmeat

Heat oil on Sauté and cook the onion for 3 minutes until soft. Stir in rice and cook for 1 minute. Pour in the wine. Cook for 2 to 3 minutes, stirring until the liquid has almost evaporated. Add vegetable stock and salt; stir.

Place a trivet on top. Arrange the broccoli and asparagus on the trivet. Seal the lid and cook on High Pressure for 8 minutes. Do a quick release. Remove the vegetables to a bowl. Fluff the rice with a fork and add in the crabmeat, heat for a minute. Taste and adjust the seasoning. Serve immediately topped with broccoli and asparagus.

Red Wine Squid

Serving Size: 4 | Total Time: 25 minutes

2 lb squid, chopped
28 oz can crushed tomatoes
2 tbsp olive oil
1 red onion, sliced
Salt and pepper to taste
2 garlic cloves, minced
½ cup red wine
1 tsp Italian seasoning
½ fennel bulb, sliced
½ cup parsley, chopped

Mix the olive oil, squid, salt, and pepper in a bowl. Pour the red wine, tomatoes, onion, garlic, Italian seasoning, and fennel in your Instant Pot and fit in a steamer basket. Put in the squid and seal the lid. Select Manual and cook for 4 minutes on High pressure. When ready, allow a natural release for 10 minutes, then perform a quick pressure release. Serve scattered with parsley.

White Wine Marinated Squid Rings

Serving Size: 3 | Total Time: 25 minutes + cooling time

1 lb fresh squid rings
2 cups fish stock
1 cup dry white wine
¼ tsp red pepper flakes
1 cup olive oil
¼ tsp dried oregano
2 garlic cloves, crushed
1 tbsp rosemary, chopped
1 lemon, juiced
1 tsp sea salt

In a bowl, mix wine, olive oil, lemon juice, garlic, flakes, oregano, rosemary, and salt. Submerge squid rings in this mixture and cover with a lid. Refrigerate for 1 hour. Remove the squid from the fridge and place it in the pot along with stock and half of the marinade. Seal the lid. Cook on High Pressure for 6 minutes. Release the pressure naturally for 10 minutes. Transfer the rings to a plate and drizzle with some marinade to serve.

Mussels With Lemon & White Wine

Serving Size: 5 | Total Time: 10 minutes

2 lb mussels, cleaned and debearded
1 cup white wine
1 tsp garlic powder
½ cup water
Juice from 1 lemon

In the pot, mix garlic powder, water, and wine. Put the mussels into the steamer basket; rounded-side should be placed facing upwards to fit as many as possible.

Insert a rack into the cooker and lower the steamer basket onto the rack. Seal the lid and cook on Low Pressure for 1 minute. Release the pressure quickly. Remove unopened mussels. Coat the mussels with the wine mixture and lemon juice and serve.

Chili Squid

Serving Size: 4 | Total Time: 35 minutes

1 lb squid, sliced into rings
¼ tsp smoked paprika
1 tsp onion powder
1 tbsp lemon juice
2 tbsp flour
1 cup vegetable broth
1 garlic clove, minced
2 tbsp butter
1 tbsp chives
Salt and pepper to taste
¼ tsp chili pepper, chopped
2 tbsp parsley, chopped

Mix the onion powder, smoked paprika, flour, garlic, chives, chili pepper, salt, and pepper in a bowl. Add in the squid slices and toss to coat. Let sit for 10 minutes.

Melt the butter in your Instant Pot on Sauté. Place in the squid mixture and cook for 3-4 minutes. Pour in the vegetable broth and seal the lid. Cook on Manual for 12 minutes on High. Once done, perform a quick pressure release and unlock the lid. Serve sprinkled with parsley.

Spicy Mussels & Anchovies with Rice

Serving Size: 4 | Total Time: 40 minutes

1 cup rice
¼ cup capers
6 oz mussels
Salt and chili pepper to taste
1 onion, finely chopped
3 tbsp olive oil
1 garlic clove, crushed
4 salted anchovies
1 tbsp dried rosemary

Add rice to the pot and pour 2 cups of water. Seal the lid and cook on Manual for 18 minutes on High. Do a quick release. Remove the rice and set aside. Grease the pot with oil, and stir-fry garlic and onion for 2 minutes on Sauté. Add mussels and rosemary. Cook for 10 more minutes. Stir in rice and season with salt and chili pepper. Serve with anchovies and capers.

Beer-Steamed Mussels

Serving Size: 4 | Total Time: 15 minutes

3 lb mussels, debearded
2 tbsp parsley, chopped
4 tbsp butter
1 cup beer
1 shallot, chopped
1 cup chicken stock
2 garlic cloves, minced

Melt butter in your Instant Pot on Sauté. Add in shallot and garlic and cook for 2 minutes. Stir in beer and cook for 1 minute. Mix in stock and mussels and seal the lid.

Select Manual and cook for 3 minutes on High pressure. Once ready, perform a quick pressure release. Discard unopened mussels. Serve sprinkled with parsley.

Basil Clams with Garlic & White Wine

Serving Size: 4 | Total Time: 15 minutes

1 lb clams, scrubbed	½ cup white wine
2 tbsp butter	½ cup chicken stock
4 green garlic, chopped	Salt and pepper to taste
1 tbsp lemon juice	2 tbsp basil, chopped

Melt the butter in your Instant Pot on Sauté. Add in the garlic and clams and cook for 3-4 minutes. Stir in lemon juice and chicken stock, white wine, salt, and pepper and seal the lid. Select Manual and cook for 3 minutes on High pressure. Once done, perform a quick pressure release and unlock the lid. Discard unopened clams. Serve topped with basil.

Saucy Clams with Herbs

Serving Size: 4 | Total Time: 15 minutes

1 lb clams, scrubbed	28 oz can crushed tomatoes
2 tsp olive oil	½ tsp basil
2 garlic cloves, minced	1 tsp rosemary
1 onion, chopped	½ tsp oregano
2 celery stalks, diced	Salt and pepper to taste
1 bell pepper, diced	¼ tsp chili pepper
1 tbsp tomato paste	

Warm the olive oil in your Instant Pot on Sauté. Place in garlic, onion, celery, and bell pepper and cook for 3-4 minutes. Add in tomato paste and cook for another 1 minute. Stir in clams, tomatoes, basil, rosemary, oregano, salt, pepper, and chili pepper and seal the lid. Select Manual and cook for 2 minutes on High pressure. Once done, perform a quick pressure release and unlock the lid. Discard unopened clams. Serve with cooked rice.

Clam & Corn Chowder

Serving Size: 4 | Total Time: 30 minutes

2 tbsp olive oil	1 red bell pepper, diced
1 onion, chopped	Salt and pepper to taste
3 potatoes, cubed	4 cups chicken broth
4 cups corn kernels	1 cup milk
12 oz canned clams, chopped	1 tbsp flour
1 green bell pepper, diced	3 tbsp butter

Warm the olive oil in your Instant Pot on Sauté. Add in onion and bell peppers and cook for 3-4 minutes until tender. Stir in potatoes, corn kernels, clams with their juice, and chicken broth.

Seal the lid, select Manual, and cook for 12 minutes on High. Once ready, perform a quick pressure release. Combine milk with flour and pour it into the pot. Press Sauté and stir in butter. Let simmer for 3-4 minutes.

Lime & Honey Scallops

Serving Size: 2 | Total Time: 15 minutes

1 lb sea scallops, shells removed

1 cup water	3 tbsp honey
1 tbsp olive oil	1 lime, juiced and zested

½ cup soy sauce	½ tsp garlic powder
½ tsp ground ginger	Salt to taste

Pour 1 cup of water into your Instant Pot and fit in a trivet. Place scallops, olive oil, honey, soy sauce, ginger, garlic powder, lime zest, and salt in a small pan and put it on the trivet. Seal the lid and cook for 6 minutes on Steam. Once ready, perform a quick pressure release and unlock the lid. Serve drizzled with lime juice.

Octopus & Shrimp with Collard Greens

Serving Size: 4 | Total Time: 30 minutes

6 oz octopus, cut into bite-sized pieces	
1 lb collard greens, chopped	4 tbsp olive oil
1 lb shrimp, whole	3 garlic cloves
1 tomato, chopped	2 tbsp parsley, chopped
3 cups fish stock	1 tsp sea salt

Place shrimp and octopus in the pot. Add tomato and fish stock. Seal the lid and cook on High Pressure for 15 minutes. Do a quick release. Remove shrimp and octopus. Drain the liquid. Heat olive oil on Sauté and add garlic and parsley and cook for 1 minute. Add in collard greens, season with salt, and simmer for 5 minutes. Serve with shrimp and octopus.

Galician-Style Octopus

Serving Size: 6 | Total Time: 30 minutes

1 lb potatoes, sliced into rounds	
2 lb whole octopus, cleaned and sliced	
1 tbsp Spanish paprika	Salt and pepper to taste
3 tbsp olive oil	

Place the potatoes in your Instant Pot and cover them with water. Place a trivet over the potatoes. Season the octopus with salt and pepper and place it onto the trivet. Seal the lid, select Manual, and cook for 15 minutes.

Once done, perform a quick pressure release and unlock the lid. Remove the octopus and let cool, then slice it into slices about half-inch thick. Transfer the sliced potatoes to a baking sheet and arrange octopus slices over the potatoes. Drizzle with olive oil and place under the broiler for 5 minutes. Sprinkle with paprika and serve.

White Wine Oysters

Serving Size: 4 | Total Time: 10 minutes

2 lb in-shell oysters, cleaned	1 garlic clove, minced
1 cup vegetable broth	Salt and pepper to taste
4 tbsp white wine	4 tbsp butter, melted
2 tbsp thyme, chopped	

Place the vegetable broth, oysters, white wine, garlic, salt, and pepper in your Instant Pot and seal the lid. Select Manual and cook for 3 minutes on High pressure. Once done, perform a quick pressure release and unlock the lid. Drain the oysters, drizzle with the melted butter, and top with thyme to serve.

PASTA & RICE

Fusilli with Chicken Bolognese Sauce

Serving Size: 4 | Total Time: 50 minutes

2 tbsp olive oil	¼ tbsp red pepper flakes
6 oz bacon, cubed	1 ½ lb ground chicken
1 onion, minced	½ cup white wine
1 carrot, minced	1 cup milk
1 celery stalk, minced	1 cup chicken broth
2 garlic cloves, crushed	Salt to taste
¼ cup tomato paste	1 lb fusilli pasta

Warm olive oil on Sauté. Add in bacon and fry for 5 minutes. Add celery, carrot, garlic, and onion and cook for 5 minutes. Mix in red pepper flakes and tomato paste, and cook for 2 minutes. Break chicken into small pieces and place them in the pot. Cook for 10 minutes as you stir until browned. Pour in the wine and simmer for 2 minutes. Add in chicken broth, salt, and milk.

Seal the lid and cook for 15 minutes on High Pressure. Release the pressure quickly. Add in the fusilli and stir. Seal the lid, and cook on High Pressure for another 5 minutes. Release the pressure quickly. Serve.

Four-Cheese Traditional Italian Pasta

Serving Size: 6 | Total Time: 20 minutes

¼ cup goat cheese, chopped	¼ cup butter, softened
¼ cup grated Pecorino	1 tbsp Italian seasoning mix
½ cup grated Parmesan	1 cup vegetable broth
1 cup heavy cream	1 lb tagliatelle pasta
½ cup grated gouda cheese	

Place the tagliatelle in your Instant Pot and cover with water. Seal the lid and cook on Manual for 4 minutes. Drain and set aside. In the pot, mix goat cheese, heavy cream, gouda cheese, broth, butter, and Italian seasoning. Press Sauté and cook for 4 minutes. Stir in the tagliatelle and Pecorino cheese and let simmer for 2 minutes. Top with Parmesan cheese and serve.

Tomato & Spinach Sausage Spaghetti

Serving Size: 4 | Total Time: 25 minutes

2 tbsp olive oil	1 tbsp dried oregano
½ cup onion, chopped	1 tbsp Italian seasoning
1 garlic clove, minced	1 jalapeño pepper, minced
1 lb pork sausage meat	1 tbsp salt
14-oz can diced tomatoes	8 oz spaghetti, halved
½ cup sun-dried tomatoes	1 cup spinach

Warm olive oil on Sauté. Add in onion and garlic and cook for 2 minutes. Stir in sausage meat and cook for 5 minutes. Stir in jalapeño pepper, 4 cups water, sun-dried tomatoes, Italian seasoning, oregano, diced tomatoes, and salt. Mix spaghetti and press to submerge into the sauce. Seal the lid and cook on High Pressure for 5 minutes. Release the pressure quickly. Stir in spinach simmer on Sauté for 3 minutes until spinach is wilted. Serve warm.

Parmesan-Coated Squash with Linguine

Serving Size: 4 | Total Time: 25 minutes

1 yellow squash, peeled and sliced	
1 cup flour	1 lb linguine pasta
Salt to taste	24 oz canned tomato sauce
2 eggs	2 tbsp olive oil
1 cup breadcrumbs	2 tbsp fresh basil, chopped
½ cup grated Parmesan	

Break the linguine in half. Put it in the pot and add enough water to cover and salt. Seal the lid and cook on High Pressure for 5 minutes. Quickly release the pressure. Combine flour and salt in a bowl. In another bowl, whisk the eggs and 2 tbsp of water. In a third bowl, mix the breadcrumbs and Parmesan cheese. Coat each squash slice in the flour. Shake off the excess flour.

Dip in the egg wash, and dredge in the breadcrumbs. Heat oil on Sauté and fry breaded squash until crispy. Remove linguine to a serving bowl and mix in the tomato sauce and sprinkle with fresh basil. Serve the squash with the linguine on the side.

Primavera Egg Noodles

Serving Size: 4 | Total Time: 20 minutes

1 lb asparagus, trimmed	2 ½ cups vegetable stock
2 cups broccoli florets	½ cup heavy cream
3 tbsp olive oil	1 cup small tomatoes, halved
Salt to taste	¼ cup chopped basil
10 oz egg noodles	½ cup grated Parmesan
2 garlic cloves, minced	

Pour the noodles, vegetable stock, and 2 tbsp olive oil, garlic, and salt in your Instant Pot. Place a trivet over. Combine asparagus, broccoli, remaining olive oil, stock, and salt in a bowl. Place the vegetables on the trivet. Seal the lid. Cook on Manual for 12 minutes.

Do a quick release. Remove the vegetables. Stir the heavy cream and tomatoes in the pasta. Press Sauté and simmer the cream for 2 minutes. Mix in asparagus and broccoli. Garnish with basil and Parmesan and serve.

Chili Mac & Cheese

Serving Size: 6 | Total Time: 15 minutes

2 cups Pecorino Romano cheese, grated	
12 oz macaroni	1 tbsp chili powder
4 cups cold water	4 tbsp butter
Salt and pepper to taste	1 ½ cups milk
2 eggs	4 cups cheddar, grated

Add salt, water, and macaroni. Seal the lid and cook for 4 minutes on High Pressure. Take a bowl and beat eggs, chili powder, and black pepper to mix well. Release the pressure quickly. Add butter to the pasta and stir until it melts. Stir in milk and egg mixture. Pour in Pecorino Romano and cheddar cheeses until melted. Cook in batches, if needed. Season to taste. Serve warm.

Tri-Color Rotini Spicy Pomodoro Sauce

Serving Size: 6 | Total Time: 15 minutes

1 lb tri-color rotini pasta	2 tsp extra-virgin olive oil
15 oz canned tomato sauce	3 tbsp basil, minced
3 garlic cloves, minced	1 cup kale, chopped
1 tsp chili flakes	¼ cup Parmesan, grated
1 tsp salt	

Add tomato sauce, salt, pasta, chili flakes, and garlic and mix well in the pot. Cover with water. Seal lid and cook for 5 minutes on High Pressure. Release the pressure quickly. Stir in kale until wilted. Plate the pasta and top with the Parmesan cheese and basil. Drizzle extra-virgin olive oil over the pasta to serve.

Pasta Caprese with Ricotta & Basil

Serving Size: 4 | Total Time: 15 minutes

1 tbsp olive oil	1 cup cherry tomatoes, halved
1 onion, chopped	1 cup water
2 garlic cloves, minced	¼ cup basil leaves
1 tbsp red pepper flakes	1 tbsp salt
2 ½ cups fusilli pasta	1 cup ricotta, crumbled
1 (15-oz) can tomato sauce	2 tbsp chopped fresh basil

Warm olive oil on Sauté. Add in red pepper flakes, garlic, and onion and cook for 3 minutes until soft. Mix in fusilli, tomatoes, basil, water, tomato sauce, and salt. Seal the lid, and cook on High Pressure for 4 minutes. Release the pressure quickly. Transfer the pasta to a serving platter and top with the crumbled cheese and remaining chopped basil.

Ziti Green Minestrone

Serving Size: 4 | Total Time: 25 minutes

¼ cup grated Pecorino Romano

3 tbsp olive oil	1 bay leaf
1 onion, diced	1 tbsp mixed herbs
1 celery stalk, diced	¼ tbsp cayenne pepper
1 large carrot, diced	Salt and pepper to taste
14 oz can diced tomatoes	1 garlic clove, minced
4 oz ziti pasta	1/3 cup olive pesto pasta
1 cup chopped zucchini	

Heat olive oil on Sauté. Cook onion, celery, garlic, and carrot for 3 minutes, stirring occasionally until the vegetables are softened. Stir in ziti, tomatoes, 3 cups water, zucchini, bay leaf, mixed herbs, cayenne, pepper, and salt. Seal the lid and cook on High for 4 minutes.

Do a natural pressure release for 10 minutes. Adjust the taste and remove the bay leaf. Ladle the soup into bowls and drizzle the pesto over. Serve topped with Pecorino cheese.

Sausage, Spinach & Tomato Rigatoni

Serving Size: 4 | Total Time: 30 minutes

1 tbsp butter	1 onion, chopped
½ cup diced red bell pepper	3 cups vegetable broth
¼ cup tomato purée	Salt and pepper to taste
4 sausage links, chopped	12 oz rigatoni pasta
½ cup milk	1 cup baby spinach
2 tbsp chili powder	½ cup Parmesan, grated

Warm butter on Sauté. Add red bell pepper, onion, and sausage and cook for 5 minutes. Mix in broth, chili, tomato pureé, milk, salt, and pepper. Stir in rigatoni pasta. Seal the lid and cook on High Pressure for 5 minutes. Naturally release pressure. Stir in spinach and let simmer until wilted. Sprinkle with Parmesan and serve.

Spinach & Cheese Filled Conchiglie Shells

Serving Size: 6 | Total Time: 45 minutes

¾ cup grated Pecorino Romano cheese

2 cups onions, chopped	2 cups ricotta, crumbled
1 cup carrots, chopped	1 ½ cups feta, crumbled
3 garlic cloves, minced	2 cups spinach, chopped
3 ½ tbsp olive oil	2 tbsp chopped fresh chives
28-oz can tomatoes, diced	1 tbsp chopped fresh dill
12 oz conchiglie pasta	Salt and pepper to taste
1 tbsp olive oil for greasing	1 cup shredded cheddar

Warm olive oil on Sauté. Add in onions, carrots, and garlic and cook for 5 minutes until tender. Stir in tomatoes and cook for another 10 minutes. Remove to a bowl. Wipe the pot with a damp cloth, add pasta, and cover with enough water. Seal the lid and cook for 5 minutes on High Pressure. Do a quick release and drain the pasta. Lightly grease olive oil on a baking sheet.

In a bowl, combine feta and ricotta cheese. Add in spinach, Pecorino Romano cheese, dill, chives, salt, and pepper and stir. Using a spoon, fill the conchiglie shells with the mixture. Spread 4 cups of the tomato sauce on a baking sheet. Place the stuffed shells over with seam-sides down and sprinkle cheddar cheese on the top. Cover with aluminum foil.

Pour 1 cup of water into the cooker and insert a trivet. Lower the baking dish onto the trivet. Seal the lid and cook for 15 minutes on High Pressure. Do a quick release. Take away the foil. Top with the remaining tomato sauce before serving.

Red Pepper & Chicken Fusilli

Serving Size: 2 | Total Time: 15 minutes

8 oz fusilli pasta	2 garlic cloves, chopped
1 cup tomato pasta sauce	½ tsp Italian seasoning
1 tbsp paprika	Salt and red pepper to taste
1 red bell pepper, sliced	1 tbsp butter
2 chicken breasts, sliced	1 cup Parmesan, grated

Stir 1 cup of water, fusilli, and pasta sauce in your Instant Pot. Add in chicken breasts, garlic, red pepper, Italian seasoning, paprika, salt, and pepper and seal the lid. Select Manual and cook for 5 minutes on High. Once over, perform a quick pressure release and unlock the lid. Stir in butter and top with Parmesan cheese to serve.

Colorful Turkey Fajitas with Rotini Pasta

Serving Size: 6 | Total Time: 15 minutes

1 ½ lb turkey breast, cut into strips
3 mixed bell peppers, cut diagonally

2 tsp chili powder	4 garlic cloves, minced
1 tsp salt	3 cups chicken broth
1 tsp cumin	1 cup pasta sauce
1 tsp onion powder	16 oz rotini pasta
1 tsp garlic powder	1 cup grated Gouda cheese
½ tsp thyme	½ cup sour cream
1 tbsp olive oil	½ cup chopped parsley
1 red onion, cut into wedges	

In a bowl, mix chili powder, cumin, garlic powder, onion powder, salt, and thyme. Reserve 1 tbsp of the seasoning. Coat turkey with the remaining seasoning.

Warm oil on Sauté. Add in turkey strips and sauté for 5 minutes until browned. Place the turkey in a bowl. Sauté the red onion and minced garlic for 1 minute in the cooker until soft. Mix in salsa and broth and scrape the bottom of any brown bits. Stir in rotini pasta and cover with bell peppers and turkey. Seal the lid and cook for 5 minutes on High Pressure. Do a quick pressure release. Open the lid, sprinkle with shredded gouda cheese and reserved seasoning, and stir well. Divide into plates and top with sour cream. Top with parsley and serve.

Creamy Fettuccine with Ground Beef

Serving Size: 6 | Total Time: 20 minutes

10 oz ground beef	1 medium onion, chopped
1 lb fettuccine pasta	2 cups tomatoes, diced
1 cup cheddar, shredded	1 tbsp butter
1 cup fresh spinach, torn	Salt and pepper to taste

Melt butter on Sauté. Stir-fry the beef and onion for 5 minutes. Add the pasta. Pour water enough to cover and season with salt and pepper. Cook on High Pressure for 5 minutes. Do a quick release. Press Sauté and stir in the tomatoes and spinach. Cook for 5 minutes. Top with shredded cheddar and serve.

Pasta Tortiglioni with Beef & Black Beans

Serving Size: 4 | Total Time: 25 minutes

2 tbsp olive oil	10 oz red enchilada sauce
1 lb ground beef	4 oz diced green chiles
16 oz tortiglioni pasta	1 cup shredded mozzarella
15 oz tomato sauce	Salt and pepper to taste
15-oz canned black beans	2 tbsp Parmesan, grated
15-oz canned corn, drained	2 tbsp chopped parsley

Heat oil on Sauté. Add ground beef and cook for 7 minutes. Mix in pasta, tomato sauce, enchilada sauce, black beans, 2 cups water, corn, and green chiles and stir. Seal the lid and cook on High Pressure for 10 minutes. Do a quick pressure release. Mix in mozzarella until melted and add pepper and salt. Garnish with parsley and Parmesan cheese and serve.

Mustard Macaroni & Cheese

Serving Size: 4 | Total Time: 20 minutes

16 oz elbow macaroni	1 tsp mustard powder
1 cup heavy cream	3 cups cheddar, shredded
Salt and pepper to taste	½ cup Parmesan, grated
1 tbsp butter	

Place macaroni and 4 cups of water in your Instant Pot. Sprinkle with salt and pepper and seal the lid. Select Manual and cook for 4 minutes on High. Once done, perform a quick pressure release. Mix in heavy cream, butter, mustard powder, and cheddar and let sit for 5 minutes. Sprinkle with Parmesan cheese and serve.

Green Goddess Mac 'n' Cheese

Serving Size: 4 | Total Time: 20 minutes

2 cups kale, chopped	4 cups chicken broth
2 tbsp cilantro, chopped	3 cups mozzarella, grated
16 oz elbow macaroni	½ cup Parmesan, shredded
3 tbsp unsalted butter	½ cup sour cream

Mix the macaroni, butter, and chicken broth in your Instant Pot and seal the lid. Select Manual and cook for 4 minutes on High. When ready, perform a quick pressure release and unlock the lid. Stir in Parmesan and mozzarella cheeses, sour cream, kale, and cilantro. Put the lid and let sit for 5 minutes until the kale wilts. Serve.

Chicken & Broccoli Fettuccine Alfredo

Serving Size: 2 | Total Time: 15 minutes

1 cup cooked chicken breasts, chopped

1 cup broccoli florets	Salt and pepper to taste
8 oz fettuccine, halved	1 tbsp parsley, chopped
1 tsp chicken seasoning	1 tbsp Parmesan, grated
1 jar (15 oz) Alfredo sauce	

Add 2 cups of water, fettuccine, and chicken seasoning to your Instant Pot. Place a steamer basket on top and add in the broccoli. Seal the lid, select Manual, and cook for 3 minutes on High. Once over, perform a quick pressure release. Drain the pasta and set aside. In a bowl, place Alfredo sauce, broccoli, parsley, and cooked chicken. Add in the pasta and mix to combine. Season with salt and pepper. Serve topped with Parmesan cheese.

Easy Brown Rice with Sunflower Seeds

Serving Size: 6 | Total Time: 30 minutes

1 tbsp toasted sunflower seeds

1 ½ cups brown rice	2 tsp olive oil
3 cups chicken broth	Salt and pepper to taste
2 tsp lemon juice	

Add broth and brown rice. Season with salt and black pepper. Seal the lid, press Manual, and cook on High for 15 minutes. Release the pressure quickly. Do not open the lid for 5 minutes. Use a fork to fluff rice. Add lemon juice, sunflower seeds, and a drizzle of olive oil and serve.

Spicy Linguine with Cherry Tomato & Basil

Serving Size: 4 | Total Time: 25 minutes

2 tbsp olive oil
1 small onion, diced
2 garlic cloves, minced
1 cup cherry tomatoes, halved
1 ½ cups vegetable stock
¼ cup julienned basil leaves

Salt and pepper to taste
¼ tsp red chili flakes
1 lb linguine noodles, halved
2 tbsp basil leaves
½ cup Parmesan, grated

Warm oil on Sauté. Add onion and Sauté for 2 minutes until soft. Mix garlic and tomatoes and Sauté for 4 minutes. Add vegetable stock, salt, julienned basil, red chili flakes, and pepper to the pot. Add linguine to the tomato mixture until covered. Seal the lid.

Cook on High Pressure for 5 minutes. Naturally release the pressure for 10 minutes. Unlock the lid. Divide into plates. Top with basil and Parmesan cheese and serve.

Marinara Turkey Linguine

Serving Size: 4 | Total Time: 20 minutes

½ cup Pecorino Romano cheese, grated
1 tsp olive oil
1 lb ground turkey
¾ tsp kosher salt
¼ onion, diced

1 clove garlic, minced
t cups marinara sauce
16 oz linguine, halved

Warm the olive oil in your Instant Pot on Sauté. Brown the ground turkey until no longer pink or about 3 minutes. Stir in garlic and onion and cook for 4 minutes. Pour linguine, marinara sauce, salt, and 4 cups of water and seal the lid. Select Manual and cook for 5 minutes on High. Once done, perform a quick pressure release and unlock the lid. Serve topped with Pecorino Romano.

Spaghetti Bolognese

Serving Size: 4 | Total Time: 20 minutes

1 tsp olive oil
1 lb ground beef
12 oz spaghetti
½ tsp dried basil
½ dried oregano

½ dried rosemary
24 oz canned tomatoes
Salt and pepper to taste
½ cup Parmesan cheese, grated

Warm the olive oil in your Instant Pot on Sauté. Add in the ground beef and cook for 4-5 minutes until browned, stirring often. Stir in basil, oregano, and rosemary and then pour in tomatoes, spaghetti, and 2 cups of water.

Seal the lid, select Manual, and cook for 5 minutes on High. When ready, perform a quick pressure release and unlock the lid. Adjust the seasoning with salt and pepper. Scatter the Parmesan cheese over the pasta and serve.

Asparagus Pasta with Pesto Sauce

Serving Size: 4 | Total Time: 15 minutes

1 cup cherry tomatoes, quartered
1 lb farfalle
1 lb asparagus, chopped

¾ cup pesto sauce
½ cup Parmesan, grated

Place the farfalle and 4 cups of salted water in your Instant Pot and fit in a trivet. Arrange the asparagus on the trivet and seal the lid. Select Manual and cook for 4 minutes on High. Once done, perform a quick pressure release. Drain the pasta and put it back in the pot. Add in the pesto sauce, asparagus, and cherry tomatoes and stir. Sprinkle with Parmesan cheese and serve.

Cheesy Mushrooms with Garganelli

Serving Size: 4 | Total Time: 20 minutes

8 oz garganelli
1 tbsp salt
1 large egg
8 oz Gruyère, shredded
2 cups mushrooms, sliced

2 tbsp chopped cilantro
3 tbsp sour cream
2 tbsp butter
3 tbsp cheddar, grated

Put the garganelli, butter, and salt into the pot and cover with water. Seal lid and cook on High Pressure for 4 minutes. Do a quick pressure release. Melt butter on Sauté and cook mushrooms for 5-6 minutes until tender.

In a bowl, whisk egg, Gruyère cheese, and sour cream. Add in garganelli and stir in the mushrooms until the cheese melts. Serve sprinkled with cheddar and cilantro.

Beef Pasta Alla Parmigiana

Serving Size: 6 | Total Time: 20 minutes

3 tsp olive oil
1 ¼ lb ground beef
1 cup white wine
1 tsp onion powder
3 beef bouillon cubes

1 lb conchiglie pasta shells
½ cup Parmesan, shredded
Salt and pepper to taste
5 basil leaves, torn

Warm olive oil in your Instant Pot on Sauté. Add in the ground beef and stir-fry until browned, about 5 minutes. Place 3 cups of water, onion powder, and bouillon cubes in a bowl and mix to combine. Pour it into the pot. Add in the white wine, pasta, salt, and pepper and seal the lid. Select Manual and cook for 5 minutes on High. Once ready, perform a quick pressure release. Sprinkle with Parmesan cheese and basil and serve.

Broccoli & Pancetta Carbonara

Serving Size: 4 | Total Time: 30 minutes

1 lb pasta rigatoni
12 oz broccoli florets
½ fennel bulb, sliced
4 large eggs, beaten

½ cup Grana Padano, grated
Salt and pepper to taste
8 oz pancetta, chopped
¼ cup heavy cream

Cover the pasta with salted water in your Instant Pot and seal the lid. Select Manual and cook for 4 minutes on High. Drain and set aside, reserving 1 cup of cooking liquid. Beat the eggs in a bowl, add the cheese, and mix to combine. Clean the pot and select Sauté. Cook the pancetta for 4 minutes then add in the fennel; cook for 2-3 more minutes. Pour in the broccoli and pasta liquid and cook for 4-5 minutes. Stir in the egg mixture and heavy cream for 2-3 minutes. Adjust the seasoning. Add the pasta and let sit for 5 minutes before serving.

Turkey Bacon & Pea Spaghetti

Serving Size: 4 | Total Time: 20 minutes

1 lb pasta	4 oz turkey bacon, diced
1 cup green peas	8 oz cheddar, grated
1 tbsp olive oil	½ cup half and half
½ tsp red chili flakes	Salt and pepper to taste

Place the pasta and 4 cup of salted water in your Instant Pot and seal the lid. Select Manual and cook for 4 minutes on High. Once done, perform a quick pressure release and unlock the lid. Drain the pasta and set aside.

Heat olive oil in your Instant Pot on Sauté. Cook the turkey bacon for 5 minutes. Add in the pasta, green peas, cheddar cheese, half and half, salt, and pepper and cook for 2 minutes. Top with red chili pepper and serve.

Spinach & Anchovy Fusilli

Serving Size: 4 | Total Time: 15 minutes

1 lb fusilli pasta	2 tbsp butter
4 cups spinach, chopped	½ tsp grated nutmeg
4 anchovy fillets, chopped	3 tbsp pine nuts, toasted
½ cup Parmesan, shredded	Salt and pepper to taste

Place fusilli pasta and 4 cups of salted water in your Instant Pot and seal the lid. Select Manual and cook for 4 minutes on High. When done, perform a quick pressure release and unlock the lid. Drain the pasta, reserving 1 cup of the liquid and set aside. Melt butter on Sauté

Add in spinach. Stir for 2 minutes and pour in the pasta liquid. Return the pasta, stir in anchovies, nutmeg, and pine nuts. Adjust the taste. Top with Parmesan and serve.

Bean Pasta with Vegetables

Serving Size: 4 | Total Time: 30 minutes

1 cup butternut squash, shredded	
1 lb penne pasta	½ zucchini, sliced
1 cup pasta sauce	½ tsp garlic powder
1 cup canned white beans	½ tsp onion powder
½ cup frozen lima beans	½ tsp ground nutmeg
½ cup black olives, sliced	½ tsp oregano
1 cup baby spinach	½ tbsp Italian seasoning

Place pasta, 3 cups of water, butternut squash, and pasta sauce in your Instant Pot. Seal the lid, select Manual, and cook for 4 minutes on High. When done, allow a natural release for 10 minutes and unlock the lid. Stir in white beans, lima beans, olives, spinach, zucchini, garlic powder, onion powder, nutmeg, oregano, and Italian seasoning and press Sauté. Cook for 5-6 minutes and adjust the seasoning. Serve right away.

Tomato & Mushroom Rotini

Serving Size: 4 | Total Time: 35 minutes

1 lb rotini pasta	2 garlic cloves, minced
2 tbsp olive oil	16 oz crushed tomatoes
½ yellow onion, diced	1 cup Mushrooms, sliced
½ tbsp grated nutmeg	Salt and pepper to taste
¼ cup basil, chopped	

Cover rotini pasta with salted water in your Instant Pot and seal the lid. Select Manual and cook for 4 minutes on High. When done, allow a natural release for 10 minutes, then perform a quick pressure release, and unlock the lid. Drain the pasta and transfer to a bowl.

Heat the olive oil on Sauté and cook the onion, mushrooms, and garlic for 3-4 minutes. Stir in tomatoes and nutmeg and simmer for 5-6 minutes. Stir in basil and cooked pasta; adjust the seasoning. Serve.

Sicilian Seafood Linguine

Serving Size: 4 | Total Time: 25 minutes

2 tbsp olive oil	16 oz linguine
1 onion, chopped	½ lb prawns, peeled
2 garlic cloves, minced	4 sardines, chopped
2 tomatoes, chopped	2 tbsp parsley, chopped
1 red bell pepper, chopped	1 tbsp tomato purée
½ cup dried white wine	Salt and pepper to taste
3 cups vegetable stock	½ cup Parmesan, grated

Warm the olive oil in your Instant Pot on Sauté. Add in the onion and garlic and cook for 3 minutes. Pour in tomatoes and bell pepper and cook for another 3-4 minutes. Stir in white wine and simmer for 3 minutes. Mix in vegetable stock, linguine, prawns, tomato puree, salt, and pepper and seal the lid. Select Manual on High.

Cook for 4 minutes on High. When ready, perform a quick pressure release and unlock the lid. Stir in sardines and parsley. Scatter with Parmesan cheese and serve.

Spicy Rice Noodles with Tofu & Chives

Serving Size: 6 | Total Time: 15 minutes

½ cup soy sauce	1 tsp fresh minced garlic
2 tbsp brown sugar	20 oz tofu, cubed
2 tbsp rice vinegar	8 oz rice noodles
1 tbsp sweet chili sauce	¼ cup chopped chives
1 tbsp sesame oil	

Heat the oil on Sauté. Fry the tofu for 5 minutes until golden brown; reserve. To the pot, add 2 cups water, garlic, vinegar, sugar, soy sauce, and chili sauce and mix until smooth. Stir in rice noodles. Seal the lid and cook on High Pressure for 3 minutes. Divide noodles between bowls. Top with tofu and sprinkle with chives and serve.

Beef Garam Masala with Rice

Serving Size: 4 | Total Time: 30 minutes

¼ cup yogurt	1 tsp ground cumin
2 cloves garlic, smashed	¼ tbsp cayenne pepper
1 tbsp olive oil	3 tbsp butter
1 lime, juiced	1 onion, chopped
Salt and pepper to taste	14-oz can puréed tomatoes
2 lb beef stew meat, cubed	1 cup beef broth
1 tbsp garam masala	1 cup basmati rice, rinsed
1 tbsp fresh ginger, grated	½ cup heavy cream
1 ½ tbsp smoked paprika	2 tbsp cilantro, chopped

In a bowl, mix garlic, lime juice, olive oil, pepper, salt, and yogurt. Add in the beef and toss to coat. In another bowl, mix paprika, garam masala, cumin, ginger, and cayenne pepper. Melt butter on Sauté and stir-fry the onion for 3 minutes. Sprinkle spice mixture over onion and cook for about 30 seconds. Add in the beef-yogurt mixture. Sauté for 3 to 4 minutes until the meat is slightly cooked. Mix in broth and puréed tomatoes.

Set trivet over beef in the Pressure cooker's inner pot. In an oven-proof bowl, mix 2 cups of water and rice. Set the bowl onto the trivet. Seal the lid and cook on High Pressure for 10 minutes. Release pressure quickly. Remove the bowl with rice and trivet. Add pepper, salt, and heavy cream into beef and stir. Use a fork to fluff rice and divide into serving plates; apply a topping of beef. Garnish with cilantro and serve.

Spinach, Garlic & Mushroom Pilaf

Serving Size: 6 | Total Time: 45 minutes

2 cups button mushrooms, sliced
1 tbsp olive oil   4 cups vegetable stock
2 cloves garlic, minced   2 cups white rice
1 onion, chopped   1 tsp salt
1 cup spinach, chopped   2 sprigs parsley, chopped

Select Sauté and heat oil. Add mushrooms, onion, and garlic, and stir-fry for 5 minutes until tender. Mix in rice, stock, spinach, and salt. Seal the lid and cook on High Pressure for 20 minutes. Release pressure naturally for 10 minutes. Fluff the rice and top with parsley. Serve.

Salmon & Tomato Farfalle

Serving Size: 4 | Total Time: 15 minutes

16 oz farfalle pasta   ¼ tsp oregano
2 tbsp olive oil   ¾ cup red wine
2 garlic cloves, sliced   4 oz smoked salmon, flaked
2 cups tomatoes, diced   10 green olives, sliced
¼ tsp chili pepper   ½ cup Parmesan, grated

Warm olive oil in your Instant Pot on Sauté. Add in garlic and cook for 1 minute. Stir in tomatoes, farfalle, chili pepper, 4 cups water, red wine, and oregano. Seal the lid.

Select Manual, and cook for 5 minutes on High. Once ready, perform a quick pressure release. Mix in salmon and green olives. Serve sprinkled with Parmesan cheese.

Vegetarian Wild Rice with Carrots

Serving Size: 6 | Total Time: 32 minutes

4 cups vegetable broth   3 tbsp butter
2 carrots, chopped   Zest and juice from 1 lemon
2 cups wild rice   Salt and pepper to taste

Add rice, carrots, lemon zest, butter, and broth. Stir, seal the lid, and cook on High Pressure for 12 minutes. Release pressure naturally for 10 minutes. Carefully unlock the lid. Sprinkle salt, lemon juice, and pepper over the rice and use a fork to gently fluff. Serve warm.

Risotto with Spring Vegetables & Shrimp

Serving Size: 4 | Total Time: 40 minutes

1 tbsp avocado oil   ¾ cup coconut milk
1 lb asparagus, chopped   1 tbsp coconut oil
1 cup spinach, chopped   1 lb shrimp, deveined
1 cup mushrooms, sliced   Salt and pepper to taste
1 cup rice   ¾ cup Parmesan, shredded
1 ¼ cups chicken broth

Warm the avocado oil on Sauté. Add spinach, mushrooms, and asparagus and sauté for 5 minutes until cooked through. Add in rice, coconut milk, and chicken broth as you stir. Seal the lid, press Manual, and cook for 20 minutes on High Pressure.

Do a quick release. Place the rice on a serving plate. Press Sauté. Heat the coconut oil. Add shrimp and cook for 6 minutes until it turns pink. Set the shrimp over rice and season with pepper and salt. Serve topped with Parmesan cheese.

Stuffed Mushrooms with Rice & Cheese

Serving Size: 4 | Total Time: 25 minutes

4 portobello mushrooms, stems and gills removed
2 tbsp melted butter   ½ cup feta, crumbled
½ cup brown rice, cooked   Salt and pepper to taste
1 tomato, chopped   2 tbsp cilantro, chopped
¼ cup black olives, chopped   1 cup vegetable broth
1 green bell pepper, diced

Brush the mushrooms with butter. Arrange them in a single layer on a greased baking pan. In a bowl, mix the rice, tomato, olives, bell pepper, feta cheese, salt, and black pepper. Spoon the rice mixture into the mushrooms. Pour in the broth.

Pour 1 cup of water into the Instant Pot and insert a trivet. Place the baking dish on the trivet. Seal the lid and cook on High Pressure for 10 minutes. Do a quick release. Garnish with fresh cilantro and serve immediately.

Risotto with Broccoli & Grana Padano

Serving Size: 6 | Total Time: 35 minutes

2 tbsp Grana Padano cheese flakes
10 oz broccoli florets   ¼ cup dry white wine
1 onion, chopped   4 cups chicken stock
3 tbsp butter   Salt and pepper to taste
2 cups carnaroli rice, rinsed 2 tbsp Grana Padano, grated

Warm butter on Sauté. Stir-fry onion for 3 minutes until translucent. Add in broccoli and rice and cook for 5 minutes, stirring occasionally. Pour wine into the pot and scrape away any browned bits of food from the pan.

Stir in stock, pepper, and salt. Seal the lid, press Manual and cook on High for 15 minutes. Release the pressure quickly. Sprinkle with grated Grana Padano cheese and stir well. Top with flaked Grana Padano cheese to serve.

Arugula & Wild Mushroom Risotto

Serving Size: 4 | Total Time: 30 minutes

½ cup wild mushrooms, chopped
4 tbsp pumpkin seeds, toasted
1/3 cup grated Pecorino Romano cheese

2 tbsp olive oil	1 cup arborio rice
1 onion, chopped	1/3 cup white wine
2 cups arugula, chopped	3 cups vegetable stock

Heat oil on Sauté and cook onion and mushrooms for 5 minutes until tender. Add the rice and cook for a minute. Stir in white wine and cook for 2-3 minutes until almost evaporated. Pour in the stock. Seal the lid and cook on High Pressure for 10 minutes. Do a quick release. Stir in arugula and Pecorino Romano cheese to melt and serve scattered with pumpkin seeds.

Yummy Mexican-Style Rice & Pinto Beans

Serving Size: 4 | Total Time: 30 minutes

3 tbsp olive oil	¼ cup tomato sauce
1 small onion, chopped	½ cup vegetable broth
2 garlic cloves, minced	1 tsp Mexican seasoning
1 serrano pepper, chopped	16 oz canned pinto beans
1 cup rice	1 tsp salt
1/3 cup red salsa	1 tbsp chopped parsley

Warm oil on Sauté and cook onion, garlic, and serrano pepper for 2 minutes, stirring occasionally until fragrant. Stir in rice, salsa, tomato sauce, vegetable broth, Mexican seasoning, beans, and salt. Seal the lid and cook on High Pressure for 10 minutes. Do a natural pressure release for 10 minutes. Sprinkle with fresh parsley and serve.

Butternut Squash with Rice & Feta

Serving Size: 4 | Total Time: 30 minutes

2 cups vegetable broth	1 cup feta cheese, cubed
1 lb butternut squash, sliced	1 tbsp coconut aminos
2 tbsp melted butter	2 tsp arrowroot starch
Salt and pepper to taste	1 cup jasmine rice, cooked

Pour the rice and broth into the pot and stir to combine. In a bowl, toss butternut squash with 1 tbsp of melted butter and season with salt and black pepper. Mix in the pot with the rice. In another bowl, mix the remaining butter, water, and coconut aminos. Toss feta in the mixture, add the arrowroot starch, and toss again to combine well. Transfer to a greased baking dish.

Lay a trivet over the rice butternut squash and place the baking dish on the trivet. Seal the lid and cook on High for 15 minutes. Do a quick pressure release. Fluff the rice with a fork and serve with feta cheese.

Avocado & Cherry Tomato Jasmine Rice

Serving Size: 6 | Total Time: 25 minutes

2 avocados, chopped	2 tsp olive oil
½ lb cherry tomatoes, halved	½ tsp salt
2 cups jasmine rice	2 tbsp cilantro, chopped

Place the rice, 2 cups water, olive oil, and salt in your Instant Pot and stir. Seal the lid, select Manual, and cook for 4 minutes on High pressure. Once done, allow a natural release for 10 minutes and unlock the lid. Using a fork, fluff the rice and add in avocados and cherry tomatoes. Top with cilantro and serve.

Date & Apple Risotto

Serving Size: 4 | Total Time: 30 minutes

1 tbsp butter	1 cup apple juice
1 ½ cups Arborio rice	2 cups milk
1/3 cup brown sugar	1 ½ tsp cinnamon powder
2 apples, cored and sliced	½ cup dates, pitted

Melt butter in your Instant Pot on Sauté and place in rice; cook for 1-2 minutes. Stir in brown sugar, apples, apple juice, milk, and cinnamon. Seal the lid, select Manual, and cook for 6 minutes on High pressure. Once done, allow a natural release for 6 minutes and unlock the lid. Mix in dates and cover with the lid. Let sit for 5 minutes.

Butternut Squash & Cheese Risotto

Serving Size: 4 | Total Time: 45 minutes

½ lb butternut squash, cubed	1 tsp thyme, chopped
3 tbsp olive oil	½ tsp nutmeg
2 cloves garlic, minced	½ tsp ginger, grated
1 yellow onion, chopped	½ tsp cinnamon
2 cups arborio rice	½ cup heavy cream
4 cups chicken stock	Salt and pepper to taste
½ cup pumpkin puree	¼ cup shaved Parmesan

Preheat the oven to 360°F. Spread the squash cubes on a baking tray and drizzle with olive oil. Roast for 20 minutes until tender. Warm oil in your Instant Pot on Sauté and add garlic and onion; cook for 3 minutes.

Stir in rice, stock, pumpkin puree, thyme, nutmeg, ginger, and cinnamon. Seal the lid, select Manual, and cook for 10 minutes on High. When done, perform a quick pressure release. Mix in heavy cream, salt, and pepper. Top with pumpkin cubes and Parmesan shaves and serve.

Spring Risotto

Serving Size: 6 | Total Time: 40 minutes

3 tbsp Pecorino Romano cheese, shredded

½ cup green peas	1 ½ cups arborio rice
1 cup baby spinach	3 ½ cups chicken stock
2 tbsp olive oil	Salt and pepper to taste
2 spring onions, chopped	

Warm olive oil in your Instant Pot on Sauté. Add spring onions and cook for 3 minutes. Pour in rice and stock. Seal the lid and cook for 15 minutes on Manual.

Once done, allow a natural release for 10 minutes and unlock the lid. Adjust the seasoning with salt and pepper. Mix in green peas and spinach and cover with the lid. Let sit for 5 minutes until everything is heated through. Top with Pecorino Romano cheese and serve.

Arroz con Pollo

Serving Size: 4 | Total Time: 40 minutes

2 tbsp olive oil	½ tsp chili powder
1 sweet onion, diced	2 carrots, diced
2 garlic cloves, minced	1 cup white jasmine rice
1 lb boneless chicken thighs	1 ½ cups chicken stock
Salt and pepper to taste	½ tsp Mexican oregano

Warm olive oil in your Instant Pot on Sauté. Add in onion and garlic and cook until fragrant, about 3 minutes. Stir in chicken, salt, and pepper and cook for 5 minutes more. Mix in carrots, rice, chili powder, chicken stock, and oregano. Seal the lid, select Manual, and cook for 10 minutes on High pressure. Once done, allow a natural release for 10 minutes and unlock the lid. Fluff the rice.

Chicken & Broccoli Rice

Serving Size: 4 | Total Time: 40 minutes

1 red chili, finely chopped	Salt and pepper to taste
2 tbsp butter	1 cup long-grain rice
1 lb chicken breasts, sliced	2 cups chicken broth
1 onion, chopped	10 oz broccoli florets
2 cloves garlic, minced	2 tbsp cilantro, chopped

Melt butter in your Instant Pot on Sauté and add chicken, onion, red chili, garlic, salt, and pepper; cook for 5 minutes, stirring often. Stir in rice, chicken broth, milk, and broccoli. Seal the lid, select Manual, and cook for 15 minutes on High. When ready, allow a natural release for 10 minutes. Sprinkle with cilantro and serve.

Hawaiian Rice

Serving Size: 4 | Total Time: 30 minutes

2 tsp olive oil	½ pineapple, and chopped
1 ½ cups coconut water	Salt to taste
1 cup jasmine rice	¼ tsp red pepper flakes
2 green onions, sliced	

Stir olive oil, water, rice, pineapple, and salt in your Instant Pot. Seal the lid, select Manual, and cook for 10 minutes on low pressure. Once over, allow a natural release for 10 minutes, then a quick pressure release. Carefully unlock the lid. Using a fork, fluff the rice. Scatter with green onions and red pepper flakes and serve.

Lime Brown Rice

Serving Size: 6 | Total Time: 45 minutes

½ bunch spring onions, chopped diagonally	
2 cups brown rice, rinsed	1 lime, juiced
2 small bay leaves	Salt to taste
2 tbsp olive oil	

Place the rice, 2 ¾ cups of water, salt, and bay leaves in your Instant Pot. Seal the lid and cook on Manual for 22 minutes on High. When done, allow a natural release for 10 minutes and unlock the lid. Drizzle with olive oil and lime juice and top with spring onions to serve.

South American Pot

Serving Size: 4 | Total Time: 30 minutes

1 cups brown rice	2 tsp chili powder
½ cup soaked black beans	Salt to taste
1 tbsp tomato paste	¼ tsp cumin
1 garlic clove, minced	1 tsp hot paprika
2 tsp onion powder	3 cups corn kernels

Place rice, beans, 4 cups water, tomato paste, garlic, onion powder, chili powder, salt, cumin, paprika, and corn in your Instant Pot and stir. Seal the lid, select Manual, and cook for 20 minutes on High pressure. Once ready, perform a quick pressure release and unlock the lid. Adjust the seasoning. Serve immediately.

Honey Coconut Rice

Serving Size: 4 | Total Time: 30 minutes

1 cup Thai sweet rice	2 tbsp honey
1 cup coconut milk	

Place rice and 1 ½ cups of water in your Instant Pot. Seal the lid, select Manual, and cook for 3 minutes on High pressure. When over, allow a natural release for 10 minutes. Warm coconut milk, and honey in a pot over medium heat until the honey has dissolved. Unlock the lid of the pressure cooker and stir in coconut mix. Cover with the lid and let sit for 5-10 minutes. Serve.

Beef & Brussels Sprout Rice

Serving Size: 6 | Total Time: 35 minutes

1 ½ cups basmati rice	3 cloves garlic, minced
1 lb ground beef, cooked	1 onion, chopped
3 cups beef broth	1 tbsp shawarma spice
½ lb Brussels sprouts, halved	Salt to taste
2 tbsp olive oil	¼ cup cilantro, chopped

Place the rice, ground beef, broth, Brussels sprouts, olive oil, garlic, onion, shawarma spice, and salt in your Instant Pot and stir. Seal the lid, select Manual, and cook for 15 minutes on High pressure. Once ready, allow a natural release for 10 minutes and unlock the lid. Serve topped with cilantro.

Pork Rice Porridge

Serving Size: 4 | Total Time: 35 minutes

2 tbsp olive oil	1 cup basmati rice, rinsed
2 cloves garlic, minced	1 ½ cups vegetable stock
1 onion, diced	Salt and pepper to taste
1 lb ground pork	2 tbsp parsley, chopped

Warm olive oil in your Instant Pot on Sauté. Add in onion and garlic and sauté for 2 minutes. Stir in ground pork and cook until get browned, about 5-6 minutes.

Pour in rice, stock, salt, and pepper. Seal the lid, select Manual, and cook for 6 minutes on High pressure. Once ready, allow a natural release for 10 minutes. Carefully unlock the lid. Serve sprinkled with parsley.

Broccoli & Ham Risotto

Serving Size: 4 | Total Time: 25 minutes

2 cups broccoli florets	3 ½ cups chicken stock
4 oz ham, cut into strips	2 tbsp Parmesan cheese, finely grated
1 tbsp olive oil	
2 tbsp butter	2 tbsp parsley, chopped
1 onion, chopped	1 tsp lemon zest, grated
1 ½ cups arborio rice	Salt and pepper to taste

Warm olive oil and 1 tbsp of butter in your Instant Pot on Sauté. Add onion and cook for 3 minutes. Stir in rice and cook for 1 minute. Mix in 3 cups of chicken stock. Seal the lid, select Manual, and cook for 5 minutes.

When over, perform a quick pressure release. Stir in broccoli and remaining stock and cook for 5-6 minutes on Sauté. Mix in Parmesan cheese, ham, parsley, remaining butter, lemon zest, salt, and pepper. Serve.

Button Mushroom Risotto

Serving Size: 4 | Total Time: 25 minutes

1 cup button mushrooms, sliced	
2 oz olive oil	¼ cup white wine
2 cloves garlic, crushed	½ cup heavy cream
1 red onion, chopped	2 tbsp Parmesan, grated
1 cup arborio rice	2 tbsp basil, finely chopped
2 cups chicken stock	Salt to taste

Warm olive oil in your Instant Pot on Sauté and add garlic, onion, and mushrooms; cook for 3 minutes. Stir in rice, stock, and wine. Seal the lid, select Manual, and cook for 10 minutes on High. Once ready, perform a quick pressure release and unlock the lid. Mix in heavy cream, Parmesan cheese, and salt. Top with basil to serve.

Provençal Rice

Serving Size: 6 | Total Time: 45 minutes

2 tbsp butter	1 tsp herbs de Provence
1 onion, diced	3 anchovy fillets, finely chopped
2 garlic cloves, minced	
2 cups brown rice	6 pitted Kalamata olives
3 cups vegetable stock	

Melt butter in your Instant Pot on Sauté and add in onion and garlic; cook for 3 minutes. Stir in rice and herbs for 1 minute and pour in the stock. Seal the lid, select Manual, and cook for 22 minutes on High. When ready, allow a natural release for 10 minutes and unlock the lid. Stir in anchovy fillets. Serve topped with Kalamata olives.

Vegetable Paella

Serving Size: 4 | Total Time: 37 minutes

2 tbsp butter	1 cup tomato sauce
1 cup long-grain rice	1 tsp cumin
1 ½ cups vegetable stock	1 tsp chili powder
A pinch of saffron	½ tsp garlic powder
1 red bell pepper, chopped	½ tsp onion powder
½ cup green peas	1 lemon, cut into wedges

Melt butter in your Instant Pot to Sauté. Add in rice and bell pepper and cook for 2 minutes. Mix in vegetable stock, tomato sauce, cumin, saffron, chili powder, garlic powder, and onion powder. Seal the lid, select Manual, and cook for 10 minutes on High pressure. Once ready, allow a natural release for 10 minutes and unlock the lid. Stir in green peas and cook for 4-5 minutes more on Sauté. Serve with lemon wedges.

Coconut Rice Breakfast

Serving Size: 4 | Total Time: 25 minutes

1 cup brown rice	¼ cup walnuts, chopped
1 cup water	¼ cup raisins
1 cup coconut milk	¼ tsp cinnamon powder
½ cup coconut chips	½ cup maple syrup

Place the rice and water in your Instant Pot. Seal the lid, select Manual, and cook for 15 minutes on High. When ready, perform a quick pressure release and unlock the lid. Stir in coconut milk, coconut chips, raisins, cinnamon, and maple syrup. Seal the lid, select Manual, and cook for another 5 minutes on High pressure. When over, perform a quick pressure release. Top with walnuts.

Prawn Basmati Rice

Serving Size: 4 | Total Time: 32 minutes

½ lb cooked prawns	1 cup basmati rice
¼ frozen peas	1 ¼ cups water
2 tbsp butter	Salt and pepper to taste

Place the rice, water, butter, and salt in your Instant Pot and stir. Seal the lid, select Manual, and cook for 6 minutes on High pressure. When ready, allow a natural release for 10 minutes and unlock the lid. Using a fork, fluff the rice and mix in prawns, peas, salt, and pepper. Let sit for 5-6 minutes until heated through. Serve.

Pomegranate Rice with Vegetables

Serving Size: 4 | Total Time: 15 minutes

¼ cup pomegranate seeds	1 cup sweet corn, frozen
2 tbsp olive oil	1 cup garden peas, frozen
1 onion, finely chopped	¼ tsp salt
2 cloves garlic, minced	1 tsp turmeric powder
1 cup basmati rice	1 ¼ cups vegetable stock

Warm oil your Instant Pot on Sauté and add onion and garlic; cook for 3 minutes until fragrant. Stir in rice, corn, peas, salt, turmeric, and stock. Seal the lid, select Manual, and cook for 4 minutes on High pressure. When ready, perform a quick pressure release and unlock the lid. With a fork, fluff the rice. Top with pomegranate and serve.

Hazelnut Brown Rice Pilaf

Serving Size: 4 | Total Time: 45 minutes

¼ cup hazelnuts, toasted and chopped	
2 tbsp olive oil	2 cups vegetable broth
1 cup brown rice	Salt and pepper to taste

Place the rice, vegetable broth, olive oil, pepper, and salt in your Instant Pot and stir. Seal the lid, select Manual, and cook for 25 minutes on High. Once ready, allow a natural release for 10 minutes and unlock the lid. Using a fork, fluff the rice. Top with hazelnuts and serve.

Vegetable Green Biryani

Serving Size: 6 | Total Time: 15 minutes

1 tbsp olive oil	1 cup broccoli florets, chopped
2 cups basmati rice	
3 tbsp butter	Salt and pepper to taste
2 garlic cloves, minced	4 tbsp cilantro, chopped
1 lb spinach, chopped	4 cups vegetable broth

Warm olive oil in your Instant Pot on Sauté. Add in the rice, butter, and garlic and cook for 1-2 minutes. In a food processor, blend the spinach, broccoli, and cilantro. Pour vegetable broth and mixed greens in the pot and stir. Season with salt and pepper. Seal the lid and cook on Manual for 6 minutes on High. Once ready, perform a quick pressure release and unlock the lid. Divide between four serving bowls and serve.

Wild Rice Pilaf

Serving Size: 4 | Total Time: 20 minutes

1 cup wild rice	Salt and pepper to taste
2 tbsp butter	2 tbsp chives, chopped

Stir the rice, butter, 2 cups of water, salt, and pepper in your Instant Pot. Seal the lid, select Manual, and cook for 5 minutes on High pressure. When ready, allow a natural release for 10 minutes and unlock the lid. Using a fork, fluff the rice. Top with chives and serve.

Spicy Indian Rice

Serving Size: 4 | Total Time: 40 minutes

2 tbsp olive oil	1 tsp ginger paste
2 garlic cloves, minced	1 ½ cups chicken broth
2 shallots, chopped	1 cup frozen green beans
1 cup basmati rice	Salt and pepper to taste
½ cup carrots, chopped	2 tbsp cilantro, chopped
2 tsp masala curry paste	

Warm olive oil in your Instant Pot to Sauté. Add in shallots, ginger, and garlic and cook until fragrant, about 3 minutes. Stir in rice, carrots, masala curry paste, chicken broth, green beans, salt, and pepper. Seal the lid and cook on Manual for 20 minutes on High. Once ready, allow a natural release for 10 minutes and unlock the lid. With a fork, fluff the rice. Scatter with cilantro and serve.

Pilau Brown Rice

Serving Size: 4 | Total Time: 20 minutes

2 tbsp olive oil	Sea salt to taste
1 bay leaf	1 ¼ cups vegetable broth
1 tsp cumin	½ tbsp turmeric
1 cup basmati brown rice	2 tbsp cilantro, chopped

Place the olive oil, bay leaf, cumin, rice, salt, vegetable broth, and turmeric in your Instant Pot and stir. Seal the lid and cook for 6 minutes on Multigrain.

When done, allow a natural release for 10 minutes and unlock the lid. Using a fork, fluff the rice. Transfer to a serving plate. Top with cilantro and serve.

Rice & Red Bean Pot

Serving Size: 4 | Total Time: 55 minutes

1 cup red beans, soaked	1 onion, diced
2 tbsp vegetable oil	1 garlic clove, minced
½ cup rice	1 red bell pepper, diced
½ tbsp cayenne pepper	1 stalk celery, diced
1 ½ cups vegetable broth	Salt and pepper to taste

Place beans in your Instant Pot with enough water to cover them by a couple of fingers. Seal the lid and cook for 25 minutes on High Pressure. Release the pressure quickly. Drain the beans and set aside.

Rinse and pat dry the inner pot. Add in oil and press Sauté. Add in onion and garlic and sauté for 3 minutes until soft. Add celery and bell pepper and cook for 2 minutes.

Add in the rice, reserved beans, vegetable broth. Stir in pepper, cayenne pepper, and salt. Seal the lid and cook for 15 minutes on High Pressure. Release the pressure quickly. Carefully unlock the lid. Serve warm.

Rice & Chicken Soup

Serving Size: 4 | Total Time: 35 minutes

1 lb chicken breasts, cubed	1 potato, finely chopped
1 carrot, chopped	1 tsp cayenne pepper
1 onion, chopped	2 tbsp olive oil
¼ cup rice	4 cups chicken broth

Heat the olive oil in your Instant Pot on Sauté. Cook the onion, carrot, and chicken for 5 minutes, stirring often. Add in rice, potato, cayenne pepper, and broth and stir. Seal the lid. Cook on Soup/Broth for 20 minutes. Do a quick pressure release. Carefully unlock the lid. Serve.

One-Pot Mexican Rice

Serving Size: 4 | Total Time: 35 minutes

2 tbsp olive oil	1 tbsp chipotle chili paste
1 onion, diced	2 mixed peppers, sliced
2 garlic cloves, sliced	1 cup salsa
1 cup long-grain white rice	Salt and pepper to taste
2 cups chicken stock	2 tbsp cilantro, chopped

Warm olive oil in your Instant Pot on Sauté and add in onion, garlic, and mixed peppers; cook for 2-3 minutes.

Add in rice and cook for another 1-2 minutes. Mix in stock, salsa, salt, and pepper. Seal the lid, select Manual, and cook for 10 minutes on High pressure.

When over, allow a natural release for 10 minutes and unlock the lid. Stir in the chipotle paste. Serve topped with cilantro. Enjoy!

BEANS & GRAINS

Stewed Spinach with Kidney Beans

Serving Size: 4 | Total Time: 50 minutes

2 tbsp olive oil	1 cup kidney beans, soaked
1 onion, chopped	1 tsp dried thyme
2 cloves garlic, minced	1 tsp dried rosemary
2 carrots, chopped	1 bay leaf
1 cup celery, chopped	1 cup spinach, torn
4 cups vegetable broth	Salt and pepper to taste

Warm olive oil on Sauté. Stir in garlic and onion, and cook for 3 minutes until tender and fragrant. Mix in celery and carrots and cook for 3 minutes until they start to soften. Add broth, bay leaf, thyme, rosemary, kidney beans, and salt.

Seal the lid and cook for 30 minutes on High Pressure. Quick-release the pressure and stir in spinach. Allow to sitting for 2 to 4 minutes until the spinach wilts and season with pepper and salt. Serve.

Spicy Three-Bean Vegetable Chili

Serving Size: 6 | Total Time: 40 minutes

1 tbsp canola oil	4 cups vegetable broth
1 onion, chopped	28-oz can tomatoes, diced
3 stalks of celery, chopped	½ cup pinto beans, soaked
1 cup green peas	½ cup black beans, soaked
10 oz broccoli florets	½ cup cannellini beans
2 tbsp minced garlic	Salt to taste
2 tbsp chili powder	2 tbsp parsley, chopped
2 tsp ground cumin	

Warm oil on Sauté. Add in onion, broccoli, and celery and cook for 5 minutes until softened. Mix in cumin, chili powder, and garlic and cook for another 1 minute. Pour in vegetable broth, tomatoes, green peas, black beans, salt, cannellini beans, and pinto beans and stir. Seal the lid and cook for 25 minutes on High Pressure. Do a quick pressure release. Dispose of the bay leaf. Adjust the seasonings. Sprinkle with parsley and serve.

Bean & Rice Stuffed Zucchini Boats

Serving Size: 4 | Total Time: 25 minutes

2 small zucchinis, halved lengthwise	
½ cup chopped toasted cashew nuts	
½ cup cooked rice	½ cup grated Parmesan
½ cup canned white beans	2 tbsp melted butter
½ cup chopped tomatoes	Salt and pepper to taste

Pour 1 cup of water into the Instant Pot and insert a trivet. Scoop out the pulp of zucchinis and chop roughly. In a bowl, mix the zucchini pulp, rice, tomatoes, cashew nuts, beans, Parmesan, melted butter, salt, and pepper.

Fill the zucchini boats with the mixture, and arrange the stuffed boats in a single layer on the trivet. Seal the lid and cook for 15 minutes on Steam on High. Do a quick release. Carefully unlock the lid. Serve immediately.

Mexican Frijoles Chili

Serving Size: 4 | Total Time: 55 minutes

¼ cup Cotija cheese, crumbled	
1 tsp olive oil	1 jalapeño pepper, diced
1 onion, chopped	1 tsp dried oregano
3 cloves garlic, minced	1 tsp dried chili flakes
6 cups vegetable broth	Salt to taste
1 cup black beans, soaked	2 tbsp cilantro, chopped

Warm oil on Sauté. Add in garlic and onion and cook for 3 to 4 minutes until fragrant. Add beans, vegetable broth, oregano, chili flakes, salt, and jalapeño pepper. Seal the lid and cook for 35 minutes on High Pressure. Quick-release the pressure. Divide into serving plates. Top with cilantro and Cotija cheese and serve.

Bell Pepper & Pinto Bean Stew

Serving Size: 6 | Total Time: 55 minutes

2 tbsp olive oil	3 cups vegetable stock
1 onion, chopped	2 cups pinto beans, soaked
1 red bell pepper, chopped	14 oz can tomatoes, diced
1 tbsp dried oregano	1 tbsp white wine vinegar
1 tbsp ground cumin	½ cup chives, chopped
1 tsp red pepper flakes	¼ cup fresh corn kernels

Set to Sauté your Instant Pot and heat oil. Stir in bell pepper, pepper flakes, oregano, onion, and cumin. Cook for 3 minutes. Mix in pinto beans, stock, and tomatoes. Seal the lid, select Manual, and cook for 30 minutes on High Pressure. Release the pressure naturally for 10 minutes. Add in vinegar. Divide among serving plates and top with corn and fresh chives to serve.

Tasty Tacos with Black Beans & Avocado

Serving Size: 6 | Total Time: 70 minutes

2 cups black beans, soaked	6 soft taco tortillas
1 cup shallots, chopped	1 avocado, sliced
1 tbsp dried oregano	Salt to taste
1 tsp chili powder	2 tbsp cilantro, chopped

Add the black beans to your Instant Pot. Mix in the shallots, oregano, salt, and chili powder. Cover with water. Seal the lid and cook on High Pressure for 60 minutes. Do a quick release. Drain and season with salt. Serve topped with taco tortillas, avocado slices, and cilantro.

Butter Beans with Pesto

Serving Size: 4 | Total Time: 40 minutes

1 cup butter beans, soaked	Salt and pepper to taste
3 cups chicken stock	½ cup heavy cream
1 tsp thyme	½ cup basil pesto

Place butter beans, chicken stock, thyme, pepper, and salt in your Instant Pot. Seal the lid, select Manual, and cook for 25 minutes on High. Once ready, perform a quick pressure release; unlock the lid. Stir in heavy cream and simmer for 5 minutes on Sauté. Serve topped with pesto.

Black Bean Tacos

Serving Size: 4 | Total Time: 45 minutes

1 cup black beans, soaked | 4 flour tortillas, warm
2 garlic cloves, minced | 1 cup cheddar, shredded
½ tsp cumin seeds | 2 tbsp cilantro, chopped
1 cup guacamole | Salt to taste

Place black beans, garlic, salt, and cumin in your Instant Pot and cover with water. Seal the lid, select Manual, and cook for 30 minutes on High pressure. When ready, allow a natural release. Strain the beans and transfer to a bowl. To assemble the tacos, divide black beans, guacamole, cheddar, and cilantro between the tortillas.

Bean & Potato Hash

Serving Size: 4 | Total Time: 15 minutes

2 cups peeled, chopped sweet potatoes
1 cup canned cannellini beans
2 tbsp olive oil | 2 tsp hot chili powder
1 onion, chopped | 1 cup veggie broth
1 clove garlic, minced | ¼ cup chives, chopped

Warm olive oil in your Instant Pot on Sauté. Place in onion and cook for 2-3 minutes. Add in garlic and cook until fragrant. Stir in sweet potatoes and chili powder and toss to coat. Mix in veggie broth. Seal the lid, select Manual, and cook for 3 minutes on High. Once over, perform a quick pressure release and unlock the lid. Stir in cannellini beans. Serve topped with chives.

Chili Black Bean & Rice Bowl

Serving Size: 4 | Total Time: 50 minutes

2 tsp olive oil | ½ cup black beans, soaked
1 clove garlic, minced | ½ tsp salt
1 onion, diced | 1 avocado, sliced
½ cup brown rice | 2 tbsp chili-garlic sauce

Warm olive oil in your Instant Pot on Sauté. Place in garlic and onion and cook for 2 minutes. Stir in rice and black beans. Add in 2 cups water and salt and seal the lid.

Select Manual and cook for 25 minutes on High pressure. When over, allow a natural release for 10 minutes. Drizzle with chili-garlic sauce and top with avocado.

Black Beans with Jalapeño Salsa

Serving Size: 4 | Total Time: 50 minutes

2 tbsp olive oil | 1 tsp cumin
1 cup black beans, soaked | Salt and pepper to taste
3 cups veggie broth | ½ cup Jalapeno-cilantro salsa
1 onion, quartered

Warm the olive oil in your Instant Pot. Place in onion and cook for 3 minutes. Stir in black beans, veggie broth, cumin, salt, and pepper. Seal the lid, select Manual, and cook for 25 minutes on High pressure. When ready, allow a natural release for 10 minutes and unlock the lid. Drizzle with Jalapeño-Cilantro Salsa and serve.

Mexican Pinto Beans

Serving Size: 4 | Total Time: 45 minutes

1 chipotle pepper in adobo sauce, minced
1 cup dried pinto beans | 1 tsp ground cumin
1 tbsp onion powder | 1 tsp Mexican oregano
2 tbsp garlic powder | Salt and pepper to taste
1 tbsp chili powder | 2 tbsp cilantro, chopped

Place pinto beans, onion powder, garlic powder, cumin, chili powder, chipotle pepper, Mexican oregano, salt, and pepper in your Instant Pot. Pour in 3 cups of water. Seal the lid, select Manual, and cook for 25 minutes on High pressure. When ready, allow a natural release for 10 minutes and unlock the lid. Serve topped with cilantro.

Bresaola & Black Eyed Peas

Serving Size: 4 | Total Time: 60 minutes

½ lb dried black-eyed peas | 3 oz bresaola, chopped
3 ½ cups chicken stock | Salt and pepper to taste

Place the black-eyed peas and chicken stock in your Instant Pot. Seal the lid, select Manual, and cook for 30 minutes on High pressure. Once ready, allow a natural release for 20 minutes and unlock the lid. Sprinkle with salt and pepper to taste. Serve topped with bresaola.

Pancetta with Black Beans

Serving Size: 4 | Total Time: 40 minutes

3 pancetta strips, halved | 1 small onion, cut in half
1 cup black beans, soaked | 1 bay leaf
3 cups chicken stock | Salt and pepper to taste
2 garlic cloves, crushed

Set your Instant Pot to Sauté. Place in pancetta and cook for 5 minutes until crispy; set aside. Stir black beans, chicken stock, garlic, onion, bay leaf, salt, and pepper in the pot. Seal the lid, select Manual, and cook for 25 minutes on High. When done, perform a quick pressure release and unlock the lid. Discard bay leaf and onion. Sprinkle with salt to taste. Serve topped with pancetta.

Fresh & Sour Bean Dip

Serving Size: 4 | Total Time: 50 minutes

1 cup white beans, soaked | 2 tsp ground cumin
1 garlic clove | ½ tsp chili flakes
4 tbsp olive oil | Salt and pepper to taste
½ tsp oregano | 3 tbsp cilantro, minced
3 tbsp lime juice

Cover the beans with salted water in your Instant Pot. Seal the lid, select Manual, and cook for 30 minutes on High pressure. When ready, allow a natural release for 10 minutes and unlock the lid. Strain the beans and let cool.

Place olive oil, garlic, oregano, cooked beans, lime juice, cumin, salt, and black pepper in a blender and pulse until well chopped. Transfer to a bowl and scatter with cilantro and chili flakes. Serve right away.

Sausage & Red Bean Stew

Serving Size: 4 | Total Time: 50 minutes

1 cup red beans, soaked	2 tbsp vegetable oil
4 sausages, sliced	1 yellow onion, diced
6 cups water	1 tomato, chopped
2 carrots, chopped	2 green onions, chopped
Salt and pepper to taste	2 tbsp cilantro, chopped

Place red beans and water in your Instant Pot. Seal the lid, select Manual, and cook for 10 minutes on High pressure. Once ready, allow a natural release for 10 minutes and unlock the lid. Drain the beans and set aside. Warm the vegetable oil in the pot on Sauté.

Add in sausage, carrots, yellow onion, salt, and pepper and cook for 5 minutes. Stir in tomatoes, green onions, cooked beans, and 1 cup of water. Seal the lid, select Manual, and cook for 15 minutes on High pressure. Once done, perform a quick pressure release and unlock the lid. Scatter with cilantro and serve.

Spinach & Kidney Beans

Serving Size: 4 | Total Time: 55 minutes

1 cup kidney beans, soaked	1 celery stick, chopped
2 tomatoes, chopped	1 onion, finely chopped
Salt and pepper to taste	3 cups chicken stock
2 tbsp olive oil	1 cup baby spinach
1 carrot, diced	2 tbsp parsley, chopped

Heat olive oil on Sauté and stir-fry onion, carrot, celery, salt, and black pepper for 3 minutes. Pour in tomatoes, chicken stock, and beans. Seal the lid, select Manual, and cook for 25 minutes on High pressure.

Once ready, allow a naturally pressure release for 10 minutes. Stir in baby spinach, press Sauté and cook for 5 minutes until the spinach wilts. Top with parsley.

Navy & Pinto Bean Pot

Serving Size: 4 | Total Time: 40 minutes

2 tbsp olive oil	3 carrots, chopped
1 onion, chopped	1 large celery stalk, chopped
2 cloves garlic, minced	1 tsp dried thyme
5 cups vegetable broth	16 oz zucchini noodles
½ cup pinto beans, soaked	Salt and pepper to taste
½ cup navy beans, soaked	

Warm oil on Sauté. Stir in garlic and onion and cook for 5 minutes. Mix in pepper, broth, carrots, salt, celery, beans, and thyme. Seal the lid and cook for 15 minutes on High Pressure. Release the pressure naturally. Mix zucchini noodles into the soup and stir until wilted. Taste and adjust the seasoning.

Greek-Style Navy Beans

Serving Size: 4 | Total Time: 45 minutes

1 cup navy beans, soaked	1 tbsp olive oil
2 spring onions, sliced	1 tsp Greek seasoning
1 garlic clove, smashed	Salt and pepper to taste

Place beans, 3 cups water, and garlic in your Instant Pot. Seal the lid, select Manual, and cook for 25 minutes on High pressure. Once done, allow a natural release for 10 minutes and unlock the lid. Drain the beans and combine with olive oil, Greek seasoning, salt, and pepper in a bowl. Serve sprinkled with green onions.

Simple Black Bean Soup

Serving Size: 6 | Total Time: 25 minutes

1 tsp olive oil	30 oz can diced tomatoes
1 onion, chopped	1 (14 oz) can black beans
2 celery stalks, chopped	¼ cup chopped cilantro
1 carrot, chopped	2 tsp ground cumin
2 serrano peppers, minced	Salt and pepper to taste
5 cups vegetable broth	

Warm oil on Sauté. Add in carrot, onion, serrano peppers, and celery. Cook for 6 to 7 minutes.

Mix in broth, sea salt, black beans, cumin, tomatoes, cilantro, and pepper. Seal lid and cook for 8 minutes on High Pressure. Release pressure naturally.

Pancetta with Garbanzo Beans

Serving Size: 6 | Total Time: 60 minutes

3 strips pancetta	2 garlic cloves, minced
1 onion, diced	½ cup ketchup
15 oz can garbanzo beans	1 tbsp mustard powder
1 cup apple cider	Salt and pepper to taste

Cook pancetta for 5 minutes until crispy on Sauté. Add onion and garlic, and cook for 3 minutes until soft. Mix in garbanzo beans, ketchup, salt, apple cider, mustard powder, 2 cups water, and black pepper. Seal the lid, press Bean/Chili, and cook on High Pressure for 30 minutes. Release pressure naturally for 10 minutes. Serve.

Chickpea & Jalapeño Chicken

Serving Size: 4 | Total Time: 40 minutes

1 lb boneless, skinless chicken legs	
½ tsp ground cumin	¼ cup chicken stock
½ tsp cayenne pepper	24 oz can crushed tomatoes
2 tbsp olive oil	28 oz can chickpeas
1 onion, minced	Salt to taste
2 jalapeño peppers, minced	½ cup coconut milk
3 garlic cloves, crushed	¼ cup parsley, chopped
2 tbsp freshly grated ginger	2 cups cooked basmati rice

Season the chicken with salt, cayenne pepper, and cumin. Set your Instant Pot to Sauté and warm the oil. Add in jalapeño peppers and onion and cook for 5 minutes, stirring occasionally until soft. Mix in ginger and garlic, and cook for 3 minutes until tender. Add ¼ cup chicken stock into the cooker to ensure the pan is deglazed. From the pan's bottom, scrape any browned bits of food.

Mix the onion mixture with chickpeas, tomatoes, and salt. Stir in the chicken to coat. Seal the lid and cook on High Pressure for 20 minutes.

Release the pressure quickly. Remove the chicken and slice into chunks. Into the remaining sauce, mix coconut milk and simmer for 5 minutes on Sauté. Split rice into 4 bowls. Top with chicken, sauce, and parsley and serve.

Chickpea & Lentil Soup

Serving Size: 6 | Total Time: 40 minutes

2 tbsp olive oil	1 cup canned diced tomatoes
1 onion, chopped	1 celery stalk, diced
3 garlic cloves, minced	1 tsp sweet paprika
2 carrots, sliced	1 tsp cumin
1 cup canned chickpeas	1 cup brown lentils, rinsed
1 sweet pepper, chopped	2 cups spinach, chopped
½ banana pepper, chopped	Salt and pepper to taste

Warm the olive oil in your Instant Pot on Sauté. Add in onion, garlic, carrot, banana pepper, sweet pepper, celery, paprika, and cumin and cook for 5 minutes.

Stir in lentils, chickpeas, tomatoes, salt, pepper, and 6 cups of water and seal the lid. Select Manual and cook for 10 minutes on High pressure. Once done, allow a natural release for 10 minutes and unlock the lid. Mix in the spinach and adjust the seasoning. Serve warm.

Quinoa Bowls with Broccoli & Pesto

Serving Size: 2 | Total Time: 15 minutes

1 bunch baby heirloom carrots, peeled	
1 cup quinoa	¼ cabbage, chopped
2 cups vegetable broth	2 eggs
Salt and pepper to taste	1 avocado, sliced
1 potato, peeled, cubed	¼ cup pesto sauce
10 oz broccoli florets	Lemon wedges, for serving

In your Instant Pot, mix the vegetable broth, pepper, quinoa, and salt. Set a trivet on top of the quinoa and place a steamer basket on the trivet. Mix carrots, potato, eggs, and broccoli in the steamer basket. Seal the lid and cook for 1 minute on High Pressure. Quick-release the pressure. Remove the trivet and basket from the pot.

Set the eggs in a bowl of ice water. Then peel and halve them. Fluff the quinoa. In two bowls, equally divide avocado, quinoa, broccoli, eggs, carrots, potato, cabbage, and pesto dollop. Serve with lemon wedges.

Homemade Veggie Quinoa

Serving Size: 6 | Total Time: 30 minutes

1 cup quinoa, rinsed	2 tbsp olive oil
2 carrots, cut into sticks	Salt to taste
1 large onion, chopped	2 tbsp cilantro, chopped

Heat olive oil in the Instant Pot on Sauté. Add in onion and carrots and stir-fry for about 10 minutes until tender and crispy. Remove to a plate and set aside. Add 2 cups of water, salt, and quinoa to the pot. Seal the lid and cook on High Pressure for 10 minutes. Do a quick release. Transfer to a serving plate and top with the carrots and onion. Serve scattered with cilantro.

Colorful Quinoa with Red Salsa

Serving Size: 4 | Total Time: 30 minutes

2 tbsp olive oil	14 oz can pinto beans
1 green bell pepper, diced	1 cup tri-color quinoa
1 red onion, diced	1 cup red salsa
1 tsp ground cumin	1 cup vegetable broth
½ tsp salt	

Warm oil on Sauté. Add red onion and green bell pepper as you stir. Add salt and cumin, and cook for 7-8 minutes until fragrant. To the vegetable mixture, add quinoa, broth, red salsa, and pinto beans. Seal the lid and cook on High Pressure for 12 minutes. Do a quick pressure release. Carefully unlock the lid. Use a fork to fluff quinoa and divide between serving bowls to serve.

Almond & Raisin Quinoa

Serving Size: 4 | Total Time: 15 minutes

1 cup quinoa	½ cup slivered almonds
1 cup raisins, soaked	¼ cup sunflower seeds

Place quinoa and 2 cups water in your Instant Pot. Seal the lid, select Manual, and cook for 10 minutes on High pressure. Once done, perform a quick pressure release. Stir in sunflower seeds, almonds, and raisins. Serve.

Saffron Quinoa Pilaf

Serving Size: 4 | Total Time: 30 minutes

1 shallot, chopped	Pinch of saffron
2 tbsp olive oil	Salt to taste
2 cloves garlic, minced	2 tbsp parsley, chopped
1 cup quinoa	

Submerge saffron in ½ cup of hot water and let soak for 10 minutes. Set your Instant Pot to Sauté. Heat the olive oil and add the garlic and shallot; sauté for 3 minutes. Stir in quinoa, saffron with the liquid, salt, and 2 cups of water. Seal the lid, select Manual, and cook for 1 minute on High pressure. Once over, allow a natural release for 10 minutes. Using a fork, fluff the quinoa. Adjust the seasoning with salt. Serve topped with parsley.

Chorizo & Veggie Quinoa

Serving Size: 4 | Total Time: 20 minutes

1 lb chorizo sausages, casings removed	
2 tbsp olive oil	2 cups chicken stock
1 sweet onion, chopped	1 cup quinoa
1 tsp turmeric powder	1 red bell pepper, chopped
½ tsp paprika	½ cup mushrooms, halved

Set your Instant Pot to Sauté. Heat the olive oil and add in chorizo sausages, onion, mushrooms, and bell pepper. Cook for 3-4 minutes until tender. Stir in turmeric and paprika, pour in chicken stock and quinoa. Seal the lid, select Manual, and cook for 1 minute on High pressure. When done, allow a natural release for 10 minutes. Using a fork, fluff the quinoa and serve.

Cilantro & Spring Onion Quinoa

Serving Size: 4 | Total Time: 15 minutes

1 cup quinoa	½ tsp salt
2 cups vegetable broth	2 spring onions, sliced
Juice of 1 lemon	2 tbsp cilantro, chopped

Place the quinoa, broth, and salt in your Instant Pot. Seal the lid, select Manual, and cook for 1 minute on High.

Once ready, allow a natural release for 10 minutes and unlock the lid. Using a fork, fluff the quinoa. Sprinkle lemon juice, cilantro, and spring onions and serve.

Chorizo & Lentil Stew

Serving Size: 4 | Total Time: 60 minutes

1 cups lentils	2 tbsp maple syrup
4 oz chorizo, chopped	2 tbsp liquid smoke
1 onion, diced	1 tbsp lime juice
2 garlic cloves, minced	2 cups brown sugar
2 cups tomato sauce	Salt and pepper to taste
2 cups vegetable broth	1 tsp chili powder
½ cup mustard	1 tsp paprika
½ cup cider vinegar	¼ tsp cayenne pepper
3 tbsp Worcestershire sauce	

Set to Sauté the Instant Pot. Add in chorizo and cook for 3 minutes as you stir until crisp. Add garlic and onion and cook for 2 minutes. Mix in tomato sauce, cider vinegar, liquid smoke, Worcestershire sauce, lime juice, mustard, and maple syrup and cook for 2 minutes.

Stir in broth and scrape the bottom to do away with any browned bits of food. Add pepper, chili, sugar, paprika, salt, and cayenne into the sauce as you stir to mix.

Stir in lentils to coat. Seal the lid and cook on High Pressure for 30 minutes. Release pressure naturally for 10 minutes and unlock the lid. Serve warm.

Easy Red Lentil Dhal with Spinach

Serving Size: 6 | Total Time: 35 minutes

2 tbsp olive oil	¼ tsp cayenne pepper
1 jalapeño pepper, minced	1 ½ cups red lentils
1 cup spinach, chopped	1 tomato, diced
4 cloves garlic, minced	¼ cup lemon juice
1 tsp fresh ginger, grated	Salt to taste
1 tbsp cumin seeds	2 tbsp cilantro, chopped
1 tbsp coriander seeds	Natural yogurt for garnish
1 tsp ground turmeric	

Heat oil on Sauté, add cayenne, red jalapeño, ginger, turmeric, cumin, garlic, and coriander, and cook for 3 minutes until seeds become fragrant and begin to pop.

Pour in 3 cups water, tomato, and lentils and stir. Seal the lid and cook on High Pressure for 10 minutes. Release pressure naturally for 10 minutes. Stir in spinach.

Cook until wilted, 5 minutes. Add lemon juice and season to taste. Garnish with yogurt and cilantro and serve.

Traditional Indian Lentil Soup

Serving Size: 6 | Total Time: 30 minutes

1 tbsp ghee	1 tomato, chopped
2 tsp cumin seeds	1 cup split yellow lentils
1 onion, chopped	2 tbsp garam masala
4 garlic cloves, minced	½ tsp ground turmeric
1-inch ginger, minced	½ tsp cayenne pepper
Salt to taste	1 tbsp cilantro, chopped

Warm ghee on Sauté. Add cumin seeds and cook for 10 seconds until they begin to pop. Stir in onion and cook for 2-3 minutes until softened. Mix in ginger, salt, and garlic and cook for 1 minute as you stir. Mix in tomato and cook for 3 to 5 minutes until the mixture breaks down. Stir in the turmeric, lentils, garam masala, and cayenne pepper. Cover with water. Seal the lid and cook for 8 minutes on High Pressure. Release the pressure quickly. Serve in bowls sprinkled with fresh cilantro.

Creamed Lentils

Serving Size: 4 | Total Time: 20 minutes

1 tbsp horseradish sauce	Salt to taste
¼ cup crème fraiche	1 tsp onion powder
1 cup brown lentils	1 tsp garlic powder
1 cup tomato sauce	1 tsp chili powder
½ tsp cumin	2 tbsp thyme, chopped

Place 3 cups of water, lentils, tomato sauce, chili powder, garlic powder, onion powder, cumin, and salt in your Instant Pot. Seal the lid, select Manual, and cook for 15 minutes on High pressure. Once ready, perform a quick pressure release and unlock the lid. Stir in horseradish sauce and crème fraiche. Scatter thyme and serve.

Lentil & Chorizo Chili

Serving Size: 4 | Total Time: 40 minutes

½ lb chorizo sausage, sliced	1 cup canned diced tomatoes
2 tbsp olive oil	1 cup lentils
1 onion, diced	3 cups vegetable broth

Warm the olive oil in your Instant Pot on Sauté. Place in onion and chorizo and sauté for 5 minutes. Add in tomatoes and cook for 1 more minute. Stir in lentils and vegetable broth. Seal the lid, select Manual, and cook for 15 minutes on High pressure. When ready, allow a natural release for 10 minutes and unlock the lid. Serve.

Lime Bulgur with Olives

Serving Size: 4 | Total Time: 30 minutes

1 tbsp olive oil	2 ½ cups vegetable broth
1 small onion, chopped	1 tbsp lime juice
2 cloves garlic, minced	10 black olives to garnish
1 tbsp cilantro	Salt and pepper to taste
1 cup bulgur	

Heat oil on Sauté. Stir in garlic and onion and cook for 5 minutes. Add in cilantro, bulgur, pepper, and salt. Place 1 tbsp of lime juice and broth into the cooker.

Seal the lid and cook on High Pressure for 15 minutes. Do a quick release. Unlock the lid. Use a fork to fluff bulgur. Serve in bowls topped with olives.

Bulgur Pilaf with Roasted Bell Peppers

Serving Size: 4 | Total Time: 25 minutes

2 tbsp olive oil	1 tsp grated lemon zest
1 garlic clove, minced	1 cup bulgur
1 onion, chopped	Salt and pepper to taste
2 cups vegetable stock	6 oz roasted bell peppers
¼ cup lemon juice	

In a bowl, toss bell peppers with some oil, salt, and pepper. Warm the remaining oil on Sauté and cook onion and garlic until soft, about 3 minutes. Stir in stock, lemon juice, lemon zest, and bulgur. Seal the lid and cook on High Pressure for 5 minutes. Do a natural pressure release for 10 minutes. Carefully unlock the lid. Fluff the rice with a fork. Top with roasted peppers to serve.

Kale & Parmesan Pearl Barley

Serving Size: 2 | Total Time: 30 minutes

1 tbsp butter	2 cups vegetable broth
1 small onion, diced	½ cup grated Parmesan
1 cup pearl barley	1 cup kale, chopped
2 garlic cloves, smashed	½ lemon, juiced

Warm butter on Sauté. Add in onion and cook for 3 minutes until soft. Stir in garlic and barley and continue cooking for 1 to 2 minutes. Mix in broth and season. Seal the lid and cook for 9 minutes on High Pressure. Release pressure naturally for 10 minutes. Add in Parmesan cheese and kale and stir until the cheese is fully melted. Drizzle with lemon juice and serve.

Pearl Barley Sloppy Joes

Serving Size: 6 | Total Time: 35 minutes

1 cup pearl barley, rinsed	1 tsp Dijon mustard
1 cup green onion, chopped	1 tsp smoked paprika
1 clove garlic, minced	1 tsp chili powder
2 cups tomato sauce	Salt and pepper to taste
2 tbsp brown sugar	6 brioche buns
2 tbsp Worcestershire sauce	Dill pickles for garnish

In the pot, mix Worcestershire sauce, 2 cups water, onion, garlic, brown sugar, barley, tomato sauce, mustard, paprika, and chili powder. Season with salt and pepper. Seal the lid and cook for 25 minutes on High Pressure. Release the pressure quickly. Carefully unlock the lid. Press Sauté and cook until the mixture becomes thick. Transfer the sloppy joe mixture to the brioche buns and top with dill pickles.

Barley & Smoked Salmon Salad

Serving Size: 4 | Total Time: 30 minutes

4 smoked salmon fillets, flaked	
1 cup pearl barley	1 cup arugula
Salt and pepper to taste	1 green apple, chopped

Place the barley, 2 cups of water, salt, and pepper in your Instant Pot. Seal the lid, select Manual, and cook for 20 minutes on High pressure.

Once ready, perform a quick pressure release and unlock the lid. Remove barley to a serving bowl. Mix in apple and salmon. Top with arugula.

Tomato & Feta Pearl Barley

Serving Size: 4 | Total Time: 30 minutes

½ cup sundried tomatoes in oil, chopped	
½ cup feta, crumbled	Salt to taste
1 cup pearl barley	2 tbsp butter, melted
2 cups chicken broth	

Place barley, chicken broth, and salt in your Instant Pot. Seal the lid, select Manual, and cook for 25 minutes on High pressure. When done, allow a natural release for 15 minutes and unlock the lid. Mix in tomatoes and top with feta and butter to serve.

Cranberry Millet Pilaf

Serving Size: 4 | Total Time: 20 minutes

½ cup dried cranberries. chopped	
2 tbsp olive oil	1 cup long-grain white rice
1 garlic clove, minced	1 cup millet
1 shallot, chopped	Salt and pepper to taste

Warm olive oil in your Instant Pot on Sauté. Add in shallot and garlic and cook for 3 minutes. Stir in rice, millet, 3 cups water, cranberries, salt, and pepper.

Seal the lid and for 10 minutes on Rice. When ready, perform a quick pressure release and unlock the lid. Using a fork, fluff the pilaf. Serve immediately.

Rich Millet with Herbs & Cherry Tomatoes

Serving Size: 4 | Total Time: 20 minutes

1 cup millet	1 tbsp fresh sage, chopped
2 cups vegetable stock	1 tsp fresh thyme, chopped
1 sweet onion, chopped	1 tsp parsley, chopped
1 cup cherry tomatoes, halved	Salt and pepper to taste

Add millet, onion, and vegetable stock. Seal the lid and cook for 10 minutes on High Pressure. Release pressure quickly. Fluff the millet with a fork, add in sage, thyme, parsley, and tomatoes, and season with pepper and salt.

Feta & Vegetable Faro

Serving Size: 4 | Total Time: 30 minutes

1 cup faro, rinsed	4 cups spinach
2 cups chicken broth	1 bell pepper, chopped
1 celery stalk, chopped	½ cup feta, crumbled

Place faro, broth, celery, spinach, and bell pepper in your Instant Pot. Seal the lid, select Manual, and cook for 10 minutes on High. When ready, allow a natural release for 10 minutes. Top with feta cheese and serve.

Harissa Chicken with Fruity Farro

Serving Size: 4 | Total Time: 45 minutes

2 tbsp dried cherries, chopped
1 lb chicken breasts, sliced
1 tbsp harissa paste
1 cup whole-grain farro
Salt to taste
3 tbsp olive oil
1 tbsp apple cider vinegar
4 green onions, chopped
10 mint leaves, chopped

In a bowl, place chicken, apple cider vinegar, 1 tbsp of olive oil, and harissa paste and combine everything thoroughly. Allow marinating covered for 15 minutes.

Heat the remaining olive oil on Sauté and cook green onion for 3 minutes. Stir in farro and salt and pour 2 cups of water. Insert a trivet over the farro and place the chicken on the trivet. Seal the lid, select Manual, and cook for 20 minutes on High. When ready, do a quick pressure release. Open the lid, remove the chicken and the trivet. Add dried cherries and mint to the farro. Stir and transfer to a plate. Top with chicken and serve.

Gluten-Free Porridge

Serving Size: 4 | Total Time: 25 minutes

1 cup buckwheat groats
2 cups rice milk
1 banana, sliced
¼ cup raisins
1 tsp ground cardamom
½ tsp vanilla
2 tbsp pistachios, chopped

Place buckwheat, milk, raisins, cardamom, and vanilla in your Instant Pot. Seal the lid, select Manual, and cook for 6 minutes on High pressure. When done, allow a natural release for 10 minutes and unlock the lid. Serve topped with banana and pistachios.

Broccoli Couscous

Serving Size: 4 | Total Time: 15 minutes

10 oz broccoli florets
2 tbsp butter, melted
1 cup couscous
Salt and pepper to taste
2 tbsp parsley, chopped

Pour 1 cup of water into the Instant Pot and add a steamer basket. Place the broccoli in the basket and seal the lid. Select Steam and cook for 3 minutes on High. Once pressure cooking is complete, use a quick release.

In a bowl cover couscous with salted boiled water. Let it stand for 2-3 minutes until the water has absorbed. Fluff with a fork and stir in broccoli and adjust the seasoning with salt and pepper. Top with parsley and serve.

Couscous with Lamb & Vegetables

Serving Size: 4 | Total Time: 40 minutes

2 tbsp olive oil
1 large onion, chopped
2 garlic cloves, minced
1 lb lamb stew meat, cubed
3 cups vegetable stock
1 carrot, grated
1 red bell pepper, chopped
1 cup Israeli couscous
½ tsp cumin
Salt and pepper to taste
2 tbsp cilantro, chopped
4 lemon wedges

Heat olive oil on Sauté and cook onion, garlic, and lamb for 6-7 minutes. Stir in carrot, bell pepper, and cumin and sauté for another 3 minutes. Pour in vegetable stock and adjust the seasoning with salt and pepper. Close and secure the lid. Select Manual and cook for 10 minutes on High. Once cooking is complete, use a natural release.

Add the couscous and select Sauté on Low. Cover with the lid and simmer for 8-10 minutes until the couscous is tender. Select Cancel and let it sit for 2-3 minutes. Fluff and top with cilantro. Serve with lemon wedges.

Salmon & Spinach Couscous

Serving Size: 4 | Total Time: 20 minutes

4 salmon fillets
2 tbsp butter
1 cup couscous
1 ¼ cups vegetable broth
2 tomatoes, chopped
1 cup spinach, chopped
4 lemon wedges
Salt and pepper to taste

Pour the vegetable broth into the Instant Pot and insert a trivet. Season the fillets with salt and pepper, and arrange them on the trivet. Seal the lid, select Steam and set to 5 minutes on high. Once ready, do a quick pressure release.

Open the lid and remove the fish and the trivet. Add butter and couscous to the broth and press Sauté. Bring to a boil, then stir in tomatoes, spinach, salt, and pepper. Cover with the lid. Let it rest for 5-7 minutes until all the liquid is absorbed and spinach is wilted. Fluff the couscous. Top with salmon and lemon wedges and serve.

Ham & Peas with Goat Cheese

Serving Size: 4 | Total Time: 40 minutes

4 goat cheese, crumbled
1 cup dried peas, rinsed
3 oz ham, diced
3 cups vegetable stock
1 tsp mustard powder
Salt and pepper to taste

Place peas, ham, mustard powder, and vegetable stock in your Instant Pot. Seal the lid, select Manual, and cook for 20 minutes on High. Once done, allow a natural release for 10 minutes and unlock the lid. Sprinkle with salt and pepper to taste. Top with goat cheese slices and serve.

Mom's Black-Eyed Peas with Garlic & Kale

Serving Size: 6 | Total Time: 20 minutes

1 cup fire-roasted red peppers, diced
15 oz can fire-roasted tomatoes
1 tsp olive oil
1 onion, chopped
2 garlic cloves, minced
½ tsp ground allspice
½ tsp red pepper, crushed
1 ½ cups black-eyed peas
1 ½ cups vegetable broth
2 cups chopped kale

Warm oil on Sauté. Add onion and garlic and cook for 5 minutes. Season with crushed red pepper, and allspice. Add broth and black-eyed peas to the pot. Seal the lid and cook on High Pressure for 5 minutes. Do a quick pressure release. Mix the peas with kale. red peppers, and tomatoes. Seal the lid and cook on High for 1 minute. Release the pressure quickly. Serve.

Apricot Steel Cut Oats

Serving Size: 2 | Total Time: 25 minutes

¾ cup dry apricots, soaked and chopped
1 tbsp butter   2 oz cream cheese, softened
1 cup steel oats   1 tsp milk
A pinch of salt   1 tsp cinnamon
2 tbsp white sugar   ¼ cup brown sugar

Melt butter in your Instant Pot on Sauté. Stir in oats for 3 minutes. Add in salt and 3 ½ cups water. Seal the lid, select Manual, and cook for 10 minutes on High pressure.

When done, allow a natural release for 5 minutes and unlock the lid. Stir in apricots and set aside. In the meantime, combine white sugar with cream cheese and milk in a bowl. In a separate bowl, mix cinnamon and brown sugar. Divide oats between bowls. Top with cinnamon and cream cheese and serve.

Honey Oat & Pumpkin Granola

Serving Size: 4 | Total Time: 45 minutes

1 tbsp soft butter   2 tsp cinnamon
1 cup steel-cut oats   A pinch of salt
1 cup pumpkin puree   ¼ cup clear honey
3 cups water   1 tsp pumpkin pie spice

Set your Instant Pot to Sauté and melt in the butter. Stir in oats and cook for 3 minutes. Add in pumpkin puree, water, cinnamon, salt, honey, and pumpkin spice and stir. Seal the lid, select Manual, and cook for 10 minutes on High. Once ready, allow a natural release for 10 minutes. Stir the granola and let sit for 10 minutes. Serve.

Kiwi Steel Cut Oatmeal

Serving Size: 4 | Total Time: 25 minutes

2 kiwi, mashed   1 tsp vanilla
2 cups steel cut oatmeal   ¼ tsp salt
¼ tsp nutmeg   ½ cup hazelnuts, chopped
1 tsp cinnamon   ¼ cup honey

Place the kiwi, oats, 3 cups water, nutmeg, cinnamon, vanilla, and salt in your Instant Pot and stir to combine. Seal the lid and cook on Manual for 10 minutes on High. When done, allow a natural release for 10 minutes and unlock the lid. Mix in hazelnuts and honey and let chill.

Southern Cheese Grits

Serving Size: 6 | Total Time: 35 minutes

2 tbsp olive oil   4 oz cheddar, shredded
1 cup stone-ground grits   3 tbsp butter
2 cups vegetable broth   Salt to taste
1 cup milk

Set your Instant Pot to Sauté. Warm the olive oil, place in grits and cook for 3 minutes until fragrant. Stir in broth, milk, cheese, butter, and salt. Seal the lid, select Manual, and cook for 10 minutes on High. Once ready, allow a natural release for 15 minutes and unlock the lid. Serve.

Coconut Cherry Steel Cut Oats

Serving Size: 4 | Total Time: 20 minutes

1 cup cherries, pitted and halved
1 cup steel-cut oats   2 cups water
1 cup coconut milk   ½ tsp vanilla extract

Place cherries, oats, milk, water, and vanilla extract in your Instant Pot. Seal the lid, select Manual, and cook for 3 minutes on High pressure. Once ready, allow a natural release for 10 minutes and unlock the lid. Serve.

Jamaican Cornmeal Porridge

Serving Size: 4 | Total Time: 25 minutes

1 cup cornmeal   1 tsp vanilla extract
1 cup coconut milk   ½ cup condensed milk
½ tsp nutmeg, ground   1 mango, sliced

Combine 1 cup of water and cornmeal in a bowl and stir. Add 3 cups of water, coconut milk, vanilla, nutmeg, and cornmeal mixture in your Instant Pot. Seal the lid, select Manual, and cook for 6 minutes on High. Once over, allow a natural release for 10 minutes and unlock the lid. Stir in condensed milk. Top with mango and serve.

Cheesy Polenta with Sundried Tomatoes

Serving Size: 4 | Total Time: 25 minutes

1 cup sun-dried tomatoes, finely chopped
2 tbsp olive oil   1 tsp kosher salt
1 cup onion, diced   4 cups vegetable stock
2 cloves garlic, chopped   ¼ cup Parmesan, shredded
2 tsp fresh oregano, minced   1 cup polenta
2 tbsp fresh parsley, minced

Warm olive oil in your Instant Pot on Sauté and add in onion and garlic. Cook for 3 minutes until fragrant. Stir in tomatoes, oregano, parsley, salt, and stock. Top with polenta. Seal the lid, select Manual, and cook for 5 minutes on High pressure. When done, allow a natural release for 10 minutes. Top with Parmesan and serve.

Garlic Mushroom Polenta

Serving Size: 4 | Total Time: 35 minutes

1 cup mixed mushrooms, sliced
2 tsp olive oil   ½ tsp cumin
4 green onions, chopped   Salt and pepper to taste
2 garlic cloves, sliced   ¼ tsp cayenne pepper
2 tbsp cilantro, minced   2 cups veggie stock
1 tbsp chili powder   1 cup polenta

Warm olive oil in your Instant Pot on Sauté and add mushrooms, garlic, and green onions. Cook for 4 minutes. Stir in chili powder, cumin, salt, pepper, cayenne, and stock. Combine polenta with 1 ½ cups of hot water in a bowl and transfer to the Instant Pot. Seal the lid, select Manual, and cook for 10 minutes on High pressure. Once done, allow a natural release for 10 minutes and unlock the lid. Top with cilantro and serve.

APPETIZERS & SIDE DISHES

Chili Deviled Eggs

Serving Size: 6 | Total Time: 15 minutes

1 cup water	¼ cup mayonnaise
10 large eggs	Salt and pepper to taste
¼ cup cream cheese	¼ tsp chili powder

Add 1 cup of water and a steamer basket in the Instant Pot. Add in the eggs. Seal the lid. Cook on Pressure cook for 5 minutes. Release the pressure quickly. Drop eggs into an ice bath to cool. Peel eggs and halve them. Transfer yolks to a bowl and use a fork to mash; Stir in cream cheese, chili powder, mayonnaise, salt, and pepper. Spoon into egg white halves.

Hard-Boiled Eggs with Paprika

Serving Size: 4 | Total Time: 20 minutes

4 large eggs	A pinch of paprika
Salt and pepper to taste	

In the pot, add 1 cup water and place a trivet. Lay your eggs on top. Seal the lid and cook for 5 minutes on High Pressure. Do a natural release for 10 minutes. Transfer the eggs to ice-cold water to cool completely. Peel and season with paprika, salt, and pepper before serving.

Traditional Italian Rice & Cheese Balls

Serving Size: 6 | Total Time: 35 minutes

1 cup canned Kernel sweet corn, drained	
½ cup + 1 tbsp olive oil	1 ½ cups grated cheddar
1 white onion, diced	¼ cup grated Parmesan
2 garlic cloves, minced	Salt and pepper to taste
5 cups chicken stock	2 cups fresh bread crumbs
½ cup apple cider vinegar	2 eggs
2 cups short-grain rice	

On Sauté, heat 1 tbsp of oil and cook onion and garlic for 3 minutes until translucent. Stir in the stock, vinegar, and rice. Seal the lid and cook on High Pressure for 7 minutes. Do a natural pressure release for 10 minutes. Stir in cheddar cheese, corn, salt, and pepper. Spoon into a bowl and let cool completely. Wipe clean the pot. In a bowl, pour the breadcrumbs.

In a separate bowl, beat the eggs. Form balls out of the rice mixture, dip each into the beaten eggs, and coat in the breadcrumb mixture. Heat the remaining oil on Sauté and fry balls until crispy. Sprinkle with Parmesan cheese and serve.

Egg Bites with Mushrooms & Arugula

Serving Size: 4 | Total Time: 15 minutes

12 oz button mushrooms, sliced	
4 oz asiago cheese, shredded	
8 oz arugula	2 tbsp butter, melted
4 eggs	½ red chili flakes

Place a trivet in the Instant Pot and pour in 1 cup water. Grease 4 heatproof cups with the butter. In a bowl, whisk the eggs and stir in the mushrooms and arugula. Pour the mixture into the cups. Top with the cheese and chili flakes. Arrange the cups on the trivet. Seal the lid and cook on Manual for 7 minutes. Do a quick release. Serve chilled.

Kale & Artichoke Cheese Bites

Serving Size: 4 | Total Time: 30 minutes

¼ cup chopped artichoke hearts	
¼ cup chopped kale	1 tsp dried basil
¼ cup ricotta cheese	1 lemon, zested
2 tbsp grated Parmesan	Salt and pepper to taste
¼ cup goat cheese	4 frozen filo dough, thawed
1 large egg white	1 tbsp extra-virgin olive oil

In a bowl, combine kale, artichoke, ricotta, parmesan, goat cheese, egg white, basil, lemon zest, salt, and pepper. Place a filo dough on a clean flat surface. Brush with olive oil. Place a second filo sheet on the first and brush with more oil. Continue layering to form a pile of four oiled sheets. Working from the short side, cut the phyllo sheets into 8 strips and half them.

Spoon 1 tbsp of filling onto one short end of every strip. Fold a corner to cover the filling and a triangle; continue folding over and over to the end of the strip, creating a triangle-shaped filo packet. Repeat the process with the other filo bites. Place a trivet and 1 cup water into the pot. Put the bites on the trivet. Seal the lid. Cook on Manual for 15 minutes. Do a quick release.

Juicy Hot Chicken Wings

Serving Size: 4 | Total Time: 15 minutes

¼ cup ranch salad dressing mix	
½ cup sriracha sauce	2 lb chicken vignettes
2 tbsp butter, melted	½ tsp paprika
Juice from ½ lemon	

Mix chicken, 1 cup water, sriracha, butter, and lemon in the inner pot. Seal the lid and cook on High Pressure for 5 min minutes. Do a quick pressure release. Serve with the paprika and ranch dressing.

Picante Chicken Wings

Serving Size: 4 | Total Time: 25 minutes

2 lb chicken wings	2 tbsp Worcestershire sauce
¼ cup hot pepper sauce	1 tsp tabasco
2 tbsp oil	4 cups chicken broth
4 tbsp butter	

Grease the pot with oil and place the chicken wings. Pour in broth and hot pepper sauce. Seal the lid and cook on Manual for 15 minutes on High. When ready, do a quick release. Unlock the lid Remove the wings and discard the broth. In the pot, melt the butter on Sauté. Brown the wings for 3 minutes, turning once. Add the Worcestershire sauce and tabasco and stir. Serve hot.

Paprika Chicken Wings

Serving Size: 4 | Total Time: 25 minutes

2 lb chicken wings	1 tsp paprika
¼ cup olive oil	1 tbsp grated ginger
2 garlic cloves, crushed	¼ cup lime juice
1 tbsp rosemary, chopped	½ cup apple cider vinegar
Salt and pepper to taste	

In a bowl, mix oil, garlic, rosemary, white pepper, salt, paprika, ginger, lime juice, and apple cider vinegar. Submerge wings into the mixture and cover. Refrigerate for one hour. Remove the wings from the marinade and pat dry.

Insert the steaming rack, 1 cup of water, and place the chicken on the rack. Seal the lid and cook on High Pressure for 8 minutes. Release the steam naturally for about 10 minutes. Serve with fresh vegetable salad.

Chicken Wings with Teriyaki Sauce

Serving Size: 6 | Total Time: 25 minutes

1 tbsp honey	2 lb chicken wings
1 cup teriyaki sauce	2 tbsp cornstarch
1 tsp black pepper	1 tsp sesame seeds

In the pot, combine honey, teriyaki sauce, and black pepper until the honey dissolves. Toss in chicken wings to coat. Seal the lid, press Manual, and cook for 10 minutes on High. Release the pressure quickly. Transfer chicken wings to a platter. Mix 2 tbsp of water with the cornstarch. Press Sauté and stir the slurry into the sauce. Cook for 4 minutes until thickened. Top the chicken wings with the thickened sauce. Add a garnish of sesame seeds and serve.

Delicious Mushroom & Garlic Pizza

Serving Size: 2 | Total Time: 1 hour 25 minutes

1 cup button mushrooms, sliced	
¾ cup all-purpose flour	¼ tsp salt
1 cup whole wheat flour	1 tbsp olive oil
½ tsp brown sugar	¼ cup gouda cheese, grated
1 tsp garlic powder	2 tbsp tomato paste
2 tsp dried yeast	½ tsp dried oregano

In a bowl fitted with a dough hook attachment, combine all-purpose flour with whole wheat flour, brown sugar, garlic powder, dried yeast, and salt. Mix well and gradually add 1 cup of lukewarm water and oil. Continue to beat until smooth dough. Transfer to a lightly floured surface and knead until completely smooth. Form into a tight ball and wrap tightly in plastic foil. Set aside for 1 hour. Line a baking dish with some parchment paper; set aside.

Roll out the dough with a rolling pin and transfer to the baking dish. Brush with tomato paste, and sprinkle with oregano, gouda, and button mushrooms. Add a trivet inside your Instant Pot and pour in 1 cup of water. Seal the lid, and cook for 15 minutes on High Pressure. Do a quick release. Cut and serve.

Lemon Hummus with Spinach

Serving Size: 4 | Total Time: 50 minutes

4 cups water	¼ cup tahini
1 cup chickpeas, soaked	1 tbsp lemon juice
2 tbsp grapeseed oil	2 cups spinach, chopped
Salt to taste	2 garlic cloves, minced

In the Instant Pot, mix 2 tbsp oil, water, salt, and chickpeas. Seal the lid and cook on High Pressure for 35 minutes. Release the pressure quickly. Mix ½ cup of the cooking liquid and drained chickpeas in a food processor and puree until no large chickpeas remain. Add in spinach, lemon juice, salt, garlic, and tahini. Process hummus for 8 minutes until smooth. Stir in the remaining 3 tablespoons of olive oil. Serve.

Classic Palak Paneer Dip

Serving Size: 4 | Total Time: 15 minutes

¼ cup milk	1 tsp minced fresh garlic
2 tsp butter	1 red onion, chopped
1 tsp cumin seeds	1 lb spinach, chopped
1 tsp coriander seeds	1 tsp salt
1 tomato, chopped	2 cups paneer, cubed
1 tsp minced fresh ginger	1 tsp chili powder

Warm butter in your Instant Pot on Sauté. Add in onion, garlic, cumin seeds, coriander, chili powder, and ginger and fry for 1 minute. Add in salt, 1 cup water, and spinach. Seal the lid and cook for 1 minute on High Pressure. Release the pressure quickly. Add spinach mixture to a blender and pulse until smooth. Transfer to a bowl. Mix in the paneer, milk, and tomato. Serve warm.

Sweet & Spicy Chili Dip

Serving Size: 6 | Total Time: 25 minutes

1 cup sour cream	1 tsp cayenne pepper
2 cups tomato sauce	½ tsp chili pepper, ground
1 cup cream cheese	Salt and pepper to taste

In a mixing bowl, add sour cream, tomato sauce, cream cheese, cayenne pepper, chili pepper, salt, and pepper and stir well to combine. Pour the mixture into the pot. Cook on High Pressure for 8 minutes. Do a natural pressure release for 10 minutes. Serve with carrots, celery, or tortilla chips.

Pork Ribs with Onions

Serving Size: 4 | Total Time: 35 minutes

1 ½ cups tomato puree	1 ¼ cups sweet onions
1 tbsp garlic, minced	½ cup carrots, thinly sliced
Salt and pepper to taste	1 lb cut pork spare ribs

Brown the ribs on Sauté. Pour in 1 ½ cups water and tomato puree. Add garlic, salt, pepper, onions, and carrots. Seal the lid and cook for 30 minutes on Pressure Cook on High. Once ready, do a quick pressure release and serve.

Mom's Beef with Prosciutto

Serving Size: 6 | Total Time: 45 minutes

2 lb beef fillets, center-cut	3 tbsp butter
1 onion, finely chopped	3 cups beef stock
¼ cup horseradish sauce	6 oz prosciutto

Melt butter on Sauté, and stir-fry the onion for 2 minutes. Add fillets and briefly brown them on both sides for 5-6 minutes. Pour in the beef stock. Seal the lid and cook on High Pressure for 30 minutes. Do a quick release. Carefully open the lid. Remove the fillets on a serving platter. In a saucepan, mix horseradish sauce with prosciutto. Warm-up and drizzle over the meat. Serve.

Beef Dumplings with Cabbage

Serving Size: 4 | Total Time: 30 minutes

½ cup savoy cabbage, shredded	
½ lb ground beef	½ tbsp melted ghee
1 carrot, grated	½ tbsp ginger powder
1 large egg, beaten	Salt and pepper to taste
1 garlic clove, minced	20 dumpling wrappers
2 tbsp coconut aminos	2 tbsp olive oil

In a bowl, mix beef, cabbage, carrot, egg, garlic, aminos, ghee, ginger, salt, and pepper. Put the dumpling wrappers on a flat surface. Spoon 1 tbsp of the beef filling into the middle of each wrapper. Run the edges of the wrapper with a little water. Fold the dough to cover the filling. Create a semi-circle shape, pinching the edges to seal.

Then, brush the dumplings with the olive oil. Arrange the dumplings in the pot. Pour in 1 cup of water, seal the lid and cook on High Pressure for 15 minutes. Do a quick release. Drain the dumplings and place them under the broiler for about 4-5 minutes.

Weekend Beef Balls

Serving Size: 4 | Total Time: 20 minutes

1 lb ground beef	1 onion, chopped
2 tbsp milk	2 eggs
2 tbsp oil	2 wheat bread slices
1 tbsp Italian seasoning	Salt and pepper to taste

Place two slices of bread in a bowl. Add ¼ cup water and let soak for 5 minutes. Mix beef, milk, oil, Italian seasoning mix, onion, eggs, salt, and pepper.

Add soaked bread and shape balls with approximately ¼ cup of the mixture. Flatten each ball with your hands and place it on a lightly floured surface. Heat the oil on Sauté. Add the meatballs and fry for 3 minutes per side. Serve immediately with garlic sauce.

Spicy Turkey Meatballs in Red Sauce

Serving Size: 6 | Total Time: 25 minutes

¼ cup cotija cheese, crumbled	
1 lb ground turkey	2 celery stalks, minced
1 carrot, shredded	¼ cup hot sauce
¼ cup bread crumbs	4 tomatoes, chopped
1 egg, beaten	Salt and pepper to taste
2 tbsp olive oil	2 tsp fresh basil, chopped

In a bowl, combine turkey, carrot, celery, cotija cheese, hot sauce, bread crumbs, and egg. Season with salt and pepper. Shape the mixture into 12 meatballs. Heat oil on Sauté and fry the meatballs in batches until lightly golden. Pour in ½ cup water , tomatoes, and salt. Seal the lid and cook on High Pressure for 5 minutes. Do a quick release. Sprinkle with basil and serve.

Mediterranean Meatballs with Mint Sauce

Serving Size: 4 | Total Time: 35 minutes

1 lb lean ground beef	½ tsp salt
¼ cup flour	2 tbsp olive oil
1 tbsp rosemary, chopped	1 cup Greek yogurt
1 cup tomato sauce	2 tbsp fresh mint
1 large egg, beaten	1 garlic clove, crushed

In a bowl, mix ground beef, rosemary, egg, flour, and salt. Lightly dampen hands and shape into balls. Warm the olive oil in your Instant Pot on Sauté. Fry the balls for 5-6 minutes on all sides. Pour in the tomato sauce and ½ cup of water. Seal the lid and cook on High Pressure for 13 minutes. When ready, do a quick release. Press Sauté and cook until the sauce thickens, about 5 minutes. In a bowl, mix the Greek yogurt, mint, and garlic. Stir well and drizzle over the meatballs. Serve and enjoy!

Saucy Carrots with Crispy Bacon

Serving Size: 4 | Total Time: 20 minutes

3 slices bacon, crumbled	1 tsp honey
2 lb carrots, chopped	1 tsp salt
½ cup orange juice	2 tsp cornstarch
¼ cup olive oil	1 tbsp cold water

Fry the bacon on Sauté until crispy, about 5 minutes. Set aside. In a bowl, mix salt, olive oil, orange juice, and honey; add the mixture and carrots to the pot and mix well to coat. Seal the lid, and cook for 6 minutes on High Pressure. Release the pressure quickly. Transfer carrots to a serving dish. Press Cancel, then press Sauté. In a bowl, mix cold water and cornstarch until dissolved. Add to the liquid remaining in the cooker. Simmer sauce as you stir for 2 minutes to obtain a thick and smooth consistency. Spoon the sauce over the carrots and scatter over the bacon. Serve.

Scrambled Eggs with Cranberries & Mint

Serving Size: 2 | Total Time: 10 minutes

4 large eggs, beaten	1 tbsp skim milk
¼ tsp cranberry extract	4-5 cranberries, to garnish
2 tbsp butter	2 tbsp fresh mint, chopped

In a bowl, whisk eggs, cranberry extract, and milk. Melt butter in your Instant Pot on Sauté. Pour the egg mixture and pull the eggs across the pot with a spatula.

Do not stir constantly. Cook for 2 minutes or until thickened and no visible liquid egg lumps. When done, press Cancel and transfer to a serving plate. Top with cranberries and garnish with fresh mint. Serve and enjoy!

Four Cheeses Party Pizza

Serving Size: 4 | Total Time: 25 minutes

1 pizza crust	5-6 mozzarella slices
½ cup tomato paste	¼ cup grated gouda cheese
1 tsp dried oregano	¼ cup grated Parmesan
1 oz cheddar, grated	2 tbsp olive oil

Grease the bottom of a baking dish with 1 tbsp of olive oil. Line some parchment paper. Flour the working surface and roll out the pizza dough to the approximate size of your Instant Pot. Gently fit the dough in the previously prepared baking dish.

In a bowl, combine tomato paste with water and dried oregano. Spread the mixture over the dough and finish with cheeses. Add a trivet inside your the pot and Pour in 1 cup of water. Seal the lid, and cook for 15 minutes on High Pressure. Do a quick release. Remove the pizza from the pot using parchment paper. Cut and serve.

Dill Marinated Gherkins

Serving Size: 6 | Total Time: 15 minutes + chilling time

1 lb cucumbers, sliced	2 tbsp dill pickle seasoning
2 cups white vinegar	2 tsp salt
1 cup sugar	1 tsp cumin

Into the pot, add cucumbers, vinegar, 1 cup water, sugar, cumin, dill pickle seasoning, and salt. Stir well to dissolve the sugar. Seal the lid and cook for 4 minutes on High Pressure. Release the pressure quickly. Ladle cucumbers into a large storage container and pour cooking liquid over. Chill for 1 hour. Serve.

Steamed Leek with Parmesan Topping

Serving Size: 2 | Total Time: 10 minutes

3 leeks, cut into 2-inches long pieces	
3 garlic cloves, crushed	3 tbsp lemon juice
1 tsp salt	½ cup Parmesan, grated
¼ cup olive oil	

Pour 1 cup of water into your Instant Pot and insert a trivet. In a baking pan, combine leeks, oil, garlic, and salt. Lower the pan onto the trivet. Cook on High Pressure for 3 minutes. Do a quick pressure release. Transfer to a plate and sprinkle with lemon juice and Parmesan cheese.

Tomato & Mozzarella Egg Scramble

Serving Size: 2 | Total Time: 20 minutes

1 cup button mushrooms, sliced	
½ cup fresh mozzarella cheese, crumbled	
4 eggs	¼ cup milk
1 large tomato, chopped	2 tbsp olive oil
2 spring onions, chopped	½ tsp salt

Warm the olive oil in your Instant Pot on Sauté. Stir-fry the spring onions for 3 minutes. Add tomato and mushrooms. Cook until liquid evaporates, about 5-6 minutes. Whisk eggs, cheese, milk, and salt. Pour into the pot and stir. Cook for 5-6 minutes, stirring often. Serve.

Beef Layer Tart with Yogurt

Serving Size: 6 | Total Time: 30 minutes

2 lb lean ground beef	½ tbsp butter, melted
4 garlic cloves, minced	1 tbsp sour cream
Salt and pepper to taste	3 cups liquid yogurt
1 (16 oz) pack pie dough	

In a bowl, mix beef, garlic, salt, and pepper until fully incorporated. Lay a sheet of dough on a flat surface and brush with melted butter. Line with the meat mixture and roll-up. Repeat the process until you have used all the ingredients. Grease a baking dish and carefully place the rolls inside. In your Instant Pot, pour in 1 ½ cups of water and place a trivet. Lay the baking dish on the trivet.

Seal the lid and cook on High Pressure for 15 minutes. When ready, do a quick pressure release. Transfer the pie to a serving plate. Mix sour cream and yogurt. Spread the mixture over the pie and serve cold.

Warm Spinach Salad With Eggs & Nuts

Serving Size: 4 | Total Time: 20 minutes

1 lb spinach, chopped	1 tbsp peanuts, crushed
3 tbsp olive oil	4 eggs
1 tbsp butter	½ tsp chili flakes
1 tbsp almonds, crushed	½ tsp salt

Pour 1 ½ cups of water into the inner pot and insert a steamer basket. Place the eggs onto the basket. Seal the lid and cook on High Pressure for 5 minutes. Do a quick release. Unlock the lid. Remove the eggs to an ice bath.

Wipe the pot clean, and heat oil on Sauté. Add spinach and cook for 2-3 minutes, stirring occasionally. Stir in 1 tbsp of butter and season with salt and chili flakes. Mix well and cook for 1 more minute. Sprinkle with nuts. Peel and slice each egg in half, lengthwise. Transfer to a serving plate and pour over spinach mixture. Enjoy!

Garlic & Herbed Potatoes

Serving Size: 4 | Total Time: 25 minutes

1 ½ lb potatoes	½ tsp fresh thyme, chopped
3 tbsp butter	½ tsp parsley, chopped
3 cloves garlic, chopped	Salt and pepper to taste
2 tbsp rosemary, chopped	½ cup vegetable broth

Use a small knife to pierce each potato to ensure there are no blowouts when placed under pressure. Melt butter on Sauté. Add in potatoes, rosemary, parsley, pepper, salt, thyme, and garlic, and cook for 10 minutes until potatoes are browned and the mixture is aromatic. Stir in the broth. Seal the lid and cook for 5 minutes on High Pressure. Release the pressure quickly. Serve and enjoy!

Chicken Drumsticks with Hot Sauce

Serving Size: 6 | Total Time: 30 minutes

2 lb chicken drumsticks, boneless and skinless
1 ½ cups hot tomato salsa   1 onion, chopped
Salt to taste   1 cup feta, crumbled

Sprinkle salt over the chicken and set in the Instant Pot. Stir in salsa, 1 cup water, and onion. Seal the lid and cook for 15 minutes on Pressure Cook. When ready, do a quick release. Unlock the lid. Press Sauté and cook for 8 minutes until excess liquid has evaporated. Top with feta.

Poached Eggs with Watercress

Serving Size: 1 | Total Time: 10 minutes

2 eggs   ¼ tsp garlic powder
1 cup watercress, chopped   Salt and pepper to taste

In a bowl, whisk eggs and ½ cup water. Add watercress, garlic powder, salt, and pepper and stir well. Transfer the mixture to a heat-proof bowl. Add 1 cup of water to the pot. Set the steamer tray and place the bowl on top. Seal the lid and cook on High Pressure for 5 minutes. When ready, do a quick release. Carefully unlock the lid. Serve.

Chili Poached Eggs with Leeks

Serving Size: 4 | Total Time: 20 minutes

1 cup leeks, chopped into 1-inch pieces
8 eggs   1 tsp mustard seeds
2 tbsp olive oil   1 tbsp dried rosemary
1 tbsp butter   ¼ tsp chili flakes

Heat the olive oil on Sauté and add mustard seeds. Stir-fry for 2-3 minutes. Add leeks and butter. Cook for 5 minutes, stirring occasionally. Crack eggs and season with dried rosemary, and chili flakes. Cook until set for about 4 minutes. Press Cancel and serve immediately.

Egg Pancake with Spinach & Herbs

Serving Size: 2 | Total Time: 15 minutes

6 oz spinach, chopped   ¼ tsp dried oregano
2 eggs   ¼ tsp dried rosemary
3 tbsp oil   ½ tsp salt
½ tsp garlic powder   10 Kalamata olives

Heat the oil in your Instant Pot on Sauté and add chopped spinach. Season with salt and garlic powder. Give it a good stir and cook for 5 minutes until soft. Crack eggs and season with oregano, rosemary, and salt. Cook until completely set for about 5 more minutes. Transfer to a serving plate and top with kalamata olives to serve.

Old-Fashioned Apple Pie

Serving Size: 6 | Total Time: 30 minutes

2 lb apples, cubed   ¼ tbsp oil
¼ cup sugar   1 egg, beaten
¼ cup breadcrumbs   ¼ cup flour
2 tsp cinnamon   Pie dough

Combine breadcrumbs, sugar, apples, and cinnamon in a bowl. On a lightly floured surface, roll out the pie dough, making 2 circle-shaped crusts. Place one pie crust on a greased baking dish. Spoon the apple mixture on top, and cover with the remaining crust. Seal by crimping edges and brush with beaten egg. Pour 1 cup of water into the Instant Pot and lay a trivet. Lower the baking sheet onto the trivet. Seal the lid and cook on High Pressure for 20 minutes. When ready, do a quick release. Carefully unlock the lid. Serve chilled.

Easy Camembert Cakes

Serving Size: 4 | Total Time: 45 minutes

1 cup Camembert cheese, cubed
2 tbsp butter   ¼ cup dry white wine
1 white onion, sliced   1 pie pastry, thawed
2 cups spinach, chopped   3 thinly sliced green onions
Salt and pepper to taste

Melt 1 tbsp of butter on Sauté and cook onion and spinach for 5 minutes until tender. Season with salt and pepper, then pour in white wine and cook until evaporated, about 2 minutes. Set aside. Unwrap the pie pastry and cut it into 4 squares. Prink the dough with a fork and brush both sides with the remaining butter. Share half of the cheese over the pie pastry squares. Cover with spinach and remaining cheese. Arrange the tarts in a buttered baking dish. Pour 1 cup of water into the pot. Insert a trivet and lower the baking dish on top. Seal the lid and cook on High Pressure for 30 minutes. Do a quick release. Serve topped with green onions.

Goat Cheese & Beef Steak Salad

Serving Size: 4 | Total Time: 55 minutes

1 lb rib-eye steak, boneless   4 hazelnuts
4 oz fresh arugula   3 tbsp olive oil
1 large tomato, sliced   2 cups beef broth
¼ cup fresh goat's cheese   2 tbsp red wine vinegar
4 almonds, chopped   1 tbsp Italian seasoning
4 walnuts, chopped

In a bowl, whisk the red wine vinegar, Italian seasoning, and olive oil. Brush each steak with the mixture and place it in your Instant Pot. Pour in the broth and seal the lid. Cook on Meat/Stew for 25 minutes on High. Release the pressure naturally for 10 minutes. Unlock the lid. Remove the steaks along with the broth. Grease the inner pot with oil and hit Sauté. Brown the steaks on both sides for 5-6 minutes. Remove from the pot and chill for 5 minutes before slicing. In a bowl, mix arugula, tomato, cheese, almonds, walnuts, and hazelnuts. Top with steaks and drizzle with red wine mixture. Serve.

Feta & Potato Salad

Serving Size: 4 | Total Time: 25 minutes + chilling time

3 lb potatoes, chopped   ¼ cup pickles
1 cup mayonnaise   1 white onion, chopped
¼ cup mustard   1 cup feta, crumbled

Place the potatoes in your Instant Pot and cover them with water. Seal the lid and cook for 6 minutes on High Pressure. Once ready, do a natural release for 10 minutes. Drain the potatoes and allow to cool. Chop into small pieces. In a bowl, mix pickles, mayonnaise, potatoes, mustard, and onion. Top with feta cheese to serve.

Healthy Kale & Egg Muffins

Serving Size: 3 | Total Time: 10 minutes

6 eggs
1 cup kale, chopped
½ cup cheddar, grated
1 small onion, chopped

½ tsp Italian seasoning
Salt and pepper to taste
2 tbsp heavy cream

In a bowl, mix eggs, salt, pepper, and heavy cream. Whisk until well combined and add cheddar, onion, kale, and Italian seasoning. Divide the mixture between greased ramekins. Add 1 cup of water in the Instant Pot and lay a trivet inside. Lower the ramekins on the trivet and seal the lid. Cook on High Pressure for 6 minutes. When ready, do a quick release. Serve.

Potatoes & Tuna Salad with Pickles

Serving Size: 4 | Total Time: 15 minutes

½ cup pimento-stuffed green olives
½ cup chopped roasted red peppers
1 lb potatoes, quartered
2 eggs
3 tbsp melted butter
Salt and pepper to taste

6 pickles, chopped
2 tbsp red wine vinegar
10 oz canned tuna, drained

Pour 2 cups of water into the pot and add potatoes. Place a trivet over the potatoes. Lay the eggs on the trivet. Seal the lid and cook for 8 minutes on High Pressure. Do a quick release. Drain and remove potatoes to a bowl.

Fill a bowl with ice water. Add in the eggs to cool. Drizzle melted butter over the potatoes and season with salt and pepper. Peel and chop the chilled eggs. Add pickles, eggs, peppers, tuna, and red wine vinegar to the potatoes and mix to coat. Serve topped with olives. Enjoy!

Grandma's Egg Salad

Serving Size: 6 | Total Time: 15 minutes

6 eggs
¼ cup crème frâiche
2 spring onions, minced
1 tbsp dill, minced

1 tbsp curry paste
2 tsp mustard
Salt and pepper to taste

Grease a cake pan with cooking spray. Carefully crack in the eggs. To the inner pot, add 1 cup water and a trivet. Set the pan with the eggs on the trivet. Seal the lid and cook for 5 minutes on High Pressure. When ready, do a quick release. Drain any water from the eggs in the pan.

Loosen the eggs on the edges with a knife. Transfer to a cutting board and chop into smaller sizes. Transfer the chopped eggs to a bowl. Add in onions, mustard, salt, dill, crème frâiche, curry paste, and pepper. Serve.

Arugula Salad with Sweet Potatoes & Eggs

Serving Size: 4 | Total Time: 20 minutes

4 sweet potatoes, peeled and diced
2 large eggs
2 ½ cups mayonnaise
¼ cup dill, chopped

1/3 cup Greek yogurt
½ cup arugula

Pour 1 cup of water into the Instant Pot and insert a steamer basket. Place in the eggs and potatoes. Seal the lid. Cook for 4 minutes on High Pressure. When ready, do a quick release. Take out the eggs and place in a bowl of ice-cold water for purposes of cooling. In a bowl, mix yogurt, mayonnaise, and dill. In a separate bowl, mash potatoes using a potato masher. Coat them with the mayonnaise mixture. Skin and dice the eggs. Add them to the potato salad and mix. Serve with arugula.

Authentic German Salad with Bacon

Serving Size: 6 | Total Time: 20 minutes

6 smoked bacon slices, chopped
6 red potatoes, peeled and quartered
½ cup apple cider vinegar
2 tsp mustard

Salt and pepper to serve
2 red onions, chopped

Set your Instant Pot to Sauté. Briefly brown the bacon for 5 minutes until crispy. Set aside. In a bowl, mix mustard, vinegar, ½ cup water, salt, and pepper. In the pot, add potatoes, bacon, and onions and top with the vinegar mixture. Seal the lid and cook for 6 minutes on High Pressure. Release pressure naturally for 10 minutes. Transfer to a serving plate. Enjoy!

Delicious Broccoli & Cauliflower Salad

Serving Size: 4 | Total Time: 10 minutes

1 lb cauliflower florets
1 lb broccoli, into florets
3 garlic cloves, crushed

¼ tbsp olive oil
1 tsp salt
1 tbsp dry rosemary

Cut the veggies into bite-sized pieces and place them in the pot. Add olive oil and 1 cup of water. Season with salt, garlic, and rosemary. Seal the lid. Cook on High Pressure for 3 minutes. When ready, do a quick release.

Greek-Style Pasta Salad

Serving Size: 6 | Total Time: 15 minutes

1 lb rotini pasta
2 plum tomatoes, halved
1 cucumber, sliced
1 red bell pepper, diced

¼ cup extra-virgin olive oil
2 tbsp white wine vinegar
1 cup feta, crumbled
2 tbsp fresh dill, chopped

Cover the rotini pasta with salted water in your Instant Pot and seal the lid. Select Manual and cook for 4 minutes on High. When ready, perform a quick pressure release and unlock the lid. Drain the pasta and set aside. Mix the extra-virgin olive oil, white wine vinegar, and salt in a large serving bowl. Add in the cooked pasta, tomatoes, cucumber, and bell pepper and toss to combine. Top with feta cheese and dill and serve.

BROTHS & SAUCES

Tasty Beef Neck Bone Stock

Serving Size: 6 | Total Time: 2 hours 10 minutes

1 carrot, chopped	1 tsp cider vinegar
2 onions, chopped	2 bay leaves
2 cups celery, chopped	10 peppercorns
2 lb beef neck bones	Salt to taste
12 cups water, or more	

Add carrot, peppercorns, salt, bay leaves, celery, vinegar, onions, and beef bones. Add enough water to cover the ingredients. Seal the lid and cook on High Pressure for 120 minutes. Release pressure naturally.

Remove the bones and bay leaves, and discard. Use a fine-mesh strainer to strain the liquid. Allow the broth to cool. From the surface, skim fat and throw away. Refrigerate for a maximum of 7 days.

Herby Chicken Stock

Serving Size: 6 | Total Time: 60 minutes

2 lb chicken wings	4 cloves garlic
4 spring onions, diced	1 small handful of parsley
2 large carrots, diced	1 bay leaf

Add chicken, carrots, parsley, onions, garlic, and bay leaf in your Instant Pot. Pour in 6 cups of water. Seal the lid and cook on High Pressure for 45 minutes. Release Pressure naturally for about 10 minutes. Carefully unlock the lid. Use a fine-mesh strainer to strain the broth and allow it to cool. Transfer the broth to containers and seal. Refrigerate for up to a week.

Best Vegetable Broth Ever

Serving Size: 6 | Total Time: 35 minutes

2 onions, chopped	A handful of rosemary
2 cups celery, chopped	A handful of parsley
2 carrots, chopped	10 peppercorns
4 garlic cloves	2 bay leaves
1 cup kale	Salt to taste
1 cup bell pepper, chopped	

Add onions, carrots, parsley, bay leaves, garlic, kale, celery, bell pepper, salt, rosemary, and peppercorns in your Instant Pot. Cover with cold water. Seal the lid and cook on High Pressure for 15 minutes. Do a natural release for 15 minutes. Use a wide and shallow bowl to hold the stock you strain through a fine-mesh strainer. Let cool. Seal into jars and refrigerate for up to 14 days.

Ginger & Vegetable Beef Broth

Serving Size: 6 | Total Time: 1 hour

2 lb beef stew meat	2 carrots, chopped
2 onions, chopped	1 tsp fresh ginger, grated
2 cups celery, chopped	4 garlic cloves
2 red chilies, chopped	Salt to taste

In the pot, mix meat, celery, garlic, carrots, onions, red chilies, and ginger. Pour in 6 cups of water. Seal the lid and cook on High Pressure for 45 minutes. Release pressure naturally for 10 minutes. Carefully unlock the lid. Use a fine-mesh strainer to strain the broth into a bowl. Season with salt. Store in sealable containers.

Homemade Chicken Stock

Serving Size: 6 | Total Time: 40 minutes

2 lb chicken carcasses	1 sprig fresh thyme
4 carrots, cut into chunks	1 bunch fresh parsley
1 cup leeks, chopped	Salt to taste
1 onion, quartered	10 peppercorns
1 cup celery, chopped	2 bay leaves
2 large garlic cloves	

Add chicken, onion, peppercorns, thyme, celery, carrots, garlic, parsley, leeks, bay leaves, and salt. Cover with water. Seal the lid and cook for 30 minutes on High Pressure. Release the pressure quickly. Unlock the lid. Use a colander to drain the broth and do away with solids. Allow cooling for about an hour before storing it.

Simple Beef Bolognese Sauce

Serving Size: 6 | Total Time: 55 minutes

4 slices bacon, chopped	3 tbsp red wine
1 tbsp olive oil	28 oz can tomatoes, diced
1 onion, minced	2 bay leaves
2 celery stalks, minced	Salt and pepper to taste
1 carrot, chopped	½ cup yogurt
1 ½ lb ground beef	¼ cup chopped basil

Set to Sauté the Instant Pot. Cook bacon until crispy, 4-5 minutes. Add in olive oil, celery, carrot, and onion and continue cooking for about 5 minutes until vegetables are softened. Add in the beef and cook for 4 minutes until golden brown. Season with salt and pepper. Stir in the wine and allow to sit for 4 more minutes. Add in bay leaves and tomatoes. Seal the lid and cook for 15 minutes on High Pressure. Release pressure naturally for 10 minutes. Carefully unlock the lid. Add yogurt and stir. Serve alongside noodles and use basil to garnish.

Authentic Neapolitan Sauce

Serving Size: 4 | Total Time: 50 minutes

1 lb mushrooms, sliced	1 tbsp olive oil
14 oz can tomatoes, diced	2 garlic cloves
1 carrot, chopped	½ tsp paprika
1 onion, chopped	1 tsp fish sauce
1 celery stick, chopped	

Heat olive oil on Sauté. Stir-fry carrot, onion, celery, and paprika for 5 minutes. Add mushrooms, garlic, and fish sauce, and pour in 1 cup water. Cook for 5-6 more minutes until the meat is slightly browned. Seal the lid. Cook on High Pressure for 10 minutes. Release the steam naturally for 10 minutes. Hit Sauté, add in tomatoes and cook for 7-8 minutes to thicken the sauce.

Cranberry Orange Sauce

Serving Size: 4 | Total Time: 20 minutes

2 cups cranberries
1 tsp orange zest
½ cup orange juice
¼ cup brown sugar
1 cup water
2 tbsp maple syrup

Combine maple syrup, water, cranberries, and orange juice in the Instant Pot. Sprinkle with orange zest. Seal the lid, and cook on High Pressure for 5 minutes. When done, release the pressure naturally for about 10 minutes. Press Sauté, add brown sugar, and stir until a thick sauce mixture is formed. Turn off the heat and transfer the sauce to the serving dish.

Herbed Squash Sauce

Serving Size: 4 | Total Time: 30 minutes

2 cups butternut squash, peeled, cubed
3 beets, trimmed, peeled, cubed
3 carrots, peeled, cubed
1 cup red wine
1 tsp dried basil
1 tbsp dried parsley
1 tsp dried oregano, ground
½ tsp garlic powder
Salt and pepper to taste

Add squash, beets, and carrots to your Instant Pot. Pour in 2 cups of water and seal the lid. Press Manual and set the timer to 10 minutes n High. Do a quick pressure release. Carefully unlock the lid. Transfer to a food processor and pulse until smooth and creamy. Add wine, basil, parsley, oregano, garlic powder, salt, and pepper and blend for a minute. Return to the pot, press Sauté, and cook for 10 minutes, stirring occasionally. Serve.

Garlic Red Bell Pepper Sauce

Serving Size: 3 | Total Time: 15 minutes

3 red bell peppers, chopped
1 cup cherry tomatoes, diced
1 onion, chopped
1 tsp garlic powder
½ cup sour cream
2 cups vegetable broth
1 tbsp balsamic vinegar
1 tbsp cayenne pepper

Combine bell peppers, cherry tomatoes, onion, garlic powder, sour cream, broth, balsamic vinegar, and cayenne pepper in a mixing bowl. Add the mixture to the Instant Pot, seal the lid, and cook on High Pressure for 6 minutes. When ready, do a quick release. Carefully unlock the lid. Transfer to your food processor and purée until the mixture is smooth. Serve and enjoy!

Quick Zucchini Sauce with Greek Yogurt

Serving Size: 4 | Total Time: 10 minutes

1 zucchini, chopped
1 cup Greek yogurt
1 cup sour cream
1 tsp garlic powder
¼ cup shallots, minced
Salt and pepper to taste

In the pot, mix zucchini, sour cream, garlic, shallots, salt, and pepper and stir until combined. Seal the lid and cook on High Pressure for 3 minutes. Do a quick release. Remove the sauce to a bowl and stir in the yogurt. Serve.

Mediterranean Tomato Sauce

Serving Size: 4 | Total Time: 15 minutes

2 cups tomatoes, diced
½ cup tomato sauce
½ cup sun-dried tomatoes
1 medium onion, chopped
3 tbsp balsamic vinegar
3 garlic cloves, chopped
1 tsp dried oregano
1 tbsp olive oil
Salt and pepper to taste

Combine tomatoes, tomato sauce, sun-dried tomatoes, onion, balsamic vinegar, garlic, oregano, oil, salt, and pepper in a mixing bowl and give it a good stir. Transfer to the Instant Pot and seal the lid. Cook on High Pressure for 6 minutes. When done, remove to serving bowls and serve with pasta or rice.

Caprese Sauce with Goat Cheese

Serving Size: 4 | Total Time: 15 minutes

1 cup goat cheese, crumbled
1 cup tomatoes, diced
3 tbsp tomato paste
1 onion, finely chopped
3 tbsp apple cider vinegar
3 garlic cloves, chopped
¼ cup mozzarella cheese
2 cups vegetable broth
Salt and pepper to taste

Add goat cheese, tomatoes, tomato paste, onion, vinegar, garlic, mozzarella cheese, broth, salt, and pepper to your Instant Pot, seal the lid and cook on High Pressure for 6 minutes. When done, press Cancel and do a quick pressure release. Serve.

Homemade Honey Applesauce

Serving Size: 4 | Total Time: 25 minutes

4 apples, cored, chopped
1 tsp ground cinnamon
1 tsp honey

Add apples, cinnamon, ½ cup water, and honey. Seal the lid and cook on High Pressure for 4 minutes. Release Pressure naturally for 10 minutes. If you desire a chunky blend, stir vigorously. For smooth applesauce, puree the mixture in a blender. Allow to cool before transferring in containers for storage.

Spicy Green Sauce

Serving Size: 4 | Total Time: 10 minutes

4 oz green jalapeño peppers, chopped
1 green bell pepper, chopped
2 garlic cloves, crushed
½ cup white vinegar
1 tbsp apple cider vinegar
1 tsp salt

Add jalapeño peppers, bell pepper, garlic, white vinegar, apple vinegar, and salt to the Instant Pot. Pour in 4 tbsp water. Seal the lid and cook on High Pressure for 2 minutes. When done, release the steam naturally for about 5 minutes. Transfer to a blender, pulse until combined, and store in jars.

SOUPS

Mushroom-Spinach Cream Soup

Serving Size: 4 | Total Time: 30 minutes

2 sweet potatoes, peeled and chopped
1 tbsp dry porcini mushrooms, soaked

8 button mushrooms, sliced	1 red onion, chopped
2 tbsp olive oil	4 cups vegetable stock
2 garlic cloves, minced	Salt and pepper to taste
1 cup spinach, chopped	1 cup creme fraiche

Set your Instant Pot to Sauté and warm the olive oil. Sauté the sliced mushrooms for 5 minutes until tender. Remove 2 tbsp of them and set aside on a plate. Add onion and garlic to the pot and cook for 3 minutes until the onion becomes translucent. Mix in the potatoes, soaked mushrooms, vegetable stock, spinach, and salt.

Seal the lid and cook on High Pressure for 5 minutes. Quick-release the pressure. Add in creme fraiche and mix. Season with salt and pepper. Using an immersion blender, whizz the mixture until smooth. Garnish with the reserved mushrooms and a drizzle of olive oil. Serve.

Red Soup with Cheesy Croutons

Serving Size: 4 | Total Time: 1 hour

2 tbsp olive oil	28 oz canned tomatoes
1 onion, chopped	1 cup heavy cream
2 garlic cloves, minced	2 Monterey Jack slices
1 carrot, chopped	4 bread slices
Salt and pepper to taste	2 gouda cheese slices
1 cup vegetable stock	2 tbsp butter, softened

Warm oil on Sauté. Stir-fry onion, garlic, carrot, pepper, and salt for 6 minutes until soft. Add in vegetable stock to deglaze. Scrape any brown bits from the pot. Mix the stock with tomatoes. Seal the lid and cook on High Pressure for 30 minutes. Allow for a natural release for 10 minutes. Transfer soup to a blender and process until smooth. Add in heavy cream and stir.

Place 1 slice Monterey Jack cheese on 1 bread slice and cover with 1 Gouda cheese slice and the second slice of bread. Brush the bread with butter. Do the same with the rest of the ingredients. Heat a skillet over medium heat. Place the sandwiches on the skillet. Cook each side for 3 to 5 minutes until browned and all cheese melts. Transfer sandwiches to a cutting board and chop them into bite-sized pieces. Divide the soup into serving plates and top with cheese croutons before serving.

Homemade Vichyssoise Soup with Chives

Serving Size: 4 | Total Time: 30 minutes

2 tbsp butter	½ cup sour cream
3 leeks, chopped	2 tbsp rosemary
2 cloves garlic, minced	Salt and pepper to taste
4 cups vegetable broth	2 tbsp chives, chopped
3 potatoes, peeled, cubed	

Melt butter on Sauté. Stir in garlic and leeks and cook for 3-4 minutes until soft. Stir in potatoes, rosemary, and broth. Seal the lid and cook on High Pressure for 15 minutes. Release pressure quickly. Transfer soup to a food processor and puree to obtain a smooth consistency. Season with salt and pepper. Top with fresh chives and sour cream. Serve

Celery-Cauliflower Soup with Blue Cheese

Serving Size: 5 | Total Time: 20 minutes

2 tbsp butter	3 cups vegetable broth
½ tbsp olive oil	Salt and pepper to taste
1 onion, chopped	2 cups milk
2 stalks celery, chopped	1 bay leaf
10 oz cauliflower florets	4 oz blue cheese, crumbled
1 potato, finely diced	

Warm oil and butter on Sauté. Add celery and onion and sauté for 3-5 minutes until fragrant. Stir in half the cauliflower and cook for 5 minutes until golden brown. Add in broth, bay leaf, potato, and the remaining cauliflower. Seal the lid. Cook on High Pressure for 5 minutes. Release the pressure quickly.

Remove the bay leaf. Puree the soup with an immersion blender until smooth. Stir in the milk. Adjust the seasoning. Top with blue cheese before serving.

Simple Chicken Soup with Fennel

Serving Size: 4 | Total Time: 55 minutes

1 lb chicken drumsticks, boneless

4 celery stalks	2 bay leaves
1 fennel bulb, chopped	Salt and pepper to taste
1 onion, diced	½ cup matzo meal
1 carrot, diced	1 egg, beaten
2 garlic cloves, minced	2 tbsp canola oil

In the pot, add chicken, bay leaves, onion, carrot, celery, pepper, garlic, salt, and fennel. Add enough water such that ingredients are covered by 2 inches. Seal the lid and cook for 30 minutes on High Pressure. Release pressure quickly. In a bowl, mix egg, canola oil, pepper, salt, and matzo meal. Use a plastic wrap to close the bowl and refrigerate for 10 minutes.

Get rid of celery stalks from the pot. Transfer chicken to a cutting board, strip, and shred it from the bones. Take back to the pot. Select Sauté and boil the soup. Roll matzo mixture into 1-inch balls and place in the boiling soup. Cook for 3 mins to heat through as you gently stir.

Broccoli, Potatoes & Cheese Cream Soup

Serving Size: 4 | Total Time: 30 minutes

1/3 cup butter	½ cup heavy cream
1 lb broccoli florets	Cheddar cheese, grated
2 cloves garlic, minced	½ cup chopped scallions
1 onion, chopped	
2 lb potatoes, chopped	
4 cups vegetable broth	

Melt butter on Sauté. Add onion and garlic and Sauté for 5 minutes. Add in broth, potatoes, and broccoli, and mix well. Seal the lid and cook for 5 minutes on High Pressure. Release pressure naturally for 10 minutes. Transfer the potato mixture to a blender and pulse until smooth. Stir in heavy cream. Divide between bowls and top with cheese and scallions. Serve.

Homemade Chicken & Quinoa Soup

Serving Size: 6 | Total Time: 25 minutes

2 tbsp canola oil
6 spring onions, chopped
2 garlic cloves, finely diced
1 carrot, chopped
2 celery stalks, chopped

2 chicken breasts, cubed
6 cups chicken broth
1 cup quinoa
Salt and pepper to taste

Heat canola oil on Sauté. Add in celery, spring onions, garlic, and carrot. Cook for 5 minutes. Add in chicken, quinoa, salt, chicken broth, and pepper. Seal the lid, select Soup/Broth, and cook for 15 minutes on High. Do a quick release. Serve.

Vegetable Soup with Coconut Milk

Serving Size: 5 | Total Time: 40 minutes

2 tbsp olive oil
1 leek, chopped
2 cloves garlic, minced
2 carrots, diced
1 celery stalk, chopped
4 potatoes, quartered

1 red bell pepper, diced
¼ tsp red pepper flakes
Salt and pepper to taste
1 ½ cups vegetable stock
2 tbsp parsley
½ cup coconut milk

Heat olive oil on Sauté. Add garlic and leek and cook for 5 minutes. Add in red bell pepper, carrots, salt, potatoes, pepper flakes, celery stalk, and pepper. Mix in stock. Seal the lid and cook for 15 minutes on High Pressure. Release pressure naturally for 10 minutes. Add parsley and coconut milk to the soup. Use an immersion blender to blitz the soup until smooth.

Black Bean & Corn Chicken Soup

Serving Size: 4 | Total Time: 25 minutes

½ lb boneless, skinless chicken thighs
5 cups chicken broth
Salt and pepper to taste
14 oz can tomatoes, diced
2 jalapeño peppers, minced
2 tbsp tomato puree
3 cloves garlic, minced
1 tbsp chili powder

1 tbsp ground cumin
½ tsp dried oregano
1 (14.5-oz) can black beans
2 cups corn kernels
Crushed tortilla chips
¼ cup cheddar, shredded
2 tbsp cilantro, chopped

Add the chicken, oregano, garlic, tomato puree, broth, cumin, tomatoes, chili, and jalapeño to your Instant Pot. Seal the lid and cook on High Pressure for 10 minutes.

Once cooking is done, release the pressure quickly. Unlock the lid. Transfer the chicken to a plate. Press Sauté and cook corn and black beans. Shred the chicken with a pair of forks, and return to the pot, stirring well.

Select Keep Warm and simmer the soup for 5 minutes until heated through. Adjust the seasoning and divide among serving plates. Garnish with cilantro, shredded cheese, and crushed tortilla chips to serve.

Traditional Italian Vegetable Soup

Serving Size: 6 | Total Time: 32 minutes

2 tbsp olive oil
1 onion, diced
1 cup celery, chopped
1 carrot, diced
1 green bell pepper, chopped
2 cloves garlic, minced
3 cups chicken broth
½ tsp dried parsley
½ tsp dried thyme

½ tsp dried oregano
Salt and pepper to taste
2 bay leaves
28 oz can diced tomatoes
1 tbsp tomato paste
2 cups kale
14 oz canned navy beans
½ cup rice
¼ cup Parmesan, shredded

Warm olive oil on Sauté. Stir in carrot, celery, and onion and cook for 5 minutes until soft. Add garlic and bell pepper and cook for 2 minutes as you stir until aromatic. Stir in pepper, thyme, broth, salt, parsley, oregano, tomatoes, bay leaves, and tomato paste. Mix in rice. Seal the lid and cook on High Pressure for 15 minutes. Do a quick release. Add kale and stir. Use residual heat to slightly wilting the greens. Discard bay leaves. Stir in navy beans and serve topped with Parmesan cheese.

Chipotle Pumpkin Soup

Serving Size: 4 | Total Time: 30 minutes

1 tbsp olive oil
1 onion, chopped
2 chipotle peppers, minced
1 tsp ground black pepper
¼ tsp grated nutmeg

¼ tsp ground cinnamon
1 butternut pumpkin, cubed
4 cups vegetable broth
1 tsp salt
1 cup half-and-half

Warm oil on Sauté and cook nutmeg, pepper, cinnamon, and onion for 3-5 minutes until translucent. Add pumpkin and cook for 5 minutes, stirring infrequently. Pour in broth and add chipotle peppers and any remaining pumpkin. Seal the lid and cook on High Pressure for 10 minutes. Release pressure quickly. Stir in half-and-half and transfer to a blender to purée until you obtain a smooth consistency. Season with salt and serve hot.

Spicy Tomato Soup with Rice

Serving Size: 4 | Total Time: 55 minutes

1 cup tomato puree
1 onion, chopped
1 garlic clove, minced
¼ cup rice
Salt and pepper to taste

2 tbsp olive oil
4 cups vegetable broth
¼ tsp cayenne pepper
1 tsp basil, chopped

Heat oil on Sauté and cook garlic and onion 3 minutes until soft. Add in tomato puree, rice, vegetable broth, and cayenne pepper. Season with salt and black pepper. Seal the lid and cook on Soup/Broth for 30 minutes on High Pressure. Release the pressure naturally for about 10 minutes. Serve in bowls sprinkled with basil.

Green Immune-Boosting Soup

Serving Size: 4 | Total Time: 35 minutes

1 lb Brussels sprouts, halved	3 tbsp sour cream
6 oz baby spinach	¼ cup celery, chopped
1 tsp salt	3 cups water
1 tbsp whole milk	1 tbsp butter

Add sprouts, spinach, salt, milk, sour cream, celery, water, and butter to the Instant Pot. Seal the lid and set the steam release. Press Soup/Broth and cook for 30 minutes on High. Do a quick release. Transfer to a food processor, and blend well to combine.

Chowder with Broccoli, Carrot & Tofu

Serving Size: 4 | Total Time: 35 minutes

1 head broccoli, chopped	1 cup soy milk
1 carrot, chopped	2 cups vegetable broth
2 tbsp sesame oil	¼ cup tofu, crumbled
1 onion, chopped	A pinch of salt
2 garlic cloves	

Heat oil on Sauté. Add onion and garlic and stir-fry for 2 minutes, or until translucent. Pour in broth, a cup of water, broccoli, salt, and carrot. Seal the lid and cook on Manual/Pressure Cook for 5 minutes on High. Do a quick release. Stir in the soy milk and transfer to a food processor. Pulse until creamy. Serve with crumbled tofu.

Vegetarian Lentil Soup with Nachos

Serving Size: 6 | Total Time: 40 minutes

2 ½ cups vegetable broth	1 tbsp smoked paprika
1 ½ cups tomato sauce	2 tsp ground cumin
1 onion, chopped	1 tsp chili powder
1 cup dry red lentils	¼ tsp cayenne pepper
½ cup prepared salsa verde	Salt and pepper to taste
2 garlic cloves, minced	Crushed tortilla chips

Add in tomato sauce, broth, onion, salsa verde, cumin, cayenne pepper, chili powder, garlic, lentils, paprika, salt, and pepper. Seal the lid and cook for 20 minutes on High Pressure. Release pressure naturally for 10 minutes. Garnish with crushed tortilla chips and serve. Enjoy!

White Cabbage & Beetroot Borscht Soup

Serving Size: 4 | Total Time: 30 minutes

1 dried habanero pepper, crushed	
2 tbsp olive oil	4 cups beef stock
1 cup leeks, chopped	1 lb white cabbage, grated
1 tsp garlic, smashed	2 tsp apple cider vinegar
2 beets, peeled and diced	¼ tsp paprika
1 tbsp cayenne pepper	Greek yogurt for garnish

Warm oil on Sauté. Stir in garlic and leeks and cook for 5 minutes until soft. Mix in the beef stock, paprika, cayenne pepper, vinegar, beets, white cabbage, and crushed habanero pepper. Seal the lid and cook on High Pressure for 20 minutes. Do a quick release. Place in serving bowls and top with Greek yogurt to serve.

Chorizo Soup with Roasted Tomatoes

Serving Size: 6 | Total Time: 25 minutes

28 oz fire-roasted diced tomatoes	
3 tbsp olive oil	½ cup tomatoes, chopped
2 shallots, chopped	½ cup raw cashews
3 cloves garlic, minced	1 tbsp red wine vinegar
Salt and pepper to taste	3 chorizo sausage, chopped
4 cups beef broth	½ cup chopped basil

Warm oil on Sauté and cook chorizo until crispy. Remove to a plate lined with paper towels. Add in garlic and shallots and cook for 5 minutes until soft. Season with salt. Stir in red wine vinegar, broth, fire-roasted tomatoes, cashews, tomatoes, and pepper into the cooker. Seal the lid and cook on High Pressure for 8 minutes. Release the pressure quickly. Pour the soup into a blender and process until smooth. Divide into bowls. Top with chorizo and decorate with basil.

Mediterranean Carrot & Chickpea Soup

Serving Size: 6 | Total Time: 15 minutes

14 oz can chickpeas	2 tbsp chopped parsley
2 carrots, chopped	2 cups vegetable broth
2 onions, chopped	2 tbsp olive oil
2 tomatoes, chopped	1 tsp salt
3 tbsp tomato paste	

Add in chickpeas, oil, onions, carrots, and tomatoes. Pour in the broth and sprinkle salt. Stir in the paste and seal the lid. Cook on High Pressure for 6 minutes. Do a quick release. Carefully unlock the lid. Remove the meal to a serving place. Sprinkle with parsley and serve.

Chili Cream of Acorn Squash Soup

Serving Size: 4 | Total Time: 25 minutes

4 cups vegetable broth	¼ tsp chili pepper
2 tbsp butter	A pinch of salt
1 onion, diced	½ cup coconut milk
1 lb acorn squash, chopped	1/3 cup sour cream
2 carrots, diced	

Melt butter on Sauté. Add onion and cook for 3 minutes until soft. Add in carrots, squash, salt, and chili pepper and stir-fry for 2 minutes until fragrant. Add the broth to the vegetable mixture. Seal the lid and cook for 12 minutes on High Pressure. Quick-release the pressure.

Add soup to a food processor and puree to obtain a smooth consistency. Take the soup back to the cooker, stir in coconut milk until you get a consistent color. Serve hot with a dollop of sour cream.

Cauliflower & Potato Soup with Parsley

Serving Size: 4 | Total Time: 30 minutes

1 lb cauliflower florets	Salt and pepper to taste
2 potatoes, chopped	¼ cup heavy cream
4 cups chicken broth	¼ cup sour cream
2 tbsp parsley, chopped	1 cup milk

Add cauliflower, potatoes, broth, parsley, salt, pepper, heavy cream, sour cream, and milk to the pot. Seal the lid and set the steam release handle. Cook on High Pressure for 20 minutes. Do a quick release. Let chill and transfer to a blender. Pulse until well-combined. Serve.

Squash Soup with Yogurt & Cilantro

Serving Size: 6 | Total Time: 50 minutes

1 lb acorn squash, peeled diced
1 tbsp olive oil
1 onion, diced
1 stalk celery, diced
1 large carrot, diced
2 garlic cloves, minced
6 cups chicken stock
Juice from 1 lemon
1 cup coconut milk
Salt and pepper to taste
2 tbsp cilantro, chopped
Yogurt for garnish

Heat oil on Sauté and stir-fry carrot, celery, garlic, salt, and onion for 4 to 5 minutes until soft. Mix acorn squash with the vegetables; cook for 1 more minute until tender. Add stock and seal the lid and cook on High Pressure for 20 minutes. Release pressure naturally for 10 minutes. Add in lemon juice and coconut milk and stir. Transfer the soup to a blender and process until smooth. Divide soup into serving plates. Garnish with cilantro, black pepper, and yogurt.

Simple Carrot & Oregano Soup

Serving Size: 4 | Total Time: 30 minutes

2 carrots, chopped
4 cups vegetable broth
1 tbsp butter
½ tsp dried oregano
½ tsp salt

Add carrots, broth, butter, oregano, and salt to the pot. Seal the lid and cook on Manual/Pressure Cook for 12 minutes on High. Do a natural release for 10 minutes. Transfer to a food processor and pulse until creamy.

Garam Masala Parsnip & Red Onion Soup

Serving Size: 4 | Total Time: 20 minutes

2 tbsp vegetable oil
1 red onion, finely chopped
3 parsnips, chopped
2 garlic cloves, crushed
2 tsp garam masala
½ tsp chili powder
1 tbsp plain flour
4 cups vegetable stock
1 whole lemon, juiced
Salt and pepper to taste
Strips of lemon rind

Heat oil on Sauté, and stir-fry onion, parsnips, and garlic for 5 minutes, or until soft but not changed color. Stir in garam masala and chili powder and cook for 30 seconds. Stir in the flour for another 30 seconds. Pour in the stock, lemon rind, and lemon juice, and seal the lid. Cook on Manual for 5 minutes on High. Do a quick release. Remove a third of the vegetable pieces with a slotted spoon and reserve. Process the remaining soup and vegetables in a food processor until smooth. Return to the pot and stir in the reserved vegetables. Press Sauté and heat the soup until piping hot. Season with salt and pepper. Garnish with strips of lemon and serve.

Fall Vegetable Soup

Serving Size: 4 | Total Time: 35 minutes

2 tbsp olive oil
1 onion, chopped
2 carrots, chopped
1 cup celery, chopped
2 cloves garlic, minced
5 cups vegetable broth
2 turnips, chopped
28 oz canned tomatoes
15 oz can garbanzo beans
1 cup frozen green peas
2 bay leaves
1 sprig fresh sage
Salt and pepper to taste
¼ cup Parmesan, grated

On Sauté, warm oil, stir in celery, carrots, and onion, and cook for 4 minutes until soft. Add in garlic and cook for 30 seconds. Add in vegetable broth, turnips, garbanzo beans, bay leaves, tomatoes, pepper, salt, peas, and sage.

Seal the lid and cook on High Pressure for 12 minutes. Allow natural pressure release for 10 minutes. Carefully unlock the lid. Serve topped with Parmesan cheese.

Farro & Vegetable Chicken Soup

Serving Size: 6 | Total Time: 45 minutes

4 boneless, skinless chicken thighs
1 tbsp olive oil
¼ cup white wine
1 cup farro
1 large onion, chopped
2 celery stalks, chopped
3 large carrots, chopped
1 tsp garlic powder
1 tsp ground cumin
1 bay leaf
6 cups chicken broth
2 tsp parsley to garnish

Warm oil on Sauté. Brown the chicken on all sides for 6 minutes. Transfer the chicken to a bowl. Into the pot, add the wine to deglaze, scraping any brown bits present at the bottom of the cooker. Mix the wine with farro, cumin, broth, onion, carrots, celery, garlic powder, and bay leaf. Seal the lid, press Meat/Stew, and cook on High for 20 minutes. Release pressure naturally for about 10 minutes. Add parsley for garnish. Serve and enjoy!.

Chili Soup with Avocado & Corn

Serving Size: 4 | Total Time: 25 minutes

1 avocado, mashed
2 tbsp lemon juice
1 tbsp vegetable oil
4 oz canned sweet corn
2 tomatoes, chopped
1 garlic clove, crushed
1 leek, chopped
1 red chili, chopped
14 oz vegetable stock
4 oz soy milk
Chopped leeks to garnish

In a bowl, mix the avocado mash with lemon juice and reserve until required. Heat the oil on Sauté and add corn, tomatoes, garlic, leek, and chili. Stir-fry for 4-5 minutes until softened. Put half of the vegetable mixture in a food processor, add the mashed avocado and process until smooth. Transfer the contents to the Instant Pot.

Pour in the stock, soy milk, and reserved vegetables, and seal the lid. Cook on Manual/Pressure Cook for 4 minutes on High. Once ready, press Cancel and release the steam naturally for about 10 minutes. Carefully unlock the lid. Garnish with chopped leeks and serve.

Kimchi Ramen Noodle Soup

Serving Size: 4 | Total Time: 20 minutes

1 chicken breast, cubed	½ tbsp kimchi paste
2 tbsp olive oil	1 cup mushrooms, chopped
½ tsp ground ginger	10 oz ramen noodles
2 tbsp garlic, minced	1 lb collard greens, trimmed
4 cups chicken stock	2 tbsp cilantro, chopped
2 tbsp soy sauce	1 red chili, chopped to serve

Warm the olive oil on Sauté. Add in the chicken and cook for 5-6 minutes until slightly browned. Add in the mushrooms, garlic, kimchi paste, and ginger and sauté for 4-5 minutes. Mix in chicken stock and soy sauce. Seal the lid and cook on High Pressure for 10 minutes. Release pressure quickly. Press Sauté and stir in the ramen noodles and collard greens and simmer for 2 minutes. Top with red chili and cilantro to serve.

Quick Mushroom-Quinoa Soup

Serving Size: 4 | Total Time: 30 minutes

4 cups vegetable broth	2 garlic cloves, smashed
1 carrot, chopped	1 tsp salt
1 stalk celery, diced	½ tsp dried thyme
2 cups quinoa, rinsed	3 tbsp butter
1 cup mushrooms, sliced	½ cup heavy cream
1 onion, chopped	

Melt the butter on Sauté. Add onion, garlic, celery, and carrot, and cook for 8 minutes until tender. Mix in broth, thyme, quinoa, mushrooms, and salt. Seal the lid and cook on High Pressure for 10 minutes. Release pressure quickly. Stir in heavy cream. Cook for 2 minutes to obtain a creamy consistency. Serve warm.

Garden Vegetable Soup

Serving Size: 4 | Total Time: 25 minutes

1 carrot, finely chopped	2 tbsp butter
2 spring onions, chopped	1 tsp vegetable oil
1 red bell pepper, chopped	4 cups vegetable broth
2 celery stalks, chopped	1 cup milk
½ cup celery, chopped	Salt and pepper to taste
½ tsp dried thyme	

Melt butter on Sauté. Add carrot, onions, bell pepper, and celery. Cook for 5 minutes, stirring constantly. Pour in vegetable broth, seal the lid and cook on Manual/Pressure Cook for 5 minutes on High. Do a quick release. Carefully unlock the lid. Stir in celery stalks, thyme, milk, oil, salt, and pepper and cook for 2-3 minutes on Sauté.

Potato-Leek Soup with Tofu

Serving Size: 4 | Total Time: 25 minutes

3 large leeks	¼ tsp nutmeg
3 tbsp butter	¼ tsp ground coriander
1 onion, chopped	1 bay leaf
1 lb potatoes, chopped	5 oz silken tofu
5 cups vegetable stock	Salt and pepper to taste
2 tsp lemon juice	2 tbsp chopped chives

Remove most of the green parts of the leeks. Slice the white parts very finely. Melt butter on Sauté. Stir-fry leeks and onion for 5 minutes. Add potatoes, stock, lemon juice, nutmeg, ground coriander, and bay leaf. Season to taste with salt and white pepper, and seal the lid. Press Manual and set the timer to 10 minutes. Cook on High. Do a quick release and discard the bay leaf. Process the soup in a food processor until smooth. Season to taste and add silken tofu. Sprinkle with chives and serve.

Delicious Chicken & Potato Soup

Serving Size: 4 | Total Time: 35 minutes

1 lb chicken breasts, cubed	2 egg yolks
1 onion, chopped	1 tsp salt
1 carrot, chopped	3 tbsp lemon juice
2 potatoes, peeled, chopped	3 tbsp olive oil
1 tsp cayenne pepper	

Add chicken, onion, carrot, potatoes, cayenne pepper, egg yolks, salt, lemon juice, oil, and 4 cups of water to the pot and seal the lid. Set the steam release handle and cook on Soup/Broth for 20 minutes on High. Release the pressure naturally for 10 minutes. Serve.

Homemade Winter Soup

Serving Size: 4 | Total Time: 40 minutes

3 sweet potatoes, chopped	1 large onion, chopped
1 tsp salt	1 tbsp coconut oil
2 fennel bulbs, chopped	4 cups water
16 oz pureed pumpkin	1 tbsp sour cream

Heat the oil on Sauté, and add onion and fennel bulbs. Cook for 3-5 minutes until tender. Add sweet potatoes, salt, pumpkin puree, and water, and seal the lid. Cook on High Pressure for 25 minutes. Do a quick release. Carefully unlock the lid. Transfer the soup to a food processor and blend for 20 seconds until creamy. Top with sour cream and serve.

Potato & Broccoli Soup with Rosemary

Serving Size: 4 | Total Time: 30 minutes

1 lb broccoli, cut into florets	½ tsp dried rosemary
2 potatoes, peeled, chopped	½ tsp salt
4 cups vegetable broth	½ cup sour cream

Place broccoli and potatoes in the pot. Pour the broth, rosemary, and seal the lid. Cook on Soup/Broth for 20 minutes on High. Do a quick release. Carefully unlock the lid and remove the soup to a blender. Pulse to combine. Stir in sour cream and add salt. Serve.

Traditional Cheesy Onion Soup

Serving Size: 4 | Total Time: 35 minutes

2 tbsp butter	2 sprigs fresh thyme
1 thinly chopped onion	2 bay leaves
Salt and pepper to taste	4 baguette slices
½ cup dry white wine	1 cup Swiss cheese, grated
4 cups beef stock	

Melt butter on Sauté. Add in onions and cook for 3-5 minutes until soft. Add in beef stock, wine, bay leaves, thyme, salt, and pepper as you stir. Seal the lid, press Manual, and cook for 15 minutes. Do a quick release. Discard bay leaves and thyme. Preheat the oven's broiler. Divide into four soup bowls. Top with ¼ cup Swiss cheese and 1 baguette slice. Transfer the bowls to a baking sheet and cook for 2-4 minutes under broiler until golden brown. Serve.

Parsley Noodle Soup with Chicken

Serving Size: 4 | Total Time: 35 minutes

1 lb chicken breasts, cubed   2 tbsp parsley, chopped
½ cup egg noodles   Salt and pepper to taste
4 cups chicken broth

Season the fillets with salt and place them in the pot. Pour the broth and seal the lid. Cook on Soup/Broth for 20 minutes on High. Do a quick release. Add in the noodles and seal the lid again. Press Manual/Pressure Cook and cook for 5 minutes on High Pressure. Release the pressure quickly. Carefully unlock the lid. Sprinkle with black pepper and parsley. Serve warm.

Creamy Broccoli-Gorgonzola Soup

Serving Size: 4 | Total Time: 35 minutes

8 oz Gorgonzola cheese, crumbled
1 cup broccoli, chopped   1 tbsp parsley, chopped
2 tbsp olive oil   Salt and pepper to taste
½ cup full-fat milk

Add broccoli, oil, milk, salt, pepper, and gorgonzola cheese to the pot and 4 cups of water. Seal the lid and cook on Soup/Broth for 30 minutes on High Pressure. Do a quick release. Carefully unlock the lid. Remove the lid and sprinkle with fresh parsley. Serve.

Rustic Soup with Turkey Balls & Carrots

Serving Size: 4 | Total Time: 45 minutes

2 tbsp olive oil   1 garlic clove, minced
6 oz turkey balls   3 large carrots, chopped
4 cups chicken broth   Salt and pepper to taste
1 onion, chopped   1 tbsp cilantro, chopped

Heat olive oil on Sauté and stir-fry onion, carrots, and garlic for 5 minutes until soft. Add turkey balls, broth, salt, and pepper to the pot. Seal the lid and press Manual. Cook for 25 minutes on HIgh. Release the pressure naturally for 10 minutes and serve sprinkled with cilantro.

Vegetable Beef Soup

Serving Size: 4 | Total Time: 45 minutes

½ lb lean beef, cut into bite-sized pieces
1 onion, chopped   2 tbsp butter
2 carrots, chopped
1 tsp cayenne pepper
Salt and pepper to taste

Melt butter on Sauté. Add onion and stir-fry for 3 minutes. Add carrots, cayenne pepper, salt, and pepper. Cook for 2 more minutes. Add the meat and pour in 4 cups of water. Seal the lid and cook on Manual for 35 minutes. Release the pressure quickly. Serve warm.

Modern Minestrone with Pancetta

Serving Size: 6 | Total Time: 30 minutes

2 tbsp olive oil   1 tbsp dried oregano
2 oz pancetta, chopped   6 cups vegetable broth
1 onion, diced   1 lb green beans, chopped
1 parsnip, chopped   1 (15-oz) can diced tomatoes
2 carrots, cut into rounds   1 (15-oz) can chickpeas
2 celery stalks   2 cups small shaped pasta
2 garlic cloves, minced   Salt and pepper to taste
1 tbsp dried basil   ½ cup grated Parmesan
1 tbsp dried thyme

Heat oil on Sauté. Add onion, carrots, garlic, pancetta, celery, and parsnip and cook for 5 minutes until they become soft. Stir in basil, oregano, beans, broth, tomatoes, pepper, salt, thyme, chickpeas, and pasta. Seal the lid and cook for 6 minutes on High Pressure. Release pressure naturally for 10 minutes. Carefully unlock the lid. Garnished with Parmesan cheese and serve.

Piri Piri Chicken Soup

Serving Size: 4 | Total Time: 40 minutes

2 chicken breasts, cubed   3 cups chicken bone broth
1 garlic clove, minced   1/3 cup Piri Piri spicy sauce
1 sweet onion, diced   1 tsp thyme
½ cup celery, diced   1 tbsp lemon juice
2 tbsp butter   Salt and pepper to taste

Melt butter in your Instant Pot on Sauté and cook onion, celery, and garlic for 3 minutes. Add in the chicken and Sauté for another 4-5 minutes, stirring occasionally. Pour in chicken broth, thyme, and spicy sauce and seal the lid. Select Manual and cook for 12 minutes on High pressure.

When done, allow a natural release for 10 minutes, then perform a quick pressure release. Carefully unlock the lid. Adjust the taste and drizzle with the lemon juice. Ladle into bowls and serve warm. Enjoy!

Turmeric Butternut Squash Soup

Serving Size: 4 | Total Time: 40 minutes

1.5 lb butternut squash, peeled and chopped
1 onion, chopped   Salt and pepper to taste
4 cups vegetable broth   2 tbsp parsley, chopped
1 tbsp ground turmeric   3 tbsp olive oil
½ tbsp heavy cream

Heat oil on Sauté and stir-fry onion for 3 minutes. Add in butternut squash, turmeric, vegetable broth, salt, and pepper and stir well. Seal the lid. Press Soup/Broth and cook for 30 minutes on High. Do a quick release. With an immersion blender, blend until smooth. Stir in heavy cream and top with freshly chopped parsley. Serve warm.

Vegetarian Soup with White Beans

Serving Size: 4 | Total Time: 30 minutes

1 cup green peas	4 cups vegetable broth
1 carrot, chopped	1 onion, chopped
2 red bell peppers, chopped	2 tbsp olive oil
½ cup white beans, soaked	Salt and pepper to taste
1 tomato, roughly chopped	¼ tsp dried oregano

Heat the olive oil on Sauté and stir-fry onion, carrot, and bell peppers for 5 minutes until tender. Stir in green peas, white beans, tomato, broth, salt, pepper, and oregano. Seal the lid. Cook on High Pressure for 20 minutes. Do a quick release. Serve warm.

Yellow Beef Soup

Serving Size: 4 | Total Time: 35 minutes

1 bay leaf	½ tsp turmeric
2 garlic cloves	2 tbsp beansprouts
½ lb beef sirloin, cubed	1 lemongrass
2 shallots	1 tsp vegetable oil
2 candlenuts	Salt and pepper to taste

In a blender, combine the shallots, garlic, candlenuts, and turmeric until smooth. Warm vegetable oil in your Instant Pot on Sauté. Place the shallot mixture and cook for 3-4 minutes, stirring often until aromatic. Add in the beef and lemongrass and stir-fry until the lemongrass is wilted, about 5 minutes. Put in 4 cups water, bay leaf, salt, and pepper and seal the lid. Select Manual and cook for 15 minutes on High. When done, perform a quick pressure release. Discard bay leaf. Mix in beansprouts and cook for 2-3 minutes until wilted. Serve warm.

Spicy Red Kidney Bean Soup

Serving Size: 4 | Total Time: 45 minutes

14.5 oz can red kidney beans	2 cloves garlic, crushed
14.5 oz canned tomatoes	2 red chilies, chopped
2 tbsp oil	1 green bell pepper, diced
1 onion, chopped	½ cup tomato sauce

Heat oil on Sauté and stir-fry garlic, chilies, and onion for 3 minutes. Add tomatoes, beans, bell pepper, tomato sauce, and 4 cups of water. Seal the lid. Cook on Manual for 25 minutes on High Pressure. Release the steam naturally for 10 minutes. Carefully unlock the lid. Serve.

Creamy Celery & Green Pea Soup

Serving Size: 4 | Total Time: 25 minutes

3 oz carrots, finely chopped	1 egg yolk
3 oz celery root, chopped	2 tbsp cream cheese
1 cup green peas	Salt and pepper to taste
2 tbsp butter	4 cups beef broth
2 tbsp parsley, chopped	

Add carrots, celery, green peas, butter parsley, egg yolk, cream cheese, salt, pepper, and broth to the Instant Pot and seal the lid. Cook on High Pressure for 10 minutes. When done, release the steam naturally for 10 minutes.

Creamy Bean & Potato Soup

Serving Size: 4 | Total Time: 35 minutes

½ cup canned beans	½ cup heavy cream
4 cups beef broth	Salt and pepper to taste
1 potato, chopped	1 tsp garlic powder

Add beans, broth, potato, heavy cream, salt, pepper, and garlic powder to the pot, seal the lid, and cook on Manual/Pressure for 10 minutes on High. Release the steam naturally for 10 minutes. Carefully unlock the lid. Transfer the ingredients to a blender. Pulse until smooth. Return the soup to the pot. Press Sauté and add a half cup of water. Cook for 5 more minutes, or until desired thickness. Let it chill for a while before serving.

Effortless Tomato-Lentil Soup

Serving Size: 4 | Total Time: 35 minutes

1 cup red lentils	2 tomatoes, chopped
1 carrot, cut into thin slices	1 onion, diced
1 tbsp tomato paste	½ tsp dried thyme
3 garlic cloves, crushed	2 tbsp olive oil
4 cups vegetable broth	

Warm oil on Sauté. Cook onion, carrot, and garlic for 5 minutes. Add in tomato paste, tomatoes, lentils, broth, and thyme. Seal the lid and cook on Soup/Broth for 15 minutes on High Pressure. Release the pressure naturally for 10 minutes. Carefully unlock the lid. Serve.

Parsley Creamy Tomato Soup

Serving Size: 4 | Total Time: 50 minutes

2 lb tomatoes, diced	1 cup vegetable broth
1 cup canned white beans	½ tsp sugar
1 small onion, diced	Salt and pepper to taste
2 garlic cloves, crushed	2 tbsp olive oil
1 cup heavy cream	2 tbsp parsley, chopped

Warm oil on Sauté. Stir-fry onion and garlic for 2 minutes. Add tomatoes, beans, broth, 3 cups of water, parsley, salt, pepper, and a little bit of sugar to balance the bitterness. Seal the lid and cook on Soup/Broth for 30 minutes on High Pressure. Release the pressure naturally for 10 minutes. Carefully unlock the lid. Top with a dollop of heavy cream and serve.

Tasty Asparagus Soup

Serving Size: 4 | Total Time: 35 minutes

2 lb asparagus, chopped	1 tbsp vegetable oil
2 onions, chopped	½ tsp salt
1 cup heavy cream	½ tsp dried oregano
4 cups vegetable broth	½ tsp paprika
2 tbsp butter	

Melt butter on Sauté, and add 1 tbsp of oil. Stir-fry the onions for 2 minutes until translucent. Add asparagus, oregano, salt, and paprika. Stir well and cook until asparagus soften for a few minutes. Pour the broth and mix well to combine.

Seal the lid and cook on Soup/Broth for 20 minutes on High. Do a quick release and whisk in 1 cup of heavy cream. Unlock the lid. Serve.

Gingery Squash & Leek Soup

Serving Size: 4 | Total Time: 35 minutes

2 cups butternut squash, chopped	
4 leeks, chopped	2 tbsp olive oil
Salt and pepper to taste	1 tsp cumin
1 tsp ginger, grated	1 tsp ginger powder
4 cups vegetable broth	

Heat the oil on Sauté, add stir-fry leeks for about 5 minutes, on Sauté. Add ginger powder and cumin. Give it a good stir and continue to cook for 1 more minute. Pour in squash, ginger, salt, pepper, and broth and seal the lid. Cook on Soup/Broth for 10 minutes on High. Release the pressure naturally for about 10 minutes.

Lentil & Carrot Soup

Serving Size: 4 | Total Time: 40 minutes

1 cup red lentils, rinsed	Salt and pepper to taste
1 red bell pepper, chopped	½ tsp cumin, ground
1 onion, chopped	2 tbsp olive oil
½ cup carrot puree	2 tbsp parsley, chopped

Heat the oil on Sauté, add stir-fry the onion for 4 minutes. Add lentils, bell pepper, carrot puree, salt, pepper, and cumin and pour in 4 cups of water. Seal the lid and cook on Soup/Broth for 30 minutes on High. Do a quick pressure release. Sprinkle with fresh parsley and serve.

Cabbage & Pork Soup

Serving Size: 6 | Total Time: 20 minutes

1 lb ground pork	3 scallions, sliced
1 onion, diced	2 tbsp butter
2 lb napa cabbage, chopped	4 cups vegetable broth
1 potato, diced	Salt and pepper to taste
6 button mushrooms, sliced	

Melt butter on Sauté and add the pork. Cook until it browned, breaking it with a spatula. Once browned, add onion and mushrooms and cook for another 4-5 minutes. Season with salt and pepper. Pour in vegetable broth and stir in cabbage, potato, and scallions. Seal the lid, cook on Pressure Cook for 6 minutes on High. Do a quick release. Carefully unlock the lid. Serve.

Millet & Beef Soup

Serving Size: 4 | Total Time: 35 minutes

½ lb beef stew meat, cubed	12 oz spicy vegetable juice
2 tbsp vegetable oil	4 cups beef bone broth
1 celery rib, chopped	Salt and pepper to taste
2 shallots, chopped	½ cup frozen peas
2 garlic cloves, minced	½ tsp dried rosemary
1 carrot, chopped	½ tsp dried sage
½ cup millet, rinsed	
1 cup canned tomatoes, diced	

Heat vegetable oil in your Instant Pot on Sauté and cook shallots, carrot, celery, and garlic for 3 minutes. Add in the beef and Sauté for another 4-5 minutes, stirring often. Pour in beef broth, tomatoes, spicy vegetable juice, millet, rosemary, and sage and seal the lid. Select Manual and cook for 15 minutes on High pressure. Once ready, perform a quick pressure release and unlock the lid. Mix in peas and let sit for 5 minutes; adjust the seasoning. Serve right away. Enjoy!

Jalapeño Chicken Soup with Tortilla Chips

Serving Size: 6 | Total Time: 50 minutes

¾ lb chicken thighs	2 tbsp butter, softened
1 onion, chopped	1 jalapeño pepper, minced
2 garlic cloves, minced	½ tsp dried basil
1 cup tomatoes, chopped	½ tsp dried oregano
1 tbsp ginger, minced	Salt and pepper to taste
2 cups collard greens	6 oz tortilla chips

Melt the butter in your Instant Pot on Sauté. Add in the onion, ginger, garlic, and jalapeño pepper and cook for 3 minutes. Add in the chicken thighs and brown for another 5 minutes, stirring occasionally. Mix in tomatoes, 6 cups of water, oregano, basil, salt, and pepper and seal the lid. Select Manual and cook for 15 minutes on High.

Once done, allow a natural release for 15 minutes. Shred the chicken and discard the bones; return it to the soup Stir in collard greens and simmer for 3 minutes on Sauté. Adjust the seasoning. Serve topped with tortilla chips.

Dilled Salmon Soup

Serving Size: 2 | Total Time: 20 minutes

¼ cup chopped green tomatoes	
½ lb salmon fillet	¼ tsp tamarind
1 cup fresh dill	1 tbsp lemon juice
2 tsp sliced shallots	1 cup water
1 tsp sliced garlic	1 bay leaf
¼ tsp ginger	½ tsp salt

Slice salmon fillet into medium dices and place them in your Instant Pot. Add in water, green tomatoes, fresh dill, shallot, garlic, ginger, bay leaf, salt, tamarind, and lemon juice. Seal the lid, select Soup, and cook for 4 minutes on High. When done, allow a natural release for 10 minutes and unlock the lid. Serve warm and enjoy!

Spicy Sweet Potato Soup

Serving Size: 2 | Total Time: 30 minutes

2 sweet potatoes, chopped	2 garlic cloves, chopped
1 carrot, chopped	Salt and pepper to taste
1 onion, chopped	1 tbsp chili flakes
2 cups chicken broth	1 tbsp olive oil

Warm oil on Sauté, and stir-fry potatoes, onion, and garlic for 3-4 minutes. Stir in carrot, broth, salt, pepper, and chili flakes, seal the lid and cook on High Pressure for 7 minutes. Do a natural release for 10 minutes. Serve.

Quick Beef Soup

Serving Size: 2 | Total Time: 40 minutes + soaking time

2 cups beef broth	1 lemongrass
2 kluwak nuts	3 kaffir lime leaves
½ lb beef sirloin	2 garlic cloves
¼ tsp ginger	2 shallots
½-inch galangal	¼ tsp turmeric
½ tsp dry coriander	½ tsp salt
¼ tsp cumin	

Place the kluwak nuts in a bowl with enough water to cover and let soak until the water turns brown. In a blender, combine the garlic, shallots, turmeric, ginger, coriander, and cumin until smooth. Cut the beef sirloin into slices and put them in your Instant Pot.

Stir in kluwak water, garlic mixture, galangal, lemongrass, lime leaves, broth, and salt. Seal the lid, select Manual, and cook for 20 minutes on High pressure. When done, allow a natural release for 10 minutes and unlock the lid. Divide between plates and serve with brown rice.

Pork Soup with Cabbage & Beans

Serving Size: 4 | Total Time: 30 minutes

2 tbsp olive oil	1 carrot, shredded
1 onion, cubed	1 garlic clove, minced
½ lb cubed pork meat	½ tsp dried rosemary
½ head cabbage, shredded	4 cups chicken broth
14 oz can cannellini beans	Salt and pepper to taste

Warm the oil in your Instant Pot on Sauté. Place the onion, garlic, and pork and cook for 4-5 minutes. Add in cabbage, carrot, broth, rosemary, salt, pepper, and cannellini beans. Seal the lid and cook on Manual for 20 minutes on High. Perform a quick pressure release.

Chicken & Potato Soup

Serving Size: 4 | Total Time: 45 minutes

2 tbsp olive oil	2 garlic cloves, minced
½ lb chicken thighs	1 celery rib, chopped
2 potatoes, cut into chunks	4 cups chicken bone broth
1 carrot, cut into chunks	Salt and pepper to taste
1 yellow onion, diced	2 tbsp parsley, chopped

Heat oil in your Instant Pot on Sauté and cook onion, carrot, celery, and garlic for 3 minutes. Add in chicken and Sauté for 4-5 minutes. Pour in broth and potatoes and seal the lid. Select Manual and cook for 15 minutes on High. Once ready, allow a natural release for 10 minutes. Adjust the taste and top with parsley. Serve.

Smoked Ham & Potato Soup

Serving Size: 4 | Total Time: 20 minutes

1 lb russet potatoes, cut into small chunks	
2 tbsp butter	½ tsp chili powder
2 garlic cloves, minced	½ lb smoked ham, diced
1 onion, diced	4 cups chicken broth
½ tsp celery seeds	2 tbsp parsley, chopped

Melt butter in your Instant Pot on Sauté. Add in garlic and onion and cook for 3 minutes. Stir in celery seeds, chili powder, and smoked ham for 1-2 minutes and pour in potatoes and broth. Seal the lid. Select Manual and cook for 10 minutes on High. Once done, perform a quick pressure release. Serve topped with parsley.

Hearty Beef Soup

Serving Size: 6 | Total Time: 65 minutes

2 tbsp olive oil	½ cup pearl barley
2 lb beef stew meat, cubed	1 bay leaf
1 leek, finely chopped	6 cups beef bone broth
2 garlic cloves, minced	½ tsp soy sauce sauce
2 carrots, chopped	Salt and pepper to taste
1 celery stalk, chopped	1 tbsp Parmesan, grated

Warm the olive oil in your Instant Pot on Sauté. Season beef with salt and pepper and cook in the pot for 10 minutes, stirring frequently; set aside. Add the leek, garlic, carrots, and celery to the pot and cook for 4 minutes. Put the beef back to the pot with pearl barley, bay leaf, beef broth, and soy sauce. Seal the lid and select Manual.

Cook for 30 minutes on High pressure. When done, allow a natural release for 10 minutes, then perform a quick pressure release and unlock the lid. Discard the bay leaf. Adjust the taste and top with Parmesan cheese.

Lentil & Pork Shank Soup

Serving Size: 6 | Total Time: 45 minutes

2 lb pork shank, trimmed of excess fat	
2 carrots, cut into chunks	½ tsp paprika
1 celery stalk, chopped	½ tsp cayenne pepper
3 garlic cloves, sliced	2 tomatoes, chopped
2 tbsp olive oil	½ lb lentils, rinsed
1 yellow onion, chopped	Salt and pepper to taste

Warm the olive oil in your Instant Pot on Sauté. Place the onion, carrots, garlic, and celery and cook for 3 minutes, stirring often. Add in pork chank, paprika, cayenne pepper, tomatoes, lentils, salt, pepper, and 6 cups water.

Seal the lid, select Manual, and cook for 25 minutes on High pressure. When over, allow a natural release for 10 minutes and unlock the lid. Serve warm.

Ukrainian-Style Borscht

Serving Size: 4 | Total Time: 40 minutes

2 tbsp grapeseed oil	2 garlic cloves, diced
½ lb beets, peeled, diced	3 cups grated red cabbage
½ lb potatoes, peeled, diced	4 cups vegetable stock
1 parsnip, diced	½ tsp ground cumin
1 celery stalk, diced	Salt and pepper to taste
1 red onion, diced	

Heat the grapeseed oil in your Instant Pot on Saué and cook celery, red onion, garlic, parsnip, and red cabbage for 4-5 minutes, stirring periodically. Pour in the vegetable stock, potatoes, beets, cumin, salt, and pepper.

Seal the lid. Select Manual and cook for 15 minutes on High pressure. When over, allow a natural release for 10 minutes and unlock the lid. Serve immediately.

Chicken & Spinach Soup

Serving Size: 6 | Total Time: 35 minutes

3 tbsp butter	2 chicken breasts, cubed
1 white onion, diced	6 cups chicken broth
3 celery stalks, diced	1 cup orzo pasta
2 carrots, diced	2 cups spinach, chopped
3 garlic cloves, minced	Salt and pepper to taste
½ tsp dried rosemary	2 tbsp fresh dill, chopped

Melt butter in your Instant Pot on Sauté. Add in onion, celery, carrot, garlic, salt, and pepper and cook for 5 minutes. Stir in chicken breasts, and rosemary and Sauté for 5 minutes. Pour in chicken broth and orzo and seal the lid. Select Manual and cook for 12 minutes on High. Once ready, perform a quick pressure release and unlock the lid. Mix in spinach and let sit covered for 5 minutes until the spinach wilts. Scatter with dill to serve.

Mom's Meatball Soup

Serving Size: 4 | Total Time: 25 minutes

2 Yukon Gold potatoes, peeled and diced	
2 tbsp canola oil	4 cups vegetable broth
1 onion, diced	½ tsp dried oregano
1 garlic clove, minced	½ tsp dried thyme
½ lb ground pork	Salt and pepper to taste
14 oz can diced tomatoes	2 tbsp parsley, chopped

Place the ground pork in a bowl and season with oregano, thyme, salt, and pepper. Mix well with your hands and form form the mixture into small balls. Warm the canola oil in your Instant Pot on Sauté. Add in the onion and garlic and cook for 3 minutes. Pour in vegetable broth, tomatoes, potatoes, and meatballs and seal the lid. Select Manual and cook for 10 minutes on High pressure. Once ready, perform a quick pressure release and unlock the lid. Sprinkle with par and serve warm.

Coconut Chicken Soup

Serving Size: 4 | Total Time: 30 minutes

2 green onions, sliced diagonally	
2 tbsp ghee	1 tbsp parsley
1 sweet onion, chopped	3 cups chicken stock
1 cup celery, chopped	1 tsp red pepper flakes
1 cup carrots, chopped	Salt and pepper to taste
6 oz rice noodles	1 cup coconut milk
½ lb chicken breasts, cubed	1 cup green peas

Melt ghee in your Instant Pot on Sauté. Add in onion, celery, and carrots and cook for 3 minutes. Stir in chicken, parsley, stock, pepper flakes, salt, and pepper. Seal the lid and select Manual. Cook for 15 minutes on High. When done, perform a quick pressure release. Stir in coconut milk, green peas, and rice noodles and cook for 3 minutes on Sauté. Serve topped with green onions.

Cilantro & Coconut Chicken Soup

Serving Size: 4 | Total Time: 20 minutes

1 tsp ground nutmeg	1 tsp paprika
2 cups diced tomatoes	1 tsp Cayenne Powder
4 chicken breasts, cubed	2 tbsp Tomato Puree
1 tbsp olive oil	1 cup Coconut Milk Whey
1 onion, chopped	1 cup Coconut Cream
1 tsp garlic powder	¼ cup Almonds, sliced
1 tsp ginger powder	¼ cup Chopped Cilantro
1 tsp turmeric	Salt to taste

Warm olive oil in your Instant Pot on Sauté. Place the onions and salt and cook for 3 minutes. Add in nutmeg, garlic powder, ginger powder, turmeric, paprika, and cayenne pepper and cook for 2 minutes, stirring often.

Mix in diced tomatoes, coconut milk, and chicken breasts and seal the lid. Select Manual and cook for 10 minutes on High pressure. When done, perform a quick pressure release. Stir in tomato puree, coconut cream, and cilantro. Adjust seasoning to taste. Serve topped with almond.

Spring Chicken Vermicelli Soup

Serving Size: 6 | Total Time: 50 minutes

2 tbsp olive oil	1 celery stalk, chopped
½ cup vermicelli	4 cups chicken stock
¾ lb chicken breasts, cubed	½ tsp oregano
2 carrots, diced	1 bay leaf
3 waxy potatoes, diced	Salt and pepper to taste
3 green onions, sliced	2 tbsp cilantro, chopped
1 green garlic stalk, sliced	

Warm the olive oil in your Instant Pot on Sauté. Add in the green onion, carrots, green garlic, and celery and cook for 3 minutes. Add in chicken and Sauté for 5 minutes, stirring often. Mix in potatoes, chicken stock, 2 cups of water, oregano, salt, pepper, and bay leaf and seal the lid. Select Manual, and cook for 20 minutes on High pressure. When over, allow a natural release for 10 minutes, then perform a quick pressure release. Discard the bay leaf, stir in vermicelli, and press Sauté. Cook for 5 minutes. Serve topped with cilantro.

Veggie & Elbow Pasta Soup

Serving Size: 2 | Total Time: 25 minutes

1 cup canned chickpeas	1 tbsp olive oil
1 carrot, diced	1 tsp dried oregano
14 oz can tomatoes, diced	2 garlic cloves, minced
½ cup elbow pasta	1 onion, diced
2 cups chicken broth	¼ cup fresh spinach
1 tsp dried basil	Salt and pepper to taste

Place the olive oil, carrot, onion, and garlic in your Instant Pot and cook until tender and soft on Sauté. Stir in oregano, basil, black pepper, salt, tomatoes, spinach, pasta, and chicken broth. Seal the lid, select Manual, and cook for 6 minutes on High. When done, allow a natural release for 10 minutes. Mix in chickpeas and serve.

Kale, Bean & Pancetta Soup

Serving Size: 6 | Total Time: 35 minutes

1 can (15-oz) pinto beans	2 tbsp tomato paste
1 tbsp olive oil	1 sprig fresh rosemary
4 slices pancetta, chopped	2 bay leaves
1 onion, chopped	4 cups chicken broth
1 carrot, chopped	3 cups baby kale
1 celery stalk, chopped	Salt and pepper to taste

Press the Sauté on your Instant Pot and heat the olive oil. Add in the pancetta and cook until it becomes crispy, about 4-5 minutes. Remove to a lined with paper towel plate. Put the onion, carrot, and celery in the pot and cook for 3 minutes. Stir in tomato paste, pinto beans, rosemary, bay leaves, and chicken broth.

Seal the lid, select Manual, and cook for 10 minutes on High. When done, allow a natural release for 10 minutes, then perform a quick pressure release and unlock the lid. Discard rosemary and bay leaves. Mix in the kale and adjust the seasoning. Serve topped with pancetta. Enjoy!

Navy Bean & Zucchini Soup

Serving Size: 4 | Total Time: 25 minutes

2 tbsp olive oil	1 cup canned navy beans
1 onion, chopped	1 tsp fresh thyme
2 garlic cloves, minced	1 bay leaf
1 zucchini, chopped	4 cups vegetable stock
1 carrot, chopped	Salt and pepper to taste
1 celery stalk, chopped	2 tbsp parsley, chopped

Warm the olive oil in your Instant Pot on Sauté. Add in onion and garlic and sweat for 4-5 minutes. Add in zucchini, carrot, and celery and cook for 5 more minutes.

Stir in beans, thyme, bay leaf, stock, salt, and pepper and seal the lid. Select Manual and cook for 8 minutes on High. When over, perform a quick pressure release. Discard bay leaf. Top with parsley and serve. Enjoy!

Turkish-Inspired Lentil Soup

Serving Size: 6 | Total Time: 30 minutes

2 tbsp olive oil	1 tbsp red pepper paste
1 white onion, chopped	¼ cup bulgur
1 celery stalk, diced	1 cup red lentils
4 garlic cloves, minced	14 oz can diced tomatoes
1 carrot, chopped	6 cups vegetable broth
1 tsp paprika	Salt and pepper to taste
½ tsp ground cumin	2 tbsp parsley, chopped
½ tsp ground coriander	

Warm the olive oil in your Instant Pot on Sauté. Add in onion, carrot, and celery and cook for 4-5 minutes. Stir in garlic, paprika, cumin, coriander, and red pepper paste and cook for another 1-2 minutes. Pour in vegetable broth, lentils, tomatoes, and bulgur and seal the lid. Select Manual and cook for 12 minutes on High. Once ready, perform a quick pressure release. Unlock the lid and adjust the seasoning. Top with parsley and serve.

Mexican Bean Soup

Serving Size: 6 | Total Time: 40 minutes

2 tbsp olive oil	4 cups vegetable broth
2 garlic cloves, minced	14 oz can diced tomatoes
1 onion, chopped	2 hot cherry peppers, sliced
1 red bell pepper, chopped	Salt and pepper to taste
½ tsp dried oregano	1 lime, cut into wedges
1 tsp ground cumin	3 tbsp cilantro, chopped
1 bay leaf	Chili oil to serve
1 lb black beans, soaked	

Warm the olive oil in your Instant Pot on Sauté. Add in garlic and onion and cook for 3 minutes. Stir in bell pepper, oregano, cumin, cherry peppers, and bay leaf and cook for another minute.

Pour in black beans, vegetable broth, tomatoes, salt, and pepper and seal the lid. Select Manual and cook for 30 minutes. Once done, perform a quick pressure release and unlock the lid. Discard the bay leaf. Drizzle with chili oil and sprinkle with cilantro. Serve with lime wedges.

Black-Eyed Pea Soup

Serving Size: 4 | Total Time: 40 minutes

2 tbsp canola oil	¼ tsp cayenne pepper
2 shallots, diced	¼ tsp dried dill
2 garlic cloves, minced	¼ tsp dried oregano
1 celery stalk, sliced	¼ tsp dried sage
1 carrot, chopped	1 cup spinach, torn
1 lb dry black-eyed peas	4 cups vegetable broth

Warm the canola oil in your Instant Pot on Sauté. Add in shallots, garlic, celery, and carrot and cook for 4 minutes. Add in black-eyed peas, cayenne pepper, dill, oregano, sage, and vegetable broth and stir well.

Seal the lid, select Manual, and cook for 10 minutes on High pressure. Once over, allow a natural release for 10 minutes, then perform a quick pressure release and unlock the lid. Stir in spinach, cover with the lid, and leave to sit in the residual heat for 5 minutes. Serve warm.

Greek-Style Fish Soup

Serving Size: 4 | Total Time: 20 minutes

1 lb codfish, cut into bite-sized pieces	
2 tbsp olive oil	½ tsp dill weed
1 onion, chopped	½ tsp Greek oregano
1 carrot, chopped	½ tsp hot sauce
2 garlic cloves, minced	4 cups seafood stock
2 tomatoes, chopped	10 Kalamata olives, chopped

Warm olive oil in your Instant Pot on Sauté. Add in onion, garlic, and carrot and cook for 4 minutes. Stir in dill weed, oregano, hot sauce, and fish and cook for 3-4 minutes. Pour in stock and tomatoes and seal the lid. Select Manual and cook for 5 minutes on High. When ready, perform a quick pressure release. Carefully unlock the lid. Sprinkle with Kalamata olives and serve.

Chicken & Lima Bean Soup

Serving Size: 6 | Total Time: 45 minutes

2 tbsp sesame oil
1 cup lima beans, soaked
¾ lb chicken breasts, cubed
1 serrano pepper, minced
½ tsp cayenne pepper
1 sweet onion, sliced
2 garlic cloves, minced

2 tomatoes, chopped
2 tbsp rosemary, chopped
6 cups vegetable broth
4 tbsp salsa
1 tsp soy sauce
Salt and pepper to taste

Press Sauté and heat the sesame oil in your Instant Pot. Cook the onion and garlic until tender and fragrant. Add the chicken, serrano pepper, cayenne pepper, salt, and black pepper and sauté for 4-5 minutes. Pour in salsa, tomatoes, vegetable broth, soy sauce, and lima beans.

Seal the lid, select Manual, and cook for 30 minutes on High pressure. Once ready, perform a quick pressure release. Sprinkle with rosemary and serve warm. Enjoy!

Zuppa Toscana

Serving Size: 4 | Total Time: 40 minutes

2 tbsp olive oil
1 white onion, diced
2 garlic cloves, minced
1 lb Italian sausages, chopped
4 oz bacon, chopped
2 potatoes, sliced
14 oz can cannellini beans

1 red pepper, crushed
4 cups chicken broth
Salt and pepper to taste
1 tsp Italian seasoning
2 cups kale, chopped
½ cup grated Parmesan

Warm the olive oil in your Instant Pot on Sauté. Add in onion, garlic, bacon, and Italian sausages and cook for 4-5 minutes. Stir in potatoes, cannellini beans, Italian seasoning, chicken broth, and red pepper and seal the lid.

Select Manual and cook for 20 minutes on High pressure. Once done, perform a quick pressure release and unlock the lid. Stir in kale and simmer for 3-4 minutes on Sauté. Adjust the seasoning and top with Parmesan to serve.

Moroccan Lentil Soup

Serving Size: 4 | Total Time: 30 minutes

2 tsp olive oil
2 garlic cloves, minced
1 onion, chopped
1 cup red lentils
2 tbsp tomato purée
1 potato, chopped
1 carrot, chopped
½ cup celery

½ tsp ground coriander
½ tsp ground cumin
½ tsp cinnamon
1 red chili pepper, chopped
4 cups water
Salt and pepper to taste
2 tbsp fresh mint, chopped

Warm olive oil in your Instant Pot on Sauté. Add in garlic, celery, carrot, and onion and cook for 3 minutes. Stir in chili pepper, tomato puree, ground coriander, cumin, salt, pepper, and cinnamon and cook for 1 minute. Pour in lentils, potato, and 4 cups of water and stir.

Seal the lid, select Manual, and cook for 10 minutes on High pressure. When done, allow a natural release for 10 minutes and unlock the lid. Sprinkle with mint and serve.

Green Soup

Serving Size: 4 | Total Time: 20 minutes

2 tbsp olive oil
1 onion, chopped
1 celery rib, chopped
10 oz broccoli florets
2 cups kale

4 cups chicken broth
Salt and pepper to taste
2 tbsp peanut butter
¼ cup heavy cream

Warm the olive oil in your Instant Pot on Sauté. Place the onion and cook for 3 minutes until translucent. Add in celery and broccoli and cook for another 2 minutes.

Pour in chicken broth and kale and seal the lid. Select Manual and cook for 5 minutes on High pressure. Once done, perform a quick pressure release and unlock the lid. Let chill, then blend it. Stir in peanut butter and heavy cream and adjust the seasonings. Serve right away.

Harvest Vegetable Soup with Pesto

Serving Size: 6 | Total Time: 30 minutes

10 oz spinach
½ cup canned white beans
2 tbsp olive oil
1 onion, chopped
2 garlic cloves, minced
1 carrot, chopped

1 celery stalk, chopped
1 can crushed tomatoes
2 tbsp parsley
6 cups chicken bone broth
Salt and pepper to taste
2 tbsp pesto

Warm the olive oil in your Instant Pot on Sauté. Add in onion, garlic, carrot, and celery and cook for 3 minutes until tender. Pour in chicken broth, white beans, parsley, and tomatoes and seal the lid. Select Manual and cook for 10 minutes on High pressure.

When done, allow a natural release for 10 minutes and unlock the lid. Stir in spinach, seal the lid, and let sit in the residual heat until the spinach wilts. Adjust the seasonings and top with pesto. Serve immediately.

Mediterranean Soup with Tortellini

Serving Size: 4 | Total Time: 40 minutes

1 cup cream of mushroom soup
½ cup mushrooms, chopped
9 oz refrigerated tortellini
1 cup green peas
2 carrots, chopped
2 tbsp olive oil
2 shallots, chopped

2 garlic cloves, minced
½ tsp oregano
3 cups vegetable broth
Salt and pepper to taste
2 tbsp Parmesan, shredded

Heat the olive oil in your Instant Pot on Sauté. Add in shallots and garlic and cook for 3 minutes until translucent. Add in the carrots and mushrooms and continue sautéing for 3-4 minutes. Pour in broth, mushroom soup, and oregano, and tomatoes and seal the lid. Select Manual and cook for 7 minutes on High.

Once over, allow a natural release for 10 minutes, then perform a quick pressure release and unlock the lid. Stir in green peas and tortellini and cook for 3-5 minutes on Sauté. Sprinkle with Parmesan cheese and serve.

Creamed Butternut Squash Soup

Serving Size: 4 | Total Time: 30 minutes

1 lb butternut squash, cut into chunks	
1 tbsp pumpkin seeds, toasted	½ tsp nutmeg
	½ tsp ground cinnamon
2 tbsp grapeseed oil	4 cups vegetable stock
1 onion, chopped	1 cup heavy cream
1 turnip, diced	Salt and pepper to taste

Heat the grapeseed oil in your Instant Pot on Sauté. Add in onion and cook for 3 minutes until softened. Stir in vegetable stock, butternut squash, turnip, nutmeg, and cinnamon and seal the lid. Select Manual and cook for 10 minutes on High pressure.

When over, allow a natural release for 10 minutes and unlock the lid. Blend the soup using an immersion blender and stir in heavy cream; adjust the seasonings. Sprinkle with pumpkin seeds and serve immediately.

French Onion Soup

Serving Size: 4 | Total Time: 45 minutes

1 cup cream of mushroom soup	
2 tbsp olive oil	4 cups chicken stock
2 tbsp butter	Salt and pepper to taste
2 lb onions, chopped	1 baguette, sliced
2 sprigs fresh thyme	1 tbsp chives, chopped
½ cup Gruyere, grated	

Heat butter and olive oil in your Instant Pot on Sauté. Add in onion and cook for 10 minutes, stirring occasionally until caramelized. Pour in the chicken stock, thyme, mushroom soup, salt, and pepper and seal the lid. Select Manual and cook for 10 minutes on High. When ready, allow a natural release for 10 minutes. Discard the thyme sprigs.

Divide the soup between four oven-safe bowls and top each one with bread slices and cheese. Cook under the broiler for 4-5 minutes until the cheese has melted and bubbly. Serve topped with chives.

Peasant Bean Soup

Serving Size: 6 | Total Time: 45 minutes

1 cup cipollini onions, chopped	
2 tbsp olive oil	1 potato, peeled, diced
1 garlic clove, minced	1 cup stewed tomatoes, diced
1 chopped celery rib	5 cups vegetable broth
1 cup chopped carrots	Salt and pepper to taste
1 cup ham, chopped	2 tbsp parsley, chopped
1 cup great northern beans	

Warm the olive oil in your Instant Pot on Sauté. Place the garlic, cipollini onions, celery, and carrots and cook for 5 minutes. Pour in vegetable broth, tomatoes, ham, great northern beans, and potato and stir. Seal the lid, select Manual, and cook for 20 minutes on High pressure. When ready, allow a natural release for 10 minutes. Adjust the seasoning. Serve topped with parsley.

Pea & Garbanzo Bean Soup

Serving Size: 4 | Total Time: 30 minutes

2 tbsp olive oil	2 Roma chopped tomatoes
½ cup shallots, sliced	4 cups vegetable broth
14 oz can garbanzo beans	Salt and pepper to taste
½ cup green peas	1 lemon, zested and juiced

Warm the olive oil in your Instant Pot on Sauté. Add in shallots and cook for 3 minutes until tender and fragrant. Pour in vegetable broth, tomatoes, lemon zest, and garbanzo beans and stir.

Seal the lid, select Manual, and cook for 10 minutes on High pressure. Once over, allow a natural release for 10 minutes, then perform a quick pressure release and unlock the lid. Stir in green peas and let it sit covered in the residual heat until warmed through. Season with salt and pepper and drizzle with lemon juice. Serve.

Cauliflower Cheese Soup

Serving Size: 4 | Total Time: 30 minutes

2 tbsp butter	1 cup heavy cream
1 onion, diced	1 tsp mustard powder
2 garlic cloves, minced	1 cup cheddar, shredded
2 russet potatoes, chopped	1 green onion, chopped
5 oz cauliflower florets	Salt and pepper to taste
4 cups vegetable broth	

Melt the butter in your Instant Pot on Sauté. Add in onion and garlic and cook for 2-3 minutes until lightly golden. Add in potato, cauliflower, mustard powder, vegetable broth, and give it a good stir.

Seal the lid, select Manual, and cook for 8 minutes on High. Once over, allow a natural release for 10 minutes and unlock the lid. Stir in heavy cream and half of the cheddar cheese and whizz until smooth, using a stick blender. Adjust the seasoning. Scatter the remaining cheddar on top and sprinkle with green onion to serve.

Minestrone with Fresh Herbs

Serving Size: 4 | Total Time: 25 minutes

2 tbsp olive oil	1 tsp rosemary, chopped
1 large onion, diced	Salt and pepper to taste
3 garlic cloves, minced	14 oz can tomatoes, diced
2 celery stalks, diced	5 curly kale, chopped
1 carrot, diced	½ cup elbow macaroni
2 tsp basil, chopped	4 cups vegetable broth
1 tsp oregano, chopped	14 oz can cannellini beans

Warm the olive oil in your Instant Pot on Sauté. Add in onion, garlic, celery, and carrot and cook for 5 minutes until tender. Stir in basil, oregano, rosemary, tomatoes, elbow macaroni, cannellini beans, and vegetable broth.

Seal the lid, select Manual, and cook for 6 minutes on High. Once done, perform a quick pressure release. Unlock the lid. Stir in kale and press Sauté. Cook for 4-5 minutes until it's wilted. Taste and adjust the seasoning.

Spicy Pumpkin Soup

Serving Size: 4 | Total Time: 25 minutes

2 tbsp butter
1 Vidalia onion, chopped
2 garlic cloves, chopped
2 carrots, diced
1 lb pumpkin, peeled, diced
½ tsp thyme

1 tsp cumin seeds
1 tbsp hot curry paste
4 cups vegetable broth
Salt and pepper to taste
1 cup heavy cream
2 tbsp cilantro, chopped

Melt the butter in your Instant Pot on Sauté. Add in onion, garlic, carrots, salt, and pepper and cook for 3 minutes. Stir in cumin seeds, thyme, hot curry paste, and pumpkin for 2 minutes and pour in vegetable broth.

Seal the lid, select Manual, and cook for 10 minutes on High. When ready, perform a quick pressure release. Blend the soup using an immersion blender and stir in heavy cream. Top with cilantro to serve.

Corn Soup with Chicken & Egg

Serving Size: 2 | Total Time: 25 minutes

1 tbsp cilantro, chopped
1 egg
½ lb chicken breasts
1 leek, chopped
1 tbsp sliced shallots

¼ tsp nutmeg
2 cups water
¼ cup corn kernels
¼ cup diced carrots
Salt and pepper to taste

Slice the chicken breasts into small cubes and place them in your Instant Pot. Add in corn kernels, water, shallots, salt, nutmeg, and black pepper. Seal the lid, select Pressure Cook, and cook for 15 minutes on High.

When done, allow a natural release and unlock the lid. Mix in carrots and leek and bring to a boil on Sauté. Beat the egg in a bowl. Once the Soup boil, pour in the beaten egg and toss until well combined and done. Divide between bowls, sprinkle with cilantro, and serve.

Mustard Carrot Soup

Serving Size: 4 | Total Time: 25 minutes

1 green bell pepper, diced
¼ cup butter
1 lb quartered carrots
3 cups chicken stock
1 tsp paprika

1 tsp ground cumin
2 tsp minced garlic
2 tbsp Dijon mustard
Salt and pepper to taste

Pour 1 cup of water into your Instant Pot; fit in a trivet. Place the carrots on the trivet and seal the lid. Select Manual and cook for 1 minute on High. When done, perform a quick pressure release; unlock the lid. Remove the carrots and pat dry the pot with a paper towel.

Melt butter in your Instant Pot on Sauté. Place the chicken stock, paprika, bell pepper, cumin, garlic, mustard, salt, black pepper, and cooked carrots. Seal the lid, select Manual, and cook for 4 minutes on High pressure.

When done, allow a natural release for 10 minutes and unlock the lid. Using an immersion blender, blend the soup until smooth and creamy. Serve right away.

Easy Veggie Soup

Serving Size: 4 | Total Time: 35 minutes

1 cup okra, trimmed
1 Carrot, sliced
1 cup Broccoli florets
1 green Bell Pepper, sliced
1 red Bell Pepper, sliced
1 Onion, sliced

2 cups vegetable broth
1 tbsp Lemon juice
4 Garlic cloves, minced
Salt and pepper to taste
2 tbsp Olive oil

Warm olive oil in your Instant Pot on Sauté. Place the onion and garlic and cook for 1 minute. Add in carrot, okra, broccoli florets, green bell pepper, and red bell pepper and cook for 5-10 minutes.

Stir in vegetable broth, salt, and black pepper and seal the lid. Select Meat/Stew and cook for 15 minutes on High pressure. When done, perform a quick pressure release and unlock the lid. Sprinkle with lemon juice and divide between bowls before serving.

Cheesy & Creamy Broccoli Soup

Serving Size: 4 | Total Time: 25 minutes

1 ½ cups grated Cheddar Cheese + extra for topping
2 tbsp cilantro, chopped
1 lb chopped Broccoli
3 cups Heavy Cream
3 cups Chicken Broth
4 tbsp Butter

4 tbsp Almond flour
1 red onion, chopped
3 garlic cloves, minced
1 tsp Italian Seasoning
Salt and pepper to taste
4 oz Cream Cheese

Melt butter in your Instant Pot on Sauté. Place the almond flour and stir until it clumps up. Slowly pour in heavy cream and stir until it gets a sauce. Remove to a bowl. Put the onions, garlic, chicken broth, broccoli, Italian seasoning, and cream cheese in the pot and stir.

Seal the lid, select Soup, and cook for 15 minutes on High pressure. When done, perform a quick pressure release and unlock the lid. Mix in butter sauce and cheddar cheese until the cheese melts. Divide between bowls and top with cheddar cheese. Serve topped with cilantro.

Gingery Carrot Soup

Serving Size: 2 | Total Time: 30 minutes

½ tsp red pepper flakes
2 cups chicken broth
½ lb carrots, chopped
½ tbsp Sriracha sauce
1 cup canned coconut milk

1 tbsp cilantro, chopped
1 tbsp unsalted butter
½ tsp fresh ginger, minced
1 garlic clove, minced
1 small onion, chopped

Place the butter and onion in your Instant Pot and cook for 2-3 minutes until soft on Sauté. Add in ginger and garlic and cook for 1 minute. Stir in carrots and cook for 2 minutes. Mix in coconut milk, chicken broth, red pepper flakes, and Sriracha and seal the lid.

Select Manual and cook for 6 minutes on High. When done, allow a natural release for 10 minutes; unlock the lid. Using an immersion blender, pulse the soup until purée. Serve topped with cilantro. Enjoy!

Carrot & Cabbage Soup

Serving Size: 4 | Total Time: 25 minutes

1 cup canned white beans	4 cup chicken broth
14 oz can diced tomatoes	1 chopped celery stalk
1 head cabbage, chopped	3 chopped carrots
3 tbsp Apple cider vinegar	1 tbsp lemon juice
4 minced garlic cloves	1 chopped onion

Place the chopped tomatoes, cabbage, apple cider vinegar, garlic, chicken broth, celery, carrots, lemon juice, and onion in your Instant Pot. Seal the lid, select Manual, and cook for 15 minutes on High pressure. When done, perform a quick pressure release and unlock the lid. Mix in white beans and cook for 2 minutes on Sauté. Serve.

Scallion Chicken & Lentil Soup

Serving Size: 4 | Total Time: 45 minutes

4 garlic cloves, sliced	1 diced tomato
6 oz skinless chicken thighs	2 tbsp chopped cilantro
½ lb dried lentils	¼ tsp oregano
½ chopped onion	½ tsp cumin
4 cups water	1 chopped scallion
¼ tsp paprika	¼ tsp salt
½ tsp garlic powder	

Place the chicken thighs, dried lentils, onion, water, paprika, garlic powder, sliced garlic, tomato, cilantro, oregano, cumin, scallion, and salt in your Instant Pot. Seal the lid, select Soup, and cook for 30 minutes. When done, allow a natural release for 10 minutes and unlock the lid. Using a fork, shred the chicken before serving.

Tomato Shrimp Soup

Serving Size: 4 | Total Time: 40 minutes

½ cup coconut Cream	¼ cup Apple Cider Vinegar
2 Tomatoes, sliced	2 Garlic cloves, minced
2 oz Shrimp	Salt and pepper to taste
4 cups Chicken broth	1 tbsp Olive oil

Warm olive oil in your Instant Pot on Sauté. Place the garlic and cook for 1 minute. Add in shrimp and cook for 10 minutes. Stir in salt, black pepper, chicken broth, tomatoes, and apple cider vinegar.

Seal the lid, select Manual, and cook for 10 minutes on High pressure. When done, allow a natural release for 10 minutes and unlock the lid. Divide between 4 bowls and top each with coconut cream. Serve warm.

Mustard Potato Soup with Crispy Bacon

Serving Size: 4 | Total Time: 30 minutes

2 Yukon gold potatoes, chopped	
2 tbsp olive oil	Salt and pepper to taste
2 garlic cloves, minced	1 tbsp Dijon mustard
1 leek, diced	4 dashes hot pepper sauce
1 tbsp onion powder	4 oz bacon, chopped
1 green bell pepper, diced	2 cups shredded mozzarella
4 cups chicken stock	1 cup milk

Warm olive oil in your Instant Pot on Sauté and cook the bacon for 5 minutes until crispy; set aside. Place garlic and leek in the pot and sauté for 3 minutes. Add in onion powder, potatoes, bell pepper, stock, salt, and pepper. Seal the lid, select Manual, and cook for 15 minutes.

When done, perform a quick pressure release. Mix in Dijon mustard, hot sauce, mozzarella cheese, and milk until thoroughly heated. Top with bacon and serve.

Curried Pumpkin Soup

Serving Size: 4 | Total Time: 20 minutes

1 tsp chili powder	1 Carrot, chopped
2 tbsp Pumpkin seeds	2 garlic cloves, minced
2 tbsp Olive oil	2 tsp Curry powder
1 onion, chopped	4 cups vegetable broth

Warm olive oil in your Instant Pot on Sauté. Place the onion and garlic and cook for 3 minutes until tender. Add in vegetable broth, pumpkin seeds, chili powder, curry powder, and carrots. Seal the lid, select Manual, and cook for 10 minutes on High. When done, allow a natural release for 10 minutes. Serve.

Nutmeg Broccoli Soup with Cheddar

Serving Size: 4 | Total Time: 25 minutes

2 garlic cloves, minced	1 cup vegetable broth
1 tbsp butter	¼ cup grated cheddar
½ lb broccoli florets	¼ cup chopped onion
¼ tsp nutmeg	¼ tsp paprika
½ tsp garlic powder	Salt and pepper to taste

Melt butter in your Instant Pot on Sauté. Place the onion and garlic and cook until wilted and aromatic. Put in vegetable broth, broccoli, black pepper, paprika, salt, nutmeg, and garlic powder. Seal the lid, select Manual, and cook for 5 minutes on High pressure.

When done, allow a natural release for 10 minutes and unlock the lid. Using an immersion blender, pulse the soup until smooth. Divide between bowls and serve.

Kielbasa Sausage Soup

Serving Size: 4 | Total Time: 60 minutes

12 oz Kielbasa smoked sausage, sliced	
2 tbsp olive oil	3 garlic cloves, pressed
1 yellow onion, chopped	1 ripe tomato, pureed
1 celery stalk, chopped	1 cup pinto beans, soaked
1 carrot, chopped	Salt and pepper to taste
2 tbsp parsley, chopped	6 oz baby kale

Warm the olive oil in your Instant Pot on Sauté. Add in onion, garlic, celery, and carrot and cook for 4 minutes. Stir in smoked sausage for another 2 minutes and pour in pinto beans, salt, pepper, and 4 cups of water. Seal the lid, select Manual, and cook for 30 minutes on High.

When over, allow a natural release for 10 minutes and unlock the lid. Stir in baby kale and tomato and let it sit covered for 5 minutes. Serve sprinkled with parsley.

Chorizo & Bean Soup

Serving Size: 6 | Total Time: 55 minutes

2 tbsp olive oil
¾ lb chorizo sausage, sliced
1 cup white beans, soaked
1 sweet pepper, sliced
14 oz can diced tomatoes

1 clove garlic, minced
1 onion, diced
½ tsp dried oregano
1 tsp chili powder
6 cups chicken broth

Warm the olive oil in your Instant Pot on Sauté. Add in onion, garlic, chorizo, sweet pepper, chili powder, and oregano and cook for 4-5 minutes. Stir in chicken broth, tomatoes, and white bean and seal the lid. Select Manual and cook for 30 minutes. Once ready, perform a quick pressure release and let sit for 10 minutes. Serve warm.

Beet & Potato Soup

Serving Size: 4 | Total Time: 45 minutes

2 tbsp olive oil
2 garlic cloves, minced
1 carrot, chopped
3 potatoes, chopped
¾ lb beets, peeled, chopped

4 cups vegetable broth
1 onion, chopped
Salt and pepper to taste
¼ cup basil leaves, chopped

Heat the olive oil in your Instant Pot on Sauté. Place the onion, carrot, and garlic paste and cook for 3 minutes. Stir in vegetable broth, beets, and potatoes and seal the lid. Select Manual and cook for 25 minutes.

Once ready, allow a natural release for 10 minutes, then perform a quick pressure release and unlock the lid. Blend the soup using an immersion blender and adjust the seasoning. Serve topped with basil.

Vegan Tomato Soup

Serving Size: 4 | Total Time: 20 minutes

2 tbsp olive oil
2 (14-oz) cans tomatoes
1 tsp caraway seeds
1 cup vegetable broth
½ tsp thyme

1 large onion, diced
2 garlic cloves, sliced
Salt and pepper to taste
¾ cup almond milk

Warm the olive oil in your Instant Pot on Sauté. Add in onion, and garlic and cook for 5-6 minutes until lightly golden. Stir in caraway seeds for 1 minute and pour in tomatoes, thyme, and vegetable broth.

Seal the lid, select Manual, and cook for 8 minutes on High. Once ready, perform a quick pressure release and unlock the lid. Stir in almond milk and adjust the seasonings. Purée the soup with an immersion blender.

Asian Tomato Soup

Serving Size: 8 | Total Time: 20 minutes

2 tbsp coconut oil
1 onion, diced
1 tbsp garlic-ginger puree
3 lb tomatoes, quartered
½ tsp ground cumin

1 tsp red pepper flakes
Pink salt to taste
3 ½ cups vegetable broth
1 cup coconut cream
2 tbsp cilantro, chopped

Heat the coconut oil in your Instant Pot on Sauté. Place the onion and garlic-ginger paste and cook for 3 minutes. Stir in tomatoes and cumin and Sauté for 3 more minutes.

Pour in the broth and salt and seal the lid. Select Manual and cook for 6 minutes. When done, perform a quick pressure release. Mix in coconut cream. Puree the soup with a stick blender until smooth. Serve topped with red pepper flakes and cilantro.

Tangy Pumpkin Soup

Serving Size: 4 | Total Time: 30 minutes

2 tbsp sesame oil
1 yellow onion, chopped
2 garlic cloves, minced
½ tbsp ginger, grated
1 lb pumpkin, cubed

Salt to taste
1 tbsp curry powder
1 tsp cayenne pepper
½ cup coconut milk
2 tbsp cilantro, chopped

Warm the sesame oil in your Instant Pot on Sauté. Add in onion and cook for 5 minutes. Stir in garlic and ginger and Sauté for 1 more minute. Stir in pumpkin, cayenne pepper, salt, and curry powder and 4 cups of water and seal the lid. Select Manual and cook for 20 minutes. Once ready, perform a quick pressure release and unlock the lid. Blend the soup using a stick blender and mix in coconut milk. Garnish with cilantro and serve.

Chicken Soup with Vegetables

Serving Size: 4 | Total Time: 35 minutes

½ lb chicken breasts, cubed
1 beet, chopped
1 carrot, diced
½ celery, diced
1 onion, chopped
1 cup mushrooms, sliced
5 cups chicken stock

2 garlic cloves, chopped
1 tsp thyme
1 tsp rosemary
2 bay leaves
2 tbsp olive oil
Salt and pepper to taste

Warm olive oil in your Instant Pot on Sauté. Place the carrots, beet, and onion and cook for 2-3 minutes. Add in garlic, celery, and mushrooms and cook for 3 minutes. Put in chicken breasts, chicken stock, thyme, rosemary, bay leaves, salt, and black pepper. Seal the lid, select Soup, and cook on Low pressure for 20 minutes. When done, perform a quick pressure release. Serve warm.

Celery & Oxtail Soup

Serving Size: 4 | Total Time: 30 minutes

4 cups vegetable broth
2 tbsp chopped' carrots
1 lb oxtails

1 tbsp chopped' celeries
¼ tsp nutmeg
Salt and pepper to taste

Place the oxtails, nutmeg, salt, and black pepper in your Instant Pot. Pour in vegetable broth and seal the lid. Select Pressure Cook and cook for 20 minutes on High.

When done, perform a quick pressure release and unlock the lid. Stir in chopped carrots and celeries and cook for 3 minutes until the carrots are tender on Sauté. Divide between bowls and serve.

Creamy Mushroom Soup with Chicken

Serving Size: 2 | Total Time: 20 minutes

1 celery stalk, chopped	½ cup water
¼ cup diced mushrooms	2 tbsp diced carrots
½ lb chicken breasts	1 tsp minced' garlic
¼ cup heavy cream	Salt and pepper to taste

Slice the chicken breast into small cubes and remove them to your Instant Pot. Add in celery, minced garlic, salt, black pepper, and water. Seal the lid, select Pressure Cook, and cook for 10 minutes on High pressure.

When done, perform a quick pressure release and unlock the lid. Stir in heavy cream, mushrooms, and carrots. Seal the lid, select Manual, and cook for 3 minutes on High pressure. When done, perform a quick pressure release and unlock the lid. Divide between bowls and serve.

Cheesy Cauliflower Soup

Serving Size: 4 | Total Time: 20 minutes

2 tbsp olive oil	1 cup vegetable broth
1 carrot, chopped	2 tsp minced garlic
¼ cup cream cheese	¼ cup chopped onion
1 ½ cups cauliflower florets	Salt and pepper to taste

Warm the olive oil in your Instant Pot on Sauté. Place the cauliflower florets, carrot, minced garlic, chopped onion, salt, and pepper and cook for 5 minutes until tender. pour in the vegetable broth. Seal the lid, select Manual, and cook for 6 minutes on High pressure.

When done, perform a quick pressure release and unlock the lid. Mix in cream cheese until well combined. Blend the soup until smooth with an immersion blender. Divide between bowls and serve.

Spicy Ground Beef Soup

Serving Size: 4 | Total Time: 30 minutes

2 tbsp butter	1 tsp chili powder
3 oz cream cheese	1 tsp ground cumin
7-oz ground beef	½ cup heavy cream
4 cups beef broth	Salt and pepper to taste
2 garlic cloves, minced	

Melt butter in your Instant Pot on Sauté. Place the ground beef and cook for 5-7 minutes and strain excess fat. Add in cream cheese, garlic, chili powder, ground cumin, heavy cream, salt, black pepper, and beef broth.

Seal the lid, select Pressure Cook, and cook for 5 minutes on High pressure. When done, allow a natural release for 10 minutes and unlock the lid. Serve warm.

Hot Spinach Soup

Serving Size: 4 | Total Time: 50 minutes

1 onion, chopped	½ cup Almond Milk
2 Garlic cloves, minced	½ tbsp Chili flakes
1 cup baby Spinach	¼ cup sour cream
2 cups Vegetable broth	2 tbsp Olive oil

Place the garlic, onion, spinach, vegetable broth, almond milk, chili flakes, and olive oil in your Instant Pot. Seal the lid, select Manual, and cook for 25 minutes on High.

When done, allow a natural release for 10 minutes and unlock the lid. Using an immersion blender, blend until creamy and put it back to the pot and cook for 6 minutes on Sauté. Serve topped with sour cream.

Asian-Style Chicken Soup

Serving Size: 4 | Total Time: 35 minutes

1 tsp soy sauce	1 tbsp fish sauce
4 cups chicken broth	1 tsp ginger
½ lb chicken breasts, cubed	1 tbsp sugar
1 tsp cinnamon	1 chopped onion
1 tsp cilantro, chopped	2 tsp minced garlic
1 tbsp olive oil	Salt and pepper to taste

Place the olive oil, garlic, and onion in your Instant Pot and cook for 2-3 minutes until soft on Sauté. Stir in chopped chicken, ginger, cilantro, sugar, cinnamon, fish sauce, soy sauce, salt, pepper, and chicken broth. Seal the lid, select Manual, and cook for 15 minutes on High. When done, allow a natural release for 10 minutes. Serve.

Egg & Chicken Soup

Serving Size: 4 | Total Time: 35 minutes

1 carrot, chopped	2 cups Chicken broth
2 Garlic cloves, minced	2 cups Water
¼ lb chicken breasts, cubed	3 tbsp Almond flour
1 onion, chopped	Salt and pepper to taste
2 Eggs, whisked	2 tbsp Olive oil

Warm olive oil in your Instant Pot on Sauté. Place the carrot, garlic, and onion and cook for 1 minute. Add in chicken pieces and cook for 10 minutes. Put in salt, black pepper, and chicken broth and simmer for 15 minutes.

Meanwhile, combine water and almond flour in a bowl and pour it slowly into the pot and cook for 2 minutes. Add in eggs and cook for 2 more minutes. Divide between bowls and serve.

Cheesy Chicken Soup

Serving Size: 4 | Total Time: 30 minutes

2 garlic cloves, minced	1 pnion, sliced
1 green bell pepper, sliced	4 oz Provolone cheese, grated
1 red bell pepper, sliced	
½ cup chicken breast strips	4 cups Chicken broth
1 tbsp canola oil	Salt and pepper to taste
1 tsp dried oregano	

Place the canola oil and chicken fillets in your Instant Pot and cook on Sauté. Mix in oregano, salt, black pepper, red bell pepper, green bell pepper, garlic, and onion and cook for 10 minutes. Pour in chicken broth and seal the lid. Select Manual and cook for 4 minutes on High pressure. When done, allow a natural release for 10 minutes and unlock the lid. Serve topped with cheese.

Brussel Sprout & Pork Soup

Serving Size: 4 | Total Time: 40 minutes

½ lb Brussels sprouts, shredded
1 cup carrot, shredded   4 cups chicken broth
½ tsp ground ginger   1 tbsp soy sauce
1 small onion, chopped   2 tbsp olive oil
½ lb ground pork   Salt and pepper to taste

Place the olive oil and ground pork in your Instant Pot and cook for 4-5 minutes until browned on Sauté. Stir in carrot, Brussels sprouts, ginger, onion, chicken broth, soy sauce, salt, and black pepper. Seal the lid, select Manual, and cook for 25 minutes on High pressure. When done, perform a quick pressure release. Serve and enjoy!

Tamarind Beef Soup

Serving Size: 2 | Total Time: 40 minutes

1 carrot, sliced   1 tsp soy sauce
¼ cup green tomatoes   2 tsp sliced garlic
1 lb beef tenderloin   2 tsp sliced shallots
1 cup water   2 tsp red chili flakes
2 tsp tamarind   ½ tsp salt

Slice the beef tenderloin into medium pieces and place them in your Instant Pot. Add in garlic, carrot, shallots, red chili flakes, salt, green tomatoes, tamarind, soy sauce, and water. Seal the lid, select Manual, and cook for 22 minutes on High. When done, allow a natural release for 10 minutes and unlock the lid. Serve warm.

Cashew & Tomato Soup

Serving Size: 4 | Total Time: 15 minutes

½ ground cumin   ½ tbsp dried basil
15 oz tomato puree   1 ½ tbsp quick oats
15 oz diced tomatoes   2 minced garlic cloves
4 tbsp cashew   Salt and pepper to taste
2 cups vegetable stock

Place the tomato puree, diced tomatoes, cashew, vegetable stock, dried basil, oats, cumin, and garlic in your Instant Pot. Seal the lid, select Manual, and cook for 4 minutes on High pressure. When done, allow a natural release. Using an immersion blender, pulse the soup until smooth. Sprinkle with salt and pepper before serving.

Pecorino Mushroom Soup

Serving Size: 4 | Total Time: 30 minutes

2 cups Pecorino, grated   2 Garlic cloves, minced
3 cups Mushrooms, chopped   2 cups Thyme, chopped
2 tbsp Butter   2 tbsp Almond flour
1 onion, chopped   3 cups Chicken stock

Place the butter and onion in your Instant Pot and cook for 2 minutes on Sauté. Mix in mushrooms, garlic cloves, thyme, chicken stock, and almond flour. Seal the lid, select Manual, and cook for 10 minutes on High. When done, allow a natural release for 10 minutes. Serve garnished with grated Pecorino cheese.

Creamy Chicken & Zucchini Soup

Serving Size: 4 | Total Time: 25 minutes

1 lb Zucchini, chopped   2 Garlic cloves, minced
1 lb Chicken breasts, cubed   4 cups Chicken broth
2 tbsp Butter   2 tbsp Nutmeg powder
1 onion, chopped   ½ cup Half and Half

Melt butter in your Instant Pot on Sauté. Mix the zucchini, chicken broth, garlic, onion, nutmeg powder, chicken cubes, and half and half. Seal the lid, select Manual, and cook for 10 minutes on High pressure. When done, allow a natural release for 10 minutes and unlock the lid. Serve right away.

Quick Chicken Soup

Serving Size: 4 | Total Time: 25 minutes

½ cup mushrooms, chopped   1 onion, chopped
½ lb Chicken Breasts   2 garlic cloves, minced
2 tbsp Olive oil   1 Green Chili Pepper, sliced
1 large Carrot, chopped   Salt and pepper to taste
1 Celery Stalk, chopped   2 cups Chicken Broth

Warm olive oil in your Instant Pot on Sauté. Place the carrot, celery, onion, garlic, salt, pepper, and green chili pepper and cook for 3 minutes. Mix in broth, chicken breasts, mushrooms, and 2 cups of water. Seal the lid, select Soup, and cook for 10 minutes on High. Do a quick pressure release. Remove the chicken, shred it, and back it to the pot. Cook for 3 minutes on Sauté and serve.

Chicken & Noodle Soup

Serving Size: 2 | Total Time: 35 minutes

8 oz egg noodles   1 Banana Pepper, minced
2 Carrots, sliced   1 garlic clove, minced
1 tbsp Olive Oil   1 small Bay Leaf
1 small onion, chopped   2 Chicken Breasts
2 Celery Ribs, diced   3 cups Chicken Broth

Warm olive oil in your Instant Pot on Sauté. Place the onion, celery, carrots, garlic, and banana pepper and cook for 4 minutes. Add in bay leaf, chicken, and broth. Seal the lid, select Manual, and cook for 15 minutes on High. When done, perform a quick pressure release. Transfer the chicken onto a cutting board and shred it. Put the chicken back in the pot with the egg noodles and cook for 7-8 minutes on Sauté. Serve.

Simple Onion Cheese Soup

Serving Size: 4 | Total Time: 10 minutes

1 onion, chopped   2 cups Monterey Jack, grated
2 tbsp all-purpose flour   2 cups milk
4 cups vegetable broth   2 tbsp butter

Melt butter on Sauté and cook the onion and flour for 2 minutes. Gradually stir in the broth and milk. Seal the lid. Cook on High Pressure for 5 minutes. Do a quick pressure release. Stir in cheese until melted. Serve.

STEWS

Curried Sweet Potato Stew

Serving Size: 4 | Total Time: 15 minutes

1 cup almond milk	½ tbsp minced ginger
2 diced sweet potatoes	1 diced onion
14 oz can diced tomatoes	1 tbsp red curry paste
½ diced bell pepper	½ tsp turmeric
½ diced zucchini	1 tsp curry powder
1 minced garlic clove	1 tbsp olive oil
1 lime juice	½ tsp sea salt

Warm olive oil in your Instant Pot on Sauté. Place the onion and cook until translucent. Add in garlic and ginger and cook for 1 minute. Pour in milk, sweet potatoes, tomatoes, bell pepper, zucchini, lime juice, curry paste, turmeric, curry powder, and salt, seal the lid, select Manual, and cook for 5 minutes on High pressure. When done, perform a quick pressure release and unlock the lid. Mix well before serving.

Vegetable & Ground Pork Stew

Serving Size: 6 | Total Time: 30 minutes

1 ¼ lb ground pork	1 red bell pepper, chopped
1 cup cabbage, shredded	1 green bell pepper, diced
½ cup chopped celery	1 yellow bell pepper, diced
2 red onions, chopped	¼ tsp cumin
2 large tomatoes, chopped	1 tsp red pepper flakes
1 carrot, shredded	Salt and pepper to taste
2 cups water	2 tbsp cilantro, chopped

Coat with cooking spray. Add the pork and cook until browned on Sauté, 6 minutes. Stir in cabbage, celery, onions, tomatoes, carrot, water, bell peppers, cumin, red pepper flakes, salt, and black pepper. Seal the lid and set to Pressure Cook for 15 minutes. Do a quick pressure release. Sprinkle with cilantro and serve.

German-Style Sauerkraut & Pork Stew

Serving Size: 4 | Total Time: 30 minutes

1 lb ground pork	1 red onion, chopped
4 cups sauerkraut, shredded	2 garlic cloves, minced
1 cup tomato puree	2 bay leaves
1 cup vegetable stock	Salt and pepper to taste

Add onion, garlic, and cook until soft and fragrant, on Sauté. Add the pork and cook it until lightly browned. Stir in sauerkraut, tomato puree, stock, and bay leaves and season with salt and black pepper. Seal the lid and cook for 20 minutes on Meat/Stew on High. When done, release the pressure quickly. Discard the bay leaves.

Chicken Stew with Bacon & Cheese

Serving Size: 4 | Total Time: 25 minutes

1 ½ cups mozzarella cheese	1 lb Chicken Breasts
10 oz Cream Cheese	1 packet ranch Seasoning
10 Bacon Slices, chopped	½ cup Water

Place the cream cheese, chicken, Ranch seasoning, and water in your Instant Pot. Seal the lid, select Manual, and cook for 15 minutes on High. When done, perform a quick pressure release. Remove the chicken and shred it. Put the chicken back in the pot with bacon and mozzarella and cook on Sauté until the cheese melts.

Classic Goulash

Serving Size: 4 | Total Time: 15 minutes

1 celery stalk, chopped	1 tbsp olive oil
1 cup diced tomatoes	4 cup chicken broth
½ lb cubed beef	1 tbsp Hungarian paprika
3 oz egg noodles	1 tsp minced garlic
1 chopped onion	Salt and pepper to taste

Warm olive oil in your Instant Pot on Sauté. Place the garlic, celery, onion, and beef and cook until the meat browns. Stir in paprika, chicken broth, egg noodles, tomatoes, pepper, and salt. Seal the lid, select Manual, and cook for 5 minutes on High pressure. When done, perform a quick pressure release. Serve warm.

Kale, Potato & Beef Stew

Serving Size: 2 | Total Time: 55 minutes

1 green bell pepper, diced	1 tbsp olive oil
2 potatoes, chopped	½ tsp garlic powder
½ lb beef stew meat, cubed	2 carrots, chopped
1 tbsp hot sauce	1 cup kale, chopped
1 small onion, chopped	2 cups beef broth
1 celery stalk, chopped	Salt and pepper to taste

Warm olive oil in your Instant Pot on Sauté Place the meat and cook for 4-5 minutes until browned. Stir in potatoes, hot sauce, onion, celery, garlic powder, bell pepper, carrots, kale leaves, beef broth, salt, and black pepper. Seal the lid, select Meat/Stew, and cook for 40 minutes. When done, perform a quick pressure release.

Pea & Beef Stew

Serving Size: 6 | Total Time: 35 minutes

1 cup mixed wild mushrooms	
1 cup green peas	½ cup dry red wine
1 cup diced potatoes	2 tbsp butter
1 lb cubed beef	1 diced onion
3 sliced carrots	2 cups beef broth
1 tsp red pepper flakes	14 oz can diced tomatoes
2 sliced garlic cloves	

Melt the butter in your Instant Pot on Sauté. Place the onion and cook for 3 minutes until soft. Add in beef cubes and cook for 5-7 minutes until the meat browns. Add in garlic and cook for 1 minute until fragrant. Pour in red wine and scrape any brown bits from the bottom.

Put in potatoes, carrots, red pepper flakes, mushrooms, beef broth, diced tomatoes, and green peas. Seal the lid, select Manual, and cook for 15 minutes on High pressure. When done, perform a quick pressure release and unlock the lid. Serve immediately.

Cauliflower Beef Stew

Serving Size: 4 | Total Time: 60 minutes

½ head cauliflower, chopped | 2 tbsp Fish sauce
1 lb Beef stew meat | 2 Garlic cloves, minced
1 large quartered Onion | 1 tsp ground Ginger
½ cup Beef or Bone broth | ½ tsp Salt
¼ cup Coconut aminos | 1 tbsp Coconut oil

Place the beef meat, onion, beef broth, coconut aminos, fish sauce, garlic, ginger, salt, and coconut oil in your Instant Pot. Seal the lid, select Manual, and cook for 35 minutes on High pressure. When done, perform a quick pressure release and unlock the lid. Put in cauliflower and simmer covered for 15 minutes on Sauté. Serve.

Rosemary Pork Belly Stew

Serving Size: 6 | Total Time: 50 minutes

3 lb sirloin pork roast | 1 tbsp rosemary
1 tbsp honey | 1 tbsp olive oil
1 tsp chili powder | Salt and pepper to taste

Combine chili powder, rosemary, salt, and pepper in a bowl and rub them onto the pork. Heat oil on Sauté and sear the pork on all sides. Stir in honey and seal the lid. Cook for 30 minutes on Meat/Stew. Do a natural pressure release for 10 minutes. Carefully unlock the lid.

Seafood Stew with Sausage

Serving Size: 4 | Total Time: 35 minutes

1 lb Andouille Sausages, sliced
1 lb halibut fillets, skinless and cut into 1-inch pieces
2 lb Mussels, debearded and scrubbed
1 lb Shrimp, peeled and deveined
1 tsp turmeric | 2 Fennel Bulb, chopped
2 (16 oz) cans Clam Juice | 4 Leeks, sliced
1 cup White Wine | 2 Bay Leaves
Salt and pepper to taste | 28 oz can Diced Tomatoes
4 tbsp Olive oil | 2 tbsp chopped Parsley
4 garlic cloves, minced

Warm olive oil in your Instant Pot on Sauté. Place sausage, fennel, and leeks and cook for 5 minutes. Stir in garlic, turmeric, and bay leaves and cook for 30 seconds. Pour in white wine and cook for 2 minutes. Add in tomatoes, clam juice, and 3 cups of water; stir. Put in mussels, fish, and shrimp and slightly cover them with the sauce.

Seal the lid, select Meat/Stew, and cook for 15 minutes on High pressure. When done, perform a quick pressure release and unlock the lid. Discard bay leaves and sprinkle with parsley, salt, and black pepper. Serve right away.

Mushroom & Spinach Chicken Stew

Serving Size: 4 | Total Time: 40 minutes

1 ¼ lb White Button Mushrooms, halved
1 celery stalk, chopped | 1 Onion, sliced
3 tbsp Olive oil | 5 garlic cloves, minced
4 Chicken Breasts, diced | Salt and pepper to taste

1 ¼ tsp Arrowroot Starch | 1 tsp Dijon Mustard
½ cup spinach, chopped | 1 ½ cup Sour Cream
1 bay leaf | 3 tbsp Chopped Parsley
1 ½ cup Chicken Stock

Warm olive oil in your Instant Pot on Sauté. Place the onion and cook for 3 minutes. Stir in mushrooms, chicken, celery, garlic, bay leaf, salt, black pepper, Dijon mustard, and chicken broth. Seal the lid, select Meat/Stew, and cook for 15 minutes on High. When done, allow a natural release for 10 minutes and unlock the lid.

Discard bay leaf. In a bowl, combine some cooking liquid with arrowroot starch until any lump left. Pour it into the pot and stir until the sauce thickens. Add in sour cream and spinach and let sit for 4 minutes. Divide between bowls and sprinkle with parsley. Serve with squash mash.

Green Pork Chili

Serving Size: 4 | Total Time: 90 minutes

1 lb Tomatillos, husks removed
1 tsp ground nutmeg | 1 Green Bell pepper, diced
2 Green Chilies | Salt and pepper to taste
1 onion, sliced | ½ tsp Cumin Powder
1 ½ lb Pork Roast, cubed | 1 tsp dried Oregano
2 tbsp Olive oil, divided into | 1 Bay Leaf
1 bulb Garlic, tail sliced off | 2 tbsp Cilantro, chopped
½ cup Chicken Broth

Preheat oven to 360°F. Place the garlic bulb, green bell peppers, onion, green chilies, and tomatillos on a baking tray and sprinkle with olive oil. Place the tray in the oven and roast for 25 minutes. Let cool the garlic before peeling. Place it in a blender with bell peppers, tomatillos, onion, and green chilies and pulse until slightly chunky.

Warm olive oil in your Instant Pot on Sauté. Sprinkle pork with salt and pepper and place it in the pot. Cook for 5 minutes until brown. Stir in oregano, nutmeg, cumin, bay leaf, green sauce, and broth. Seal the lid, select Manual, and cook for 35 minutes on High. When done, let sit for 10 minutes and allow a natural release for 5 minutes Stir in salt and pepper. Top with cilantro. Serve immediately.

Cheesy Turkey Stew

Serving Size: 4 | Total Time: 20 minutes

1 tbsp soy Sauce | ¼ cup grated Parmesan
1 lb Turkey Breast | 1 tsp Dijon Mustard
1 ½ cups Chicken Broth | ¼ tsp Garlic Powder
1 cup Sour Cream | Salt and pepper to taste

Place the turkey breast and chicken broth in your Instant Pot. Seal the lid, select Manual, and cook for 10 minutes on High pressure. When done, perform a quick pressure release. Transfer the turkey onto a cutting board and cut it into cubes. Discard the broth and wipe the pot out.

Mix in soy sauce, sour cream, Parmesan cheese, Dijon mustard, garlic powder, salt, black pepper, and cubed chicken and cook for 2 minutes on Sauté. Serve.

Chicken Stew with Potatoes & Broccoli

Serving Size: 4 | Total Time: 25 minutes

1 lb potatoes, chopped	¼ tsp Red Chili Flakes
2 tbsp Butter	2 tbsp Dried Parsley
3 Chicken Breasts, cubed	10 oz broccoli florets
2 Onions, chopped	1 cup cheddar cheese, grated
2 cups Chicken Broth	
Salt and pepper to taste	

Sprinkle chicken breast with salt and pepper. Melt butter in your Instant Pot on Sauté. Place the chicken and cook for 8 minutes on both sides until browns. Add in onion and cook for 5 minutes, stirring often.

Put chicken broth, black pepper, salt, red pepper flakes, potatoes, chicken, and parsley and seal the lid. Select Manual and cook for 4 minutes on High pressure.

When done, perform a quick pressure release and unlock the lid. Min in broccoli and cook until tender on Sauté. Serve right away topped with cheddar cheese.

Taco-Style Chicken Stew

Serving Size: 4 | Total Time: 25 minutes

2 tbsp butter	Salt and pepper to taste
1 lb Chicken Breasts	1 ½ cups Diced Tomatoes
1 Carrot, chopped	1 lb cubed Butternut Squash
1 Celery stalk, chopped	2 cups Chicken Broth
1 Onion, chopped	1 tsp Lime Juice
3 garlic cloves, minced	4 Lime Wedges
3 tbsp Taco Seasoning	2 tbsp Chopped Cilantro

Melt butter in your Instant Pot on Sauté. Place the celery, onion, carrots, garlic, taco seasoning, black pepper, and salt and cook for 5 minutes, stirring often. Mix in chicken breast, tomatoes, butternut squash, broth, and lime juice. Seal the lid, select Soup and cook for 10 minutes.

When done, perform a quick pressure release. Transfer the chicken onto a cutting board and shred it. Put the chicken back in the pot and divide between bowls. Serve topped with cilantro and lime wedges.

One-Pot Sausages with Peppers & Onions

Serving Size: 4 | Total Time: 20 minutes

2 red bell peppers, cut into strips	
4 pork sausages	¼ cup white wine
1 sweet onion, sliced	1 tsp garlic, minced
1 tbsp olive oil	Salt and pepper to taste
½ cup beef broth	

On Sauté, add the sausages and brown them for a few minutes. Remove to a plate and discard the liquid. Press Cancel. Wipe clean the cooker and heat the oil on Sauté. Stir in onion and bell peppers. Stir-fry them for 5 minutes until soft. Add garlic and cook for a minute. Add the sausages and pour in broth and wine. Season with salt and pepper. Seal the lid and cook for 5 minutes on High pressure. Once done, do a quick pressure release. Serve.

Cheesy Duck & Spinach Stew

Serving Size: 4 | Total Time: 25 minutes

1 onion, chopped	8 oz Cream Cheese
2 cups Spinach	¼ cup Chicken Broth
1 lb Duck Breasts	1 tbsp Olive oil
¼ cup grated Parmesan	1 tsp minced Garlic
1 cup Heavy Cream	Salt and pepper to taste

Warm olive oil in your Instant Pot on Sauté. Place the garlic and onion and cook for 1 minute. Add in duck breasts and cook for 6-8 minutes on both sides until golden brown. Remove to a plate and slice thinly. Mix the spinach, Parmesan cheese, heavy cream, cream cheese, broth, garlic, salt, and pepper in the pot and top with the sliced duck. Seal the lid, select Manual, and cook for 5 minutes on High pressure. When done, perform a quick pressure release and unlock the lid. Serve warm.

Sausage & Cannellini Bean Stew

Serving Size: 6 | Total Time: 35 minutes

1 cup cannellini beans	1 sprig fresh sage
2 tbsp olive oil	1 sprig fresh rosemary
1 lb Italian sausages, halved	1 bay leaf
1 celery stalk, chopped	2 cups vegetable stock
1 carrot, chopped	3 cups fresh spinach
1 onion, chopped	1 tsp salt

Warm oil on Sauté in your Instant pot. Add in sausage pieces and sear for 5 minutes until browned; set aside on a plate. To the pot, add celery, onion, bay leaf, sage, carrot, salt, and rosemary; cook for 3 minutes to soften slightly. Stir in vegetable stock and beans. Arrange seared sausage on top of the beans. Seal the lid, press Bean/Chili, and cook on High for 10 minutes. Release pressure naturally for 10 minutes. Get rid of bay leaf, rosemary, and sage. Mix in spinach and serve.

Tuscan Chicken Thighs

Serving Size: 4 | Total Time: 35 minutes

3 cups kale	2 tsp Olive oil
6 Chicken Thighs	2 cups Chicken Broth
6 oz Cream Cheese	1 ½ cups Milk
½ cup Sundried Tomatoes	3 tbsp Heavy Cream
2 tbsp Chicken Seasoning	3 tsp Italian Seasoning
½ cup Parmesan, grated	Salt and pepper to taste
4 garlic cloves, minced	2 tbsp chopped parsley

Sprinkle chicken thighs with salt, black pepper, and Italian seasoning. Warm olive oil in your Instant Pot on Sauté. Place the chicken and cook for 6 minutes. Add in milk, chicken stock, and chicken seasoning. Seal the lid, select Manual, and cook for 15 minutes on High.

When done, perform a quick pressure release. Remove the chicken to a plate. Put the tomatoes, heavy cream, cheese cream, Parmesan, kale, and garlic in the pot and cook for 5 minutes on Sauté. Put the chicken back to the pot and toss to combine. Serve topped with parsley.

Spicy Pumpkin Curry

Serving Size: 4 | Total Time: 30 minutes

4 spring onions, chopped into lengths
1 ½ lb pumpkin, chopped
4 cups chicken stock
½ cup buttermilk   ¼ tsp cayenne pepper
2 tbsp curry powder   2 bay leaves
1 tsp ground turmeric   Salt and pepper to taste
½ tsp ground cumin   2 tbsp cilantro, chopped

In the pot, stir in pumpkin, buttermilk, curry, turmeric, spring onions, stock, cumin, and cayenne. Season with pepper and salt. Add bay leaves to the liquid and ensure they are submerged. Seal the lid, press Soup/Broth and cook for 10 minutes on High.

Naturally release the pressure for 10 minutes. Discard bay leaves. Transfer the soup to a blender and process until smooth. Use a fine-mesh strainer to strain the soup. Garnish with cilantro before serving.

Vegetables with Veal & Pork

Serving Size: 4 | Total Time: 25 minutes

12 oz button mushrooms, sliced
1 lb veal cuts, cut into bite-sized pieces
1 lb pork tenderloin, cubed   1 tbsp cayenne pepper
3 carrots, chopped   Salt and pepper to taste
2 tbsp butter, softened   3 oz celery root, chopped
2 tbsp olive oil

Heat the olive oil and butter in the Instant Pot on Sauté. Add in veal, pork, mushrooms, carrots, salt, pepper, cayenne pepper, and celery, and cook for 5 minutes. Stir in 2 cups of water. Seal the lid and cook on High Pressure for 15 minutes. Do a quick release Open the lid and adjust the seasoning. Serve warm.

Aromatic Lamb Stew

Serving Size: 4 | Total Time: 60 minutes

1 ½ lb lamb stew meat, cubed
2 tbsp olive oil   ½ cup pomegranate juice
3 garlic cloves, chopped   ½ tsp allspice
1 onion, chopped   1 tsp ground cumin
3 cups mushrooms, sliced   ½ tsp ground bay leaf
1 celery stalk, chopped   ½ tsp curry powder
1 carrot, chopped   1 tsp ground coriander
28-oz can tomatoes, diced   Salt and pepper to taste
3 cups chicken broth

In a bowl, mix the allspice, ground cumin, ground bay leaf, curry powder, ground coriander, salt, and pepper and add in the lamb; toss to coat. Warm the olive oil in your Instant Pot on Sauté. Add in the lamb and cook for 5-6 minutes until browned. Add in garlic, onion, celery, carrot, and mushrooms and sauté for 5 minutes. Pour in tomatoes, pomegranate juice, and chicken broth.

Seal the lid, select Manual, and cook for 30 minutes on High pressure. When over, allow a natural release for 10 minutes, then perform a quick pressure release. Serve.

Flemish Beef Stew

Serving Size: 4 | Total Time: 60 minutes

1 ½ lb stew meat, cubed   1 cup tomatoes, diced
2 tbsp olive oil   1 tbsp yellow mustard
1 onion, chopped   1 cup Belgian ale beer
2 garlic cloves, minced   2 sprigs thyme
1 cup beef broth   Salt and pepper to taste

Warm the olive oil in your Instant Pot on Sauté. Place in meat and brown for 7 minutes on all sides, stirring occasionally. Add in onion and garlic and cook for another 3 minutes. Stir in beef broth, beer, mustard, bay leaf, thyme sprigs, salt, and pepper and seal the lid.

Select Manual and cook for 30 minutes on High pressure. When done, allow a natural release for 10 minutes, then a quick pressure release, and unlock the lid. Discard bay leaf and sprigs. Serve right away.

Grandma's Beef & Vegetable Stew

Serving Size: 6 | Total Time: 70 minutes

¼ cup flour   1 tbsp Italian seasoning
1 tsp paprika   2 tsp Worcestershire sauce
2 lb beef chuck, cubed   4 cups potatoes, diced
2 tbsp olive oil   2 celery stalks, chopped
2 tbsp butter   3 cups carrots, chopped
1 onion, diced   3 tomatoes, chopped
3 garlic cloves, minced 2 bell peppers, chopped
1 cup dry red wine   Salt and pepper to taste
2 cups beef stock   2 tbsp parsley, chopped

In a bowl, mix beef, flour, paprika, salt, and pepper. Toss the ingredients and ensure the beef is well-coated. Warm butter and oil on Sauté. Add in beef and cook for 8-10 minutes until browned. Set aside on a plate. To the same fat, add garlic, onion, celery, and bell peppers and cook for 4-5 minutes. Deglaze with wine, scrape the bottom to get rid of any browned beef bits.

Pour in beef stock, Worcestershire sauce, and Italian seasoning. Return beef to the pot; add carrots, tomatoes, and potatoes. Seal the lid, press Meat/Stew, and cook on High Pressure for 35 minutes. Release pressure naturally for 10 minutes. Taste and adjust the seasonings as necessary. Serve on plates and scatter over the parsley.

Chili Goose Stew

Serving Size: 6 | Total Time: 20 minutes

1 onion, chopped   1 tbsp Sweetener
1 cup Chicken Broth   3 tbsp Chili Sauce
1 lb Goose Breasts   Salt and pepper to taste
3 tbsp Tamari Sauce   ½ cup water

Sprinkle goose breasts with salt and pepper. Place them in your Instant Pot. Mix the chicken broth, tamari sauce, sweetener, onion, chili sauce, salt. pepper, and water in a bowl and pour it over the goose. Seal the lid, select Manual, and cook for 15 minutes on High. Perform a quick pressure release. Serve topped with sauce.

Delicious Pork & Garbanzo Bean Chili

Serving Size: 10 | Total Time: 60 minutes

1 lb garbanzo beans, soaked overnight	2 tbsp ground cumin
	Salt to taste
1 tbsp olive oil	1 tsp smoked paprika
2 onions, finely chopped	1 tsp dried oregano
2 ½ lb ground pork	1 tsp garlic powder
1 jalapeño pepper, minced	¼ tsp cayenne pepper
6 garlic cloves, minced	2 ½ cups beef broth
¼ cup chili powder	1 tbsp tomato puree

Add the beans and pour in cold water to cover 1 inch. Seal the lid and cook for 20 minutes on High Pressure. Release the pressure quickly. Drain beans and rinse with cold water. Set aside. Wipe clean the pot and set to Sauté. Warm olive oil, add the onions and sauté for 3 minutes until soft. Add jalapeño, pork, and garlic, and stir-fry until it is cooked through, about 5 minutes.

Stir in chili powder, salt, garlic powder, paprika, cumin, oregano, and cayenne, and cook until soft, about 30 seconds. Pour in broth, beans, and tomato puree. Seal the lid and cook for 20 minutes on High Pressure. Release the pressure naturally. Open the lid, press Sauté, and cook as you stir until desired consistency is attained. Spoon chili into bowls and serve.

Red Wine Pork Stew with Tomatoes

Serving Size: 4 | Total Time: 45 minutes

1 lb pork tenderloin, cubed	½ tbsp red wine
1 onion, peeled, chopped	½ tbsp beef broth
2 tbsp vegetable oil	A handful of fresh basil
4 tomatoes, peeled, diced	Salt and pepper to taste

Heat oil and stir-fry the onion until translucent. Add the meat, salt, pepper, wine, tomatoes, and basil. Cook for 10 minutes. Pour in broth, seal the lid and cook on High Pressure for 25 minutes. Do a quick release. Serve.

Creamy Mushroom Chicken Stew

Serving Size: 4 | Total Time: 20 minutes

1 lb Button Mushrooms, sliced	
2 tbsp butter	1 can heavy Cream
¼ tsp Garlic Powder	2 tbsp Arrowroot
4 Chicken Breasts	Salt and pepper to taste
1 cup Chicken Broth	

Place the chicken broth in your Instant Pot. Add in butter, garlic powder, salt, and black pepper. Sprinkle chicken breasts with salt and black pepper and place it in the pot. Add in mushrooms and seal the lid. Select Manual and cook for 10 minutes on High pressure.

When done, perform a quick pressure release and unlock the lid. Remove the chicken to a plate. In a bowl, combine 2 tbsp water with arrowroot and pour it into the pot. Cook for 2 minutes until the sauce thickens on Sauté. Stir in heavy cream and put the chicken back and cook for 1 more minute. Serve warm.

Herby Whole Chicken Stew

Serving Size: 6 | Total Time: 50 minutes

1 tsp cumin	1 Onion, quartered
1 tbsp Butter	1 ½ tsp Ranch Seasoning
1 Lemon, halved	½ tsp Lemon Pepper
1 (3-lb) Chicken	1 Rosemary Sprig
1 ½ cups Chicken Broth	2 Garlic Cloves

Combine the Ranch seasoning and lemon pepper in a bowl. Brush the chicken with the mixture. Melt butter in your Instant Pot on Sauté. Place the chicken and sear on all sides until golden brown. Set aside.

Fill the chicken with lemon, onion, garlic, cumin, and rosemary and place it in the pot with chicken broth. Seal the lid, select Poultry, and cook for 30 minutes on High pressure. When done, perform a quick pressure release. Let chill for 10 minutes before serving.

Rabbit & Veggie Stew

Serving Size: 6 | Total Time: 55 minutes

1 rabbit, cut into chunks	2 celery stalks, chopped
4 tbsp olive oil	2 tomatoes, diced
1 cup dry red wine	1 tbsp tomato paste
1 onion, chopped	1 bunch rosemary sprigs
2 garlic cloves, minced	1 bay leaf
1 carrot, chopped	3 cups chicken broth
1 cup mushrooms, sliced	Salt and pepper to taste
1 zucchini, chopped	2 tbsp parsley, chopped

Sprinkle rabbit with salt and pepper. Warm the olive oil in your Instant Pot on Sauté. Place in rabbit chunks and cook for 5 minutes on all sides; reserve. Stir onion, garlic, carrot, celery, mushrooms, and zucchini for 4-5 minutes until tender. Add in red wine tomatoes, tomato paste, bay leaf, and rosemary and cook for 5 minutes.

Mix in chicken broth, return the rabbit, and seal the lid. Select Manual and cook for 15 minutes on High pressure. Once done, allow a natural release for 10 minutes, then perform a quick pressure release, and unlock the lid. Adjust season to taste and discard rosemary sprigs and bay leaf. Serve topped with parsley.

Thyme Chicken Pot with Cheese

Serving Size: 4 | Total Time: 30 minutes

1 carrot, chopped	2 oz Parmesan cheese, grated
1 lb Chicken breasts, cubed	
1 Onion, chopped	Salt and pepper to taste
3 Garlic cloves, minced	¼ tbsp Thyme
	2 tbsp Butter

Melt butter in your Instant Pot on Sauté. Add in onion and garlic and sauté for 2-3 minutes until translucent. Put in chicken breast and cook until golden brown, 6-8 minutes. Stir in carrot, salt, black pepper, thyme, and 3 cups of water. Seal the lid, select Manual, and cook for 20 minutes on High pressure. When done, perform a quick pressure release. Serve sprinkled with Parmesan.

Coconut & Cauliflower Curry

Serving Size: 4 | Total Time: 25 minutes

2 tbsp butter	½ tsp cardamom
1 onion, chopped	½ tsp cumin
3 cups chicken broth	1 head cauliflower, chopped
1 cup coconut milk	1 tbsp cilantro, chopped
2 tbsp red curry paste	

Melt the butter in your Instant Pot on Sauté. Place the onion and cook for 4-5 minutes. Add in chicken broth, cauliflower, coconut milk, curry paste, cardamon, and cumin and seal the lid. Select Manual and cook for 10 minutes on High pressure. When ready, perform a quick pressure release and unlock the lid. Blend the soup using an immersion blender. Serve topped cilantro.

Pancetta & Cheese Chicken Thighs

Serving Size: 4 | Total Time: 30 minutes

4 Bacon Slices, cooked and crumbled

1 cup Chicken Broth	¼ tsp Garlic Powder
4 Chicken Thighs	¼ tsp Italian Seasoning
8 oz Cream Cheese	Salt and pepper to taste
½ cup shredded Cheddar	2 tbsp Arrowroot

Combine the chicken broth, cream cheese, garlic powder, Italian seasoning, salt, and black pepper in your Instant Pot. Add in chicken thighs and seal the lid. Select Manual and cook for 18 minutes on High pressure. When done, perform a quick pressure release and unlock the lid. Transfer the chicken to a plate. Add the arrowroot to the pot and cook for 2 minutes until the sauce thickens on Sauté. Mix in pancetta and chicken and serve right away.

Habanero Chicken Stew

Serving Size: 4 | Total Time: 25 minutes

1 habanero pepper, diced	1 cup Heavy Cream
2 tbsp Butter	2 cups shredded Cheddar
½ cup Hot Sauce	2 Chicken Breasts
1 ½ cups Chicken Broth	1 Celery Stalk, diced
½ Onion, diced	½ cup chopped Cauliflower
2 Garlic Cloves, minced	Salt and pepper to taste

Place the butter, hot sauce, chicken broth, onion, garlic, habanero pepper, chicken breasts, celery, cauliflower, salt, and pepper in your Instant Pot. Seal the lid, select Manual, and cook for 15 minutes on High. When done, perform a quick pressure release and unlock the lid. Mix in heavy cream and cheddar cheese. Serve.

Chinese-Style Chicken Stew with Broccoli

Serving Size: 4 | Total Time: 20 minutes

1 tsp Chinese Five-Spice seasoning

1 cup Coconut Aminos	1 garlic clove, minced
4 Chicken Breasts	Salt and pepper to taste
1 cup Chicken Broth	4 cups Broccoli Florets
3 tbsp Olive oil	1 tbsp Sesame seeds
½ tsp Fish Sauce	2 tbsp Arrowroot Flour
1 inch Ginger, grated	

Place the chicken breasts, chicken broth, olive oil, garlic, ginger, coconut aminos, Chinese five-spice seasoning, black pepper, and salt in your Instant Pot. Seal the lid, select Manual, and cook for 8 minutes on High pressure.

When done, perform a quick pressure release. Whisk the arrowroot with 2 tbsp water in a bowl and pour it into the pot. Add in broccoli and cook for 5 minutes on Sauté. Stir in fish sauce. Serve garnished with sesame seeds.

Hot Beef Chili

Serving Size: 4 | Total Time: 35 minutes

1 lb ground beef	2 carrots, chopped
2 tbsp olive oil	1 tsp chili powder
1 red bell pepper, chopped	2 tbsp Worcestershire sauce
1 yellow bell pepper, diced	2 tsp paprika
1 onion, chopped	2 tbsp parsley, chopped
2 cups tomatoes, chopped	Salt and pepper to taste

Select Sauté and add the olive oil and ground beef. Cook the beef until it browns while stirring occasionally for about 8 minutes. Top it with the onion, bell peppers, tomatoes, carrots, chili powder, Worcestershire sauce, paprika, salt, and pepper. Stir the ingredients well. Seal the lid, and select Soup/Broth on High Pressure and cook for 20 minutes. Once the timer has ended, do a quick pressure release. Sprinkle with parsley and serve.

Delicious Thai Vegetable Stew

Serving Size: 4 | Total Time: 20 minutes

1 tbsp coconut oil	1 orange bell pepper, diced
1 cup onion, chopped	1 (14-oz) can coconut milk
1 tbsp fresh ginger, minced	1 cup bok choy, chopped
2 garlic cloves, minced	½ cup water
3 carrots, chopped	2 tbsp red curry paste
1 red bell pepper, chopped	Salt and pepper to taste

Melt coconut oil on Sauté. Add in onion, garlic, and ginger and cook for 3 minutes until soft. Mix in orange bell pepper, red bell pepper and carrots and cook for 3 minutes until the peppers become soft and tender.

Add curry paste, bok choy, coconut milk, and water and stir well to obtain a consistent color of the sauce. Seal lid. Cook for 1 minute on High Pressure. Release the pressure quickly. Adjust the seasoning and serve hot.

Garbanzo Stew with Onions & Tomatoes

Serving Size: 5 | Total Time: 35 minutes

1 lb chickpeas, soaked	3 cups vegetable broth
3 purple onions, chopped	1 tbsp paprika
2 tomatoes, chopped	2 tbsp olive oil
2 oz fresh parsley, chopped	

Warm olive oil on Sauté and stir-fry the onions for 3 minutes. Add chickpeas, tomatoes, broth, parsley, and paprika. Seal the lid and cook on the Meat/Stew for 30 minutes on High. Do a quick release. Serve warm.

VEGAN & VEGETARIAN

Mashed Potato Balls with Tomato Sauce

Serving Size: 4 | Total Time: 55 minutes

2 potatoes, peeled
1 onion, peeled, chopped
1 lb spinach, torn
¼ cup mozzarella, shredded
2 eggs, beaten
Salt and pepper to taste
TOMATO SAUCE:

1 tsp dried oregano
1 cup whole milk
¼ cup flour
¼ cup cornflour
2 garlic cloves

1 lb tomatoes, chopped
1 onion, chopped
2 garlic cloves, minced
3 tsp olive oil
¼ cup white wine

1 tsp sugar
1 tsp dried rosemary
½ tsp salt
1 tsp tomato paste

Place the potatoes in your Instant Pot and add enough water to cover. Seal the lid and cook on High Pressure for 13 minutes. Do a quick release. Add 1 cup of milk and mash with a potato masher. Whisk in eggs, add onion, spinach, mozzarella, salt, pepper, oregano, flour, cornflour, and garlic, and mix with hands. Shape into balls and set aside. Press Sauté, warm olive oil, and stir-fry onion and garlic until translucent.

Stir in tomatoes and cook until tender, about 10 minutes. Pour in the wine and add sugar, rosemary, and salt. Stir in 1 tsp of tomato paste and mix well. Cook for five more minutes. Place the potato balls in the cooker and seal with the lid. Cook on High Pressure for 5 minutes. Do a natural release for 10 minutes. Ser

Weekend Burrito Bowls

Serving Size: 4 | Total Time: 30 minutes

2 tbsp olive oil
1 onion, chopped
2 garlic cloves, minced
1 tbsp chili powder
2 tbsp ground cumin
2 tbsp paprika
Salt and pepper to taste
¼ tbsp cayenne pepper

1 cup quinoa, rinsed
14.5-oz can diced tomatoes
1 (14.5-oz) can black beans
1 ½ cups vegetable stock
1 cup frozen corn kernels
2 tbsp chopped cilantro
2 tbsp cheddar, grated
1 avocado, chopped

Warm oil on Sauté. Add in onion and stir-fry for 3-5 minutes until fragrant. Add garlic and Sauté for 2 more minutes until soft and golden brown. Add in chili powder, paprika, cayenne pepper, salt, cumin, and black pepper and cook for 1 minute until spices are soft. Pour quinoa into onion and spice mixture and stir to coat quinoa thoroughly in spices. Add tomatoes, black beans, vegetable stock, and corn; stir to combine.

Seal the lid and cook for 7 minutes on High Pressure. Release the pressure quickly. Open the lid and let sit for 6 minutes until flavors combine. Use a fork to fluff quinoa and season with pepper and salt. Stir in cilantro and divide into plates. Top with cheese and avocado slices and serve.

Plant-Based Indian Curry

Serving Size: 4 | Total Time: 20 minutes

1 tsp butter
1 onion, chopped
2 cloves garlic, minced
1 tsp ginger, grated
1 tsp ground cumin
1 tsp red chili powder
1 tsp salt

½ tsp ground turmeric
1 (15-oz) can chickpeas
1 tomato, diced
1/3 cup water
2 lb collard greens, chopped
½ tsp garam masala
1 tsp lemon juice

Melt butter on Sauté. Add in the onion, ginger, cumin, turmeric, red chili powder, garlic, and salt and cook for 30 seconds until crispy. Stir in tomato. Pour in ⅓ cup of water and chickpeas. Seal the lid and cook on High Pressure for 4 minutes. Release the pressure quickly. Press Sauté. Into the chickpea mixture, stir in lemon juice, collard greens, and garam masala until well coated. Cook for 2 to 3 minutes until collard greens wilt on Sauté. Serve over rice or naan.

Spicy Vegetable Pilaf

Serving Size: 4 | Total Time: 40 minutes

3 tbsp olive oil
1 tbsp ginger, minced
1 cup onion, chopped
1 cup green peas
1 cup carrots, chopped
1 cup mushrooms, chopped
1 cup broccoli, chopped
1 tbsp chili powder

½ tbsp ground cumin
1 tbsp garam masala
½ tbsp turmeric
1 cup basmati rice
2 cups vegetable broth
1 tbsp lemon juice
Salt and pepper to taste

Warm 1 tbsp olive oil on Sauté. Add in onion and ginger and cook for 3 minutes. Stir in broccoli, green peas, mushrooms, and carrots and cook for 5 minutes. Stir in the turmeric, chili powder, garam masala, salt, pepper, and cumin for 1 minute. Add ¼ cup broth and scrape the bottom to get rid of any browned bits. Add the remaining broth and rice. Seal the lid and cook for 20 minutes on High Pressure. Release the pressure quickly. Drizzle with lemon juice and serve.

Quick Farro with Greens & Pine Nuts

Serving Size: 6 | Total Time: 20 minutes

6 oz spinach, chopped
6 oz collard greens, torn
3 oz Swiss chard, chopped
3 tbsp parsley, chopped
1 leek, chopped

1 ½ cups farro
2 tbsp olive oil
2 ¼ cups vegetable broth
1 tbsp salt
½ cup toasted pine nuts

Add farro and vegetable broth to the Instant Pot. Season with salt and seal the lid. Cook on Manual for 9 minutes on High. Do a quick release and open the lid. Fluff the farro with a fork and set aside. Wipe the pot clean.

Warm the olive oil in the pot on Sauté. Add the leek and stir-fry for 4-5 minutes until slightly caramelized. Add in the spinach, Swiss chard, and salt and sauté for another 4-5 minutes until the greens are wilted. Toss in the farro, sprinkle with pine nuts, and serve.

Quinoa with Brussels Sprouts & Broccoli

Serving Size: 2 | Total Time: 25 minutes

1 cup quinoa, rinsed	½ lb Brussels sprouts
Salt and pepper to taste	2 eggs
1 beet, peeled, cubed	1 avocado, chopped
1 cup broccoli florets	¼ cup pesto sauce
1 carrot, chopped	Lemon wedges, for serving

In the pot, mix 2 cups of water, salt, quinoa and pepper. Set trivet over quinoa and set steamer basket on top. To the steamer basket, add eggs, Brussels sprouts, broccoli, beet cubes, carrots, pepper, and salt. Seal the lid and cook for 1 minute on High Pressure. Release pressure naturally for 10 minutes. Remove the steamer basket and trivet from the pot and set the eggs in a bowl of ice water. Peel and halve the eggs. Use a fork to fluff the quinoa. Divide quinoa, broccoli, avocado, carrots, beet, Brussels sprouts, eggs between two bowls, and top with a pesto dollop. Serve with lemon wedges.

Vegetarian Green Dip

Serving Size: 4 | Total Time: 15 minutes

10 oz canned green chiles, drained, liquid reserved	
2 cups broccoli florets	½ tsp sea salt
1 green bell pepper, diced	¼ tsp chili powder
¼ cup raw cashews	¼ tsp garlic powder
¼ cup soy sauce	¼ tsp cumin

In the pot, add cashews, broccoli, green bell pepper, and 1 cup water. Seal the lid and cook for 5 minutes on High Pressure. Release the pressure quickly. Carefully unlock the lid. Drain water from the pot. Add reserved liquid from canned green chiles, salt, garlic powder, chili powder, soy sauce, and cumin. Use an immersion blender to blitz the mixture until smooth. Stir in chiles and serve.

Cauliflower & Potato Curry with Cilantro

Serving Size: 4 | Total Time: 40 minutes

1 tbsp vegetable oil	1 tomato, chopped
10 oz cauliflower florets	1 jalapeño pepper, minced
1 potato, peeled and diced	1 tbsp curry paste
1 tbsp ghee	1 tbsp ground turmeric
2 tbsp cumin seeds	½ tsp chili pepper
1 onion, minced	Salt and pepper to taste
4 garlic cloves, minced	2 tbsp cilantro, chopped

Warm oil on Sauté. Add in potato and cauliflower and cook for 8 to 10 minutes until lightly browned; season with salt. Set the vegetables in a bowl. Add ghee to the pot. Mix in cumin seeds and cook for 10 seconds until they start to pop; add onion and cook for 3 minutes until softened. Mix in garlic and pepper; cook for 30 seconds.

Add in tomato, curry paste, chili pepper, jalapeño pepper, and turmeric; cook for 4 to 6 minutes. Return potato and cauliflower to the pot. Stir in 1 cup water. Seal the lid and cook on High Pressure for 4 minutes. Quick-release the pressure. Unlock the lid. Top with cilantro and serve.

Parmesan Topped Vegetable Mash

Serving Size: 6 | Total Time: 15 minutes

3 lb Yukon gold potatoes, chopped	
2 cups cauliflower florets	¼ cup milk
1 carrot, chopped	1 tsp salt
1 cup Parmesan, shredded	1 garlic clove, minced
¼ cup butter, melted	2 tbsp parsley, chopped

Into the pot, add potatoes, cauliflower, carrot and salt; cover with enough water. Seal the lid and cook on High Pressure for 10 minutes. Release the pressure quickly. Drain the vegetables and mash them with a potato masher. Add garlic, butter, and milk. Whisk until well incorporated. Top with Parmesan cheese and parsley.

Steamed Artichokes with Lime Aioli

Serving Size: 4 | Total Time: 20 minutes

2 large artichokes	Salt and pepper to taste
2 garlic cloves, smashed	Juice of 1 lime
½ cup mayonnaise	

Using a serrated knife, trim about 1 inch from the top of the artichokes. Into the pot, add 1 cup of water and set trivet over. Lay the artichokes on the trivet. Seal lid and cook for 14 minutes on High Pressure. Release the pressure quickly. Mix the mayonnaise, garlic, and lime juice. Season with salt and pepper. Serve artichokes on a platter with garlic mayo on the side.

Buttery Mashed Cauliflower

Serving Size: 4 | Total Time: 15 minutes

2 cups water	Salt and pepper to taste
1 head cauliflower	¼ cup heavy cream
1 tbsp butter	1 tbsp parsley, chopped

Into the pot, add water and set trivet on top. Lay cauliflower head onto the trivet. Seal the lid and cook for 8 minutes on High Pressure. Release the pressure quickly. Remove trivet and drain the liquid from the pot. Take back the cauliflower to the pot. Add heavy cream, butter, salt, and pepper. Use an immersion blender to blend until smooth. Top with parsley and serve.

Vegetarian Chili with Lentils & Quinoa

Serving Size: 4 | Total Time: 45 minutes

28-oz can diced tomatoes	2 garlic cloves, minced
1 cups cashew, chopped	1 tsp chili powder
1 cup onion, chopped	1 tsp salt
½ cup red lentils	1 cup carrots, chopped
½ cup red quinoa	1 (15-oz) can black beans
2 chipotle peppers, minced	¼ cup parsley, chopped

In the pot, mix tomatoes, onion, chipotle peppers, chili powder, lentils, cashew, carrot, quinoa, garlic, and salt. Cover with water. Seal the lid, Press Soup/Stew, and cook for 30 minutes on High Pressure. Release the pressure quickly. Add in black beans. Simmer on Sauté until heated through. Top with parsley and serve.

Minestrone Soup with Green Vegetables

Serving Size: 4 | Total Time: 15 minutes

2 tbsp olive oil	1 zucchini, chopped
10 oz broccoli florets	1 cup green beans
4 celery stalks, chopped	2 cups vegetable broth
1 leek, chopped thinly	2 cups chopped kale

Add broccoli, leek, beans, zucchini, and celery. Mix in vegetable broth, oil, and enough water to cover. Seal the lid and cook on High Pressure for 4 minutes. Release pressure naturally for 5 minutes, then release the remaining pressure quickly. Stir in kale on Sauté and cook until tender. Serve.

Homemade Gazpacho Soup

Serving Size: 4 | Total Time: 2 hours 20 minutes

1 lb trimmed carrots	1 red onion, chopped
1 lb tomatoes, chopped	2 cloves garlic
1 cucumber, peeled, cubed	2 tbsp white wine vinegar
¼ cup olive oil	Salt and pepper to taste
2 tbsp lemon juice	

Add carrots, salt, and enough water to cover the carrots. Seal the lid and cook for 10 minutes on High Pressure. Do a quick release. In a blender, add carrots, cucumber, red onion, pepper, garlic, oil, tomatoes, lemon juice, vinegar, 4 cups of water, and salt. Blend until very smooth. Place gazpacho into a serving bowl, chill while covered for 2 hours. Serve and enjoy!

Easy Tahini Sweet Potato Mash

Serving Size: 4 | Total Time: 15 minutes

1 cup water	¼ tsp ground nutmeg
2 lb sweet potatoes, cubed	2 tbsp chopped chives
2 tbsp tahini	Salt and pepper to taste

Into the cooker, add 1 cup water and insert a steamer basket. Put potato cubes into the steamer basket. Seal the lid and cook for 8 minutes at High Pressure. Release the pressure quickly. In a bowl, add cooked sweet potatoes and slightly mash. Using a hand mixer, whip in nutmeg and tahini until the sweet potatoes attain desired consistency. Add salt and pepper and top with chives.

Parsley Lentil Soup with Vegetables

Serving Size: 4 | Total Time: 20 minutes

1 tbsp olive oil	1 ½ cups lentils, rinsed
1 onion, chopped	4 carrots, halved lengthwise
1 cup celery, chopped	½ tsp salt
2 garlic cloves, chopped	2 tbsp parsley, chopped
3 cups vegetable stock	

Warm olive oil on Sauté. Add in onion, garlic, and celery and sauté for 5 minutes until soft. Mix in lentils, carrots, salt, and stock. Seal the lid and cook on High Pressure for 10 minutes. Release the pressure quickly. Serve topped with parsley.

Simple Cheese Spinach Dip

Serving Size: 6 | Total Time: 20 minutes

2 cups cream cheese	Salt and pepper to taste
1 cup baby spinach	½ cup scallions
1 cup mozzarella, grated	1 cup vegetable broth

Place cream cheese, spinach, mozzarella cheese, salt, pepper, scallions, and broth in a mixing bowl. Stir well and transfer to your Instant Pot. Seal the lid and cook on High Pressure for 5 minutes. Release the steam naturally for 10 minutes. Serve with celery sticks or chips.

Savory Spinach with Mashed Potatoes

Serving Size: 6 | Total Time: 20 minutes

3 lb potatoes, peeled	2 tbsp chopped chives
½ cup milk	Salt and pepper to taste
⅓ cup butter	2 cups spinach, chopped

Cover the potatoes with salted water in your Instant Pot. Seal the lid and cook on High Pressure for 8 minutes. Release the pressure quickly. Drain the potatoes, and reserve the liquid in a bowl. Mash the potatoes. Mix with butter and milk; season with pepper and salt. With reserved cooking liquid, thin the potatoes to attain the desired consistency. Put the spinach in the remaining potato liquid and stir until wilted; Season to taste. Drain and serve with potato mash. Garnish with chives.

Coconut Milk Yogurt with Honey

Serving Size: 6 | Total Time: 15 hours

2 cans coconut milk	1 tbsp probiotic powder
1 tbsp gelatin	Zest from 1 lime
1 tbsp honey	

Into the pot, stir in gelatin and coconut milk until well dissolved. Seal the lid, Press Yogurt until the display is reading "Boil". Once done, the screen will then display "Yogurt". Ensure milk temperature is at 180°F. Remove steel pot from Pressure cooker base and place into a large ice bath to cool milk for 5 minutes to reach 112°F.

Remove the pot from the ice bath and wipe the outside dry. Into the coconut milk mixture, add probiotic powder, honey, and Lime zest, and stir to combine. Return steel pot to the base of the Instant Pot. Seal the lid, press Yogurt, and cook for 10 hours. Once complete, spoon yogurt into glass jars with rings and lids; place in the refrigerator to chill for 4 hours to thicken.

Tofu with Noodles & Peanuts

Serving Size: 4 | Total Time: 15 minutes

1 package tofu, cubed	2 tbsp vinegar
8 oz egg noodles	1 tbsp sesame oil
2 bell peppers, chopped	1 tbsp sriracha
¼ cup soy sauce	¼ cup roasted peanuts
¼ cup orange juice	3 scallions, chopped
1 tbsp fresh ginger, minced	

In the Instant Pot, mix tofu, bell peppers, orange juice, sesame oil, ginger, egg noodles, soy sauce, vinegar, and sriracha. Cover with enough water. Seal the lid and cook for 2 minutes on High Pressure. Release the pressure quickly. Divide the meal between 4 plates and top with scallions and peanuts to serve.

Mushroom & Gouda Cheese Pizza

Serving Size: 4 | Total Time: 30 minutes

4 oz button mushrooms, chopped
½ cup grated gouda cheese   1 tbsp dried oregano
1 pizza crust   2 tbsp olive oil
½ cup tomato paste   12 olives
1 tbsp sugar   1 cup arugula

Grease the bottom of a baking dish with one tbsp of olive oil. Line some parchment paper. Flour the working surface and roll out the pizza crust to the approximate size of your Instant Pot. Gently fit the dough in the previously prepared baking dish.

In a bowl, combine tomato paste, ¼ cup water, sugar, and oregano. Spread the mixture over the crust, make a layer with button mushrooms and grated gouda. Add a trivet inside the pot and pour in 1 cup water. Seal the lid and cook for 15 minutes on High Pressure. Do a quick release. Sprinkle the pizza with the remaining oil and top with olives and arugula. Serve.

Chickpea Stew with Onion & Tomatoes

Serving Size: 4 | Total Time: 40 minutes

6 oz chickpeas, soaked   2 tbsp olive oil
2 tomatoes, chopped   2 tbsp butter
1 red onion, chopped   2 tbsp parsley, chopped
1 tbsp cumin seeds   Salt and pepper to taste
2 cups vegetable broth

To the Instant Pot, add olive oil, tomatoes, onion, cumin seeds, chickpeas, and pour in the broth. Seal the lid and set the steam handle. Cook on Manual for 30 minutes on High. Do a quick release and set aside to cool for a while.

Transfer the soup to a food processor and season with salt and pepper. Process until pureed and spoon onto a serving bowl. Stir in 2 tbsp of butter. Top with freshly chopped parsley and serve.

One-Pot Swiss Chard & Potatoes

Serving Size: 4 | Total Time: 15 minutes

1 lb Swiss chard, chopped   1 tsp salt
2 potatoes, peeled, chopped   1 tsp Italian seasoning
¼ tsp oregano

Add Swiss chard and potatoes to the pot. Pour water to cover all and sprinkle with salt. Seal the lid and select Manual. Cook for 3 minutes on High. Release the steam naturally for 5 minutes. Transfer to a serving plate. Sprinkle with oregano and Italian seasoning and serve.

Green Bean Salad with Cheese & Nuts

Serving Size: 6 | Total Time: 15 minutes

Juice from 1 lemon   1 cup feta, crumbled
2 lb green beans, trimmed   6 tbsp olive oil
1 cup toasted pine nuts   Salt and pepper to taste

Add water and set rack over the water and the steamer basket on the rack. Loosely heap green beans into the steamer basket. Seal lid and cook on High Pressure for 5 minutes. Release pressure quickly. Drop green beans into a salad bowl. Top with olive oil, feta cheese, salt, lemon juice, black pepper, and pine nuts.

Power Green Soup with Lasagna Noodles

Serving Size: 4 | Total Time: 25 minutes

1 tsp olive oil   ½ lb broccoli, chopped
1 cup leeks, chopped   ¼ cup dried green lentils
2 garlic cloves minced   2 tsp Italian seasoning
1 cup tomato paste   Salt to taste
1 cup tomatoes, chopped   2 cups vegetable broth
1 carrot, chopped   3 lasagna noodles

Warm olive oil on Sauté. Add garlic and leeks and cook for 2 minutes until soft; add tomato paste, carrot, Italian seasoning, broccoli, tomatoes, lentils, and salt. Stir in vegetable broth and lasagna noodles. Seal the lid and cook on High Pressure for 3 minutes. Release pressure naturally for 10 minutes. Divide into bowls and serve.

Stuffed with Rice Grape Leaves

Serving Size: 4 | Total Time: 50 minutes

32 wine leaves   2 garlic cloves, crushed
1 cup long grain rice   ¼ cup lemon juice
½ cup olive oil   Salt and pepper to taste

In a bowl, mix rice with 3 tbsp of olive oil, garlic, salt, and pepper. Place 1 wine leaf at a time on a working surface and add 1 tbsp of filling at the bottom. Fold the leaves over the filling towards the center. Bring the 2 sides in towards the center and roll them up tightly.

Grease the Instant Pot with 2 tbsp olive oil. Make a layer of wine leaves. Transfer the previously prepared rolls. Add the remaining olive oil, 2 cups water, and lemon juice. Seal the lid and cook on High Pressure for 30 minutes. Do a natural release for 10 minutes. Remove the dolmades from the pot and chill overnight.

Spanish-Style "Tortilla de Patatas"

Serving Size: 3 | Total Time: 40 minutes

5 eggs, beaten   1 cup heavy cream
1 cup spinach, torn   Salt and pepper to taste
1 potato, chopped   1 tbsp olive oil

In a bowl, mix eggs, heavy cream, and potato. Sprinkle with salt and pepper and stir to combine. Heat olive oil on Sauté and cook the spinach for 3 minutes or until wilted. Remove the spinach to the egg mixture.

Transfer all to an oven-safe dish. Add 1 cup of water, insert the trivet, pour 1 cup of water, and place the oven-safe dish on top. Seal the lid and cook on High for 20 minutes. Release the steam naturally for 10 minutes.

Parsnip & Cauliflower Mash with Chives

Serving Size: 8 | Total Time: 15 minutes

1 ½ lb parsnips, cubed	¼ cup sour cream
10 oz cauliflower florets	¼ cup grated Parmesan
2 garlic cloves	1 tbsp butter
Salt and pepper to taste	2 tbsp minced chives

In the pot, mix parsnips, garlic, 2 cups water, salt, cauliflower, and pepper. Seal the lid and cook on High Pressure for 4 minutes. Release the pressure quickly. Drain parsnips and cauliflower and return to pot. Add Parmesan, butter, and sour cream. Use a potato masher to mash until the desired consistency is attained. Top with chives and place to a serving plate. Serve.

Traditional Italian Pesto

Serving Size: 4 | Total Time: 20 minutes

3 zucchini, peeled, chopped	½ cup basil-tomato juice
1 eggplant, peeled, chopped	½ tbsp salt
3 red bell peppers, chopped	2 tbsp olive oil

Add zucchini, eggplant, bell peppers, basil-tomato juice, salt, and olive oil to the pot and give it a good stir. Pour 1 cup of water. Seal the lid and cook on High Pressure for 15 minutes. Do a quick release. Set aside to cool completely. Serve as a cold salad or a side dish.

Mozzarella & Eggplant Lasagna

Serving Size: 2 | Total Time: 30 minutes

1 large eggplant, chopped	2 tomatoes, sliced
4 oz mozzarella, chopped	¼ cup olive oil
3 oz mascarpone cheese	Salt and pepper to taste

Grease a baking dish with olive oil. Slice the eggplant and make a layer in the dish. Cover with mozzarella and tomato slices. Top with mascarpone cheese. Repeat the process until you run out of ingredients.

In a bowl, mix olive oil, salt, and pepper. Pour the mixture over the lasagna, and add ½ cup of water. In your pot, pour 1 cup of water and insert a trivet. Lower the baking dish on the trivet, seal the lid and cook on High Pressure for 4 minutes. Do a natural release for 10 minutes.

Mushroom & Ricotta Cheese Manicotti

Serving Size: 4 | Total Time: 35 minutes

6 oz button mushrooms, chopped	
8 oz pack manicotti pasta	3 oz butter
12 oz spinach, torn	¼ tbsp salt
3 oz ricotta cheese	1 tbsp sour cream
¼ cup milk	

Melt butter on Sauté and add mushrooms. Cook until

soft, 5 minutes. Add spinach and milk and continue to cook for 6 minutes. Stir in cheese and season with salt. Line a baking dish with parchment paper. Fill manicotti with spinach mixture. Transfer them on the baking sheet. Pour 1 cup water into the Instant Pot and insert a trivet. Lay the baking sheet on the trivet. Seal the lid and cook on High Pressure for 15 minutes. Do a quick release. Top with sour cream and serve.

Mixed Vegetables Medley

Serving Size: 4 | Total Time: 20 minutes

10 oz broccoli florets	5 oz green beans
16 asparagus, trimmed	2 carrots, cut on bias
10 oz cauliflower florets	Salt to taste

Add 1 cup of water and set trivet on top. Place a steamer basket over the water. In an even layer, spread green beans, broccoli, cauliflower, asparagus, and carrots in the steamer basket. Seal the lid and cook on Steam for 3 minutes on High. Release the pressure quickly. Remove basket from the pot and season with salt.

Carrot & Chickpea Boil with Tomatoes

Serving Size: 4 | Total Time: 25 minutes

½ cup button mushrooms, chopped	
1 cup canned chickpeas	2 carrots, chopped
1 onion, peeled, chopped	2 garlic cloves, crushed
1 lb string beans, trimmed	4 cherry tomatoes
1 apple, cubed	1 tbsp grated ginger
½ cup raisins	½ cup orange juice

Place mushrooms, chickpeas, onion, beans, apple, raisins, carrots, garlic, cherry tomatoes, ginger, and orange juice in the Instant Pot. Pour enough water to cover. Cook on High Pressure for 8 minutes. Do a natural release for 10 minutes. Serve warm.

Amazing Vegetable Paella

Serving Size: 4 | Total Time: 25 minutes

½ cup green peas	3 oz celery root, chopped
2 carrots, chopped	1 tbsp turmeric
1 cup fire-roasted tomatoes	2 cup vegetable broth
1 cup zucchini, chopped	1 cup long-grain rice

Place green peas, carrots, tomatoes, zucchini, celery, turmeric, and broth in the Instant Pot. Stir well and seal the lid. Cook on Manual for 15 minutes on High. Do a quick release, open the lid, and stir in the rice. Seal the lid and cook on High pressure for 3 minutes. When ready, release the pressure naturally for about 10 minutes.

Delicious Mushroom Goulash

Serving Size: 4 | Total Time: 50 minutes

6 oz portobello mushrooms, sliced	
1 cup green peas	1 celery stalk, chopped
1 cup pearl onions, minced	2 garlic cloves, crushed
2 carrots, chopped	2 potatoes, chopped

1 tbsp apple cider vinegar 2 tbsp butter
1 tbsp rosemary 4 cups vegetable stock
Salt and pepper to taste

Melt butter on Sauté and stir-fry onions, carrots, celery stalks, and garlic for 2-3 minutes. Season with salt, pepper, and rosemary. Add mushrooms, peas, potatoes, vinegar, and stock and seal the lid. Cook on High Pressure for 30 minutes. When ready, release the pressure naturally.

Stuffed Peppers with Rice & Mushrooms

Serving Size: 4 | Total Time: 40 minutes

4 bell peppers, seeds and stems removed
6 oz button mushrooms, chopped
1 onion, peeled, chopped ½ cup rice
2 garlic cloves, minced ½ tbsp paprika
2 tbsp olive oil 2 cups vegetable stock

Warm the olive oil on Sauté. Add onion, garlic, and mushrooms, and stir-fry until tender for about 5 minutes. Press Cancel and set aside. In a bowl, combine rice with the mixture from the pot. Sprinkle with paprika.

Stuff each bell pepper with this mixture. Place them in the Instant Pot, filled side up, and pour in the stock. Seal the lid and cook on High Pressure for 15 minutes. Release the pressure naturally for about 10 minutes.

Celery & Red Bean Stew

Serving Size: 4 | Total Time: 25 minutes

6 oz red beans, cooked 2 cups vegetable broth
2 carrots, chopped 3 tbsp olive oil
2 celery stalks, chopped 1 tbsp salt
1 onion, chopped 2 tbsp parsley, chopped
2 tbsp tomato paste 1 tbsp flour
1 bay leaf

Warm olive oil on Sauté and stir-fry the onion for 3 minutes. Add celery and carrots. Cook for 5 more minutes. Add red beans, bay leaf, salt, and tomato paste. Stir in 1 tbsp of flour and pour in the vegetable broth. Seal the lid and cook on High Pressure for 5 minutes. Do a natural release for about 10 minutes. Sprinkle with some fresh parsley and serve warm.

Penne Pasta with Shiitake & Vegetables

Serving Size: 4 | Total Time: 20 minutes

6 oz shiitake mushrooms, chopped
6 oz penne pasta
2 garlic cloves, crushed 4 oz baby spinach
1 carrot, chopped into strips 3 tbsp oil
6 oz zucchini cut into strips 2 tbsp soy sauce
6 oz finely chopped leek 1 tbsp ground ginger
  ½ tbsp salt

Heat oil on Sauté and stir-fry carrot and garlic for 3-4 minutes. Add mushrooms, penne, zucchini, leek, spinach, soy sauce, ginger, and salt and pour in 2 cups of water. Cook on High Pressure for 4 minutes. Quick-release the pressure and serve.

Thyme Asparagus Soup

Serving Size: 4 | Total Time: 15 minutes

1 carrot, chopped 3 tbsp Coconut oil
2 cups sour cream ½ tsp dried Thyme
½ lb Asparagus, chopped 5 cups Bone broth
1 sliced Onion 1 Lemon, juiced, zested
3 Garlic cloves, minced

Melt coconut oil in your Instant Pot on Sauté. Place the onions and garlic and cook for 2 minutes, stirring often. Add in thyme and cook for 1 minute. Put in bone broth, asparagus, carrot, and lemon zest and seal the lid. Select Manual and cook for 5 minutes on High pressure. When done, perform a quick pressure release and unlock the lid. Mix in sour cream and serve.

Gingery Butternut Squash Soup

Serving Size: 6 | Total Time: 25 minutes

1 lb peeled and diced Butternut Squash
2 garlic cloves, minced 1 cup Heavy cream
1 tbsp Ginger powder 2 tbsp vegetable oil
4 cups Chicken broth Salt and pepper to taste

Place the vegetable oil and half of the butternut squash cubes and cook for 5 minutes until browns on Sauté. Add in the remaining cubes, garlic, ginger powder, chicken broth, heavy cream, salt, and black pepper. Seal the lid, select Manual, and cook for 10 minutes on High pressure. When done, perform a quick pressure release and unlock the lid. Using an immersion blender, pulse until purée. Serve immediately.

Vegan Lentil & Quinoa Stew

Serving Size: 4 | Total Time: 35 minutes

10 sun-dried tomatoes, chopped
1 cup quinoa 4 cups vegetable broth
1 cup tomatoes, diced 1 tsp salt
1 cup lentils 1 tsp red pepper flakes
1 tsp garlic, minced

Add sun-dried tomatoes, quinoa, tomatoes, lentils, garlic, broth, salt, and red pepper flakes to your Instant Pot. Seal the lid and adjust the steam release handle. Cook on High Pressure for 20 minutes. Release the steam naturally for about 10 minutes. Carefully unlock the lid.

Spinach Tagliatelle with Mushrooms

Serving Size: 4 | Total Time: 25 minutes

8 oz spinach tagliatelle ¼ cup grated Parmesan
6 oz mixed mushrooms 2 garlic cloves, crushed
3 tbsp butter ¼ cup heavy cream
¼ cup feta cheese 1 tbsp Italian seasoning

Melt butter on Sauté and stir-fry the garlic for a minute. Stir in feta, Italian seasoning, and mushrooms. Add the tagliatelle, 2 cups water, and heavy cream. Cook on High Pressure for 4 minutes. Quick-release the pressure. Top with Parmesan cheese. Serve and enjoy!

Pasta Orecchiette with Broccoli & Tofu

Serving Size: 4 | Total Time: 25 minutes

1 (9 oz) pack orecchiette	3 tbsp olive oil
16 oz broccoli, chopped	1 tbsp grated tofu
2 garlic cloves	Salt and pepper to taste

Place the orecchiette and broccoli in your Instant Pot. Cover with water and seal the lid. Cook on High Pressure for 10 minutes. Do a quick release. Drain the broccoli and orecchiette. Set aside. Heat the olive oil on Sauté. Stir-fry garlic for 2 minutes. Stir in broccoli, orecchiette, salt, and pepper. Cook for 2 minutes. Stir in tofu to serve.

English Vegetable Potage

Serving Size: 4 | Total Time: 50 minutes

1 lb potatoes, cut into bite-sized pieces	
2 carrots, peeled, chopped	3 tbsp olive oil
3 celery stalks, chopped	2 cups vegetable broth
2 onions, peeled, chopped	1 tbsp paprika
1 zucchini, sliced	Salt and pepper to taste
A handful of celery leaves	2 bay leaves
2 tbsp butter, unsalted	

Warm olive oil on Sauté and stir-fry the onions for 3-4 minutes until translucent. Add carrots, celery, zucchini, and ¼ cup of broth. Continue to cook for 10 more minutes, stirring constantly. Stir in potatoes, paprika, salt, pepper, bay leaves, remaining broth, and celery leaves. Seal the lid and cook on Meat/Stew for 30 minutes on High. Do a quick release and stir in butter.

Spicy Split Pea Stew

Serving Size: 4 | Total Time: 40 minutes

2 cups split yellow peas	2 tbsp butter
1 cup onion, chopped	2 garlic cloves, crushed
1 carrot, chopped	1 tbsp chili pepper
2 potatoes, chopped	4 cups vegetable stock

Melt butter on Sauté and stir-fry the onion for 3 minutes. Add peas, carrot, potatoes, and garlic and cook for 5-6 minutes until tender. Stir in chili pepper. Pour in the stock and seal the lid. Cook on Meat/Stew for 25 minutes. Do a quick release. Serve.

Speedy Mac & Goat Cheese

Serving Size: 4 | Total Time: 20 minutes

1 lb elbow macaroni	1 tsp dried oregano
2 oz goat's cheese, crumbled	1 tsp Italian seasoning
½ cup skim milk	2 tbsp olive oil
1 tsp Dijon mustard	5 oz olives, sliced

Add macaroni in the Instant Pot and cover with water. Seal the lid and cook on High Pressure for 4 minutes. Do a quick release. Drain the macaroni and set aside. Press Sauté on the pot and add the olive oil, mustard, milk, oregano, and Italian seasoning. Cook for 3 minutes. Stir in macaroni and cook for 2 minutes. Top with fresh goat's cheese and olives and serve.

Two-Cheese Carrot Sauce

Serving Size: 4 | Total Time: 25 minutes

1 carrot, shredded	1 cup Gruyere, crumbled
1 cup cream cheese	Salt and pepper to taste
½ cup Gorgonzola cheese	1 tsp garlic powder
3 cups vegetable broth	1 tbsp parsley, chopped

Combine carrot, cream cheese, gorgonzola cheese, broth, gruyere, salt, pepper, garlic powder, and parsley in a large bowl. Pour in the Instant Pot, seal the lid and cook on High Pressure for 8 minutes. Do a natural release for 10 minutes. Store for up to 5 days.

Curly Kale Soup

Serving Size: 4 | Total Time: 20 minutes

4 cups curly kale	1 tbsp Olive oil
2 tbsp Ginger, minced	1 cup Heavy cream
4 Garlic cloves, minced	2 cups vegetable broth
1 tbsp Mustard seeds	1 tbsp Cumin powder

Warm olive oil in your Instant Pot on Sauté. Place the mustard seeds, garlic, ginger, cumin powder, vegetable broth, curly kale, and heavy cream. Seal the lid, select Manual, and cook for 10 minutes on High pressure. When done, perform a quick pressure release and unlock the lid. Serve warm.

Cauliflower Rice with Peas & Chili

Serving Size: 2 | Total Time: 20 minutes

10 oz cauliflower florets	1 tsp chili powder
2 tbsp olive oil	¼ cup green peas
Salt to taste	1 tbsp chopped parsley

Add 1 cup water, set rack over water and place the steamer basket onto the rack. Add cauliflower into the steamer basket. Seal the lid and cook on High Pressure for 1 minute. Release the pressure quickly. Remove rack and steamer basket. Drain water from the pot. Set it to Sauté and warm oil. Add in cauliflower and stir to break into smaller pieces like rice. Stir in chili powder, peas and salt. Serve the cauliflower topped with parsley.

Sweet Potato Medallions with Garlic

Serving Size: 4 | Total Time: 25 minutes

1 tbsp fresh rosemary	2 tbsp butter
1 tbsp garlic powder	Salt to taste
4 sweet potatoes	

Add 1 cup water and place a steamer rack over the water. Use a fork to prick sweet potatoes all over and set onto the steamer rack. Seal the lid and cook on High Pressure for 12 minutes. Release the pressure quickly. Transfer sweet potatoes to a cutting board. Peel and slice them into ½-inch medallions. Melt butter in the on Sauté. Add in the medallions and cook each side for 2 to 3 minutes until browned. Season with salt and garlic powder. Serve topped with rosemary.

Steamed Artichokes & Green Beans

Serving Size: 4 | Total Time: 20 minutes

4 artichokes, trimmed
½ lb green beans, trimmed
1 lemon, halved
1 tbsp lemon zest
1 tbsp lemon juice

3 cloves garlic, crushed
½ cup mayonnaise
Salt to taste
2 tbsp parsley, chopped

Rub the artichokes and green beans with lemon. Add 1 cup water into the pot. Set steamer rack over water and set steamer basket on top. Add in artichokes and green beans and sprinkle with salt. Seal lid and cook on High Pressure for 10 minutes.

Release the pressure quickly. In a mixing bowl, combine mayonnaise, garlic, lemon juice, and lemon zest. Season to taste with salt. Serve with warm steamed artichokes and green beans sprinkled with parsley.

Stuffed Potatoes with Feta & Rosemary

Serving Size: 4 | Total Time: 50 minutes

1 cup button mushrooms, chopped
6 whole potatoes
¼ cup olive oil
3 garlic cloves, minced
¼ cup feta cheese

1 tsp rosemary, chopped
½ tsp dried thyme
1 tsp salt

Rub the potatoes with salt and place them in the Instant Pot. Add enough water to cover and seal the lid. Cook on High Pressure for 30 minutes. Do a quick release and remove the potatoes. Let chill for a while.

In the pot, mix oil, garlic, rosemary, thyme, and mushrooms. Sauté until the mushrooms soften, 5 minutes on Sauté. Stir in feta. Cut the top of each potato and spoon out the middle. Fill with cheese mixture and serve.

Grandma's Asparagus with Feta & Lemon

Serving Size: 4 | Total Time: 20 minutes

1 lb asparagus spears
1 tbsp olive oil
Salt and pepper to taste

1 lemon, cut into wedges
1 cup feta cheese, cubed

Into the pot, add 1 cup of water and set trivet over the water. Place steamer basket on the trivet. Place the asparagus into the steamer basket. Seal the lid and cook on High Pressure for 1 minute. Release the Pressure quickly. Add olive oil in a bowl and toss in asparagus until well coated. Season with pepper and salt. Serve with feta and lemon wedges.

Turmeric Stew with Green Peas

Serving Size: 4 | Total Time: 35 minutes

2 cups green peas
1 onion, chopped
4 cloves garlic, minced
3 oz of olives, pitted
1 tbsp ginger, shredded

1 tbsp turmeric
1 tbsp salt
4 cups vegetable stock
3 tbsp olive oil

Heat olive oil on Sauté. Stir-fry the onion and garlic for 2-3 minutes, stirring a few times. Add peas, olives, ginger, turmeric, salt, and stock and press Cancel. Seal the lid, select Manual, and cook on High Pressure for 20 minutes. Once the timer goes off, do a quick release before opening the lid. Serve with a dollop of yogurt.

Spicy Shiitake Mushrooms with Potatoes

Serving Size: 4 | Total Time: 45 minutes

1 lb shiitake mushrooms
2 potatoes, chopped
3 garlic cloves, crushed
2 tbsp olive oil
1 tsp garlic powder
1 tbsp cumin seeds

½ tbsp chili powder
1 large zucchini, chopped
1 cup onions
2 cups vegetable stock
1 cup tomato sauce

Warm olive oil on Sauté. Stir-fry cumin seeds for one minute. Add onions, chili powder, garlic, and garlic powder. Cook for 3 minutes, stirring constantly. Add mushrooms and continue to cook on Sauté for 3 more minutes. Add potatoes, zucchini, stock, and tomato sauce and seal the lid. Cook on High Pressure for 20 minutes. When done, release the pressure naturally. Serve warm.

Creamy Turnips Stuffed with Cheese

Serving Size: 4 | Total Time: 20 minutes

½ cup chopped roasted red bell pepper
4 small turnips
¼ cup whipping cream
¼ cup sour cream
1/3 cup grated Parmesan

1 tsp Italian seasoning
1 ½ cups grated mozzarella
4 green onions, chopped

Pour 1 cup of water into the pot and insert a trivet. Place the turnips on top. Seal the lid and cook on High for 10 minutes. Do a quick pressure release. Remove the turnips to a cutting board and allow cooling. Cut the turnips in half. Scoop out the pulp into a bowl and mash it with a potato mash. Mix in the whipping and sour cream until smooth. Stir in the roasted bell pepper.

Add in Italian seasoning and mozzarella cheese. Fetch out 2 tbsp of green onions and put into the turnips. Fill the turnip skins with the mashed mixture and sprinkle with Parmesan cheese. Arrange on a greased baking dish and place on the trivet. Seal the lid and cook on High pressure for 3 minutes. Do a quick pressure release. Top with the remaining onions to serve.

Sautéed Spinach with Roquefort Cheese

Serving Size: 2 | Total Time: 10 minutes

½ cup Roquefort cheese, crumbled
9 oz fresh spinach
2 leeks, chopped
2 red onions, chopped

2 garlic cloves, crushed
3 tbsp olive oil

Grease the inner pot with oil. Stir-fry leeks, garlic, and onions for about 5 minutes on Sauté. Add spinach and give it a good stir. Press Cancel, transfer to a serving dish, and sprinkle with Roquefort cheese. Serve right away.

Roman Stewed Beans with Tomatoes

Serving Size: 6 | Total Time: 30 minutes

2 cups cranberry beans	3 tbsp olive oil
2 onions, chopped	2 tbsp parsley, chopped
3 carrots, chopped	2 cups water
3 tomatoes, peeled, diced	Salt and pepper to taste

Heat olive oil on Sauté, and stir-fry the onions for 3-4 minutes until translucent. Add in carrots and tomatoes. Stir well and cook for 5 minutes. Stir in beans, salt, black pepper and water, and seal the lid. Cook on High Pressure for 15 minutes. Do a quick release and serve hot sprinkled with fresh parsley.

Cannellini Beans with Garlic & Leeks

Serving Size: 4 | Total Time: 45 minutes

1 lb cannellini beans	3 garlic cloves, whole
1 onion, chopped	Salt and pepper to taste
2 large leeks, finely chopped	

TOPPING

2 tbsp vegetable oil	1 tbsp cayenne pepper
2 tbsp flour	

Add beans, onion, leeks, garlic, salt, and pepper to the Instant Pot. Press Manual/Pressure Cook and cook for 20 minutes on High. Heat the vegetable oil in a skillet. Add flour and cayenne pepper. Stir-fry for 2 minutes and set aside. When done, do a quick release. Pour in the cayenne mixture and give it a good stir. Let it sit for 15 minutes before serving.

Stuffed Avocado Bake

Serving Size: 2 | Total Time: 20 minutes

1 avocado, halved	1 tbsp dried oregano
2 eggs	Salt and pepper to taste
3 tbsp butter, melted	1 tomato, chopped

Grease a baking dish with butter. With a spoon, remove some of the avocado flesh to create more space for the eggs. Reserve the flesh for garnish. Place the avocado in the baking dish. Crack an egg into each avocado half. Season with salt and oregano. Add 1 cup of water and place the trivet in the pot. Lower the baking dish on top.

Seal the lid, select Manual, and cook on High Pressure for 10 minutes. When done, do a quick release before opening the lid. Mix the reserved avocado flesh with the tomato, season with salt and pepper and serve with the baked avocado.

Corn & Lentil Hummus with Parmesan

Serving Size: 6 | Total Time: 45 minutes

1 lb lentils, cooked	2 tbsp Parmesan cheese
1 cup sweet corn	1 tbsp salt
2 tomatoes, diced	½ tbsp red pepper flakes
3 tbsp tomato paste	3 tbsp olive oil
½ tbsp dried oregano	¼ cup red wine

Heat olive oil on Sauté and add tomatoes, tomato paste, and ½ cup of water. Sprinkle with salt, pepper flakes, and oregano and stir-fry for 5 minutes. Add lentils, sweet corn, and red wine. Pour in ½ cup of water and seal the lid. Cook on High Pressure for 2 minutes. Do a quick release. Set aside to cool completely and refrigerate for 30 minutes. Sprinkle with Parmesan cheese before serving.

Indian Dhal with Veggies

Serving Size: 4 | Total Time: 35 minutes

1 cup lentils	¼ tbsp parsley, chopped
2 tbsp almond butter	½ tbsp chili powder
1 carrot, peeled, chopped	2 tbsp ground cumin
1 potato, peeled, chopped	1 tbsp garam masala
1 bay leaf	3 cups vegetable stock

Melt almond butter on Sauté. Add carrots, potatoes, and bay leaf. Stir and cook for 10 minutes. Add lentils, chili powder, cumin, garam masala, and stock and press Cancel. If the mixture is very thick, add a bit of water. Seal the lid, select Manual, and cook on High Pressure for 15 minutes. Once the timer goes off, do a quick release. Serve sprinkled with parsley.

Acorn Squash with Sweet Glaze

Serving Size: 4 | Total Time: 15 minutes

1 lb acorn squash, cut into 2-inch chunks	
3 tbsp honey	1 tbsp cinnamon
2 tbsp butter	Salt and pepper to taste
1 tbsp dark brown sugar	

In a small bowl, mix 1 tbsp honey, butter and ½ cup water. Pour into the pot. Add in acorn squash, seal the lid and cook on High Pressure for 4 minutes. Release the pressure quickly. Transfer the squash to a serving dish. **Set on Sauté.** Mix sugar, cinnamon, the remaining 2 tbsp honey and the liquid in the pot. Cook as you stir for 4 minutes to obtain a thick consistency and turn caramelized and golden. Spread honey glaze over squash; add pepper and salt to taste.

Vegan Sloppy Joe's

Serving Size: 6 | Total Time: 40 minutes

3 tbsp olive oil	1 tsp chili powder
1 chopped onion	1 tbsp mustard powder
1 red bell pepper, diced	1 tbsp brown sugar
3 cups vegetable broth	Salt and pepper to taste
1 cup green lentils	6 hamburger buns
14 oz can diced tomatoes	3 dill pickles, sliced

Warm the olive oil in your Instant Pot. Place in onion and bell pepper and cook for 5 minutes. Stir in vegetable broth, lentils, tomatoes, mustard powder, chili powder, brown sugar, salt, and pepper. Seal the lid, select Manual, and cook for 15 minutes on High pressure. Once over, allow a natural release for 10 minutes and unlock the lid. To assemble, toast each bun and top with lentil mixture and a dill slice. Serve right away.

Sweet Polenta with Pistachios

Serving Size: 4 | Total Time: 20 minutes

½ cup honey	½ cup heavy cream
5 cups water	¼ tsp salt
1 cup polenta	¼ cup pistachios, toasted

Set your Instant Pot to Sauté. Place honey and water and bring to a boil, stirring often. Stir in polenta. Seal the lid, select Manual, and cook for 12 minutes on High.

When ready, perform a quick pressure release and unlock the lid. Mix in heavy cream and let sit for 1 minute. Sprinkle with salt to taste. Top with pistachios and serve.

Almond & Cherry Millet

Serving Size: 4 | Total Time: 25 minutes

½ cup chopped dried cherries	
1 cup millet	2 tbsp coconut oil
½ cup almond milk	2 tbsp shaved almonds

Place millet, milk, 2 cups of water, cherries, and coconut oil in your Instant Pot. Seal the lid; select Manual, and cook for 10 minutes on High. Once done, allow a natural release for 10 minutes. Top with almonds and serve.

Basil Parmesan Sauce

Serving Size: 4 | Total Time: 10 minutes

1 cup fresh basil, torn	1 tbsp olive oil
1 cup cream cheese	Salt and pepper to taste
2 tbsp Parmesan, shredded	2 cups vegetable broth

In the Instant Pot, stir basil, cream cheese, Parmesan, oil, salt, pepper, and broth. Seal the lid and cook on High Pressure for 5 minutes. Do a quick pressure release and unlock the lid. Serve immediately.

Coconut Milk Millet Pudding

Serving Size: 4 | Total Time: 25 minutes

1 cup millet	4 dried prunes, chopped
1 cup coconut milk	Maple syrup for serving

Place the millet, milk, and prunes in your Instant Pot. Stir in 1 cup water. Seal the lid, select Manual, and cook for 10 minutes on High pressure. When ready, allow a natural release for 10 minutes. Drizzle with maple syrup.

Blueberry & Quinoa Porridge

Serving Size: 4 | Total Time: 20 minutes

½ cup quinoa	½ tsp vanilla extract
1 ½ cups milk	3 tbsp blueberries
2 tbsp honey	

Place the quinoa, vanilla extract, milk, and ½ cup of water in your Instant Pot and stir. Seal the lid, select Manual, and cook for 1 minute on High pressure. Once ready, allow a natural release for 10 minutes and unlock the lid. Top with honey and blueberries and serve.

Carrot & Sweet Potato Thick Soup

Serving Size: 4 | Total Time: 40 minutes

4 sweet potatoes, cut into bite-sized pieces	
2 carrots, chopped	1 tbsp celery, chopped
1 onion, chopped	1 tbsp parsley, chopped
6 tbsp olive oil	Salt and pepper to taste
2 tbsp tomato sauce	

Heat olive oil on Sauté. Add onion, carrots, celery, and potatoes. Stir-fry for 2 minutes. Stir in 4 cups of water and tomato sauce. Seal the lid and cook for 25 minutes on High Pressure. Do a quick release. Open the pot and add celery, parsley, salt, and pepper. Seal again, and cook for 5 minutes on High. Do a quick release.

Coconut Millet Porridge

Serving Size: 2 | Total Time: 25 minutes

½ cup millet	2 tbsp coconut flakes
½ cup coconut milk	1 tbsp honey

Place millet, milk, and 1/2 cup of water in your Instant Pot. Seal the lid, select Manual, and cook for 10 minutes on High pressure. When over, allow a natural release for 10 minutes and unlock the lid. Drizzle with honey, top with coconut flakes, and serve.

Cheddar Cheese Sauce with Broccoli

Serving Size: 4 | Total Time: 15 minutes

1 cup broccoli, chopped	3 cups chicken broth
1 cup cream cheese	Salt and pepper to taste
1 cup cheddar, shredded	2 tsp dried rosemary

Mix broccoli, cream cheese, cheddar, broth, salt, pepper, and rosemary in a large bowl. Pour the mixture into the Instant Pot. Seal the lid and cook on High Pressure for 8 minutes. Do a quick release. Store for up to 5 days.

Hot Tofu Meatballs

Serving Size: 4 | Total Time: 35 minutes

1 lb tofu, crumbled	2 tbsp olive oil
2 tbsp butter, melted	3 tbsp hot sauce
¼ cup almond meal	2 tbsp chopped scallions
1 garlic clove, minced	Salt to taste

Mix the almond meal, tofu, garlic, salt, and scallions in a bowl. Make meatballs out of the mixture. Warm olive oil in your Instant Pot on Sauté. Place the meatballs and cook for 10 minutes until browned.

In the meantime, microwave the butter and hot sauce in a bowl. Combine and set aside. Place the meatballs in the pot and top with hot sauce and 1 cup of water. Seal the lid, select Manual, and cook for 15 minutes on High pressure. When done, perform a quick pressure release and unlock the lid. Serve immediately.

DESSERTS & DRINKS

Vanilla Cheesecake with Cranberry Filling

Serving Size: 8 | Total Time: 1 hour + chilling time

1 cup coarsely crumbled cookies
2 tbsp butter, melted
1 cup mascarpone cheese
½ cup sugar
2 tbsp sour cream

½ tsp vanilla extract
2 eggs
1/3 cup dried cranberries

Fold a 20-inch piece of aluminum foil in half lengthwise twice and set on the Instant Pot. In a bowl, combine butter and crumbled cookies. Press firmly to the bottom and about 1/3 of the way up the sides of a cake pan. Freeze the crust. In a separate bowl, beat mascarpone cheese and sugar to obtain a smooth consistency. Stir in vanilla and sour cream. Beat one egg and add into the cheese mixture to combine well. Do the same with the second egg.

Stir cranberries into the filling. Transfer the filling into the crust. Into the pot, add 1 cup water and set the steam rack. Center the springform pan onto the prepared foil sling. Use the sling to lower the pan onto the rack.

Fold foil strips out of the way of the lid. Seal the lid, press Manual, and cook on High Pressure for 40 minutes. Release the pressure quickly. Transfer the cheesecake to a refrigerator for 3 hours. Use a paring knife to run along the edges between the pan and cheesecake to remove the cheesecake and set to the plate.

Orange New York Cheesecake

Serving Size: 6 | Total Time: 1 hour + freezing time

FOR THE CRUST
1 cup graham crackers crumbs
2 tbsp butter, melted   1 tsp sugar

FOR THE FILLING
2 cups cream cheese   Zest from 1 orange
½ cup sugar   A pinch of salt
1 tsp vanilla extract   2 eggs

Fold a 20-inch piece of aluminum foil in half lengthwise twice and set on the Instant Pot. Grease a parchment paper and line it to a cake pan. In a bowl, combine melted butter, sugar, and graham crackers. Press into the bottom and about ⅓ up the sides of the pan. Transfer the pan to the freezer as you prepare the filling.

In a separate bowl, beat sugar, cream cheese, salt, orange zest, and vanilla until smooth. Beat eggs into the filling, one at a time. Stir until combined. Add the filling over the chilled crust in the pan. Add 1 cup water and set a trivet into the pot. Put the pan on the trivet.

Seal the lid, press Cake, and cook for 40 minutes on High. Release the pressure quickly. Cool the cheesecake and then transfer it to the refrigerator for 3 hours. Use a paring knife to run along the edges between the pan and cheesecake to remove the cheesecake and set to the plate.

Pie Cups with Fruit Filling

Serving Size: 6 | Total Time: 40 minutes + chilling time

FOR THE CRUST:
2 cups flour   1 tbsp sugar
¾ tsp salt   ½ cup ice water
¾ cup butter, softened

FOR THE FILLING:
½ fresh peach   1 tbsp sugar
½ cup apples, chopped   ½ tsp cinnamon
¼ cup cranberries   1 egg yolk, for brushing
2 tbsp flour

Place flour, salt, butter, sugar, and water in a food processor and pulse until dough becomes crumbly. Remove to a lightly floured work surface. Divide among 4 equal pieces and wrap in plastic foil. Refrigerate for an hour. Place apples, peach, cranberries, flour, sugar, and cinnamon in a bowl. Toss to combine and set aside. Roll each piece into 6-inch round discs. Add 2 tablespoons of the apple mixture at the center of each disc and wrap to form small bowls. Brush each bowl with egg yolk and gently Transfer to an oiled baking dish. Pour 1 cup of water into the pot and insert the trivet. Place the pan on top. Seal the lid, and cook for 25 minutes on High Pressure. Release the pressure naturally. Serve cool.

Homemade Lemon Cheesecake

Serving Size: 6 | Total Time: 1 hour + chilling time

CRUST:
4 oz graham crackers   3 tbsp butter, melted
1 tsp ground cinnamon

FILLING:
1 lb mascarpone cheese,   1 tsp vanilla extract
softened   1 tsp lemon zest
¾ cup sugar   1 tbsp lemon juice
¼ cup sour cream, at room   A pinch of salt
temperature   1 cup strawberries, halved
2 eggs

In a food processor, beat cinnamon and graham crackers to attain a texture almost same as sand; mix in melted butter. Press the crumbs into the bottom of a 7-inch springform pan in an even layer. In a stand mixer, beat sugar, mascarpone cheese, and sour cream for 3 minutes to combine well and have a fluffy and smooth mixture. Scrape the bowl's sides and add eggs, lemon zest, salt, lemon juice, and vanilla. Carry on to beat the mixture until you obtain a consistent color and all ingredients are completely combined. Pour filling over crust.

Into the inner pot, add 1 cup water and set in a trivet. Place the springform pan on the trivet. Seal the lid, press Cake, and cook for 40 minutes on High. Release the pressure quickly. Remove the cheesecake and let it cool. Garnish with strawberry halves on top. Use a paring knife to run along the edges between the pan and cheesecake to remove it and set it to a plate. Serve.

Classic French Squash Tart

Serving Size: 6 | Total Time: 35 minutes

15 oz mashed squash	½ tsp salt
6 fl oz milk	3 large eggs
½ tsp cinnamon, ground	½ cup granulated sugar
½ tsp nutmeg	1 pack pate brisee

Place squash puree in a large bowl. Add milk, cinnamon, eggs, nutmeg, salt, and sugar. Whisk together until well incorporated. Grease a baking dish with oil. Gently place pate brisee creating the edges with hands. Pour the squash mixture over and flatten the surface with a spatula. Pour 1 cup of water into the pot and insert the trivet. Lay the baking dish on the trivet. Seal the lid, and cook for 25 minutes on High Pressure. Do a quick release. Transfer the pie to a serving platter. Refrigerate.

Walnut & Pumpkin Tart

Serving Size: 6 | Total Time: 70 minutes

1 cup packed shredded pumpkin

3 eggs	1 tsp vanilla extract
½ cup sugar	1 tsp ground cinnamon
1 cup flour	½ tsp ground nutmeg
½ cup half-and-half	½ cup chopped walnuts
¼ cup olive oil	2 cups water
1 tsp baking powder	

FROSTING:

4 oz cream cheese, room temperature	½ cup confectioners sugar
8 tbsp butter	½ tsp vanilla extract
	½ tsp salt

In a bowl, beat eggs and sugar to get a smooth mixture. Mix in oil, flour, vanilla extract, cinnamon, half-and-half, baking powder, and nutmeg. Stir well to obtain a fluffy batter. Fold walnuts and pumpkin through the batter. Add batter into a cake pan and cover with aluminum foil. Into the pot, add 1 cup water and set a trivet. Lay cake pan onto the trivet.

Seal the lid, select Manual, and cook on High Pressure for 40 minutes. Release pressure naturally for 10 minutes. Beat cream cheese, confectioners' sugar, salt, vanilla, and butter in a bowl until smooth. Place in the refrigerator until needed. Remove cake from the pan and transfer to a wire rack to cool. Over the cake, spread frosting and apply a topping of shredded carrots.

Cottage Cheesecake with Strawberries

Serving Size: 6 | Total Time: 35 minutes +cooling time

10 oz cream cheese	1 tsp lemon extract
¼ cup sugar	3 tbsp sour cream
½ cup cottage cheese	1 cup water
1 lemon, zested and juiced	10 strawberries, halved to decorate
2 eggs, cracked into a bowl	

Blend with an electric mixer, the cream cheese, quarter cup of sugar, cottage cheese, lemon zest, lemon juice, and lemon extract until a smooth consistency is formed.

Adjust the sweet taste to liking with more sugar. Add the eggs. Fold in at low speed until incorporated. Spoon the mixture into a greased baking pan. Level the top with a spatula and cover with foil. Fit a trivet in the pot and pour in water. Place the cake pan on the trivet.

Seal the lid. Select Manual and cook for 15 minutes. Mix the sour cream and 1 tbsp of sugar. Set aside. Once the timer has gone off, do a natural pressure release for 10 minutes. Use a spatula to spread the sour cream mixture on the warm cake. Let cool. Top with strawberries.

Yogurt Cheesecake with Cranberries

Serving Size: 6 | Total Time: 45 minutes + chilling time

2 lb Greek yogurt	2 tsp lemon zest
2 cups sugar	1 tsp lemon extract
4 eggs	1 cheesecake crust

FOR TOPPING:

7 oz dried cranberries	1 tsp vanilla sugar
2 tbsp cranberry jam	1 tsp cranberry extract
2 tsp lemon zest	¾ cup lukewarm water

In a bowl, combine yogurt, sugar, eggs, lemon zest, and lemon extract. With a mixer, beat well until well-combined. Place the crust in a greased cake pan and pour in the filling. Flatten the surface with a spatula. Leave in the fridge for 30 minutes. Combine cranberries, jam, lemon zest, vanilla sugar, cranberry extract, and water in the pot. Simmer for 15 minutes on Sauté. Remove and wipe the pot clean. Fill in 1 cup water and insert a trivet. Set the pan on top of the trivet and pour cranberry topping. Seal the lid and cook for 20 minutes on High Pressure. Do a quick release. Run a sharp knife around the edge of the cheesecake. Refrigerate. Serve and enjoy!

Lemon-Apricot Compote

Serving Size: 6 | Total Time: 20 minutes

2 lb fresh apricots, sliced	1 tsp ground nutmeg
1 lb sugar	10 cups water
2 tbsp lemon zest	

Add apricots, sugar, water, nutmeg, and lemon zest. Cook, stirring occasionally until half of the water evaporates, on Sauté. Press Cancel and transfer the apricots and the remaining liquid into glass jars. Let cool. Refrigerate.

Banana Chocolate Bars

Serving Size: 6 | Total Time: 25 minutes

½ cup almond butter	2 tbsp cocoa powder
3 bananas	

Place the bananas and almond butter in a bowl and mash finely with a fork. Add the cocoa powder and stir until well combined. Grease a baking dish. Pour the banana and almond butter into the dish. Pour 1 cup water into the cooker and lower a trivet. Place the baking dish on the trivet and seal the lid. Select Pressure Cook for 15 minutes on High. When it goes off, do a quick release. Let cool for a few minutes before cutting into squares.

Cherry & Chocolate Marble Cake

Serving Size: 6 | Total Time: 45 minutes

1 cup flour	3 tbsp butter, softened
1 ½ tsp baking powder	3 eggs
1 tbsp powdered stevia	¼ cup cocoa powder
½ tsp salt	¼ cup heavy cream
1 tsp cherry extract	

Combine flour, baking powder, stevia, and salt in a bowl. Mix well to combine and add eggs, one at a time. Beat well with a dough hook attachment for one minute. Add heavy cream, butter, and cherry extract. Continue to beat for 3 more minutes. Divide the mixture in half and add cocoa powder in one-half of the mixture. Pour the light batter into a greased baking dish. Drizzle with cocoa dough to create a nice marble pattern. Pour in one cup of water and insert the trivet. Lower the baking dish on top. Seal the lid and cook for 20 minutes on High Pressure. Release the pressure naturally for 10 minutes.

Chocolate Glazed Cake

Serving Size: 6 | Total Time: 40 minutes + chilling time

3 cups yogurt	1 cup oil
3 cups flour	2 tsp baking soda
2 cups granulated sugar	3 tbsp cocoa

FOR THE GLAZE:

7 oz dark chocolate	10 tbsp milk
10 tbsp sugar	5 oz butter, unsalted

In a bowl, combine yogurt, flour, sugar, oil, baking soda, and cocoa. Beat well with an electric mixer. Transfer a mixture to a large springform pan. Wrap the pan in foil. Insert a trivet in the Instant Pot. Pour in 1 cup water and place the pan on top. Seal the lid and cook for 30 minutes on High Pressure. Do a quick release, remove the pan, and unwrap. Chill well. Microwave the chocolate and whisk in butter, milk, and sugar. Beat well with a mixer and pour the mixture over the cake. Refrigerate for at least two hours before serving.

Molten Chocolate Cake

Serving Size: 6 | Total Time: 40 minutes

1 cup butter	Powdered sugar to garnish
4 tbsp milk	7 tbsp flour
2 tsp vanilla extract	5 eggs
1 ½ cups chocolate chips	1 cup water
1 ½ cups sugar	

Grease the cake pan with cooking spray and set aside. Fit the trivet at the pot, and pour in water. In a heatproof bowl, add the butter and chocolate and melt them in the microwave for about 2 minutes. Stir in sugar. Add eggs, milk, and vanilla extract and stir again. Finally, add the flour and stir it until smooth. Pour the batter into the greased cake pan and use a spatula to level it. Place the pan on the trivet, inside the pot, seal the lid, and select Manual at High for 15 minutes.

Do a natural pressure release for 10 minutes. Remove the trivet with the pan on it and place the pan on a flat surface. Put a plate over the pan and flip the cake over onto the plate. Pour the powdered sugar in a fine sieve and sift over the cake. Cut the cake into slices and serve.

Best Tiramisu Cheesecake

Serving Size: 6 | Total Time: 35 minutes + chilling time

1 ½ cups ladyfingers, crushed

1 tbsp Kahlua liquor	2 tbsp powdered sugar
1 tbsp granulated espresso	½ cup white sugar
1 tbsp butter, melted	1 tbsp cocoa powder
16 oz cream cheese	1 tsp vanilla extract
8 oz mascarpone cheese	2 eggs

In a bowl beat the cream cheese, mascarpone, and white sugar. Gradually beat in the eggs, the powdered sugar, cocoa powder, and vanilla. Combine Kahlua liquor, espresso, butter, and ladyfingers, in another bowl. Press the ladyfinger crust at the bottom. Pour the filling on a greased cake pan. Cover the pan with aluminum foil. Pour 1 cup of water into your pressure cooker and lower a trivet. Place the pan inside and seal the lid. Select Manual and set to 25 minutes at High pressure. Release the pressure quickly. Allow cooling completely.

Catalan-Style Crème Brûlée

Serving Size: 4 | Total Time: 15 minutes

5 cups heavy cream	4 tbsp sugar
8 egg yolks	1 vanilla extract
1 cup honey	1 cup water

In a bowl, combine heavy cream, egg yolks, vanilla, and honey. Beat well with an electric mixer. Pour the mixture into 4 ramekins. Set aside. Pour water into the pot and insert the trivet. Lower the ramekins on top. Seal the lid and cook for 10 minutes on High Pressure. Do a quick pressure release. Remove the ramekins from the pot and add a tablespoon of sugar to each ramekin. Burn evenly with a culinary torch until brown. Chill well and serve.

Simple Apple Cinnamon Dessert

Serving Size: 6 | Total Time: 30 minutes

TOPPING:

½ cup rolled oats	½ cup granulated sugar
½ cup oat flour	¼ cup olive oil

FILLING:

5 apples, cored, and halved	1 tsp ground cinnamon
2 tbsp arrowroot powder	¼ tsp ground nutmeg
½ cup water	½ tsp vanilla paste

In a bowl, combine sugar, oat flour, rolled oats, and olive oil to form coarse crumbs. Spoon the apples into the Instant Pot. Mix water with arrowroot powder in a bowl. Stir in nutmeg, cinnamon, and vanilla. Toss in the apples to coat. Apply oat topping to the apples. Seal the lid and cook on High Pressure for 10 minutes. Release the pressure naturally for 10 minutes.

Easy Lemon Cake

Serving Size: 6 | Total Time: 30 minutes

2 eggs
2 cups sugar
1 cup vegetable oil
LEMON TOPPING:

½ cup flour
1 tsp baking powder

1 cup sugar
1 cup lemon juice

1 tbsp lemon zest
1 lemon, sliced

In a bowl, combine eggs, sugar, oil, and baking powder. Gradually add flour until the mixture is thick and slightly sticky. Shape balls with hands and flatten them to half-inch thick. Place in a baking pan. Pour 1 cup of water, insert a trivet, and lower the pan onto the trivet. Cover the pan with foil and seal the lid. Cook on High Pressure for 20 minutes. Do a quick release. Let cool at room temperature. Add sugar, lemon juice, lemon zest, and lemon slices to the Instant Pot. Press Sauté and stir until the sugar dissolves. Pour the hot topping over the cake.

Honey Homemade Almond Milk

Serving Size: 4 | Total Time: 15 minutes

1 cup raw almonds, peeled
2 dried apricots, chopped
2 tbsp honey

1 vanilla bean
½ tsp almond extract

In the Instant Pot, mix a cup of water with almonds and apricots. Seal the lid and cook for 1 minute on High. Release the pressure quickly. The almonds should be soft and plump, and the water should be brown and murky. Use a strainer to drain almonds and apricots. Rinse with cold water. To a blender, add the rinsed almonds and apricots, almond extract, vanilla bean, honey, and 4 cups water. Blend for 2 minutes until well combined and frothy. Line a cheesecloth to the strainer. Place the strainer over a bowl and strain the milk. Use a wooden spoon to press milk through the cheesecloth and get rid of solids. Place almond milk in an airtight container and refrigerate.

Amazing Fruity Cheesecake

Serving Size: 6 | Total Time: 35 minutes

1 ½ cups graham cracker crust
1 cup raspberries
3 cups cream cheese
1 tbsp fresh orange juice
3 eggs

½ stick butter, melted
¾ cup sugar
1 tsp vanilla paste
1 tsp orange zest

Insert the tray into the pressure cooker, and add 1 cup of water. Grease a springform. Mix in graham cracker crust with sugar and butter in a bowl. Press the mixture to form a crust at the bottom. Blend the raspberries and cream cheese with an electric mixer. Crack in the eggs and keep mixing until well combined. Mix in orange juice, vanilla paste, and orange zest. Pour this mixture into the pan, and cover the pan with aluminum foil. Lay the springform on the tray. Select Pressure Cook and cook for 20 minutes on High. Once the cooking is complete, do a quick pressure release. Refrigerate the cheesecake.

Chocolate Quinoa Bowl

Serving Size: 4 | Total Time: 15 minutes

12 squares dark chocolate, shaved
2 tbsp cocoa powder
1 cup quinoa
2 tbsp maple syrup

½ tsp vanilla
A pinch of salt
1 tbsp sliced almonds

Put the quinoa, cocoa powder, maple syrup, vanilla, 2 ¼ cups water, and salt in your Instant Pot. Seal the lid, select Manual, and cook for a minute on High pressure. When ready, allow a natural release for 10 minutes and unlock the lid. Using a fork, fluff the quinoa. Top with almonds and dark chocolate and serve.

Simple Apple Cider with Orange Juice

Serving Size: 6 | Total Time: 20 minutes

6 green apples, chopped
¼ cup orange juice

2 cinnamon sticks

In a blender, add orange juice, apples, and 3 cups water and blend until smooth; use a fine-mesh strainer to strain and press using a spoon. Get rid of the pulp. In the pot, mix the apple puree and cinnamon sticks. Seal the lid and cook for 10 minutes on High Pressure. Release the Pressure naturally. Strain again and do away with the solids.

Spiced & Warming Mulled Wine

Serving Size: 6 | Total Time: 20 minutes

3 cups red wine
2 tangerines, sliced
¼ cup honey
6 whole cloves
6 whole black peppercorns

2 cardamom pods
8 cinnamon sticks
1 tsp fresh ginger, grated
1 tsp ground cinnamon

Add red wine, honey, cardamom, 2 cinnamon sticks, cloves, tangerine slices, ginger, and peppercorns. Seal the lid and cook for 5 minutes on High Pressure. Release pressure naturally for 10 minutes. Using a fine mesh strainer, strain the wine. Discard spices. Divide the warm wine into glasses. Garnish with cinnamon sticks to serve.

Walnut & Dark Chocolate Brownies

Serving Size: 6 | Total Time: 30 minutes

2 eggs
1/3 cup granulated sugar
¼ cup olive oil
1/3 cup flour
1/3 cup cocoa powder

1/3 cup dark chocolate chips
1/3 cup chopped walnuts
1 tbsp milk
½ tsp baking powder
1 tbsp vanilla extract

Add 1 cup of water and set a steamer rack into the cooker. Line a parchment paper on the steamer basket. In a bowl, beat eggs and sugar to mix until smooth. Stir in oil, cocoa, milk, baking powder, chocolate chips, flour, walnuts, vanilla, and sea salt. Transfer the batter to the prepared steamer basket. Arrange into an even layer. Seal the lid, press Cake, and cook for 20 minutes on High. Release the pressure quickly. Let cool before cutting into squares. Use powdered sugar to dust and serve.

Quick Coconut Treat with Pears

Serving Size: 2 | Total Time: 15 minutes

¼ cup flour	2 pears, peeled and diced
1 cup coconut milk	¼ cup shredded coconut

Combine flour, milk, pears, and shredded coconut in your Pressure cooker. Seal the lid, select Pressure Cook and set the timer to 5 minutes at High pressure. When ready, do a quick pressure release. Divide the mixture between two bowls. Serve.

Homemade Walnut Layer Cake

Serving Size: 6 | Total Time: 25 minutes

½ cup vanilla pudding powder	
3 standard cake crusts	10.5 oz chocolate chips
¼ cup granulated sugar	¼ cup walnuts, minced
4 cups milk	

Combine vanilla powder, sugar, and milk in the inner pot. Cook until the pudding thickens, stirring constantly on Sauté. Remove from the steel pot. Place one crust into a springform pan. Pour half of the pudding and sprinkle with minced walnuts and chocolate chips. Cover with another crust and repeat the process. Finish with the final crust and wrap in foil.

Insert the trivet, pour in 1 cup of water, and place springform pan on top. Seal the lid and cook for 10 minutes on High Pressure. Do a quick release. Refrigerate.

Creme Caramel with Whipped Cream

Serving Size: 4 | Total Time: 30 minutes + cooling time

½ cup granulated sugar	½ tsp vanilla extract
4 tbsp caramel syrup	½ tbsp milk
3 eggs	5 oz whipping cream

Combine milk, whipping cream, and vanilla extract in your Instant Pot. Press Sauté, and cook for 5 minutes, or until small bubbles form. Set aside. Using an electric mixer, whisk the eggs and sugar. Gradually add the cream mixture and whisk until well combined. Divide the caramel syrup between 4 ramekins. Fill with egg mixture and place them on the trivet. Pour in 1 cup water. Seal the lid and cook for 15 minutes on High Pressure. Do a quick release. Remove the ramekins and cool.

Plum & Almond Dessert

Serving Size: 6 | Total Time: 1 hour 50 minutes

6 lb sweet ripe plums, pits removed and halved	
2 cups white sugar	1 cup almond flakes

Drizzle the plums with sugar. Toss to coat. Let it stand for about 1 hour to allow plums to soak up the sugar. Transfer the plum mixture to the Instant Pot and pour 1 cup of water. Seal the lid and cook on High Pressure for 30 minutes. Allow the Pressure to release naturally for 10 minutes. Serve topped with almond flakes.

Homemade Spanish-Style Horchata

Serving Size: 4 | Total Time: 20 minutes

4 cups cold water	Zest from 1 lemon
½ cup short-grain rice	2 tbsp sugar
¼ stick cinnamon	1 tbsp cinnamon powder

In the pot, combine cinnamon stick, rice and 2 cups of water. Seal the lid cook on High Pressure for 5 minutes. Release pressure naturally for 10 minutes. In a blender, puree the rice mixture with the lemon zest and sugar. Strain the blended mixture into the remaining water. Mix well and place in the refrigerator until ready for serving. Serve sprinkled with cinnamon.

Grandma's Fruit Compote

Serving Size: 6 | Total Time: 45 minutes

7 oz Turkish figs	3 tbsp cornstarch
7 oz fresh cherries	1 tsp cinnamon, ground
7 oz plums	1 cup sugar
3 ½ oz raisins	1 lemon, juiced
3 large apples, chopped	

Combine figs, cherries, plums, raisins, apples, cornstarch, cinnamon, sugar, and lemon juice in the Instant Pot. Pour in 3 cups water. Seal the lid and cook for 30 minutes on High pressure. Release the pressure naturally for 10 minutes. Store in big jars.

Pumpkin Pudding with Apple Juice

Serving Size: 4 | Total Time: 20 minutes

1 lb pumpkin, chopped	4 cups apple juice
1 cup granulated sugar	1 tsp cinnamon, ground
½ cup cornstarch	3-4 cloves

In a bowl, combine sugar and apple juice until sugar dissolves completely. Pour the mixture into the pot and stir in cornstarch, cinnamon, cloves, and pumpkin. Seal the lid, and cook for 10 minutes on High Pressure. Do a quick release. Pour in the pudding into 4 serving bowls. Let cool at room temperature and refrigerate overnight.

Banana & Walnut Oatmeal

Serving Size: 2 | Total Time: 20 minutes

1 banana, chopped	¼ teaspoon cinnamon
1 cup rolled oats	1 tbsp chopped walnuts
1 cup milk	½ tsp white sugar

Pour 1 cup of water into your Instant Pot and fit in a steam rack. Place oats, sugar, milk, cinnamon, and ½ of water in a bowl. Divide between small-sized cups. Place on the steam rack. Seal the lid, select Manual, and cook for 5 minutes on High pressure. When done, allow a natural release for 10 minutes and unlock the lid. Top with banana and walnuts and serve.

RECIPE INDEX

H

Habanero Beef Brisket with Red Wine, 69

Habanero Chicken Stew, 149

Haddock with Edamame Soybeans, 92

Ham & Egg Cups, 19

Ham Omelet with Red Bell Pepper, 19

Ham & Peas with Goat Cheese, 116

Hard-Boiled Eggs with Paprika, 118

Harissa Chicken Thighs, 44

Harissa Chicken with Fruity Farro, 116

Harvest Vegetable Soup with Pesto, 137

Hawaiian Rice, 107

Hazelnut Brown Rice Pilaf, 108

Hazelnut Brussels Sprouts with Parmesan, 26

Healthy Kale & Egg Muffins, 123

Hearty Beef Soup, 134

Hearty Beef Stew with Vegetables, 73

Herbed Poached Salmon, 87

Herbed Squash Sauce, 125

Herby Chicken Stock, 124

Herby Chicken with Peach Gravy, 42

Herby Crab Legs with Lemon, 97

Herby Trout with Farro & Green Beans, 89

Herby Whole Chicken Stew, 148

Hoisin Spare Pork Ribs, 63

Homemade Braised Pork Belly, 58

Homemade Chicken Puttanesca, 45

Homemade Chicken & Quinoa Soup, 127

Homemade Chicken Stock, 124

Homemade Cuban Ropa Vieja, 70

Homemade Gazpacho Soup, 152

Homemade Honey Applesauce, 125

Homemade Lemon Cheesecake, 160

Homemade Spanish-Style Horchata, 164

Homemade Turkey Pepperoni Pizza, 48

Homemade Veggie Quinoa, 113

Homemade Vichyssoise Soup with Chives, 126

Homemade Walnut Layer Cake, 164

Homemade Winter Soup, 130

Honey Butternut Squash Cake Oatmeal, 17

Honey Coconut Rice, 107

Honey-Glazed Turkey, 51

Honey Homemade Almond Milk, 163

Honey-Lemon Chicken with Vegetables, 33

Honey Oat & Pumpkin Granola, 117

Honey & White Wine Pork, 54

Hot Beef Chili, 149

Hot Chicken with Coriander & Ginger, 35

Hot Chicken with Garlic & Mushrooms, 37

Hot Paprika & Oregano Lamb, 84

Hot Pork Chops with Cheddar Cheese, 64

Hot Shrimp & Potato Chowder, 96

Hot Spinach Soup, 142

Hot Tofu Meatballs, 159

Hungarian-Style Turkey Stew, 50

I

Indian Dhal with Veggies, 158

Indian Prawn Curry, 97

Indian-Style Chicken, 45

Italian Egg Cakes, 17

Italian Meatballs with Pomodoro Sauce, 69

Italian Roast Beef, 78

Italian Sausage & Lentil Pot, 60

Italian Steamed Sea Bream with Lemon, 92

Italian-Style Brussels Sprouts, 27

J

Jalapeño Chicken Soup with Tortilla Chips, 133

Jalapeño Shrimp with Herbs & Lemon, 96

Jamaican Chicken with Pineapple Sauce, 44

Jamaican Cornmeal Porridge, 117

Japanese-Style Pork Tenderloin, 64

Juicy Hot Chicken Wings, 118

Juicy Pork Butt Steaks, 64

K

Kale & Artichoke Cheese Bites, 118

Kale, Bean & Pancetta Soup, 136

Kale & Parmesan Omelet, 19

Kale & Parmesan Pearl Barley, 115

Kale, Potato & Beef Stew, 144

Kielbasa Sausage Soup, 140

Kimchi Ramen Noodle Soup, 130

Kiwi Steel Cut Oatmeal, 117

Korean-Style Chicken, 43

L

Lamb Chops with Mashed Potatoes, 86

Lamb Chorba, 86

Lamb Shanks with Garlic & Thyme, 84

Lamb Stew with Lemon & Parsley, 85

Lamb with Tomato & Green Peas, 84

Lazy Steel Cut Oats with Coconut, 16

Lebanese-Style Chicken with Couscous, 31

Leftover Beef Sandwiches, 80

Leg of Lamb with Garlic and Pancetta, 85

Lemon-Apricot Compote, 161

Lemon Chicken Wings, 32

Lemon Hummus with Spinach, 119

Lemon & Leek Tilapia, 92

Lemon Salmon with Blue Cheese, 89

Lemon & Thyme Chicken, 47

Lentil & Carrot Soup, 133

Lentil & Chorizo Chili, 114

Lentil & Pork Shank Soup, 134

Light & Fruity Yogurt, 18

Lime Brown Rice, 107

Lime Bulgur with Olives, 114

Lime & Honey Scallops, 99

Lime Trout with Spinach & Tomatoes, 90

MEASUREMENTS & CONVERSIONS

	US STANDARD	US STANDARD (OUNCES)	METRIC (APPROXIMATE)
VOLUME EQUIVALENTS (LIQUID)	2 tablespoons	1 fl. oz.	30 mL
	¼ cup	2 fl. oz.	60 mL
	½ cup	4 fl. oz.	120 mL
	1 cup	8 fl. oz.	240 mL
	1 ½ cups	12 fl. oz.	355 mL
	2 cups or 1 pint	16 fl. oz.	475 mL
VOLUME EQUIVALENTS (DRY)	¼ teaspoon		1 mL
	½ teaspoon		2 mL
	1 teaspoon		5 mL
	1 tablespoon		15 mL
	¼ cup		59 mL
	⅓ cup		79 mL
	½ cup		118 mL
	⅔ cup		156 mL
	¾ cup		177 mL
	1 cup		235 mL
	2 cups or 1 pint		475 mL
	3 cups		700 mL
	4 cups or 1 quart		1 L
WEIGHT EQUIVALENTS	½ ounce		15 g
	1 ounce		30 g
	2 ounces		60 g
	4 ounces-		115 g
	8 ounces		225 g
	12 ounces		340 g
	16 ounces or 1 pound		455 g

	FAHRENHEIT (F)	CELSIUS (C) (APPROXIMATE)
OVEN TEMPERATURES	250°F	120°F
	300°F	150°F
	325°F	180°F
	375°F	190°F
	400°F	200°F
	425°F	220°F
	450°F	230°F

INSTANT POT COOKING TIME CHARTS

BEANS, LEGUMES & LENTILS	DRY	SOAKED
Black beans	20-25	6-8
Black-eyed peas	14-18	4-5
Chickpeas	35-40	10-15
Cannellini beans	20-25	6-8
Great Northern beans	25-30	7-8
Kidney beans	20-25	7-8
Lima beans	12-14	6-10
Navy beans	20-25	7-8
Pinto beans	25-30	6-9
Soy beans	35-45	18-20
Peas	16-20	10-12
Lentils, red or yellow, split	8-10	N/A
Lentils, green or brown	1-2	N/A

RICE & GRAINS	WATER RATIO (GRAIN:WATER)	COOKING TIME
Rice, white/Basmati/Jasmin	1:1,5	5
Oats, quick-cooking/ steel-cut	1:2/1:3	2-3/3-5
Millet	1:1.75	10-12
Barley, pearl	1:2.5	20-22
Couscous	1:2	2-3
Corn, dried, halved	1:3	5-6
Quinoa	1:1.25	1
Porridge, thin	1:6-1:7	5-7

VEGETABLES	FRESH	FROZEN
Asparagus, whole	9-11	11-13
Artichoke, heart	4-5	5-6
Beans	1-2	2-3
Beetroot, small/large	11-13/20-25	13-15/25-30
Broccoli, florets	1-2	2-3
Brussels sprouts, whole	2-3	3-4
Cabbage	3	4
Carrots, sliced or shredded	2-3	3-4
Cauliflower florets	2-3	3-4
Celery, chunks	2-3	3-4
Collard greens	4-5	5-6
Corn	2-4	3-5
Eggplant	3-4	3-4
Onions, sliced	2-3	3-4

Potatoes, cubed/whole	3-4/10-12	4-5/14-16
Peas (green)	1-2	2-3
Pumpkin	5-8	6-7
Spinach	1-2	2-3
Tomatoes, quarters	2-3	4-5

FISH & SEAFOOD	FRESH	FROZEN
Fish, whole	4-5	5-7
Fish, fillet	2-3	3-4
Fish, steak	3-4	4-6
Crab, whole	2-3	4-5
Lobster	2-3	3-4
Mussels	1-2	2-3
Shrimp or prawns	1-3	2-4

MEAT	COOKING TIME (PER POUND)
Beef, stew meat	20
Beef ribs	20-25
Beef roast, 2–3" pieces	15-20
Beef, meatballs	5
Beef, oxtail	40-50
Beef, shanks	2-30
Pork, loin	20
Pork, butt	15
Pork, ribs	15-20
Ham, steaks	9-12
Ham, picnic shoulder	8
Chicken breasts boneless	6-8
Chicken, whole	8
Turkey breast (boneless)	7-9
Turkey leg	15-20
Duck	12-15
Lamb, leg	15
Lamb, stew meat	12-15
Veal, chops	5-8
Veal, roast	12

Made in the USA
Monee, IL
23 January 2021